DOGMA and ECUMENISM

DOGMA and ECUMENISM

Vatican II and Karl Barth's *Ad Limina Apostolorum*

EDITED BY

Matthew Levering, Bruce L. McCormack,
and Thomas Joseph White, OP

The Catholic University of America Press
Washington, D.C.

The paper used in this publication meets the minimum requirements of American National Standards for Information Science—Permanence of Paper for Printed Library Materials, ANSI Z39.48-1984.
∞

Library of Congress Cataloging-in-Publication Data
Names: Levering, Matthew, 1971– editor. | McCormack, Bruce L., editor. | White, Thomas Joseph, 1971– editor.
Title: Dogma and ecumenism : Vatican II and Karl Barth's "Ad Limina Apostolorum" / edited by Matthew Levering, Bruce L. McCormack, Thomas Joseph White.
Description: Washington, D.C. : The Catholic University of America Press, 2020. | Includes bibliographical references and index. | Identifiers: LCCN 2019044576 | ISBN 9780813232409 (paperback) | ISBN 9780813232416 (ebook)
Subjects: LCSH: Vatican Council (2nd : 1962–1965 : Basilica di San Pietro in Vaticano) | Barth, Karl, 1886–1968. Ad limina apostolorum. | Catholic Church—Doctrines. | Protestant churches—Doctrines. | Catholic Church—Relations—Protestant churches. | Protestant churches—Relations—Catholic Church.
Classification: LCC BX830 1962 .D546 2020 | DDC 262/.52—dc23
LC record available at https://lccn.loc.gov/2019044576

For John Webster and Richard Schenk, OP

Two great companions in the theological search for the truth

Contents

Acknowledgments

This book owes its genesis to a theological symposium cosponsored by the Barth Center at Princeton Theological Seminary and the Pontifical Faculty of the Immaculate Conception at the Dominican House of Studies in Washington, D.C., in September 2016. We would like to thank all those who made this project possible, in particular, Fr. John Langlois, OP; Fr. Thomas Petri, OP, of the PFIC; and the staff of the Barth Center and the Thomistic Institute. Prof. Thomas Adam Van Wart and David L. Augustine graciously served as assistant editors for many of the essays, for which we are very grateful. David Augustine prepared the manuscript for the final submission to the Catholic University of America Press, and he also put together the bibliography; we are greatly in his debt. We also give many thanks to Jason Paone, a doctoral candidate in systematic theology at the Catholic University of America, for his work in preparing the index. John Martino skillfully guided the book through CUAP's acquisition process. Most of all we are grateful to the participant writers who prepared such substantive theological essays in the service of a profound encounter among fellow baptized Christians.

DOGMA and ECUMENISM

Introduction

Vatican II and the Future of Catholic-Protestant Ecumenism

Thomas Joseph White, OP

Thomas Aquinas famously argues that the intellect has a kind of priority over the will, because knowledge informs the desires of the heart. The will can move only toward that which it first loves and it can love only what it first knows. Consequently, we act by knowledge, through love; or negatively stated, we cannot love what we do not know. It is precisely because we first come to know what is truly good that we begin to appreciate and love it, and in turn to seek it out habitually. Knowledge of the other leads one to frequent or dwell with the other whom one loves. This is true whether we speak of God, or persons, books, or activities like prayer.

The will can in turn also influence the intellect, since we will to turn our mind attentively to the things we love best. We pay preferential intellectual attention to what we love most. In that sense, it is also true to say, for Aquinas, that love has a certain priority over the intellect, not in the knowledge of the truth, but in the concrete exercise of the search for the truth. The intellect, then, has priority in the order of specification because our knowledge informs or specifies our will's desires, while the will has priority in the exercise of agency, as we give attention to and learn from the things we begin to love and love best.[1]

A corollary to this idea exists in the domain of more general truths about life: human beings and cultures of human beings organically develop over

1. See on these matters, Thomas Aquinas, *De malo*, q. 6, and the helpful study by Michael Sherwin, *By Knowledge and by Love: Charity and Knowledge in the Moral Theology of Thomas Aquinas* (Washington, D.C.: The Catholic University of America Press, 2011).

time global interpretations of existence by reference to a body of teachings and norms of right actions by reference to those teachings. These are the theories and codes or norms by which human beings seek to safeguard that which they love best, and consider to be true. It is this inevitably diverse, broad body of interpretations of human existence that we might call *doctrina*, using the Latin word, or doctrines. In this sense, the human being simply is, naturally speaking, a "doctrinal being"—*ens doctrinae*—a being that is led through teaching to develop a sense of meaning and to explain the world thematically.

Christian theology claims of course that there is a higher doctrine or teaching available to human beings than any that derives from mere human culture or religious invention, one that is rendered available by means of the revelation of God to Israel, achieved in the person of Christ, and communicated by the inspired scripture of the Old and New Testaments, read in and through the tradition of the apostolic Church. Given that this is the case, that God does disclose his identity to us through divine revelation, theology is a science or study of sacred doctrine, *sacra doctrina*.[2] If the human being is naturally doctrinal, the Christian person is inevitably "dogmatic" insofar as he seeks to articulate in theory and practice the truth of the Christian faith. What is the essential content of divine revelation and how must we speak and act if we are to confess Christ truthfully, and if we aspire to speak the truth of Christianity in terms that are universally accessible both within the Church and outside of it?

This is a book that treats Catholic-Protestant ecumenism as a subject of both fraternal encounter in Christ and rigorous doctrinal argument. That is to say, it presupposes that doctrine matters integrally to Christian arguments about the truth of revelation. The exchanges in this book take their inspiration from two major influences in modern theology: the documents of the Second Vatican Council and the dogmatic work of Karl Barth. The choice of the two is natural. The Second Vatican Council is a preeminent modern doctrinal expression of Catholic teaching. The Council sought self-consciously to present traditional Catholic truths to both Christians and non-Christians in the contemporary world; it spoke on a host of significant topics, in a markedly modern tone. The documents of the Council contain also thematic, sophisticated treatments of ecumenism and ecclesiology that speak directly to Catholic-Protestant relations, even while they note the

2. On theology and *sacra doctrina*, see Thomas Aquinas, *Summa theologiae* (*ST*) I, q. 1.

central place of doctrine within ecumenical discussion.[3] For the fathers of the Second Vatican Council, doctrine and modern Christian identity are in no way at odds. On the contrary, as the Council notes, the Church exists down through time only if she has a continuous and clear proclamation of revealed truth to share with the world, by which she signifies her faith in a universal way, manifesting the inward meaning of the hope and charity that inspire her inward life with Christ.[4]

These are not ideas alien to Barth. Barth's work from the early 1930s onward was clearly motivated by the concern to recover dogmatic thinking in modern Protestant thought. His famous reaction to what he called "liberal Protestant modernism" led progressively to the emergence of a large-scale ambitious plan: to reflect in a disciplined and principled way on the content of Christian revelation by taking into account classical doctrinal theories while reexamining these anew, in light of his own particular Reformed convictions and in the context of modern secular intellectual culture.

Barth characterizes his own theological writing as a form of "dogmatics," since theology as he understands it is only ever a reflection on the truth of revelation disclosed in Christ to the Church, through the medium of the apostolic preaching.[5] To think out the meaning of human existence in light of Christ just is a doctrinal activity, and one that is central to the very life and self-expression of the Church. If this is the case, then dogmatics is always something "ever ancient," accountable to the ancient monuments of tradition and its classical formulae, but also something "ever new," since it must confront the mentality and challenges of a contemporary setting, including that unique context that secular modernity presents. Of course, this is something different from what Catholics mean by "dogma," since it does not entail reference to the magisterium of the bishops as successors of the apostles, as it develops organically through history. There is a reason, however, that Barth's modern exercise in dogmatic exploration has been so influential among modern theologians of various confessional traditions,

3. Second Vatican Council, Decree on Ecumenism, *Unitatis Redintegratio* §11: "The way and method in which the Catholic faith is expressed should never become an obstacle to dialogue with our brethren. It is, of course, essential that the doctrine should be clearly presented in its entirety. Nothing is so foreign to the spirit of ecumenism as a false irenicism, in which the purity of Catholic doctrine suffers loss and its genuine and certain meaning is clouded." (Unless otherwise indicated, all translations from the Second Vatican Council are taken from the official translations present at www.vatican.va.)

4. See for example, *Lumen Gentium* §25.

5. Karl Barth, *Church Dogmatics* I/1, 82: "Concrete dogma, indeed, is simply the kerygma tested, provisionally purified, and reduced to a correct formula by the Church." Hereafter "*CD*." All citations of the *CD* are taken from the English translations by G. W. Bromiley and T. F. Torrance (London: T&T Clark), 2004.

including Catholics. He pursues the thematic articulation of the content of revealed truth in a disciplined way, both in reference to the traditions of the past and in conversation with the challenges of the contemporary era. It is not surprising in this respect that many who have read Barth seriously have been led progressively to become Roman Catholic, even as Barth's work continues to serve as a central point of reference for many who seek a firm foundation for the defense of classically Reformed principles in a modern context. After all, Barth took Catholic dogma very seriously even when he did not always agree with it, and he saw it as a living intellectual option for a modern person enlightened by Christ.

Barth was very supportive of the ecumenical thrust of Vatican II and many of its core claims, but also wary of the Catholic triumphalism that he saw emerging in the late 1960s in the wake of the Council. He noted an emergent tendency among his Catholic brethren that he had encountered decades earlier in what he called Protestant modernism: the temptation to do away with the distinction between the gospel and the world, and to accommodate to a secular mentality and philosophy, under the pious auspices of missionary engagement and intellectual openness.[6] In that sense he is a dialogue partner for ecumenical conversation well suited to the post–Vatican II era. His form of engagement is not one marked by facile irenicism. As Barth saw rightly, the need for doctrine is presupposed by the very aims of the modern ecumenical movement, as a conversation between Christians—even amidst controversy—about the actual content of divine revelation.[7] What is really true about divine revelation? This is the central question of any real Christian ecumenism. After all, it is only when and as Christians discover and identify clearly, in light of the truth of Christ, what they have in common that they can in turn clarify where their differences lie and also where there are relational forms of convergence that might emerge. To think in these terms is precisely to think in doctrinal ways about the truth content of the revelation of Christ.

6. See the reflections on this theme in *CD* I/1, 35–36, 250–54. In the last years of his life, after the Second Vatican Council, Barth was to revisit some of these themes in his conversations with the Catholic protagonists of that era.

7. See the developed argument to this effect by the Catholic theologian Charles Morerod in *Tradition et Unité des Chrétiens. Le dogme comme condition de possibilité de l'oecumenisme* (Paris: Parole et Silence, 2005).

Vatican II, Karl Barth, and *Ad Limina Apostolorum*

Every ecumenical engagement has particular parameters. This book takes its framework from the signature theological initiative of the Second Vatican Council, which was not primarily an ecumenical event but which clearly had important ecumenical aspects and has had major consequences for Catholic-Protestant ecumenism in the time since the Council. Karl Barth was invited to Rome in 1966 after the Council to meet with Pope Paul VI and to discuss the conciliar documents with major representatives involved in their composition and interpretation. It was this engagement that led to Barth's later book *Ad Limina Apostolorum: An Appraisal of Vatican II*.[8] In this volume Barth considers from his theologically distinctive but characteristically Protestant vantage point the ways in which the Council engages Protestant Christians, and he in his turn responds to the ideas of the Council by posing questions about each document. Barth was involved in profound discussion with Catholic theologians throughout his life, and he conversed with them as both a seriously critical Reformed thinker and a person who allowed Catholic claims to challenge him. This was no less true in the late chapter in his life. At the same time, the late Barth also sees ambiguities in the conciliar documents, places where interpretations can open up in a variety of ways. In this respect, his questions are often quite contemporary; they speak to our own time half a century later when we can perceive more clearly both the accomplishments and the limitations of Catholic theology just after the Council, and of the postconciliar ecumenism, its advances and subsequent problems.[9] It is with open eyes toward the situation of today that we can look to Barth's doctrinal form of engagement with Vatican II and learn from it what shape a constructive, doctrinally informed ecumenism might have today, and under what conditions.

8. Karl Barth, *Ad Limina Apostolorum: An Appraisal of Vatican II*, trans. K. R. Crim (Eugene, Ore: Wipf and Stock, 2016). German original: *Ad Limina Apostolorum* (Zurich: EVZ-Verlag, 1967).

9. Here, for example, is the telling list of "general questions" Barth posed about the Council as a whole, before proceeding to specific documents: "1. Do the actions of the Council have a definite central point of emphasis? 2. Was Vatican II a reforming council? (This is sometimes disputed.) 3. What does *aggiornamento* mean? ('Accommodation' to what?) 4. Was the main concern a renewal of the Church's theoretical and practical understanding of itself in light of the revelation on which it is founded, or a renewal of her thinking, speaking, and acting today in light of the modern world? 5. If both, in the interests of the pastoral task, which was it primarily? 6. On which of these two types of renewal will the stress be placed in the period after the Council? 7. Are the adherents of the 'progressive' majority of the Council, who opt for the latter, aware of the danger, that might result in an undesired repetition of the errors committed in modern Protestantism?" (*Ad Limina Apostolorum*, 20).

Karl Barth as a Resource for Dialogue with Catholic Theologians

If doctrinal thinking is essential to theology and to ecumenical engagement, then conversations between Catholics and Protestants can always develop along at least three lines. One pertains to the exploration of shared doctrinal convictions, such as the common exploration of the content of the Chalcedonian doctrine of the one person and two natures of Christ as a way of understanding New Testament Christology, or the shared conviction that the Bible is the inspired Word of God. Another approach treats doctrines that have historically elicited opposition; this convergentist approach seeks historical context for the initial elaboration of the disputed doctrinal differences and seeks to identify ways of thinking about one's own tradition and that of the other confession in ways that can converge. A third form of engagement is relational or dialectic: it seeks to understand how Catholic-Protestant relations develop in opposition or in mutual reaction, to think out distinct and different doctrinal options, often in response to a perceived error or danger on the other side.

We find all of these patterns of engagement in Barth's theology. In fact, it is his willingness to openly revisit anew so many "settled matters" in the Christian tradition at large or in the Reformed tradition specifically that makes Barth a highly original and intriguing thinker. Consequently one even might ask whether Barth is a sufficient representative of the classical Lutheran and Reformed viewpoints, especially in light of his own often highly original (even idiosyncratic) notions of biblical inspiration, election and predestination, sources of tradition, natural knowledge of God (or the lack thereof), sacramental efficacy, or church polity. A contrasting position could be stated as well. Barth is deeply polemical at times when treating Catholic themes: doctrinal infallibility, philosophical knowledge of God, Mariology, the sacramental life.[10] Perhaps his lack of profound sympathy would seem artificially constricted, to such an extent that his intellectual potential for partnership in a dialogue would remain always tenuous at best.

How should we answer these reasonable queries? The first point to be noted is that Barth does maintain characteristically Reformed views in a number of respects. In fact, a much stronger version of this thesis would be warranted: Barth is clearly one of the most successful and intellectually

10. On doctrinal nonreformability and infallibility, see Karl Barth, *Church Dogmatics* I/2, 544–72; on natural knowledge of God, the famous passages in *CD* I/1, xiii, 35–44; on Mariology see *CD* I/2, 138–47; on the sacraments, consider *CD* I/2, 228–32, and the famous baptismal "fragment" of *CD* IV/4.

powerful theological protagonists of the Reformation in the modern era. His mature theological project represented especially by the *Church Dogmatics* is characterized by the decision to articulate the core tenets of Reformed Christianity even at the heart of the modern intellectual epoch in a profound and wide-ranging way, one that is both intellectually cosmopolitan and deeply theoretically demanding. This trajectory of his thinking was long in the making, since Barth's break in the 1930s with what he characterized as modernist liberal Protestantism was also meant to be a return to the sources of Protestantism, albeit articulated in a new key, and this motivation seems to characterize his intellectual project up to the end of his life.[11] Indeed, Barth's sense of responsibility for the Protestant heritage is easily perceptible when one observes his consistent treatment in the *Church Dogmatics* of classical Protestant themes: the centrality of Christ within revelation and with regard to all true knowledge of God, the primacy of scripture, its unique authority over all subsequent tradition, and the inherent reformability of the Church's magisterial proclamations, the extrinsic origins of grace with respect to all human mediations, the centrality of imputed justification as a key concept for understanding God's election of humanity in Christ, the radical depravity of the human condition apart from Christ, the necessity of revelation as the sole key to rightly interpreting human nature and ethical life, the centrality of word and proclamation as a measure of the inward meaning of the sacraments.

Nevertheless, it is also the case that Barth was not invulnerable to or intellectually disengaged from Catholicism. On the contrary, one noteworthy aspect of his thought is that he weighs Catholic claims seriously and engages with them earnestly precisely so as to determine where and under what conditions he may or may not consent to them as a Reformed theologian and fellow Christian. A helpful example can be found in Barth's treatment of the topic of the Catholic understanding of dogma and infallibility in *CD* I, 1.[12] There it is clear that he allows himself to be deeply challenged by the claims of the Catholic Church regarding doctrinal infallibility, and actually places the burden of dissent from this teaching on the Protestant theologian, for understandable reasons. After all, revelation is of divine origin and God's revelation in Christ is itself free from error or falsehood. Furthermore, the Church is able to proclaim this truth of the revelation of God only be-

11. See *CD* I/1, 34–36, 251–59. See Barth's similar warning about liberal Protestantism to Karl Rahner in his late correspondence in 1968, in *Letters 1961–1968*, ed. Jurgen Fangmeier and Hinrich Stoevesandt, trans. G. W. Bromiley (Grand Rapids, Mich.: Eerdmans, 1981), 287–88.

12. *CD* I/1, 265–75.

cause she has first encountered and come to know the mystery of Christ. Consequently, proclamation of the Gospel and the articulation of theology itself presupposes some latent appeal to divinely revealed knowledge without error that the Church has truly come to possess.[13] The history of creed and doctrine is central to the life of the Church, and seems to emerge as a virtual practical inevitability once one takes seriously the magisterial burden of the Church to present the gospel clearly in a public fashion. One witnesses this dynamic not only in the Catholic tradition but also in the Lutheran magisterial tradition as evidenced by the Formula of Concord.[14] In conclusion, then, it would seem for both speculative and practical reasons that the Church in her concrete history of reception of the gospel must in some respect make appeal to fundamental defining doctrines of Christian revelation that she claims to know to be true infallibly in virtue of their origin in the self-revelation of God.

Barth responds to this query not by caricaturing or trivializing his opponents' views but by re-contextualizing the claim to infallibility in his own typically Reformed terms. He does so by appeal to the twin notions of human fallibility and eschatological resolution of the truth. In the scope of this world, human beings are inherently fallible and incapable of holding divine truth habitually in their own possession in such ways as to control or wield it for institutional and ecclesiastical usage.[15] Claims to the contrary are suspect since they can readily stem from a nonevangelical, all too human will to power. Though the Church can and does often proclaim revealed truth, she cannot guarantee her capacity to do so in any intrinsic habitual way.[16] However, the Church is actualized by God's revelation in this life, by God's providence and mercy, in view of a sustained, pure, and plenary possession of the truth that is to be brought to perfection in the eschatological state.[17]

13. *CD* I/1, 265: "Dogma is the agreement of Church proclamation with the revelation attested in Holy Scripture."

14. Barth discusses this problem at some length in *CD* I/2, 552–72.

15. *CD* I/1, 266–67: "The proximity of *dogmata ecclesiastica* to *dogmata haereticorum* should be enough to remind us of the basic vulnerability of the dogma defined by the Church and also to ward off the idea of an infallible dogma of this kind. It may also be pointed out that according to Roman Catholic teaching itself not all dogmas have yet been confessed or defined by the Church, that even if revealed truth is substantially closed there is still dogmatic progress . . . and that ultimately it is the material content (*sensus*) rather than the formula that is said to be the unchangeable and infallible truth in dogmatic formulations."

16. *CD* I/1, 267: "The dogma which dogmatics investigates cannot, then, be the *veritas ab Ecclesia definita*. The *veritas ab Ecclesia definita* is itself the question of dogma. It can and should guide dogmatics. But it cannot seek to be the dogma which is the goal of dogmatics. . . . [W]hile dogma which dogmatics investigates is not the truth of revelation, it aims at the truth of revelation."

17. *CD* I/1, 269: "If questioning ceased . . . if the agreement of specific Church proclamation with the Word of God and therefore the Word of God itself in this specific Church proclamation could be

Therefore the Church in her history in this world dialectically seeks the truth through ever reformable arguments between her members, always made in subjection to scripture, while Christians live in hope in an eschatological infallible knowledge of God, one that is already breaking into the world in Christ, albeit imperfectly and in a way that humbles human pretensions.

What is interesting about this example is that it actually invites a deeper conversation between Catholicism and Protestantism. For example, Roman Catholic theology traditionally does distinguish infallible ecclesial dogma quite clearly from divine revelation as such and claims that the former is subordinate to the latter, though adequate in part (imperfectly) to the truth communicated by God. Barth's formulations about Catholicism do not always engage sufficiently the traditional Catholic distinctions on this point.[18] Furthermore, the Catholic theologian can readily acknowledge Barth's concern about human fallibility and his confidence in the eschatological revelation of Christ as reasons not for denying but rather for advancing the Catholic affirmation of the infallibility of the Church (and its concrete instances in dogmatic formulae). After all it is only if the Church is assisted and sustained in the midst of argument by the capacity to come to discernments of clear teaching concerning the content of revelation that she can in turn orient herself toward eschatological fulfillment, even in the midst of the moral and epistemological obscurity that characterizes our current human state.[19] Even when there is not consensus, then, on a major point of Catholic-Protestant division, Barth's way of engaging with the deeper principles that the Catholic and Reformed controversies evoke or imply provides grounds for identifying shared premises and for thinking through the consequences of differentiated oppositions. Barth's is an ecumenism without compromise but also a depth ecumenism. It invites Christians to become deeply themselves amidst dispute, as they also seek to understand the real shape of their own deepest doctrinal commitments to the truth.

---

demonstrated, then dogmatics would be at an end along with the *ecclesia militans*, and the kingdom of God would have dawned.... To this extent one may call dogma an 'eschatological concept.'"

18. See, for example, the classical treatment by Charles Journet in *L'Église du Verbe Incarné*, vol. I, *La hiérarchie apostolique* (Paris: Saint Augustin, 1998), 294–335 690–722; Yves Congar, *Tradition and Traditions: An Historical and a Theological Essay*, trans. M. Naseby and T. Rainborough (London: Burns and Oates, 1966), 376–493, which engages Barth positively and constructively; and more recently Guy Mansini, *Fundamental Theology* (Washington, D.C.: The Catholic University of America Press, 2018), 122–40.

19. See the brief but interesting argument to this effect by Hans Urs von Balthasar at the end of his book on Barth, *The Theology of Karl Barth: Exposition and Interpretation*, trans. E. Oakes (San Francisco: Ignatius, 1992), 386–89; and the classic argumentation by Yves Congar, in *Vrai et fausse réforme dans l'église* (Paris: Cerf, 1950).

In fact, Barth's contact with modern Catholic theology is evident throughout his corpus and his life of relationships. If we consider this chronologically, we could readily identify the following instances: Barth's engagement with Erich Przywara in the early 1930s regarding the *analogia entis*; his sustained interest in the theology of Matthias Scheeben on topics of grace, ecclesial authority, and Mariology, evidenced in early volumes of the *CD*; his analysis of and reaction to the work of Gottlieb Söhngen again on the topic of the *analogia entis*; the sustained intellectual dialogue and friendship with Hans Urs von Balthasar centered on Christology and Trinitarian ontology; the supervision of the thesis of Hans Küng on justification; encounters in later life with Congar, Rahner, and Ratzinger on topics related to Vatican II; and of course his meeting with Paul VI near the end of his life.[20]

Why was Barth a sustained dialogue partner for these many Catholic theologians who were themselves central protagonists in twentieth-century debates? Clearly in one respect simply because of Barth's own stature as a modern Christian thinker and characteristic representative of the rebirth and refashioning of Protestant thought under modern conditions. However, there are other arguably deeper reasons stemming from Barth's own methodological approach to theology. Catholics could perceive in him a kind of fellow traveler in key respects.

Most fundamentally, there is the fact that Barth seeks continually in his theology to rearticulate traditional dogmatic formulae of the ancient Church in a modern idiom. In his first volume of the *Church Dogmatics* for example, he takes ancient Arianism and Sabellian modalism as two erroneous extremes of thinking about the mystery of God: a monotheism that denies the divinity of Christ and a Trinitarianism that denies the real distinction of persons.[21] Barth wishes to find a way to present the classical Trinitarian notion of God in a contemporary way. In this he follows Schleiermacher in intent, but not in content, since the latter leaned decisively toward a kind of Sabellianism and (arguably) a Nestorian adoptionism in his later work.[22]

20. Clear evidence of his engagement with several of these figures near the end of his life can be seen in *Letters 1961–1968*.

21. See *CD* I/1, 348–58.

22. Friedrich Schleiermacher, *The Christian Faith*, 2 vols., ed. H. R. Mackintosh and J. S. Stewart (New York: Harper and Row, 1963). On the Trinity, see especially vol. I, §§70–72, 282–304; vol. II, §§93–99, 377–424; §§117–20, 536–60; §§160–62, 707–713; §§170–72, 738–51. Vol. II, §170, 738–39: "An essential element of our exposition in this Part has been the doctrine of the union of the Divine Essence with human nature, both in the personality of Christ and in the common Spirit of the Church; therewith the whole view of Christianity set forth in our Church teaching stands and falls. For unless the being

Barth's own Trinitarian theology in the early *Church Dogmatics* centers the discussion around revelation and historical disclosure: The Trinity is God who reveals himself in his Word in and through the historical life, death, and resurrection of Christ, as in the sending of the Spirit of Christ. This historical manifestation of God sets out the pattern of Trinitarian distinction of persons as truly distinct modes of being in God's own life as it is given to us to know in time.[23] Undoubtedly this way of thinking about the Trinity was to influence later Catholic authors like Rahner and Balthasar, albeit in different ways.[24] The point is that Barth's efforts to think dogmatically in a modern key were not imitated materially by his Catholic colleagues but were influential to them, since they were experiments in typically modern Christian dogmatic thinking. In this sense, there is even a parallelism (with significant differences!) between the Second Vatican Council itself and Barth's own work. Each was attempting, in significantly different ways, to articulate the traditional doctrines of Christianity to contemporary human beings, in the thought idioms of modernity.

Theology in this period was also marked by ecumenical engagement, as Protestants and Catholics each confronted problems in relation to modernity that were common to the two traditions. What is the place of historical-critical study of the Bible with regard to traditional the Christological dogmas? How ought one to understand the relationship of theology and clas-

---

of God in Christ is assumed, the idea of redemption could not be thus concentrated in his Person. And unless there were such a union also in the common Spirit of the Church, the Church could not thus be the Bearer and Perpetuator of the redemption thorough Christ.... But at this point we would call a halt; we cannot attach the same value to the further elaboration of the dogma, which alone justifies the ordinary term. For the term, 'Trinity' is really based on the fact that each of the two above-mentioned unions is traced back to a separate distinction posited independently of such union, and eternally, in the Supreme Being as such; further, after the member of this plurality destined to union with Jesus had been designated by the name 'Son,' it was felt necessary to posit the Father in accordance therewith as a special distinction. The result was the familiar dualism—unity of Essence and trinity of Persons. But the assumption of an eternal distinction in the Supreme Being is not an utterance concerning the religious consciousness, for there it could never emerge. Who would venture to say that the impression made by the divine in Christ obliges us to conceive such an eternal distinction as its basis?"

23. *CD* I/1, 371: "To the unity of the Father, Son and Spirit among themselves corresponds their unity *ad extra*. God's essence and work are not twofold but one. God's work is His essence in its relation to the reality that is distinct from Him and which is to be created or is created by Him. The work of God is the essence of God as the essence of Him who ... is revealer, revelation and being revealed, or Creator, Reconciler and Redeemer. In this work of His, God is revealed to us."

24. See most notably Karl Rahner, *The Trinity*, trans. J. Donceel (London: Burns & Oates, 1967). Rahner's articulation of his "Trinitarian Grundaxiom" (that the immanent Trinity is ontologically identical with the economic Trinity and vice versa) bears evident similarities to the work of Barth in *CD* I/1 and references that work at several junctures. For a very different application of the idea, evidently influenced by Barth, see Hans Urs von Balthasar, *Theo-Logic; Theological Logical Theory*, Vol. II, *Truth of God*, trans. Adrian Walker (San Francisco, Calif.: Ignatius, 2004), 173–218.

sical metaphysics in a post-Enlightenment age? What is the relationship between theology and modern natural science and its discoveries of the past two centuries? How ought Christians to respond to the rise of modern secular democratic societies and nonreligious culture as well as antireligious ideologies? How should Christians address and learn from the Jewish people in a way that moves beyond the pattern of polemical diatribes and all too frequent horrible violence? Can anything positive be learned by one side of the Reformation divide from the other side, and can anything positive be said about the status of the billions of people who live today as adherents of non-Christian religions? In answering these typically modern challenges, Catholics and Protestants alike could take advice from one another theologically, even if they also maintained key differences, as one sees for example in the early Christological work of Wolfhart Pannenberg, which clearly engages very deeply with the modern Christological reflection of Karl Rahner, and self-consciously so.[25] Barth was a more polemical writer than Pannenberg, to be sure, but his own pattern of engaging with modern Catholic thinkers contributed to the rise of this dynamic of ecumenically interactive (and dialectical!) doctrinal thinking.

We might consider a few notable examples in this respect, starting with the reaction of Barth to the *analogia entis* theories of Przywara. Paradoxically, it is Barth's way of responding and reacting to the analogy of being doctrine of the Jesuit that came to color his thought in ways that are typically Catholic. How can this be? It is often the case that one becomes like what one reacts to, especially if that reaction is constructive and creative. Barth perceived a challenge in Przywara's controversial (and arguably problematic) claim that the analogy of being is the fundamental form of Catholic theology (a claim Söhngen and Balthasar would dispute, even while still differing from Barth).[26] Barth sought to give expression to a distinctively reformed Protestant form of theology in reaction to Pryzwara's vision of Catholicism, one characterized by his own sense of what he called the analogy of faith (the likeness between God and creatures revealed only in Christ).

25. Wolfhart Pannenberg, *Jesus—God and Man*, second edition, trans. L. L. Wilkins and D. A. Priebe (Philadelphia: Westminster, 1968), especially 317–52, where the engagement with Rahner is manifest repeatedly and even thematically.

26. See this idea in Erich Przywara, Analogia Entis; *Metaphysics: Original Structure and Universal Rhythm*, trans. John Betz and David Bentley Hart (Grand Rapids, Mich.: Eerdmans, 2014), Part II, chap. 2, "The Scope of Analogy as a Fundamental Catholic Form," 348–99; and the criticisms of it in Gottlieb Söhngen, "The Analogy of Faith: Likeness to God from Faith Alone?" *Pro Ecclesia* 21, no. 1 (2012): 56–76, and "The Analogy of Faith: Unity in the Science of Faith," *Pro Ecclesia* 21, no. 2 (2012): 169–94, trans. K. Oakes; as well as the criticisms by Balthasar in *Theo-Logic* II: *The Truth of God*, 94–95n16, and on 273n109.

However, in doing so, Barth also focused in a distinctive way on ontological questions and oriented his dogmatic thinking toward the speculative horizon, the search for an integrated understanding of the structure of reality undertaken in light of Christology: the two natures of Christ, the doctrine of election in Christ as it affects all creaturely existence, the revelation of the inward identity of God the Trinity in the event of Christ's being human, his death and resurrection.[27] The overtly ontological character of this vision, and its speculative amplitude, clearly bear some important similitudes to the high medieval form of thinking Aquinas calls *sacra doctrina*, just as it does to various forms of early modern Reformed scholasticism, and Barth was quite well aware of this fact.[28] In other words, Barth's Christological ontology is not entirely novel; it has clear roots and precedents in patristic Chalcedonian theology, as well as in both medieval and modern scholastic theologies (all the while containing deeply novel elements).[29] Precisely for this reason, Barth's Christological ontology in important respects bears inevitable likenesses to traditional Catholic thought, which as Przywara rightly noted, is always characterized by a profound reference to the metaphysics of creaturely being as a way of thinking about the likeness *and the nonsimilitude* between the Holy Trinity and the creature, illuminated especially in the light of Christ. This ontological parallelism between Catholic theology and Barth's distinctively Reformed theology is unmistakable, even if Barth's methodology emerges from the rejection of a classical Catholic model of *sacra doctrina* in its use of philosophical reason. In a manner internal to his own particular epistemological principles, Barth continually explores the great tradition of patristic, medieval, and modern Christian thought, engaging with the themes he finds in Augustine, Anselm, Aquinas, Scheeben, and Pryzwara as much as with those of Luther, Calvin, or Schleiermacher.

At the same time, Barthian ontology is characterized profoundly throughout his corpus by the distinctive form of Protestant thinking that he developed in reaction to both liberal Protestantism and Roman Catholicism. When Barth confronts an enigma of ontology that philosophers debate he frequently advances by a twofold process. First he will claim that the philosophical aporias surrounding the question are signs of the impotence of human reasoning to resolve the question in a nonskeptical manner. Second he will appeal to revelation (formally) not only to resolve the matter but also

27. This is particularly clear in Barth's Christological ontology present in *CD* II, 1–2 and IV, 1–2.

28. Balthasar presents an influential argument in this regard in *The Theology of Karl Barth*, especially pp. 114–67.

29. As exemplified in the Chalcedonian-inspired Christology of *CD* IV/1 and 2.

to signify ontologically that the answer to the question simply lies outside the sphere of human natural perception, and is only present in Christ and in the elective covenant. So for example, Barth considers the ontological question of what human personhood is and of our continuing identity through time as a speculative enigma of human reason that is resolved effectively only by recourse to the theology of election. It is precisely because God in Christ has designated us for self-hood and personal *identity in Christ* that we are able to decipher a narrative of continual existence that is grounded in something transcendent and real.[30] Likewise Barth contests the foundations in revelation for the immaterial nature of the human soul or its subsistence after death, which the Catholic tradition affirms to be both truths of divine revelation and necessary conclusions of sound philosophical reasoning.[31] Instead, Barth treats all questions regarding the eschatological existence of the person after death within the context of the ontology of Christ resurrected and his re-creative activity alone. This leads Barth toward a skeptical reserve concerning the question of personal "survival" after death.[32] Clearly this point of view differs radically from that of Catholicism, but it anticipates "death-in-resurrection" theories of eschatology that emerged in Lutheran thought in the late twentieth century, in which hope is placed in God's complete re-creation of human persons after death, in light of the elective covenant in Christ.[33]

Other examples could be given: Human freedom is understood only in light of the mystery of God's election and gift of justification.[34] Knowledge of creation is made possible only in Christ and in light of the Incarnation.[35] Human nature is truly intelligible only in light of the human life, death,

30. See in this respect the extremely instructive discussion of Descartes and the nature of the human being in *CD* III/1, 350–63. Man has knowledge of his enduring identity principally and above all as a covenant partner of God, elected by him in Christ. The ontological stability emerges first and foremost from something outside of man's own natural being and self-knowledge.

31. See *CD* III/2, 573–55, on the question of the origins of the human soul, and 587–640 on the final state of man in light of death.

32. *CD* III/2, 632–33: "Death is man's step from existence into non-existence.... Man as such, therefore, has no beyond. Nor does he need one, for God is his beyond.... Man as such, however, belongs to this world. He is thus finite and mortal.... He does not hope for redemption from the this-sidedness, finitude and mortality of His existence. He hopes positively for the revelation of its redemption as completed in Jesus Christ, namely the redemption of his this-sided, finite existence."

33. See the theological analysis and criticism of these views in Joseph Ratzinger, *Eschatology: Death and Eternal Life*, trans. Michael Waldstein (Washington, D.C.: The Catholic University of America Press, 1988; 2nd ed., 2007), and in the 1979 document from the Congregation for the Doctrine of the Faith, "Letter on Certain Questions Concerning Eschatology," available at www.vatican.va; and the *Catechism of the Catholic Church*, §§365–66; 1021–42.

34. See *CD* III/1, 265–76.

35. See *CD* III/1, 3–41.

and resurrection of Christ.[36] The sacraments and holy scripture are efficacious means of grace only if and when God should choose to employ them to manifest himself and act in the power of the Holy Spirit, but God is never committed to these means in such a way that human beings might have any guarantee to encounter God in and through them.[37]

In all these examples we find a number of confluent principles: God in his sovereignty, transcendence, and freedom is the true and unique author of grace, and the only one who can reveal himself to man. There is a unilateral relationship that is always established by the prior initiative of God. Deep understanding of the structures of reality is available to us only in light of the election of God, made manifest in Christ, as a gift of grace, never by the prior initiative of man, whether that initiative be moral or epistemological. The visible sphere of creation is never the place that human beings have a right or guarantee to initiate their relationship with God, nor even a final form of self-understanding of an adequate and complete human philosophy. No ecclesial structures are adequate to the mystery of God, and every human instance of ecclesial life is marked by limitation, finitude, and fallibility. Consequently there is always a nonparallelism and inadequateness between what members of the Church are doing and what God may or may not be doing above and beyond or even over and against them. In all this Barth was clearly attempting to explore what he took to be the ontological implications of Luther's notion of justification, not only in moral terms (the primacy of God's grace and its first initiative in the order of salvation) but also in ontological and epistemological terms (following Calvin, as Barth interpreted him): election and covenant are the inward ground of our very being, made manifest to us only in Christ.[38]

36. See *CD* III/2, 19–74, at 48: "The sinlessness, purity and freedom of human nature in Jesus consists precisely in the fact that, laden with the sin which is alien to His own nature, He causes Himself to be condemned and rejected with us. Thus the sin of our human nature is not only covered by Him but rightfully removed and destroyed. But this means that it is truly buried and covered, so that before God and in truth there now remains only the pure and freed humanity of Jesus as our own humanity.... The purity, freedom, peace and clarity of the human nature of Jesus does not remain His privilege alone, but for His sake this privilege becomes ours as well. As God knows Him, He also knows us." See 73: "If it is the case in relation to the man Jesus that in His humanity we are confronted immediately and directly with the being of God, then necessarily, assuming that there is similarity between Him and us in spite of all dissimilarity, every man is to be understood, at least mediately and indirectly, to the extent that he is conditioned by the priority of this man, in his relation with God."

37. See *CD* I/2, 226–32; 512–37.

38. In his book *Nein! Antwort an Emil Brunner*, Barth argues against Brunner that the Reformers rightly emphasized the sufficiency and unique authority of scripture over and above tradition and the primacy of grace over against human operations, but that they did not adequately treat the question of human knowledge as it relates to revealed truth. The argument against natural theology that Barth undertakes then is to be seen as an extension of the Reformed principle. The real and foundational

It is a mistake, however, to characterize Barth's thought in primarily reactive or negative terms, as a reaction against alternatives, even in view of positive traditional Reformed ends. As Hans Urs von Balthasar noted, Barth's theology is intended above all to signify the inward content of the revelation of Christ as God and man.[39] In this sense, it is a theology of proclamation but even more a theology concerned with speculative truth and beauty, a conceptual hymn of praise oriented in its distinctive way toward the mystery of God, conducted with the intent of sincere submission to apostolic revelation, and in confession of human sin and brokenness, but also with confidence in Christ as an extrinsic source of activity and justification, *simul justus et peccator*.[40]

Hans Urs von Balthasar famously attempted to depict Barth's thought as one that developed in his *Church Dogmatics* from "dialectic to analogy," from an ontology of oppositions of God's activity and human activity to one of similitude and alignment, a harmony initiated by God's grace and brought into fulfillment in Christ. Alternative interpretations, such as that of Bruce McCormack, have sought to underscore the persistence of the dialectical and distinctively Reformed elements of Barth's thought in his mature work.[41] Reinhard Hütter helpfully characterizes these dual elements or tendencies in Barth's thought by speaking of his dialectical ecclesiology: God does reveal the similitude of God and man in the person and event of Christ, and does so in and through the Church, her proclamation, and her sacramental life.[42] But God also does this despite and in a sense always over and against the finite limitations of these features of created reality that cannot adequately sustain or guarantee the presence of God in creation, from the side of human perceptions and activities, inside or outside the Church.

knowledge of ontology is knowledge given theologically from the revelation of the ontology of Christ. See the English translation "No!" in Emil Brunner and Karl Barth, *Natural Theology* (Eugene, Ore.: Wipf and Stock, 2002), particularly on p. 102, where Barth gives an account of his theoretical standpoint.

39. Balthasar, *The Theology of Karl Barth*, 114–21, 169.

40. See Balthasar, *The Theology of Karl Barth*, 157, describing Barth's Christocentric Protestant vision of sinful man, so that even man's sin has to be understood now within the encompassing sphere of Christ's reconciliation: "There is still a contradiction to God in man, but now it is bracketed in the truth of the Redeemer. One could echo *The Epistle to the Romans* and say that the contradiction is at its most rebellious where it is closest to being dissolved: in the Church, among the redeemed. But it is nonetheless an 'impossible possibility': impossible in Christ, who has broken the contradiction; but a possibility in man, who, although he is a brother of Christ, has said No to this fact. When the sinner opposes God's summons with his own contradiction, he thereby contradicts himself and his own nature."

41. Bruce L. McCormack, *Karl Barth's Critically Realistic Dialogical Theology: Its Genesis and Development 1909–1936* (Oxford: Clarendon, 1995).

42. See Reinhard Hütter, "Karl Barth's 'Dialectical Catholicity': Sic et Non," *Modern Theology* 16, no. 2 (2000): 137–57; also "Barth between McCormack and von Balthasar. A Dialectic," *Pro Ecclesia* 8, no. 1 (1999): 105–9.

We might add to Hütter's line of analysis the idea of Barth as offering us a "dialectical" ontology of the visible Church, in which the limitations and opaqueness of the created order send us ever back to a uniquely Christological understanding of being, one made manifest in the ontology of the elective covenant of God in Christ.

One may of course wonder whether Barth's particular form of Reformed theology (itself subject to complex internal disputes) is really too idiosyncratic and personal a project to sustain a deep conversation with Catholicism. The arguments in this book of both Catholics and Protestants alike are not based on the premise that Barth's theology constitutes the unique or exclusive paradigm of Protestant thought. They do presuppose that Barth's theology contains many representative Protestant ideas, that his thought is a sophisticated and forceful defense of the Protestant tradition in a modern key, and that Barth posed good questions about the documents of the Second Vatican Council from a distinctively Protestant point of view. In this sense, the dialogue represented in this book is not about the adjudication of Barth's thought or even its internal coherence and integrity as a Protestant form of thought. Rather, it is about the ways that Barth's own engagements with Catholic theology allow those who come after him to engage in a helpful (if limited) form of constructive dispute. Barth's own analysis of the Council serves to help us now, fifty years later, identify clearly Catholic doctrinal principles as they relate to Protestant ones, and to dispute the inner contours and potential promise (or perhaps limitation) of the Council as a "place" of Catholic-Protestant encounter. What is at stake? The most fundamental commonality shared by Catholics and Protestants is their common search for the truth about God. Theological dispute is above all the shared search for the truth about divine revelation itself, pursued in the charity of Christ. This is the case also in ecumenical engagement.

Vatican II as a Resource for Catholic-Protestant Ecumenism

That the Second Vatican Council is of importance for ecumenism is beyond dispute. The Council document *Unitatis Redintegratio* is the signature treatment of the subject by the modern Roman Catholic magisterium. Nevertheless, the topic is also approached in a variety of other documents. *Dei Verbum*, the Apostolic Constitution on Divine Revelation, treats the subjects of scripture, tradition, and magisterial authority in ways that are distinctively Catholic, yet sensitive to the concerns or opposing viewpoints of both Orthodox sister-Churches and Protestant ecclesial communities. Arguably the most important document of the Council, *Lumen Gentium*, contains an important theological consideration of non-Catholic Christians as they relate to the visible Catholic Church, in paragraphs 14–16. *Nostra Aetate* treats the subject of the Church's regard toward non-Christian religions. By this very fact however, the document also speaks explicitly of the Christocentric character of revelation and salvation, themes that are at the center of Christian theology for non-Catholics, who must also think seriously about their own relations to Jews, as well as Muslims and members of other religious traditions. *Gaudium et Spes* is a document addressed to the larger world of non-Christians, and so similarly, it provides a potential model of how Christians may choose to present Christ and the mystery of Christianity to non-Christian and indeed to secular modern human beings. The promise or peril of this particular model may be subject to dispute (as indeed the document has been subsequently *within* the Catholic Church itself). At the same time, it is one that invites non-Catholic Christians to consider how Christianity can rightly and confidently be proclaimed to modern nonreligious persons, and how this might be done by Christians, including the question of what pertains to the natural law, as clarified in light of Christian revelation.

Ecumenism in the Twenty-First Century

Of course, a great deal has changed since the time of the Second Vatican Council and since the time of Barth's engagement with the Council in his book *Ad Limina Apostolorum*. First, the world situation of Christianity has changed greatly. The Council did not foresee a number of new factors that have emerged since and that affect Christianity in our own time. How truly "contemporary" are these documents today, in light of important historical changes that have occurred since its publication? One can think here of the fall of communism, the global expansion of capitalist liberalism, the growth of Christianity in the global south, the widescale secularization of Europe and North America, the philosophical influence of postmodernity on ontology and ethics, the sexual revolution (stemming from the widespread use of contraception, the prevalence of abortion, co-habitation, divorce, and the increasing cultural acceptance of homosexuality), the discovery of the human genome and the bioethical practices to which it has given rise, the expansion of Islam, the widespread crisis in Catholic religious orders, the cultural transformation enacted by modern social media, especially through the use of the computer and internet. None of these events were foreseen by the Council, and all of them are more central to the culture of the twenty-first century than many of the "signs of the times" alluded to in *Gaudium et Spes*. Protestants and Catholics have not always negotiated these changes in the same ways or each found ways to respond to change that are unambiguously linked to their own core doctrinal traditions. Controversies about Christian identity ensue within both traditions that are substantive.

Furthermore, as Yves Congar rightly noted, in the postconciliar period, modern ecumenism must not be utopian or naively a-doctrinal. It is marked by relational (dialectical) modes of engagement and not only by convergentist accounts.[43] Discussions between Catholics and Protestants in our own era must be characterized then by at least three concerns: First to ascertain what really pertains to the content of divine revelation and the Christian doctrinal and natural law tradition, with reference to each one's own doctrinal patrimony and magisterial expression (including the controversies over human sexuality that continue to exist in discussions between Catholics and Protestants); Second, to think about what core principles are present that allow for convergence or better mutual understanding; and Third, to identify where there exist true points of contrast, tension or ongoing dispute, including disputes about the nature of the Church, her visible institutional structure and sacraments. Without honesty and clarity about these issues, presented in charity and fraternal trust, there cannot be a thorough-going and robust ecumenism in the contemporary context. It is this kind of search for theological truth, conducted in charity, that this volume seeks to advance.

The Structure of This Book as an Ecumenical Engagement

The conversation of this book is structured around five major documents from the Second Vatican Council, each of which Barth commented upon in his work *Ad Limina Apostolorum*. Consequently, in each case, the consideration of the questions raised by the document and their ecumenical importance is framed in large part by reference to Barth's critical questions. We begin first, however, with an overview of Barth's engagement of the council fathers, in the wake of the event of the Council, and a consideration

43. See Yves Congar, *Diversity and Communion*, trans. J. Bowden (London: SCM Press, 1984).

of Barth's influence upon Catholic theology in the modern era, specifically with respect to Barth's insistence that theology be explicitly (though not exclusively) engaged with the text of holy Scripture. This framing essay is provided by Matthew Levering. Then we move to the five documents themselves. We begin thematically with *Dei Verbum*, the Apostolic Constitution on Divine Revelation, since that document looks at the sources of revelation (scripture, tradition and the magisterium). The document has modern historical study of scripture and tradition squarely in view as touching upon the human and historical dimension of revelation. In this first section, then, we present Katherine Sonderegger's reflections on scripture and Lewis Ayres's reflections on tradition, as complementary and interactive analyses of the text of Vatican II.

From here the conversation moves to the Apostolic Constitution on the Church, *Lumen Gentium*, which obviously touches upon central differences of Catholic and Protestant self-understanding. Christoph Schwöbel provides a substantive and positive analysis of visible ecclesial identity as conceived in a Protestant context, in convergence with but not identical to the Roman Catholic conception, while Thomas Joseph White analyzes Barth's characteristically Reformed criticisms of the Catholic notion of continual, visible, institutional structures in the Church. In continuity with some of Barth's Christological premises, he argues in view of the reality and fittingness of instrumental mediations in Christ himself and in the apostolic and post-apostolic Church.

In the exchange on *Nostra Aetate*, Bruce L. McCormack offers a timely reflection on the Council's treatment of Islam. Is it true to say that Muslims worship (in some way) the same God as Christians, and, if so, to what does this commit one theologically? Barth presents contrasting reflections to the Council on this point, and the topic is one that theologians continue to explore in our own historical moment. Bruce D. Marshall, meanwhile, considers the Council's reflections on the Jewish people as distinct from other non-Christian religious traditions, and how all of this touches upon the mystery of the Church and her self-understanding of non-Christian peoples.

The reflection on *Gaudium et Spes* is marked by a helpfully rich ecumenical engagement. John Bowlin looks at the document on the Church in the modern world as a Reformed theologian, and seeks to make use of the thought of Thomas Aquinas to consider the promise and perils of the theological vision of this work as a "Pastoral Constitution." Francesca Murphy, meanwhile, as a Catholic theologian, considers the response of George

Lindbeck, the Lutheran theologian, to the Council document, and engages critically with his analysis.

The final pair of essays is concerned with *Unitatis Redintegratio*, the Council document on principles for Catholic ecumenicism. Hans Boersma presents an analysis of that document that seeks to show how it is always already marked by deeply Catholic ecclesiological presuppositions, and why this is consequential for Catholic-Protestant relations in the wake of the Council. Reinhard Hütter considers Barth's questions regarding the document in systematic fashion and argues that *Unitatis Redintegratio* constitutes a genuine "development of Catholic doctrine" in the sense in which John Henry Newman understood that phrase. In this sense, the document proceeds from genuine Catholic ecclesiological principles and holds the key to subsequent forms of Catholic ecumenical engagement.

The analysis of the volume is brought to a conclusion with an essay on the nature of ecumenism by the Dominican theologian Richard Schenk. Fr. Schenk's lifelong commitment to Roman Catholic–Protestant ecumenism both in Europe and in North America provides him with a fitting vantage point from which to speak to the topic of "true and false ecumenism" in the postconciliar period. His essay provides an appropriate concluding statement to the volume, since it formulates an analysis of and embodies in practice the kind of ecumenical reflection that the volume at large aspires to accomplish.

This volume came about more generally because of the sustained discussions of the faculty of the Dominican House of Studies in Washington, D.C., and that of Princeton Theological Seminary, characterized in this regard by their two institutes, the Thomistic Institute and the Center for Barth Studies. Of course Aquinas and Barth represent very distinctive and in some ways contrasting visions of theology, but also in some ways convergent ones, and each of these thinkers continues to inform vividly his respective ecclesial tradition of confessional thinking and doctrinal expression. We hope this volume shows, then, how fruitful doctrinal commitments can be in the context of ecumenical discussion, and how real ecumenical discussion presupposes and proceeds from doctrinal commitments, and the shared search for the truth concerning the authentic inward content of the revelation of Christ.

Chapter 1

Biblical Renewal and Vatican II

Karl Barth's Contributions

Matthew Levering

Due to ill health, Karl Barth declined an invitation to attend the final two sessions of the Council as an observer. In May 1966, however, Barth felt well enough to propose a visit to Rome to discuss the documents of the recently completed Council. In response to his proposal, he received a "very friendly and cordial" response from the Secretariat for Christian Unity, which (in Barth's words) "did everything needed to open the way for me to meet a great number of persons and groups who are characteristic of the situation in Rome since the Council."[1] The visit took place September 22–29, 1966, and Barth prepared for it by developing "a total of ten sets of questions on the pronouncements of the Council that seemed to me the most important—one general set of questions and nine double sets: Questions for Clarification and Critical Questions" (*ALA*, 11). During his week in Rome, Barth discussed these prepared questions in three-hour sessions with invited Catholic theologians; the conversations were held in French. He explains with appreciation that "[o]n both sides the atmosphere in which this took place was always characterized by brotherly trust, frankness, and relevance" (*ALA*, 12).

In his *Karl Barth, Catholic Renewal and Vatican II*, Benjamin Dahlke shows that Barth's September 1966 engagement with Vatican II did not come out of nowhere, but in fact reflects forty years of sustained engagement and friendship between Barth and numerous German-speaking Cath-

1. Karl Barth, *Ad Limina Apostolorum: An Appraisal of Vatican II*, trans. Keith R. Crim (Edinburgh: The Saint Andrew Press, 1969), 10. (Hereafter, *ALA*; citations will be given parenthetically in the text.)

olic theologians and philosophers. For most of these Catholic interlocutors, Barth's theology functioned in relation to neo-scholastic theology. Whereas neo-scholastic theologians generally found Barth's theology to be sharply lacking, some important opponents of neo-scholastic theology found in Barth a significant resource for the formulation of their own perspective. The goal of these Catholic opponents of neo-scholastic theology, as stated by Dahlke, was "to replace a Neo-Scholastic theology focused on metaphysics with a theology oriented by salvation history."[2] Not surprisingly, Dahlke reports that "Barth was heavily in favour of this project from the beginning."[3] In Dahlke's words, the "main characteristic" of the *nouvelle théologie* "was the emphasis on the historicity of revelation and the development of dogmas along with an increasing recourse to the Bible."[4] Describing Hans Urs von Balthasar's 1950 book on Barth (in light of a related 1953 article by Balthasar), Dahlke observes that Balthasar wished to replace neo-scholastic theology's "tendency ... to measure revelation philosophically and reappraise it rationally" with a new focus on "God's saving acts in history," above all "God's address to humanity in Jesus Christ."[5]

Dahlke draws attention to the fact that in 1953, Barth praised von Balthasar, along with "quite a chorus of German and especially French friends," for seeking from a Catholic perspective "to look again to the centre, to the 'author and finisher of our faith' (Heb. 12:2)" and for setting in motion a Catholic "christological renaissance"—even if it is one in which the relationship between the doctrine of justification and the doctrine of sanctification remains too close.[6] Barth's praise here for the Catholic theologians of the *nouvelle théologie*, who in 1953 were still smarting under the effects of the ecclesiastical crackdown flowing from Pope Pius XII's 1950 encyclical *Humani Generis*, is quite accurate with respect to their goals. Remarks made by the young theologian Joseph Ratzinger at the outset of Vatican II describe well a major impetus of the *nouvelle théologie*, namely, the desire to respond to apologetic problems that had arisen from historical-critical research and which neo-scholastic theology (with its focus on philosophical issues and on the scientific coherence of dogmatic theology, and with its relative avoidance of the issues raised by historical criticism) could not sufficiently an-

2. Benjamin Dahlke, *Karl Barth, Catholic Renewal and Vatican II* (London: Bloomsbury, 2012), 83.
3. Dahlke, *Karl Barth, Catholic Renewal and Vatican II*, 83.
4. Dahlke, *Karl Barth, Catholic Renewal and Vatican II*, 129.
5. Dahlke, *Karl Barth, Catholic Renewal and Vatican II*, 131.
6. Karl Barth, *Church Dogmatics*, vol. IV: *The Doctrine of Reconciliation*, Part 1, trans. G. W. Bromiley (Edinburgh: T&T Clark, 1956), 768; cited in Dahlke, *Karl Barth, Catholic Renewal and Vatican II*, 149.

swer: "Among the theological questions open to serious discussion were the relationship of scripture to tradition and the way in which faith is related to history. Also under discussion was a proper understanding of inspiration and of the historicity of events narrated in scripture."[7] Describing Vatican II in September 1966, Ratzinger argues that these questions were (and are) important because they have to do with how contemporary believers can encounter and understand Jesus Christ. Ratzinger states that "the measure of the renewal is Christ, as scripture witnesses him. And if the renewal seeks to think through and to speak the Gospel of Christ in a way understandable to contemporary man—i.e., in a contemporary fashion (*aggiornamento* means bringing up to date), then the objective is precisely that Christ may become understood."[8]

In his *Reforming Rome: Karl Barth and Vatican II*, Donald Norwood points out that in talking with students at the Ecumenical Institute at Bossey in January 1967, Barth strongly praised the Catholic Christocentrism and direct engagement with Scripture to which Ratzinger refers. Speaking about Vatican II to these students, Barth perceives "a clear tendency to make Scripture the real governing element in the Church," and "[i]f Scripture is important then Jesus Christ becomes important."[9]

In what follows, I examine how Barth's 1966 *Ad Limina Apostolorum* expresses this positive view of developments within Catholicism. Barth considers the renewal of scriptural authority to be an opportunity for the Catholic Church to ask itself further "Critical Questions" that will continue, he suggests, the advance of Vatican II. Of Barth's approximately forty Critical Questions, nineteen rely explicitly upon the authority of Scripture and ask whether the Catholic Church, in particular positions taken in documents of Vatican II, has taken scriptural teachings seriously enough. If Scripture is now the "governing element" in the Catholic Church, Barth suggests, then the Catholic Church must respond by seeking to be ever more conformed to Scripture.

My perspective in what follows is shaped by a twofold conviction. First, I agree with Barth that scriptural authority is crucial. If Scripture did not authoritatively and truthfully witness to Jesus Christ, then divine revelation could not possess cognitive content. And if that were so, then God would

7. Joseph Ratzinger, *Theological Highlights of Vatican II*, trans. Henry Traub, SJ (New York: Paulist Press, 2009), 43.

8. Ratzinger, "Preface to the English Edition," in *Theological Highlights of Vatican II*, vii–ix, at ix.

9. Karl Barth, *Gespräche 1964–1968* (Zurich: Theologischer Verlag, 1997), 582, cited in Donald W. Norwood, *Reforming Rome: Karl Barth and Vatican II* (Grand Rapids, Mich.: Eerdmans, 2015), 61, 63.

not really have revealed anything to us, and Christian faith and practice would be nothing other than human cultural constructs gesturing toward the ineffable and seeking to build the best possible human religious institution (rather than receiving the *gift* of communion with *God*). We would still be enslaved to sin and death, rather than having been redeemed by Christ, who heals, sanctifies, and divinizes us. *Dei Verbum* §11 strongly affirms the authority of Scripture: "The divinely revealed realities . . . are contained and presented in the text of sacred Scripture," and "the books of Scripture, firmly, faithfully, and without error, teach that truth which God, for the sake of our salvation, wished to see confided to the sacred Scriptures."[10]

Second, I recognize that Catholic theology today is struggling with deep doubts about the authority and truth of Scripture. This theological struggle both reflects and contributes to the massive loss of faith among baptized (but now nonpracticing) Catholics that has taken place in much of Europe, North America, and elsewhere.[11] In light of the striking growth of popular atheism, Ratzinger's observation at the outset of the Council about "the way in which faith is related to history" and "the historicity of events narrated in scripture" is only more pressing today.[12] Dahlke observes matter-of-factly that after the Council "[t]he ascending historical focus plunged Catholic theology into a crisis with which it has been plagued ever since," given that "modern historical understanding ties truth claims to their original context and thus qualifies their absoluteness."[13] Although in this postconciliar context, historicist Catholic theologians continue to appeal broadly to "the gospel" (generally for the purpose of undermining the teachings of the

10. *Dei Verbum*, §11, in *Vatican Council II*, vol. 1: *The Conciliar and Post Conciliar Documents*, rev. ed., ed. Austin Flannery, OP (Northport, N.Y.: Costello Publishing Company, 1996), 750–65, at 756–57.

11 See especially Stephen Bullivant, *Mass Exodus: Catholic Disaffiliation in Britain and America since Vatican II* (Oxford: Oxford University Press, 2019); Stephen Bullivant, Hannah Vaughan-Spruce, and Catherine Knowles, *Why Catholics Leave, What They Miss, and How They Might Return* (New York: Paulist Press, 2019); Guillaume Cuchet, *Comment notre monde a cessé d'être chrétien. Anatomie d'un effondrement* (Paris: Seuil, 2018).

12. Ratzinger, *Theological Highlights of Vatican II*, 43. For background on the growth of popular atheism after World War I and on the *nouvelle théologie* as an apologetically motivated enterprise, see Jon Kirwan, *An Avant-garde Theological Generation: The Nouvelle Théologie and the French Crisis of Modernity* (Oxford: Oxford University Press, 2018). For the current situation, see bestsellers such as Richard Dawkins, *The God Delusion* (Boston: Houghtin Mifflin Harcourt, 2006); Reza Aslan, *Zealot: The Life and Times of Jesus of Nazareth* (New York: Random House, 2013) and Bart D. Ehrman, *How Jesus Became God: The Exaltation of a Jewish Preacher from Galilee* (New York: HarperCollins, 2014). Ratzinger, as Pope Benedict XVI, sought to combat this situation by publishing his trilogy on Jesus: *Jesus of Nazareth: From the Baptism in the Jordan to the Transfiguration*, trans. Adrian J. Walker (New York: Doubleday, 2007); *Jesus of Nazareth*, Part Two: *Holy Week: From the Entrance into Jerusalem to the Resurrection*, trans. Vatican Secretariat of State (San Francisco: Ignatius Press, 2011); *Jesus of Nazareth: The Infancy Narratives*, trans. Philip J. Whitmore (New York: Random House, 2012).

13. Dahlke, *Karl Barth, Catholic Renewal and Vatican II*, 158.

Church), for the regnant historicist perspective the biblical texts can exemplify *praxis*, but cannot convey truths that are enduring or authoritative, since the truth-claims of texts are utterly inextricable from the cultures and conceptual frameworks of their authors. On this view, there is no enduring cognitive content of "the gospel" (whether in the biblical texts themselves or as developed dogmatically over the centuries) to which appeal can really be made, since Scripture's truth-claims cannot be retrieved in any way that is authoritative for all generations. Not only is there no doctrinally knowable "gospel," there is also no enduring ecclesiastical subject, since "the Church" means quite a different thing in the first century than it does in the fourth, and the Church of the fourth century is profoundly different from the Church in the thirteenth—and also since only local instantiations of the Church exist.[14] Barth was quite familiar with liberal historicizing of this kind, and John Henry Newman had already identified and responded to it.

One finds a nuanced version of this historicizing in Cardinal Walter Kasper's recent book *Pope Francis' Revolution of Tenderness and Love*. Discussing his own rationale for allowing certain divorced and remarried persons to receive communion (without receiving an annulment of their first marriage), Kasper effectively rules out appeal to truth-claims made by Christ according to the New Testament, by arguing that such an appeal to the New Testament inevitably constitutes a case of flat-footed biblicism, given the historical complexities of the transmission of these *logia*. Kasper states that the question of how the situation of divorced and remarried persons should be handled is really a question "of divine faithfulness (*emet*) in a concrete situation"; and he drives home his point by rejecting Scripture's ability (let alone Tradition's ability) to convey authoritatively Christ's actual words or actual meaning: "This question, as many recent exegetical investigations show, cannot be decided merely by quoting the words of Jesus (Mark 10:2–12 and parallels), which were transmitted differently already in the New Testament."[15] What seem to be clear teachings of Jesus are not in fact clear at all, due to the difficulties in transmission. The unavoidable implication is that other much less clear teachings of Jesus are unlikely to have accessible meanings either.

14. I discuss these points, with extensive bibliographical references, in my *Engaging the Doctrine of Revelation: The Mediation of the Gospel through Church and Scripture* (Grand Rapids, Mich.: Baker Academic, 2014); and my *An Introduction to Vatican II as an Ongoing Theological Event* (Washington, D.C.: The Catholic University of America Press, 2017). For examples of historicist Catholic theological thought, see Terrence W. Tilley, *Inventing Catholic Tradition* (Maryknoll, N.Y.: Orbis Books, 2000); and Tilley, *The Disciples' Jesus: Christology as Reconciling Practice* (Maryknoll, N.Y.: Orbis Books, 2008).

15. Walter Kasper, *Pope Francis' Revolution of Tenderness and Love: Theological and Pastoral Perspectives*, trans. William Madges (New York: Paulist Press, 2015), 43.

The historicism that is at work here is further illuminated by the fact that consistent interpretation of these biblical texts in the Church's Tradition does not here count for much and, indeed, can for practical purposes be discarded.[16]

Barth's *Ad Limina Apostolorum*, then, functions in two ways for me. First, Barth's book provides an outline (via his Critical Questions) of important paths that Catholic theology should take today in order both to receive the Council more deeply and to go constructively beyond the Council (though not by rupturing definitive doctrine). Second, Barth's book represents an opportunity to recommit ourselves to the Christ-centered vision of the Church and of theology to which Vatican II calls us, grounded in Scripture's trustworthy cognitive communication of Christ and rejecting a historicist hermeneutic that cut us off from divine revelation as mediated by Scripture.[17] In reaffirming the Council's vision, Catholics should now also proceed with a greater appreciation for Thomas Aquinas in particular and for the dogmatic project of neo-scholastic theology in general, especially since, given his own scriptural commitments, Aquinas offers profound resources for a contemporary theology whose primary source is Scripture and whose center is Christ and the Trinity.[18]

16 For further discussion, see my *The Indissolubility of Marriage:* Amoris Laetitia *in Context* (San Francisco: Ignatius Press, 2019).

17. For an effort to renew this commitment to the Council's Christ-centered vision, see Robert P. Imbelli, *Rekindling the Christic Imagination: Theological Meditations for the New Evangelization* (Collegeville, Minn.: Liturgical Press, 2014). Dahlke is quite right when he observes in the conclusion to his book (even if his view of neo-scholastic theology is too limited): "Barth's work was also studied intensively on the Catholic side after the period covered here [i.e., after the Council], a situation which continues even up until the present. Yet the context of Catholic theology has, to state the obvious, changed considerably, as what is at stake is no longer the renewal of Catholic thought in the face of the fossilization of Neo-Scholasticism, but of its reconstruction in the light of the problems modernity presents and the apparent arbitrariness of post-modernism. Barth now offers his services as a debating partner for very different reasons, not least because of the fact that he recalls theology to its particular and genuine task" (*Karl Barth, Catholic Renewal and Vatican II*, 159). By comparison, Donald Norwood engages Barth's relationship to Catholic theology from a perspective that, with regard to contemporary hot-button theological debates, often criticizes both Barth's position and the Catholic Church's. For example, Norwood writes, "If Protestant feminists like Elisabeth Wendel-Moltmann found little support from Barth, and if Roman Catholic feminists rarely troubled to look for help in his direction, this need not be the last word. We can have a shared concern for the good of the church as a whole and the Roman Catholic Church in particular. By her attitude to women, the Roman Catholic Church continues to alienate many of her most faithful women supporters. Pope John XXIII may have opened a window in the Vatican so that the Holy Spirit could blow in, but as far as women like Deborah Halter are concerned, it is a case of 'Vatican II: A Window Unopened'" (*Reforming Rome*, 158).

18. See Jean-Pierre Torrell, OP, *Saint Thomas Aquinas*, vol. 2: *Spiritual Master*, trans. Robert Royal (Washington, D.C.: The Catholic University of America Press, 2003). See also my *Paul in the "Summa Theologiae"* (Washington, D.C.: The Catholic University of America Press, 2014).

Karl Barth's Good Impression of Vatican II and Rome

The first impression given by Barth's *Ad Limina Apostolorum*, most of which recounts his trip to Rome, is one of joyful appreciation. One sees it in his highly positive appraisal of the Catholic theologians whom he meets in Rome. As he says of his trip to Rome, "*Ultra montes* I met so many Christians with whom I could not only speak candidly and seriously, but also join in hearty laughter" (*ALA*, 17). One sees it, too, in his appreciative remarks about Pope Paul VI, remarks that are both theological and personal. Theologically, he states vigorously: "The Pope is not the Antichrist!" (*ALA*, 17). He also describes a theological conversation that he had with Pope Paul VI, in which he understood the pope to agree with his (Barth's) emphasis on the word "brethren" in the phrase "separated brethren" (*fratres sejuncti*) that the Council employs when speaking of Protestants.

During the conversation, Barth raised his concerns about "Mariology" to the pope, specifically about Mary's elevation "to the position of Queen of heaven" and about whether Joseph, who contributes nothing of his own, offers a better model of the Church than does Mary (*ALA*, 15). Wittily, Barth states that the pope's response to these concerns about the Catholic Church's teaching on the role of Mary was to "[assure] me that he would pray for me, that in my advanced age I would be given deeper insight into this problem" (*ALA*, 15).

Barth underscores that the theological conversation was a real one, and the personal bonds were real as well. He says with reference to a then well-known proverb about the Vatican ("Who is so smart as not to find his master in the Vatican"), "no one there made the slightest attempt to master me" (*ALA*, 15). Instead, he takes pleasure in the respect with which he was treated, and he remarks that "I count the full hour which Pope Paul VI gave me as among the most pleasant memories of our week" (*ALA*, 15). As Barth twice points out, Paul VI showed himself aware of Barth's *Church Dogmatics* and praised Barth's efforts. Barth appreciated the Pope's personal present of "a magnificent facsimile edition of the text of the Gospels of the Codex Vaticanus, the sight of which will give pleasure to my grandchildren and great-grandchildren" (*ALA*, 16).

On a personal level, Paul VI seems to have impressed Barth. Barth describes him as "an intelligent and, in his own way, a definitely humble, pious person," and adds that "[t]he way in which Paul VI received us and took leave of us was dignified and human in the highest sense" (*ALA*, 16). He praises Paul VI for his effort "to serve the cause of true freedom and that of necessary order" in the Catholic Church, and he reflects upon "how hard it must be, in the midst of already existing problems and those which have newly developed," to serve as pope (*ALA*, 16). Most strongly, he praises Paul VI for "his courageous and persistent commitment to peace among the nations, and especially in Vietnam" and his refusal to "[bless] any weapons." (*ALA*, 16–17).

Barth also felt generously welcomed by the theologians and priests in Rome, except for by those in charge of the Lateran University. Guided during his time in Rome by Bishop Jan Willenbrands and Fr. Magnus Löhrer, Barth had the opportunity to discuss the documents of the Second Vatican Council with leading Catholic theologians at the Vatican's Secretariat for Christian Unity and at various residences and universities. Whenever a question failed to produce an adequate response, he did not press the question, since he did not wish "to quarrel" but rather wished to "dialogue" (*ALA*, 12–13). He has particular praise for the Jesuit theologians with whom he held an amicable discussion while seated "on the battlements of their Gregoriana ... looking directly at the dome of St. Peter's" (*ALA*, 12).

Barth expresses appreciation for the willingness of Cardinal Alfredo Ottaviani and Archbishop Pietro Parente, both known as exponents of a conservative theological line during the Council, to discuss the conciliar documents with him. Even though he deems Cardinal Augustin Bea's theology to be "rather conventional," he was glad to meet with him and he praises him as "an undeniably good man in the service of an undeniably good cause" and "rightly honored in the non-Roman ecumenical movement" (*ALA*, 13). Barth attended a Sunday Mass and he reports that he "received a courteous welcome from the officiating priest" (*ALA*, 13). He was able to take part in an International Congress of Catholic theologians, where, as he says, "I was greeted by applause, honored by a respectful greeting, personally introduced together with the cardinals who were present (as if I were one of them, except that I lacked the red hat), and then seated in an armchair a little removed from them, but on the same level" (*ALA*, 14). This occasion was followed by a meeting with Karl Rahner, Joseph Ratzinger, and Otto Semmelroth, the leading German-speaking theologians of the day and influential *periti* at the Council.

These signs of respect are mentioned by Barth not in a spirit of self-aggrandizement, but rather so as to indicate the ecumenical graciousness that he encountered in Rome. He concludes that his trip to Rome gave him "a close acquaintance with a church and a theology which have begun a movement, the results of which are incalculable and slow but clearly genuine and irreversible" (*ALA*, 17). This movement, he thinks, is the same one as the "christological renaissance" that he praised in 1953.

The Biblical "Movement" and Barth's "Critical Questions"

In *Ad Limina Apostolorum*, Barth includes an essay that he wrote for a conference organized by Yves Congar on *Dei Verbum*. Barth's essay bears the title "'Conciliorum Tridentini et Vaticani I Inhaerens Vestigiis'?" (*ALA*, 43). This title comes from a portion of the Prologue of *Dei Verbum*, in which the Council Fathers state: "Following, then, in the steps of the Councils of Trent and Vatican I, this Synod wishes to set forth the true doctrine on divine Revelation and its transmission."[19] Although *Dei Verbum* follows in the footsteps of Trent and Vatican I, it does not merely repeat these earlier Councils. Thus, as Barth says, they "are not quite adequate" and "should not be the final word on the subject" of "divine Revelation and its transmission" (*ALA*, 44). Specifically (and uncontroversially), Barth argues that *Dei Verbum* goes beyond Trent and Vatican I by deliberately seeking to give prominence to Scripture in Catholic piety and theology.

Citing passages from throughout *Dei Verbum*, Barth praises the "high evaluation of Holy Scripture in the context of the transmission of divine revelation" and notes that one can see a sharp contrast with Trent and Vatican I in the fact that among *Dei Verbum*'s six chapters, "four (16 of the 26 sections) are given over to a consistent doctrine of Holy Scripture" (*ALA*, 47). Although he finds chapter 2 of *Dei Verbum* to be a disappointing exception to this rule, he comments that the new emphasis on Scripture emerges from what Hans Urs von Balthasar called the "'trend to the Bible,'" a movement that in Barth's view "is completely foreign to Trent and Vatican I."[20] As an example, Barth compares the chapters of *Dei Verbum* with Vatican I's *Dei Filius*, a Dogmatic Constitution on Catholic Faith that contains a chapter on revelation. In *Dei Filius*, Barth observes, "There is literally no word at all in

19. *Dei Verbum*, §1, in *Vatican Council II*, 750.

20. *ALA*, 47. Criticizing chapter 2 of *Dei Verbum*, Barth remarks (echoing a fundamental concern of the Reformation): "Is it not mandatory to distinguish fundamentally between the respect and the love accorded there [in Catholicism] to a sainted teacher of the Church or to the 'Holy Father' in Rome and here [in Protestantism] to a charismatic theologian or churchman on the one hand, and on the other, the obedience of faith with which we are to heed ... the witness of the biblical prophets and apostles to revelation?" (*ALA*, 51). For Barth, the Catholic view of Tradition and the Magisterium cannot stand, since it places mere humans over divine revelation.

any of the four chapters about the origin, object, and content of the Catholic faith" (although *Dei Filius* does frequently cite Scripture, a point that Barth does not mention here), whereas *Dei Verbum* frames its whole treatise as a response to and proclamation of the Word of God, by "appealing to what is written in 1 John 1" (*ALA*, 52). In *Dei Verbum*, the key to the obedience of faith is the encounter with the revealing Word, Jesus Christ. By comparison, Barth finds in *Dei Filius* a paramount concern with philosophical distinctions, including an insistence upon "natural" knowledge of God. Barth concludes that *Dei Verbum* (with the exception of its chapter 2) is suffused with a new awareness of "the *supreme* authority of Holy Scripture for the Church and theology," and thus of the supreme authority of the incarnate Word Jesus Christ (*ALA*, 54).

This return to the authority of Scripture (and thus of Christ over the Church) makes Vatican II, in Barth's estimation, a true "reforming Council" in the Reformation sense of the phrase (*ALA*, 55). Admittedly, even in the best chapters of *Dei Verbum*, Barth sees "minor difficulties and lapses" that take something away from its overall achievement (*ALA*, 54). Barth's "Critical Questions" about the conciliar documents expand upon these concerns, which are more prevalent for some documents than for others. Let me quote here the nineteen Critical Questions that are based explicitly upon challenges drawn from Scripture (I have condensed three Critical Questions about *Dignitatis Humanae* into one):

- "Had the eucharistic celebration already taken on in the New Testament church the primary significance ascribed to it here [*Sacrosanctum Concilium*] and in the other documents of Vatican II?" (*ALA*, 22).
- "Why is it that among the four marks of the church in Acts 2:42 (devotion to the apostles' teaching, fellowship, breaking of bread, and prayers) it is the third (Eucharist) that is designated [in *Lumen Gentium*] as constitutive for the life of the church?" (*ALA*, 23–24).
- "Where in the allusions to the eschatological dimension of the church (e.g., 48–50; 65 [of *Lumen Gentium*]) do we find the return of Christ as the judge? Where do we find the 'new Jerusalem,' the holy city that comes down from God out of heaven (Rev. 21:2), and does not ascend to him?" (*ALA*, 24).
- "Is the exegesis alluded to in 55–58 [of *Lumen Gentium*] able to support the Mariology erected on it? Can it support the exhortation to a special cult of Mary (66)?" (*ALA*, 24).
- "If, according to 4, 2 [of *Dei Verbum*], there is no new 'public revelation,'

and if (7f.) the tradition consists only in handing on and testifying to the revelation which the apostles received and bore witness to, and if (10, 2) the teaching office is not above the Word of God (which in 24 is equated with the Scripture!) but is in its service, then why is tradition given precedence over Scripture (7, 2; 9; 10, 1; 10, 3)?" (*ALA*, 25–26).

- "Does the thorough optimism of this Constitution [*Gaudium et Spes*] over the possibilities of the development of the world correspond to the emphases of the Synoptic Gospels and the Letters of Paul?" (*ALA*, 27).
- "Is 3, 5 [of *Unitatis Redintegratio*] intended to imply that the party of Cephas mentioned in 1 Corinthians 1:12, in distinction from the other three, was the one complete Catholic Church?" (*ALA*, 30).
- "Why is the most grievous, the fundamental schism—the opposition of Church and synagogue (Rom. 9–11; Eph. 2)—not dealt with here [in *Unitatis Redintegratio*] ... ?" (*ALA*, 30).
- "If Mary (4, 9 [of *Apostolicam Actuositatem*]) is the 'perfect example' of the apostolate of the laity, and as such the 'Queen of Apostles' (and therefore of Peter and his colleagues and successors), is it not then necessary to speak of the superiority of the apostolate of the laity to all other forms of the apostolate of the Church?" (*ALA*, 32).
- "Is not the concept of testimony, which is used in this decree [*Apostolicam Actuositatem*] (11, 2; 11, 5; 13, 1, etc.) to designate the task of the laity, a suitable designation of the task of the whole Church in her relation to the world (Acts 1:8; 2:32, etc.)?" (*ALA*, 32).
- "Again and again, is it the Church which *saves* and *renews* the world (1, 2 [of *Ad Gentes*]? Is not her task of testifying to Christ through the proclamation of the gospel between his first and his second coming, great and magnificent enough?" (*ALA*, 34).
- "In what passages in the Old or New Testaments is there an analogy to the presentation and interpretation of 'non-Christian religions' in the historical and analytical manner that dominates this Declaration [*Nostra Aetate*]?" (*ALA*, 36).
- "Would not the justifiable human concern of the Declaration [*Nostra Aetate*] have been expressed better by adhering to the proven methods of Paul, the apostle to the Gentiles, in which he proclaimed nothing to Jews or Greeks but the One who had been crucified for them—a stumbling block to the first and folly to the others—in order to address them as men from that point, and to call them to a realization of their common humanity?" (*ALA*, 36).

- "On what grounds does the Declaration (4, 1ff. [of *Nostra Aetate*]) speak of the past and present history of Israel in the same breath with Hinduism, Buddhism, and Islam as a 'non-Christian' religion, while (a) the Old Testament does not present a 'religion' at all but the original form of the one revelation of God, (b) and in the existence of later and contemporary Judaism (believing or unbelieving) we have the sole natural (i.e., in terms of world history) proof of God?" (*ALA*, 36).
- "When or where did the witnesses in the Old and New Testaments demand a legally assured scope for their life and the proclamation of their faith, and for the presentation of other religions? When or where did they defend their freedom to act by reference to the natural dignity of the human person? When or where did they react to the threats of oppression which the ruling powers raised against freedom in any other manner than by resisting and suffering?" (*ALA*, 40).
- "Why does this Declaration [*Dignitatis Humanae*] (except for the final sentence in 15, 5) have nothing to say about the true freedom for which the Son makes us free (John 8:36), which is there where the Spirit of the Lord is present (2 Cor. 3:17), and nothing about the liberating 'law of the Spirit of life in Christ Jesus' (Rom. 8:2), into which the Church continuously looks (James 1:25) and which is itself judgment (James 2:12)? In short, why does it say nothing about the 'glorious liberty of the children of God' (Rom. 8:21)?" (*ALA*, 40).
- "Could not the Church, which is called to *this* freedom (Gal. 5:13) and stands in it (Gal. 5:1), by speaking to and for itself have given more powerful testimony to governments and to all mankind about 'religious freedom' than it did in this Declaration [*Dignitatis Humanae*]?" (*ALA*, 40).

In every case, Barth's point of concern is rooted in the question of fidelity to the scriptural witness. Consider for example the first question, about whether the Eucharist, in the apostolic Church, really had the significance that *Sacrosanctum Concilium* attributes to it. After all, although Barth does not say it here, the risen Jesus' command to his apostles does not include celebrating the Eucharist, even supposing Jesus commanded this at the Last Supper; instead the risen Jesus emphasizes preaching and baptizing: "Go therefore and make disciples of all nations, baptizing them in the name of the Father and of the Son and of the Holy Spirit, teaching them to observe all that I have commanded you" (Mt 28:19–20). Similarly, Paul speaks of his mission in terms of "proclaiming ... the testimony of God" (1 Cor 2:1) and he underscores that "Christ did not send me to baptize but to preach the gospel" (1 Cor 1:17). When Paul instructs Timothy about how to continue on when Paul is absent, Paul urges: "Till I come, attend to the public reading of scripture, to preaching, to teaching.... Practice these duties, devote yourself to them, so that all may see your progress. Take heed to yourself and to your teaching" (1 Tim 4:13, 15–16). In the Book of Acts, we find a great deal of preaching and baptizing, but only a very few references to the Eucharist (assuming, that is, that at least some of the following passages refer to the Eucharist: Acts 2:42, 46; Acts 20:7, 11; Acts 27:35).

Of course, the Church today can make a scriptural case for the centrality of the Eucharist in the earliest Church without denying the importance (then and now) of preaching and baptizing. But the key point is that the scriptural testimony matters, both to Barth and—crucially—to *Sacrosanctum Concilium* itself, which reminds believers that Christ "is present in his word since it is he himself who speaks when the holy scriptures are read in the Church."[21] To be sure, this is Scripture as liturgically "read in the Church" and thus by no means a Scripture abstracted from the interpretative and worshipping community or from Tradition. Nonetheless it is *Christ* who speaks to the community "through Scripture" and therefore the Church is accountable to what Christ speaks "through Scripture." Barth himself is well aware that the Church is the appropriate locus for the interpretation of Scripture, but he insists that Christ judges and corrects the Church's inadequacies and failures by speaking to the Church through Scripture. The Catholic Church must continually submit to the test of Scripture, through which Jesus Christ challenges, purifies, and leads his Church. Barth himself, therefore, employs Scripture to submit the Council's documents to just such a testing, just as the *nouvelle théologie* similarly did prior to the Council.

Let me paraphrase and reorganize his questions in order to exhibit their combined force. Barth first and foremost offers questions that engage the Council's doctrine of the Church. Why should not baptism and proclaiming the Word of God (rather than the Eucharist) be the center of the life of the Church, as it is in the Book of Acts? And if Christians are simply witnesses to Christ, why differentiate laity and clergy so sharply, in a manner that the New Testament hardly seems to do? Why credit the Church with being the extension of the Incarnation, since it seems that although the Church witnesses to Christ, the Church (as we find already in Paul's letters) always falls far short of its Lord? Is it not Christ, rather than the Church, who brings about new Christians in the world, as Pentecost shows? Who commanded

21. *Sacrosanctum Concilium*, §7, in *Vatican Council II*, 1–36, at 5.

the Church to proclaim the unique glories of Mary, whose presence in the life of the Catholic Church seems out of proportion with her presence in Scripture? Has the element of the judgment of the world, so prominent in New Testament eschatology, been stripped from the Catholic Church's vision, with the result that it is no longer clear that the New Jerusalem descends from heaven rather than being an ecclesiological ascension? If Catholics (unlike Protestants) can identify themselves by observing that they "belong to Cephas [Peter]" (1 Cor 1:12), how is it that this does not divide the unity that, as Paul emphasizes, can be truly found only in Christ? How can the Catholic Church be the one Church—truly possessed of the unity willed by Christ for his people—given the schism with the synagogue that (far before any other divisions) deprived the Church of any cause for boasting in its unity? Does not what the Catholic Church proclaims about Mary make the state of the laity far superior to that of the clergy, including the pope, who should thereby be chastened in their claims to interpretative authority over nonordained Christians?

In a related way, Barth also offers questions that engage the doctrine of revelation and the Church's role in proclaiming divine revelation to the world which so urgently needs God's Word. Given that Scripture hands on the utterly unrepeatable apostolic witness to Jesus Christ, as we find in the New Testament, how then can or should the determinations of later Church authorities be (*de facto* or *de jure*) on the same level as Scripture's own statements? Where in Scripture is there an emphasis on dialogue with the world (rather than on proclamation), and where in Scripture is there an optimism about the spiritual condition of the world? Is it not troubling that the task of testifying to Christ in the midst of the world should be given by the Catholic Church to the laity, rather than being the definitive task of the whole Church, as in Acts? Has the Catholic Church taken the place of Christ, when it claims any salvific mission in the world other than its New Testament mission of testifying to Christ? Where in the Catholic Church's encounter with "non-Christian religions" (which certainly should not include Israel/ Judaism, which is the bearer of divine revelation rather than a mere "religion") is there now a place for Paul's criticism of idolatry, his awareness of the necessity of the Cross for human salvation, and his emphasis that the foundation of evangelization is not a generic common humanity but rather the crucified Christ who is the creator and redeemer?

Lastly, Barth offers questions that pertain to the true freedom of the Christian. When the Catholic Church makes common cause with the state, as it has done in numerous formal pacts over the centuries, is this befitting the Lord who made clear how radically distinct his kingdom is from that of the world? What biblical basis is there for seeking legal recognition for Christian life and faith, as though God's sovereignty and the blood of those whom God configures to Christ do not suffice by comparison with the decree of a mere human state? Should Christians defend their freedom of action by means of suffering and resistance rooted in faith in the power of Christ's love, or by means of an appeal to a generic shared humanity and to the best interests of states? When speaking of true "freedom," is it necessary to root oneself in the *Christian* freedom described so powerfully in the New Testament, or can such descriptions be ignored? Should the Church, when teaching about freedom, teach a generic freedom, or teach the freedom from sin and death that Christ offers to all humankind?

These questions can be boiled down to two fundamental concerns that he has about the Council's documents, despite his appreciation of the "movement" driving the Council. The first concern is that the Catholic Church, in its own perception, still stands on an equal level with the Word of God, Jesus Christ, who speaks through Scripture. (Inscribed within this first concern is Catholic doctrine about Mary.) The second concern has to do with the Church's effort to speak to the world on the basis of our shared humanity, as though Christ's coming (which cannot be separated from his people Israel) had not radically changed matters for the whole world, with the result that we must reconfigure everything around Christ.

To my mind, the concerns that Barth raises remain the central theological-exegetical ones of our time, insofar as they ask to what degree God enables mere humans to participate effectively (by the grace of the Holy Spirit) in the work of salvation that Christ performs, and to what degree created powers and natures remain in operation after the Fall (so that Christians can still appeal to them in speaking *ad intra* and *ad extra*). I agree with Barth that these questions should be answered by attending to authoritative Scripture, though I would underscore that this scriptural attentiveness must intrinsically involve the Church's long engagement with Scripture—an engagement that includes, rather than precludes, reasoning borrowed from philosophers. Today we need to engage Scripture in light of historical-critical insights into the cultures in which the biblical texts were written under divine inspiration and guided by divine providence. But the presence of divine providence, worked out through the historical missions of the Son and Holy Spirit, indicates why we cannot read Scripture *qua* Scripture without adhering to the dogmatic tradition.

For Barth, the "turn to the Bible" implies that all theology should be explicitly centered upon Scripture. Although with *Dei Verbum* I hold that "the 'study of the sacred page' should be the very soul of sacred theology," because "[t]he Sacred Scriptures contain the Word of God, and ... truly are the Word of God," I do not think that all theologians need to focus their work biblically.[22] In formulating his phrase about the "turn to the Bible," Hans Urs von Balthasar had in view a turn away from neo-scholastic theologies. It was in this sense a "turn" to an older theology, since when one compares (for example) Réginald Garrigou-Lagrange's *Reality: A Synthesis of Thomistic Thought* to Aquinas himself, or to a Church Father, one finds a large difference in the frequency and functions of biblical citations. For instance, in the section on "Redemptive Incarnation" in Garrigou-Lagrange's book, there are nine citations of Scripture, whereas Aquinas's discussion of the same topics (in *Summa theologiae* III, qq. 1–59) contains 483 citations of the Pauline corpus alone, as well as abundant citations of the Old Testament and the other parts of the New Testament. Garrigou-Lagrange intends to set forth the "Thomistic synthesis" that "reached definitive form in the *Summa theologiae*," but his account of this synthesis lacks a central dimension, namely the vast biblical erudition of the *Summa*.[23]

Even so, given that there are a number of theological tasks (including the inevitably philosophical task of penetrating more deeply into the intelligibility of revealed dogma) that do not require focusing on Scripture, theological renewal today—while grounded in the "turn to the Bible"—should appreciate and value works such as Garrigou-Lagrange's. Garrigou-Lagrange's *Reality* introduces significant theological debates involving such teachers as John Duns Scotus, John Capreolus, Cajetan, the Carmelites of Salamanca, Dominic Bañez, Luis de Molina, Francisco Súarez, John of St. Thomas, Alphonsus Liguori, and others. Neglecting or despising these past debates deprives the Church of valuable doctrinal and pastoral resources. Moreover, when theologians neglect or despise centuries of Catholic theology, they undermine the reality of divine providence at work within the Church's ongoing doctrinal tradition. The point is that a theology that presses biblical questions and that shows that the study of Scripture is the soul of theology, as Vatican II calls for, must not overlook or suppress the dogmatic and historical insights of neo-scholastic treatises.

22. *Dei Verbum* §24, in *Vatican Council II*, 763–64.

23. Réginald Garrigou-Lagrange, OP, *Reality: A Synthesis of Thomistic Thought*, trans. Patrick Cummins, OSB (Lexington, Ky.: Ex Fontibus, 2009), xiv.

In my view, therefore, Barth's rightful appreciation of the biblical "movement" underway at Vatican II does not mean that his rejection of neo-scholastic theology was appropriate.[24] Like Barth, neo-scholastic theologians were deeply concerned about the influence of rationalist philosophy upon theology and biblical exegesis. Theologians such as Garrigou-Lagrange contended correctly that Kantian philosophy undercuts our ability to perceive the action of God, to recognize in Jesus Christ the divine Person of the Son, and to appreciate the intellectual coherence and value of theology as a domain of knowledge (rooted in divine revelation). Given these concerns, Garrigou-Lagrange emphasized both the "scientific" character of theology in its bringing together "supernatural truths with the truths of the natural order," and also Aquinas's status as an anti-rationalist contemplative: "To solve difficulties, he [Aquinas] would pray before the tabernacle. He never, we might say, went out of the cloister, he slept little, passed much of the night in prayer."[25] Barth's efforts in his *Church Dogmatics* to correlate Catholic neo-scholastic theology with classical Protestant liberalism, since both are willing to build in certain ways upon nonrevealed sources of knowledge, have never seemed fair or accurate to me, not least because Barth's position displays an equal misunderstanding of the patristic approach to similar issues.[26]

Conclusion

In an appendix included in *Ad Limina Apostolorum* and titled "Thoughts on the Second Vatican Council" (originally published in 1963), Barth suggests that the opening stages of the Council, not least with regard to the rejection of the original *schema* on divine revelation, reveal "a certain landslide that is taking place in the Roman Church, a *spiritual* movement actually taking place there" (*ALA*, 68). The Council's "majority," says Barth, exhibits the signs of "the beginning of a reorganization—precisely around the gospel,"

24 I agree here with the late John Webster and other contemporary Reformed theologians whose appreciation for Barth has not stopped them from increasingly valuing the major exponents of Reformed scholasticism (as well as Thomas Aquinas). See for example Steven J. Duby, *Divine Simplicity: A Dogmatic Account* (London: Bloomsbury, 2018); Tyler R. Wittman, *God and Creation in the Theology of Thomas Aquinas and Karl Barth* (Oxford: Oxford University Press, 2018).

25. Garrigou-Lagrange, *Reality*, xii–xiii. See also Torrell, *Saint Thomas Aquinas*, vol. 2: *Spiritual Master.*

26. For the patristic approach, see Jaroslav Pelikan, *Christianity and Classical Culture: The Metamorphosis of Natural Theology in the Christian Encounter with Hellenism* (New Haven, Conn.: Yale University Press, 1993); see also my *Proofs of God: Classical Arguments from Tertullian to Karl Barth* (Grand Rapids, Mich.: Baker Academic, 2016).

and he adds enthusiastically that "[t]he Bible ... was obviously for a long time past read more industriously and fruitfully in clerical (and not only in clerical) circles of the Roman Church than we had noticed or properly judged" (*ALA*, 69). Barth expresses delight that through the "presence of the prophetic and apostolic Scriptures," Jesus Christ has "stepped anew into the center of faith of the Roman Christians and the thought of the Roman theologians" (*ALA*, 69). Given Catholic doctrines about Mary and the papacy, Barth admits that "[t]here is no reason for anyone to dream that the Roman Catholics might become 'evangelical' in *our* sense, whether tomorrow, the day after tomorrow, or at any other time" (*ALA*, 70). But he holds that it is of the utmost significance that the Catholic Church has allowed itself to be awakened, disturbed, and challenged by Jesus Christ.

Having been awakened, disturbed, and challenged, however, Catholic theologians have had trouble in the postconciliar period giving a persuasive account of how the divine Word speaks authoritatively today through the ancient texts that make up Scripture. Many Catholic theologians no longer defend the claim that the Church's handing on of Scripture in the Tradition truly and faithfully makes present the gospel delivered by Jesus Christ. Instead, historical questions about the development of the scriptural texts and the development of dogma have shaken Catholic belief that divine revelation, if it even occurred, has been truthfully communicated in the past and is knowable today.

These questions already characterized the modernist crisis at the end of the nineteenth century. Attempting to respond constructively to this crisis, theologians such as Yves Congar and (later) Joseph Ratzinger sought both before and after the Council to combine a biblical theology schooled by historical-critical scholarship with erudition in the history of dogma. Congar, Ratzinger, and most of their allies were profoundly concerned to defend theologically (not simply historically, but dogmatically and in a philosophically realist way) the truthfulness of the Church's mediation of the gospel over the centuries under the guidance of the Holy Spirit. At the same time, they were trained under a neo-scholastic regimen that gave them intellectual access to the achievements of the medieval scholastics (Bonaventure as well as Aquinas) and also to the achievements of the patristic theologians whose writings, by the late fourth century, display deeply "scholastic" erudition, as anyone who reads the literature of the semi-Arian or Nestorian controversies can perceive.

Lacking scholastic training, postconciliar generations of Catholic theologians have proven to be intellectually weaker and less able to integrate the dogmatic, philosophical, and historical tasks.[27] A theology that fails to learn dogmatic insight and metaphysical rigor from the scholastics and the Fathers will also fail to appreciate how deeply biblical and Christ-centered scholastic and patristic theology actually are, and thus will fail to draw upon key resources for the biblical renewal of contemporary theology. As a result, today Catholic theology is much more susceptible to the liberal modernism against which the *nouvelle théologie*, like neo-scholastic theology, sought (with some exceptions) to contend.

In "A Letter about Mariology," which is included in *Ad Limina Apostolorum* and which in October 1966 Barth sent to an unidentified young Catholic theologian who had asked for Barth's criticisms, Barth strenuously rejects "Mariology" but first pauses to mention another source of worry. He reports serious "alarm over the way in which you throughout bring together and separate the concepts 'history' and 'faith.' By so doing you are traveling down (in Rome also I noted that you are not the only young Catholic theologian of our day to do so) the steep path to Schleiermacher and Bultmann" (*ALA*, 60). Barth warns that the separation of history and faith will have dire consequences if pursued in Catholic theology. From this path, says Barth, "you cannot in the end expect to harvest good fruit either in your theme [Mariology] ... or in the treatment of other, genuine theological problems" (*ALA*, 60).

This letter balances out Barth's general enthusiasm about the Council's biblical "movement" with a stern warning about the danger of theological liberalism. The "turn to the Bible" can enrich contemporary dogmatic theology with a deeper direct contact with divine revelation at its Christological source. But the danger is that theologians will lack the metaphysical training and integrative power necessary to hold together historical and dogmatic elements. As a result, they will see no alternative but to separate history and faith. Barth in 1966 finds young Catholic theologians going down this disastrous path, and Ratzinger, Congar, and Henri de Lubac voiced the same concern directly after the Council.[28] Historicism

27. For further discussion of the current situation (and its sources), see Thomas Joseph White, OP, "The Precarity of Wisdom: Modern Dominican Theology, Perspectivalism, and the Tasks of Reconstruction," in *Ressourcement Thomism: Sacred Doctrine, the Sacraments, and the Moral Life*, ed. Reinhard Hütter and Matthew Levering (Washington, D.C.: The Catholic University of America Press, 2010), 92–123. See also White's *The Incarnate Lord: A Thomistic Study in Christology* (Washington, D.C.: The Catholic University of America Press, 2015) and Reinhard Hütter's *Bound for Beatitude: A Thomistic Study in Eschatology and Ethics* (Washington, D.C.: The Catholic University of America Press, 2019).

28. For discussion, see my *An Introduction to Vatican II as an Ongoing Theological Event*.

quickly became widespread in postconciliar Catholic theology. In my view, therefore, one of the central purposes of Catholic-Protestant ecumenism inspired by Barth is to ensure that the "turn to the Bible"—which Barth's outreach to Catholics consistently aimed to strengthen—does not instead mire the Catholic Church in a Catholic version of the liberalism against which Barth so assiduously fought. As many young Reformed Barthians have realized in recent years, this will require, among other things, pairing the "turn to the Bible" with a turn to scholasticism and Thomas Aquinas. It is precisely this that Catholic "Ressourcement Thomism" attempts to do.

Chapter 2

Holy Scripture as a Mirror of God

Katherine Sonderegger

I was a schoolgirl when the Holy Gospel of the New Testament was enthroned in the *aula* of St Peter's Basilica at the opening of the Second Vatican Council. A child of the Reformation, I was deeply moved by the sight of that magnificent codex in the splendor of that nave, the solemnity and dignity given to that Holy Book. Some fifty years on, I am moved still by the majesty of that long-ago image, and even more by the faithfulness of that whole body of the Church Catholic, bishops, *periti*, observers, Pope and cardinals, all gathered by and under the *Dei Verbum*. It is an honor to reflect on the Council in this anniversary season, and most especially to participate in ecumenical gatherings, such as this one, working together with other scholars to understand, receive, and reflect upon the great decrees, declarations, and constitutions of that remarkable Council. I consider the work and words of the Second Vatican Council a gift and treasure of the whole Church; the dogmatic constitution, *Dei Verbum*, a crown jewel.

"The Dogmatic Constitution on Divine Revelation," *Dei Verbum*, is widely considered the central or foundational text of Vatican II. That does not mean it is considered perfect—or even fully consistent, transparent, or self-interpreting! To be a "classic," theologian David Tracy tells us,[1] is to give rise in later generations to steady conflict, reappraisal, rereading, reappropriation; a classic cannot remain inert but rather becomes generative, a living word in the midst of its living readers. A classic, if I might borrow the idiom of the Council itself, exemplifies both *aggiornamento* and

1. This idea can be found in many places in Fr. Tracy's work, but most prominently in *The Analogical Imagination: Christian Theology and the Culture of Pluralism* (New York: Crossroad, 1981).

ressourcement. Dei Verbum is a classic in just this sense. To this reader, the "Constitution on Divine Revelation" shows in our day some signs of wear—how transformed would be the brief section on the Old Testament were it written today!—and the seams that run along differing layers and voices that compose the final text catch our eye from time to time. Consider now a few of these fault lines, those distinct themes and texts forged, melded, and joined, under the tremendous pressure of a relentless calendar, of the conflict of the schools, of scholars, of prelates, of commissions and previous magisterial teaching, and of the great urgency of the Holy Spirit himself—a mighty downward pressure to bring out of varying and competing schemas a single document, joined and seamed together, for the pastoral guidance of the whole Church. These seams were visible to the fathers of the Council even as they are to us today. Here are some celebrated ones, then and now.

Just how does the magisterium at once exercise a "divinely conferred commission" to make all biblical interpretation "subject to the judgement of the Church," yet remain not "superior but servant" to the Word of God?[2] Or we might wonder how we are to at once affirm that the Holy Scriptures are the "speech of God as it is put down in writing under the breath of the Holy Spirit," teaching the "truth of God" in that famous phrase, "firmly, faithfully, and without error" and also that the Gospels are the words and work of human authors, mere mortals who receive, collate, edit, and present the life of Christ in the "conventions of the people of the time" of the Evangelist?[3] Or again, we might ask just how we are to understand the celebrated claim of *Dei Verbum,* that Holy Scripture and tradition "make up a single sacred deposit of the Word of God," is to be interpreted in light of the exhortation but a few lines earlier, that "both Scripture and Tradition"—two elements!—"must be accepted and honored with equal feelings of devotion and reverence."[4] How do the varying passages of the document express or heighten the anxious worry over the "material sufficiency" of Holy Scripture? Or, to lean upon the blunt language of Karl Barth in his book, *Ad Limina Apostolorum*:

> For my part, I regard this second chapter [on The Transmission of Divine Revelation] as the great fit of weakness which befell the Council in the editing of our text. By the way in which the holy tradition and, in 10, the teaching office of the Church also

2. *DV* §§10, 12. Unless otherwise noted all quotations of *DV* are taken from *The Documents of Vatican II*, ed. Austin P. Flannery, new revised edition (Grand Rapids, Mich.: Eerdmans, 1975).

3. *DV* §§9, 11, 12.

4. *DV* §§9, 10.

are placed alongside the Holy Scriptures, this chapter obscures the unmistakable declaration of chapter I in reference to revelation itself and of chapters III–VI in reference to Scripture, and thereby to some extent the intent of the whole document.[5]

Or, more telegraphically, here is Barth on the seam that shows between the piety expressed for Trent and Vatican I—these are the famous "footsteps" Vatican II seeks to follow—and the silence that awaits so much of the doctrine of revelation in Vatican I in the heart of *Dei Verbum*: "Why does this Constitution," Barth asks, "not have a first chapter 'on God,' parallel to the chapter that opens and dominates the corresponding Constitution from Vatican I? Why is it that in chapter I of this Constitution the knowledge of God is spoken of only at the end of the chapter (6,2) and then not in explanation of the main statement of Vatican I but only by quoting it?"[6]

Students of *Dei Verbum* will know that I am hardly the first reader who has puzzled over these questions or wrestled with these tensions. They are the *crux interpretum* of the document, and authorities on the Constitution, from Cardinal Bea, to *peritus* Joseph Ratzinger, to observer George Lindbeck, struggle over the proper weighting, order, and purpose of these disparate claims about divine revelation. *Dei Verbum* could scarcely have given shape to an entire Council and generated the vibrant glory that is Catholic biblical scholarship if it did not contain such a rich admixture of elements, insights, and yes, distinct sources (even contradictions). In my view, the "Constitution on Divine Revelation" shines forth, and gathers its greatness, from its reflection of the complex character of Holy Scripture itself, an echo of that one voice that sounds from the end times, in and as many voices and as mighty thunder. *Dei Verbum*, I would say, points to, teaches, and reflects the one thing needful, yet it does so in many and varied ways, each witness standing side by side, each speaking and showing, and none silenced or put under constraint, but all radiating the infinite glory who is God. That, I believe, is the lasting gift and strength of *Dei Verbum*. So I seek to honor the richness of this constitution, the way it mirrors the infinite richness of the good God.

I would like to do that, at least in part, by reflecting on a rather odd question that the constitution raises in my mind. Just what sort of book is Holy Scripture? Or, perhaps more pointedly, is Holy Scripture properly a book at all? I have already aired my enchantment with the Greek practice,

5. Karl Barth, *Ad Limina Apostolorum: An Appraisal of Vatican II*, trans. Keith R Crim, (Richmond, Va.: John Knox Press, 1967), 48. (Hereafter, *ALA*.)

6. *ALA*, 25.

adopted by the Council, of processing and ceremonially seating the Book of the Gospels at the start of each deliberative session. But have I in truth captured the spirit of this constitution when I focus on the codex, the late Roman form of writing that was to give shape to all literature in the western world? Are the troubled and troubling questions of authorship, of divine and human speaking and writing, the neuralgic questions about historical or doctrinal or moral error, in truth bettered or advanced by notions of writers and texts, of sources and forms, composition and coherence? Should the Bible be thought of first as a book, so that the venerable tradition of God as "Author" should be conformed to the complex relation of writer and text—a relation at once so very familiar to us, and yet so very odd? Of course I acknowledge that these are odd questions, indeed, to ask about an artefact whose very title "bible" simply means "book," and whose more formal title, "Holy Scripture," simply means "sacred writing." But these are the odd questions that emerge, I believe, with many ancient cultural artefacts; in this sense it is a perfectly general question. Are the great sagas of Homer works of literature, we might ask; are they species of writing? Are Euripidean or Shakespearian plays most properly scripts, written roles? Is music the score? The very concept of notation or of dictation casts a shadowy light on the space between a cultural work and its expression as book or drama or musical score. How much more might we wonder about this book of books! Is it in truth a codex at all?

Now, I ask these questions because *Dei Verbum* itself quietly asks them—forces our hand, really. The constitution in several places advances several analogies and images of Holy Scripture that undermine or set aside the dominant one of the book. I want to settle on one, more minor image—Holy Scripture as mirror—but not without briefly consulting its kindred images, scattered through the text. The resistance to Holy Scripture as a book forms a widespread underground movement in *Dei Verbum*, and its allies are everywhere.

Think for a moment about the formal title of the entire document: the "Dogmatic Constitution on Divine Revelation." Now Barth, as we have seen, was quick to note the obscurity that appeared to swallow up the very idea of revelation the hour of its announcement. And it is very true that *Dei Verbum* mentions but does not develop a theological epistemology of the kind firmly advanced in Vatican I. But I think, in the idiom of ecclesial statements, the title and chapter headings do more work in the text as a whole than Barth seems willing to credit. For what does it mean to title an entire dogmatic constitution on the Bible, divine revelation? Do we not here approach the event-centered language Barth adopted throughout the first volume of the *Church Dogmatics*, where divine revelation is the explosion of the Word of God in its threefold form?[7] Recall that at critical junctures *Dei Verbum* relies upon the notion of speech: revelation is the *viva vox* of the self-disclosing God. The constitution does not set aside, but rather strongly affirms, the notion of natural knowledge of God in creation; revelation may take the form of created order, contingency, and purpose. But the center of gravity in *Dei Verbum* remains the living God as he bends down, draws near, gives and gives away his love and law and grace. Holy Scripture speaks still, *Dei Verbum* tells us. The revelation of the one God takes place now as it did of old, and, in the intimate language of the constitution, we are invited to confess that "in the sacred books the Father who is in heaven comes lovingly to meet his children, and talk with them."[8] A divine colloquy springs from this theme of revelation, so that Holy Scripture is not so much a collation of divine truths or propositions, seeking our assent, but rather a tender *tête-à-tête*: "God, who spoke in the past, continues to converse with the spouse of his beloved Son."[9] Scripture as revelation is the event of disclosure; it is prophecy, address, promise; it is above all *communio*—conversation and intimate exchange.

Think now too of another cluster of images *Dei Verbum* gives us for reflecting upon the reality of Holy Scripture. The Bible, our constitution tells us, springs from and remains preaching, *kerygma*. This image is tied expressly to the origin of the New Testament. In a programmatic statement, *Dei Verbum* affirms: "The apostles preached, as Christ had charged them to do, and then, under the inspiration of the Holy Spirit, they and others of the apostolic age handed on to us in writing the same message they had preached, the foundation of our faith: the fourfold Gospel, according to Matthew, Mark, Luke and John."[10] Now, it is easy to spot the contemporary influences on this account of Scripture as kerygmatic speech; we can simply mention the great names of Gunkel, Lightfoot, and Bultmann and the form critical schools that made a study of literary genres, saying sources, layers of oral tradition and their tradents, and the vital *sitz im leben*, all household words in biblical studies. And the explicit affirmation of historical sourc-

7. Karl Barth, *Church Dogmatics*, trans. G. W. Bromiley and T. F. Torrance (Edinburgh: T&T Clark, 1936–69), I/1, §4; I/2, §19.

8. *DV* §21.

9. *DV* §8.

10. *DV* §18.

es, editing, and expression were hard-won victories for biblical scholars, cementing and extending the liberty declared in *Divino Afflante Spiritu* of Pius XII. But more central to the constitution than this mandate for Catholic higher criticism is the conviction that the Bible should be understood as divine address, proclamation. Holy Scripture is a word that goes forth: not simply a word disclosed, not simply a truth conveyed, but a promise, a herald, a daring confidence in the saving God who declares to each generation: "See, I am putting no obstacle in your way. Now is the acceptable time! Now is the day of salvation!"[11]

It is from this joining of preaching and apostolic witness that the tangled threads of Scripture and tradition can be discerned, sorted, and firmly knit together. Of course it is a far greater topic than I could undertake here to spell out just how the notion of preaching at once distinguishes and unites tradition and Scripture; these two terms mark out the raw and well-furrowed field occupied and burned over by the children of Geneva and the children of Trent since the division of Christendom in the sixteenth century—a sad legacy. But it may well be a herald of glad tidings that Barth himself, no stranger to bitter words over revelation, can affirm, in a calm and irenic fashion, that Protestants too "appeal with one accord to the Councils of the first several centuries[.] And were we not justified in developing the traditions that became fixed in the various 'confessions' (up to and including the Theological Declaration of Barmen in 1934) and also unwritten traditions?"[12] *Dei Verbum* teaches us to say that preaching, in season and out, joins the living voice of the Church with the living voice of the God who reveals. That simple confidence brings us some healthy distance away from Holy Scripture as book, standing sovereign and alone, or perhaps accompanied by a second volume, a book of the Church. The whole shelf is dismantled here.

I want to examine one final image that in its own way de-centers and reworks the notion of Scripture as book. And that is the central image, noted too by Barth, of the Word of God as Christology—no, as the living presence of Jesus Christ. Here we have the vital center of the Second Vatican Council, the Christological concentration that focuses and grounds the whole college of documents which emerges from those debates. The great constitutions on liturgy, on the Church, on the formation of priests and religious, on the relation of Christianity to non-Christian religions—all these are unthinkable apart from Christology. *A fortiori*, Jesus Christ is living Lord of *Dei Verbum*.

11. Cf. 2 Corinthians 6:2.
12. Barth, *ALA*, 49.

Throughout the text, all things are seen as moving, pressing forward, hurrying toward the Incarnation and then the final revelation of Jesus Christ. The Old Testament can scarcely say a word apart from the promises it receives about the coming savior. The New Testament speaks hardly a word outside the Gospels proper. It is the life of the Savior we see and receive and hear in the holy words of God. Two places in *Dei Verbum* make explicit the likeness of Holy Scripture to Christology. In the ringing conclusion to Chapter III, "On Divine Inspiration and Interpretation," the fathers of the Council write: "Indeed the words of God, expressed in the words of human beings, are in every way like human language, just as the Word of the eternal Father, when he took on himself the flesh of human weakness, became like humankind."[13] Here we uncover the foundation for the much-discussed rubric for reading the Bible as at once divine word and human, never separated, never confused or mixed, but both strongly one: one revelation, one person of our redemption. So strongly has this analogy taken hold that some Bible scholars can view fundamentalist interpretations of Scripture as a form of "monophysitism" that the Church rightly reproves.

The second place where Christology emerges boldly into the text of *Dei Verbum* is the Holy Eucharist, the substantial presence of Christ under the accidents of the creaturely gifts. The constitution can speak, in a famous metaphor, of the "One Table of Word of God and the Body of Christ."[14] But more plainly still, it can tie devotion to the sacrament to the fealty and love the faithful show and should show to the Word of God: "Just as from constant attendance at the eucharistic mystery the life of the Church draws increase, so a new impulse of spiritual life may be expected from increased veneration of the Word of God, which 'stands forever.'"[15] These are the final words of the whole constitution, an unmistakable affirmation of Holy Scripture as sacramental mystery.

All these images and notes allow us to reconsider and re-fashion our notion of the Bible, Old Testament and New. But I want to devote closer attention to one image that I believe offers a radical re-shaping of our doctrine of Scripture: the image of the Bible as mirror. Here is the tantalizingly brief passage where the simile is set out. "This sacred Tradition, then, and the sacred Scripture of both Testaments, are like a mirror, in which the Church, during its pilgrim journey here on earth, contemplates God, from whom she

13. *DV* §13.
14. *DV* §21.
15. *DV* §26.

receives everything, until such time as she is brought to see him face to face as he really is."[16] What a passage! I cannot think of another section that so clearly joins together the main affirmations of *Dei Verbum* as does this one long sentence. Here we have what observer George Lindbeck called the "eschatological" impulse of Vatican II.[17] Not simply "development," nor mere movement from the first garden to the last, splendid city, but rather dynamism, historical life, under the impress and calling of the *eschaton*, the final and last things. The kingdom of God, preached by the one Son of Man, invades this old world of ours, defining and limiting it, driving it to its fulfillment in the future that is God's very life. This "discovery of the eschatological" that dominated biblical studies from the years of Johannes Weiss forward, now finds its place in *Dei Verbum*: stirred up by the Spirit, driven onward, the pilgrim people move out from bondage into the liberty of the children of God, straining forward until the day that God is seen, face to face. Not the familiar traditional honorifics for the Church here. Nothing static or complete, but rather that great red thread of the Council as a whole, the Church as people of God, journeying *a Patre ad Patrem*, a pilgrim band.

Lying behind such rich, scriptural idiom is surely the great Pauline hymn to love, found in 1 Corinthians 13. After every garland is laid on the divine gift of love, Paul moves to the remarkable, complex coda of the whole: "For now we see in a mirror dimly"—a glass darkly, the King James Version has us say—"but then face to face. Now I know only in part, then I will know fully, even as I have been fully known. And now faith, hope and love abide, these three; but the greatest of these is love." Here we see the great pairings that frame an eschatological universe, now and then; part and whole. Standing in the midst of time, our "life-time" as Barth puts this, we seek only the partial, the enigmatic, the first fruits. For this reason, *Dei Verbum* dares to affirm, we must learn to hear the Word of God more deeply, to "advance toward the plenitude of Divine truth, until eventually the words of God are fulfilled in her."[18] Surprisingly, *Dei Verbum* does not cite 1 Corinthians here, but rather a different passage, from 1 John 3:2: "Beloved, we are God's children now; what we will be has not yet been revealed. What we do know is this: When he is revealed we shall be like him, for we shall see him as he is." But perhaps this is not so surprising after all, for this has

16. *DV* §7.

17. In his well-known, exuberant, and controversial reflections on the Council, written when a young academic, new at Yale Divinity School: George Lindbeck, *The Future of Roman Catholic Theology* (Philadelphia: Fortress Press, 1970).

18. *DV* §8.

usually been read as a Christological passage, fully eschatological, fully immersed in the language of revelation and fulfillment. As in the Pauline text, the Johannine letter revolves around the axis of the partial and the whole, the glimpse, then the full vision, the grace given but then the plentitude, poured out and made perfect. Taken together, and ordered to Augustine's great conception of the pilgrim city of God, these scriptural texts teach us how to expound and meditate upon the dense analogy of the mirror of God.

Let me begin with a theme that the mirror image implies—a rich and significant one—that has not made its appearance until now: the notion of "mediation," or "instrument." Of course such terms are rife within the modern treatment of the doctrine of inspiration; they play prominent roles in Fr. Smith's discussion of inspiration and inerrancy in the early *Jerome Biblical Commentary*,[19] and also in *The Word of God and Mankind*, Cardinal Bea's exploration of *Dei Verbum*.[20] But both these authors rely heavily upon the image and framework of the book, the author and compiler and reader—the very architecture that walls in so many problems in the doctrine of Scripture. Let's look at "mediation" and "instrument" once again under the impress, this time, of the mirror, the reflection of God for the pilgrim people. Here we have the familiar notion and practice of indirect vision, of seeing ourselves or some object in something else. We stand in the neighborhood here of Karl Rahner's celebrated concept of "mediated immediacy." In a mirror—we can borrow here from our daily practice of checking our appearance in the hallway mirror—we see ourselves, our face, our clothing, in a reliable image (or so we hope!) and we learn to adjust all that by reading what's left hand on us as right hand in the mirror, a reversal that is all the same trustworthy. Now the element that I consider most revealing in this practice is the conviction, so ordinary and everyday that we do not record any surprise at it, that something of an entirely different order and kind—an artefact, or perhaps a deep well of water—can reliably reveal to us our own image and likeness. This, in part, is just what we mean by mediation. Something can be conveyed by an instrument of another sort, yet the object conveyed is not the instrument but the original subject.

How very odd this is can be measured by how strongly we resist this notion of mirroring in, say, our doctrine of sacraments. There, across many communions of the Christian family, Christ is understood to be present in

19. Richard F. Smith, "Inspiration and Inerrancy," in *Jerome Biblical Commentary*, vol. 2, ed. Raymond S. Brown, Joseph A. Fitzmyer, Ronald E. Murphy (Englewood Cliffs, N.J.: Prentice-Hall, Inc., 1968), 499–514.

20. Augustin Cardinal Bea, *The Word of God and Mankind* (London: Geoffrey Chapman, 1967).

the elements of another kind. This is just what a mirror does not convey. A mirror can be a "looking glass," a shard of glass silvered over; it could be a polished leaf of metal, the mirrors of the ancient Roman world; it can be the odd reflective surface, a window or smooth table top, that happens to convey our image on its face. A mirror, that is, can mediate in the sense that a catalyst can bring about a chemical reaction: it is essential, yet it does not enter into the process or the result. Note the distance here from author and text! In the very notion of the book or text, we lean upon sameness, not difference: the word *in intellectu*, if I may borrow from St. Anselm here, is captured, expressed, recorded *in re*. From such likeness or indeed, identity, spring the vexed notions of causality—the Bible is the effect of God's speaking—or inerrancy, as the divine Word guards, guarantees, and brings about a full and proper expression of the divine intention. Now, of course there are ways to resist such conclusions! We might well think of Thomas's marvelous notion of a universal or equivocal cause; or again of the likeness to "two nature" Christology; indeed, of the very idea of incarnation itself. I do not mean, that is, that the Bible should never be thought of as book; we would scarcely enter the ante-room of the tradition were we to harshly exclude the idea of sacred writing. But a mirror affords us an alternative that opens up attractive space around the *Verba Dei*. We can, for example, acknowledge in this idiom that the Bible could be something entirely other than the revelation or speech of God, an entirely human artefact, say, and perhaps not even a wholly attractive one; yet it remains reliable. We see God there, though the mirror is not God, not even the direct effect of his self-disclosure.

You'll note there that I opened the door a bit to notions of fallibility, of scriptural error. Now this is no small topic, no abstract or cool tenet of the schools, but rather a "painful school of honesty," to borrow Schweitzer's celebrated phrase, a testing crisis of the Christian faith in modernity. *Dei Verbum*, you remember, forged a delicate sentence to capture the wide-ranging opinions of the Fathers and *periti* on the doctrine of inerrancy. The full sentence—itself a master of joinery!—reads: "Since all that the inspired authors, or sacred writers, affirm should be regarded as affirmed by the Holy Spirit, we must acknowledge that the books of Scripture, firmly, faithfully and without error, teach that truth which God, for the sake of our salvation, wished to see confided to the sacred Scriptures."[21] Now an entire treatise could be written on this complex sentence so I will not pretend to do it justice here. But commentators have been quick to point out that this truth

21. *DV* §11.

God “wishes to see confided to the sacred Scriptures” is for our salvation; we are not in the presence here of a mere scrupulously correct instruction book. God’s intention or will for the creature, the liberation and healing of the whole world, is the proper subject-matter of the Holy Bible. Now it seems to me that the image of the mirror would allow us the wide-open vista of a reflection that is itself true and without error, even if the reflective instrument is itself flawed, partial, even woefully inadequate. I see my gray hair quite accurately, unmistakably even, in the poorest Woolworth looking-glass. There are limits, to be sure. Cardboard does not reflect; even the components, glass without the silvering, show nothing. But we might, in this image of the mirror, capture something of the infinite distance between God and his creatures, including the works of their hands, yet remain still children of the Word, seeing in part and in a riddle, yet truly, faithfully, and in confidence of the whole that will be seen one day, God willing, face to face.

Let me close with one final recommendation for this rich and stunning image of Holy Scripture. I have spoken both of reflection and of mediation, but I think we might better say, a double mediation or reflection. For note what is seen in the Holy Bible itself: the covenant history of Israel, the neighbors and allies and enemies of this great nation, and the Jews and Gentiles drawn together by the one Jew, born under the law, born of a woman, born to die and live again as *Salvator Mundi*. In the mirror of Scripture, that is, we catch a glimpse not simply of words, of teaching or of commandment, but, as *Dei Verbum* stresses, events, deeds, the *gesta* of the history of salvation. These, in Augustine’s famous words, are “things become signs.” The mirror of the Bible holds before our eyes these objective signs that speak of another, that speak of God. We see Israel; we behold Jesus Christ; we see in a mirror darkly the one who sent them. Just as we can catch sight of something other or something beyond our own face in a mirror, angling its surface now one way and now another, so Holy Scripture as a mirror shows not our face, as reader or as believer, but rather the prophets and apostles, the widows and orphans, the suffering and the delivered, the mighty nations, their chariots and their chariot drivers, and the Prince of Peace who will overcome and still them all. In these we are to glimpse and long for the face of God; but in our pilgrimage here below, we look directly and with loving eyes on the mortal creatures and incarnate servant who walk in and out among us. For this reason, deeper and fuller truths can be awaited and sought in the one Holy Bible, under the guidance of the Holy Spirit. In the famous words of *Dei Verbum*: “The spouse of the incarnate Word, which is the Church ... strives to reach day by day a more profound understanding of the sacred Scriptures, in order to provide her children with food from the divine words."[22] Just so we can look in the mirror of our lives many times; but only in faith and love can we really see.

The Bible as mirror of God cannot exhaust the riches of *Dei Verbum*; many images and many notions must, side by side, reflect and express the complex insight of this great constitution. But all of us who love the Holy Scriptures, as all Christians are awakened to do, must be grateful for this dogmatic constitution and for the wisdom it affords us in this, our earthly pilgrimage, until that last day, the day of grace and glory, when we see God, face to face. Then temple and sacrifice and Scripture cease, and God is all, in all.

22. *DV* §23.

Chapter 3

Totius Traditionis Mirabile Sacramentum

Toward a Theology of Tradition in the Light of *Dei Verbum*

Lewis Ayres

I have yet many things to say to you, but you cannot bear them now. When the Spirit of Truth comes, he will guide you into all the truth.

—John 16:12–13

The reassertion of what is old with a luminousness of explanation which is new, is a gift inferior only to that of revelation itself.

—St. John Henry Newman

The organizers of the meeting from which these essays flow posed to speakers a number of questions.[1] One ran thus: "How, ... in our own secularized era can the documents [of Vatican II] serve the tasks of theology, and advance the cause of Christian unity?" This chapter suggests an answer to at least the first part of this question, and it does so with respect to *Dei Ver-*

Epigraph by Newman is from "The Benedictine Schools," in *Historical Sketches* 2 (London: Longmans, Green and Co., 1888), 476, reprinted, with original pagination, in John Henry Newman, *Rise and Progress of Universities and Benedictine Essays*, with introduction and notes by Mary Katherine Tillman (Notre Dame: University of Notre Dame Press, 2001).

1. This paper was presented first to colleagues at the Institute for Religion and Critical Inquiry of the Australian Catholic University in Melbourne, then to the *Ad Limina Apostolorum* conference in Washington, D.C., and finally to the systematic theology seminar of St Mary's College at St Andrews University. I am particularly grateful to Fr. Dominic Langevin, OP, for his comments on and help with revision of the paper.

bum. The council's constitution on divine revelation should be a central resource for thinking about the nature and tasks of theology today, but many of its most important passages have been oddly under-exploited in the half-century it has been ours. I think this to be particularly the case with respect to the famous second chapter of this text, the chapter that concerns the "handing on" of revelation, the theology of tradition. Recent decades have seen few attempts to think with this section of the document, attempts to offer theologies of tradition that embrace the charge *Dei Verbum* issues.

In this chapter I offer a constructive reflection on principles that are central to that second chapter. The constitution's insistence on the Spirit's role in the unfolding of Christian faith encourages me to argue that we should treat the act of *traditio*—the act of handing on and reflecting on the faith—as sacramental within the broader context of the Church understood as sacrament. Pushing a little further, I will argue that the act of *traditio* is the fundamental theological act because of fundamental Christological and Trinitarian dynamics, and as the fundamental theological act it is an effective sign of and may effect the gradual restoration of the intellect that is intrinsic to life in Christ. As a sign of this restoration the act of "handing on" is also a sign of the fundamental unity of humanity under God and in Christ. These arguments about tradition understood as act will also suggest some principles for considering the role of tradition understood as content. The final section of the essay turns briefly to the topic of doctrinal "development," suggesting that the 15th of Newman's *University Sermons* and the careful wording on the subject to be found in *Dei Verbum*'s second chapter still provide a basis for considering this question, despite a persistent critique of the very idea over the past half century.

But how does this essay also serve an ecumenical purpose? The Catholic discussions of Scripture, Tradition, and Revelation during the 1950s and 1960s that formed the background to *Dei Verbum* were often focused toward the emergent context of ecumenical engagement. But two distinct emphases are apparent, often in the same author. At times these authors dig for a common biblical and dogmatic core, trying to emphasize that which is shared between our traditions and, at least temporarily, putting aside distinctively Catholic emphases. At other times, they follow a different path and aim at exposing the roots of the Catholic difference in the gospel itself, not hiding that difference but claiming for it a necessity that follows from its presence at the source of our common faith, and opening a conversation about the most fundamental contents of the gospel. Both strategies are those of *res-*

sourcement, but they are rather different in tone. My essay today is an example of this second path: my goal is to think with and celebrate some themes at the heart of *Dei Verbum*, presenting them as central to the divine economy and bringing to light questions that should draw us all into conversation. For Karl Barth, of course, the second chapter of *Dei Verbum*, was its low point; in an age when there is a broader interest in the concept and theology of tradition across Christian traditions, I pray that my own arguments are received less negatively![2]

On Reading the Council

In developing a notion of tradition as sacramental on the foundation of *Dei Verbum* we face one problem. The document uses the term *sacramentum* only once, and that in quotation of Ephesians 1:9, speaking of the "mystery" of the divine will. We are faced then with a methodological question—a useful one, in fact, that will help us raise questions about how we should read and develop conciliar documents more widely. I take for granted the relevance of the principles, sparsely sketched in the *Code of Canon Law*, that understanding of "ecclesiastical laws" involves interpreting texts in appropriate context, if necessary also attending to parallel texts and to what we can usefully say about the intentions of those framing them.[3] But how and where these principles apply to conciliar texts that often avoid legal precision in order to speak in biblical and patristic terms of core Christian belief is a complex question. I would like to suggest the usefulness of two further principles.[4]

2. Karl Barth, *Ad Limina Apostolorum. An Appraisal of Vatican II*, trans. Keith R. Crim (Edinburgh: St. Andrews Press, 1969): 48: "[Chapter II] which Stakemeier ... calls the 'heart, midpoint, and focus of the whole Constitution.' How differently we can read and judge! For my part I regard this second chapter as the great fit of weakness which befell the Council in the editing of our text."

3. *CIC* §17: "Leges ecclesiasticae intellegendae sunt secundum propriam verborum significationem in textu et contextu consideratam; quae si dubia et obscura manserit, ad locos parallelos, si qui sint, ad legis finem ac circumstantias et ad mentem legislatoris est recurrendum."

4. The two methodological assumptions I highlight here are not intended to be sufficient. In a more exhaustive treatment one would need also, for example, to comment on the concept of theological "notes" attached to conciliar texts. Even here, though, the discussion becomes quite complex. While a "note" is attached only to *Lumen Gentium*, §25 of that text seems to presume something like the divisions the tradition of "notes" offered; more recent theological writing reveals an ongoing conflict over this tradition. On this tradition see for example Francis G. Morrisey, *The Canonical Significance of Papal and Curial Pronouncements* (Hartford, Conn.: Canon Law Society of America, 1974) and then idem, "Papal and Curial Pronouncements: Their Canonical Significance in the Light of the 1983 Code of Canon Law," *The Jurist* 50 (1990): 102–25. See also Harold E. Ernst, "The Theological Notes and the Interpretation of Doctrine," *Theological Studies* 63 (2002): 813–25. I am not convinced by the second half of Ernst's article, but he draws on the denser work of Francis A. Sullivan, *Creative Fidelity: Weigh-*

The first is the principle that we best interpret one of the four conciliar constitutions in the light of the others, and all in the light of the combined emphases of *Lumen Gentium* and *Dei Verbum*.[5] In this particular case, I am concerned to read some key sentences of *Dei Verbum*'s second chapter in the light of the appearance of sacramental language in both *Sacrosanctum Concilium* and *Lumen Gentium*. The second principle may seem a little more quixotic. In legal terms I am neither a strict constructionist nor a strict textualist with regard to magisterial texts. I certainly think that careful historical investigation into the work of those who framed these documents provides an essential feature of good investigation. And, at the same time, I take it that the words of the council's texts are delivered us by providence in this form and not another—not only as a powerful synthesis of the Church's teaching phrased with care in biblical and patristic teaching, but also with their ambiguities, their often carefully chosen reticence, and their hesitations. To say this is certainly a form of textualism, but one which emphasizes that ambiguity is also a providentially ordered invitation.

We might, in this regard, draw a parallel between *Dei Verbum*'s treatment of tradition and its treatment of biblical study. The constitution asserts both the necessity of reading Scripture in the light of Christian faith, and the necessity of certain modern historical-critical approaches. However, the text does not so much negotiate between these necessities as simply state the tension between them. But this acknowledgment may itself be a conciliar gift. No clear negotiation was at that point possible, and thus an agenda was commended to future generations. Similarly with the council's account of tradition: some basic orientation is offered but many questions concerning how one might develop and explore these emphases are simply left open.[6] Through such ambiguity the theologian is drawn to careful spec-

ing and Interpreting Documents of the Magisterium (New York: Paulist Press, 1996). Taking up critically some of the lines of thought pursued in the wake of Sullivan is Lawrence J. Welch, "*Quaestio Disputata.* Reply to Richard Gaillardetz on the Ordinary Universal Magisterium and to Francis Sullivan," *Theological Studies* 64, no. 3 (2003): 598–609.

5. For a particularly perceptive introduction to this principle see Christian D. Washburn, "The Theological Priority of 'Lumen Gentium' and 'Dei Verbum' for the Interpretation of the Second Vatican Council," *The Thomist* 78, no. 1 (2014): 107–34.

6. Indeed, some of the most important ambiguities concerning the role of Tradition in *Dei Verbum* flow from its discussion of the relationship between Scripture and tradition. The manner in which *DV* §9 attempts to incorporate the language of the two as a duality into the document's final emphasis on their unity (see *DV* §10)—"in a certain way" they "merge"—leaves open many avenues for us to explore. We might also note the famous statement of *DV* §12: "But since sacred Scripture must be read and interpreted with its divine authorship in mind, no less attention must be devoted to the content and unity of the whole of Scripture, taking into account the Tradition of the entire Church." How does one integrate readings of Scripture undertaken in the light of the tradition with readings developed on the basis of the using modern-historical critical methods to determine the intentions of the human authors? Again

ulation and expansion. We should certainly learn to worry when we find ourselves thinking against the world of those who drew up these texts, but we should also be prepared to think with them, heeding the calls to further work that they issue.[7]

Moritur Christus ut fiat ecclesia[8]

Where, then, to begin with Chapter II of *Dei Verbum*? At the end of the chapter we find:

> It is clear, therefore, that sacred tradition, sacred Scripture and the teaching authority of the Church, in accord with God's most wise design, are so linked and joined together that one cannot stand without the others, *and that all together and each in its own way, under the action of the one Holy Spirit, contribute effectively to the salvation of souls.*[9]

Discussions of tradition in Catholic theology tend not to reflect on what is here presented as central: the use of Tradition by God for salvific purpose. Two comments on this text will set an agenda for the rest of my argument. First, note an ambiguity in the very word "tradition." Nowhere does *Dei Verbum* define the term; while the title of the chapter—*De diviniae revelationis transmissione / On the transmission/handing on of divine revelation* focuses on the act of handing on, the matter of the chapter speaks both of the act itself and of that which is handed on. Once again, ambiguity opens multiple appropriate lines of possible speculation, and I will focus on tradition as act. Second, this passage's emphasis on the effective contribution of tradition to our salvation invites us to find ways of conceptualizing how tradition

---

the text opens for us a theological task. An essential resource for studying the manner in which the final text of *Dei Verbum* still incorporates earlier formulations and reveals some of the tensions between the document's architects is Francisco Gil Hellin, *Concilii Vaticani II Synopsis. Constitutio Dogmatica De Divina Revelatione Dei Verbum* (Città del Vaticano: Libreria Editrice Vaticana, 1993). Throughout this paper I have used the translations found in Austin Flannery, ed. *Vatican Council II. The Conciliar and Post Conciliar Documents*, rev. ed. (Dublin: Dominican Publications, 1992). I have made occasional changes to the translation but have not noted them individually.

7. And in this sense my principles are, I hope, consistent with Benedict XVI's famous call for us to read the Council in a "hermeneutic of reform." See his "Address of His Holiness Benedict XVI to the Roman Curia, December 22nd 2005 Offering Them His Christmas Greetings," http://w2.vatican.va/content/benedict-xvi/en/speeches/2005/december/documents/hf_ben_xvi_spe_20051222_roman-curia.html (accessed October 11th 2016).

8. Augustine, *In Iohannes Evangelium Tractatus* 9.10.

9. *DV* §10: "Patet igitur Sacram Traditionem, Sacram Scripturam et Ecclesiae Magisterium, iuxta sapientissimum Dei consilium, ita inter se connecti et consociari, ut unum sine aliis non consistat, omniaque simul, singula suo modo sub actione unius Spiritus Sancti, ad animarum salutem efficaciter conferant." The text is available in *Decrees of the Ecumenical Councils: Volume II (Trent–Vatican II)*, ed. Norman Tanner SJ (Washington, D.C.: Georgetown University Press, 1990) and at www.vatican.va.

does so contribute. I propose to do so by locating the act of "handing on" within the notion of the Church's sacramentality, which is such a strategically important feature of *Lumen Gentium*.[10] Thus I cannot proceed without sketching some theological foundations, without setting out a basic sense of what it means to call the Church a "sacrament."

The recovery of this language that began in the nineteenth century has served a number of goals, the most important of which is probably to emphasize the centrality of the incarnate Christ as the heart of all sacramental action.[11] For it is Christ who is the "great sacrament" of 1Tim 3.16. Scheeben, the greatest modern theologian of Christian mystery, makes the links that we need:

Here [in the case of Christ] the supernatural in the most exalted sense is really and most closely united to the visible humanity, the flesh, as the humanity is called from its visible side, and in such a way that, although it is substantially and personally present in the flesh, it remains hidden under the flesh. As the hypostatic union of

10. *LG* §1: "Since the Church is in Christ like a sacrament or as a sign and instrument both of a very closely knit union with God and of the unity of the whole human race (*veluti sacramentum seu signum et instrumentum intimae cum Deo unionis totiusque generis humani unitatis*)." *LG* §9: "God gathered together as one all those who in faith look upon Jesus as the author of salvation and the source of unity and peace, and established them as the Church that for each and all it may be the visible sacrament of this saving unity (*ut sit universis et singulis sacramentum visibile huius salutiferae unitatis*)" (quoting Cyprian, *ep.* 69.6). *LG* §48: "Christ, having been lifted up from the earth, has drawn all to Himself. Rising from the dead He sent His life-giving Spirit upon His disciples and through Him has established His Body which is the Church as the universal sacrament of salvation (*Ecclesia ut universale salutis sacramentum constituit*). Sitting at the right hand of the Father, He is continually active in the world that He might lead men to the Church and through it join them to Himself and that He might make them partakers of His glorious life by nourishing them with His own Body and Blood."

11. For the history of the theme "the Church as sacrament" in modern Catholic thought see Jean-Marie Pasquier, *L'Eglise Comme Sacrement. Le development de l'idée sacramentelle de l'Eglise de Moehler à Vatican II* (Fribourg: Academic Press Fribourg, 2008) (on the theme at Vatican II, pp. 191–273). For other commentary on the theme in *Lumen Gentium* and in other texts from Vatican II see Aloys Grillmeier in *Commentary on the Documents of Vatican II*, vol. I, ed. Herbert Vorgrimler, trans. L. Adolphus et al. (New York: Herder and Herder, 1967), 138–52; Peter Smulders, SJ, "L'Eglise Sacrement du Salut," in *L'Église de Vatican II. Études autour de la Constitution conciliaire sur l'Église*, vol. II, ed. G. Baraúna and Y. Congar (Paris: Cerf, 1966): 313–38; Yves Congar, "The Church, Universal Sacrament of Salvation," in *This Church That I Love*, trans. Lucien Delafuente (Denville, N.J.: Dimension Books, 1969): 39–61. One of the very best extended discussions in recent Catholic theology is to be found in Benoît-Dominique de La Soujeole, OP, *Introduction to the Mystery of the Church*, trans. Michael J. Miller (Washington, D.C.: The Catholic University of America Press, 2014). See also idem, "The Economy of Salvation: Entiative Sacramentality and Operative Sacramentality," *The Thomist* 75 (2011): 537–53. The theme is discussed in a broader context in Henri de Lubac, "How Is the Church a Mystery?" and "Lumen Gentium and the Fathers of the Church," in *The Church: Paradox and Mystery*, trans. James R. Dunne (Staten Island, N.Y.: Ecclesia Press, 1969): 13–29 and 30–67. In this essay I have said little about the centrality of this theme to the liturgical movement. Were I to do so, Odo Casel's 1932 *Das christliche Kultmysterium* would demand central place, translated as *The Mystery of Christian Worship and Other Writings*, ed. Burkhardt Neunheuser (London: DLT, 1962). I have also learnt a great deal from the inventive work on sacramentality and the Church pursued in Jean-Philippe Revel, *Traité des sacraments I. Baptême et sacramentalité 1. Origine et signification du baptême* (Paris: Cerf, 2004).

Christ's flesh with the Logos is the mystery in the sacrament of the flesh, so this flesh itself is raised by the power of the divinity to a supernatural, spiritual mode of existence, to the mystery in the sacrament of the Eucharist.... Thereupon also the Church, by virtue of its connection with the Incarnation and the Eucharist, becomes a great sacrament, a sacramental mystery.[12]

For Scheeben, thus, the Church may be described as a sacrament because of the connection that Christ effects between his transformed flesh and his body.

The same dynamic is explained with particular clarity in the early text by Edward Schillebeeckx, *Christ the Sacrament of Encounter with God*. Because of the hypostatic union, Christ's humanity and his earthly life become the means through which the Word brings about our salvation. As such, salvation is intrinsically sacramental; it occurs through the enactment of divine activity in an outwardly perceptible form. The acts of Jesus' life are expressions of the man Jesus's love for and worship of the Father.[13] And as such, Jesus's human life manifests the true character of humanity's intended relationship with the Father; it does so because Jesus's life is that of the incarnate Word. Indeed, we can go further and say that in his human love and worship Christ reveals the eternal love of the Son for the Father. Christ in this theological context is *the* sacrament; all other sacramental realities are named so analogically (although expanding this distinction would require that much more be said about the unique status of the Eucharist).[14]

The Father responds to the love manifest in Christ's life to the cross by raising him from the dead and drawing him to his right hand at the Ascension, establishing Christ as Lord and the objective redemption of humanity (Heb 8–9).[15] The glorified is Christ eternally our high priest, worshipping the Father, sending the Spirit, and being the grace that he bestows (Heb 7.25).[16] Christ has, thus, gone from our sight in order that he may be glorified, and that he may send the Spirit. Christ's sending of his Spirit alters neither the

12. Matthias Scheeben, *The Mysteries of Christianity*, trans. Cyril Vollert, SJ (London: Herder, 1947): 560–61.

13. Edward Schillebeeckx, *Christ the Sacrament of the Encounter with God*, trans. Paul Barrett, OP (London: Sheed and Ward, 1963): 15–18. See now also the reflections of Thomas G. Weinandy, *Jesus Becoming Jesus: A Theological Interpretation of the Synoptic Gospels* (Washington, D.C.: The Catholic University of America Press, 2018).

14. This way of describing the matter is thus rather different from that which presents the Church as the primary sacrament. E.g. Karl Rahner, *The Church and the Sacraments*, Quaestiones Disputatae 9, trans. W. J. O'Hara (New York: Herder and Herder, 1963). But even here (e.g., p. 15), we find that "Christ in his historical existence is both reality and sign, *sacramentum* and *res sacramenti*, of the redemptive grace of God."

15. Schillebeeckx, *Christ the Sacrament*, 32–33.

16. Schillebeeckx, *Christ the Sacrament*, 37–39.

fundamental nature of our need for visible sacramental signs nor the centrality of Christ's humanity as the locus of our salvation. Hence, the glorified Christ extends to us visible and corporeal signs that enable our encounter with him; Christ acts among us through a sacramental Spirit-led economy to make present both "his continual intercession for us and his active gift of grace."[17] In this perspective, "the sacraments are the saving mystery of the worship of Christ himself in ecclesial visibility."[18] And the Father always responds to that love and worship from his Son. But this guarantee—which Schillebeeckx treats as an explanation of the true meaning of the traditional "*ex opere operato*"—is, of course, not one that denies the mystery of human freedom. Divine love's expressive gesture draws us, and grace is given that we may respond, but respond we still must.

This sacramental economy is, however, misunderstood unless it is seen within the context of the Church's sacramentality as a whole. Christ stands as a representative of fallen humanity before the Father, and in his redemptive activity he wins for the Father a redeemed human community. That redeemed community is the body of Christ in which Father, Son, and Spirit dwell, and which Christ has chosen to be united to his person.[19] The visible society of the Church is that mystical body, "a sign raised up among the nations" of the eschatological community (Is. 11.12).[20] Schillebeeckx here reiterates an insistence in recent Catholic ecclesiology found implicitly in Pius XII's 1943 encyclical *Mystici corporis* and stated very clearly at Vatican II in *Lumen Gentium* 8.1 that the visible social community of the Church *is* the mystical body; there is no separation between the soul of the Church, an inner communion with the grace of Christ, and the visible body.[21] And thus

17. Schillebeeckx, *Christ the Sacrament*, 45. See also 44: "from the moment, that, by his ascension, the 'primordial sacrament' leaves the world, the economy of the 'separated sacraments' becomes operative." With reference to this point Schillebeeckx quotes Thomas, *SCG* 4.76.7: "Christ Himself perfects all the sacraments of the Church: it is He who baptizes; it is He who forgives sins; it is He, the true priest, who offered Himself on the altar of the cross, and by whose power His body is daily consecrated on the altar—nevertheless, because He was not going to be with all the faithful in bodily presence, He chose ministers to dispense the things just mentioned to the faithful."

18. Schillebeeckx, *Christ the Sacrament*, 70–79.

19. My allusion here is to Augustine's discussion of the third of three ways in which we may speak of Christ: *serm*. 341.11: "The third way is how the whole Christ is predicated with reference to the Church, that is as head and body. For indeed head and body form one Christ. Not that he isn't complete without the body, but that he was prepared to be complete and entire together with us too, though even without us he is always complete and entire, not only insofar as he is the Word, the only-begotten Son equal to the Father, but also in the very man whom he took on, and with whom he is both God and man together."

20. Schillebeeckx's use of Isaiah here references that found at Vatican I, *Dei Filius* 3 (DS 3014).

21. LG §8: "[T]he society structured with hierarchical organs and the Mystical Body of Christ, are not to be considered as two realities, nor are the visible assembly and the spiritual community, nor the

the visible social reality of the Church as a social communion is sacramental, an effective sign of Christ's salvation. The particular order of the seven sacraments identified by the Church presents to us seven clear points of entry into this community, into Christ himself.[22]

Now, identifying the Church as a sacrament in relationship to Christ the true sacrament brings with it a number of dangers. In particular one runs the danger of attributing to all aspects of the life of the Church the guaranteed sacramental efficacy that attends upon the seven. Thus, for clarity, in what follows I have reserved to the Church itself and to the seven sacraments the term "sacrament" and I speak of other aspects of the Church's life adjectivally as "sacramental."[23]

In order to complete the sketch on the basis of which I hope to address directly the particular topic of tradition conceived as sacramental, it will be helpful to identify four key themes, grouped into two pairs.[24]

Mystery and Act

Once again Scheeben identifies some essential points:

> It pertains to the essence of the sacramental mystery that the mystery remain a mystery.... This would not be the case if the sacrament would literally manifest the mystery. Something must be, and remain, hidden in the sacrament, within its interior.

---

earthly Church and the Church enriched with heavenly things; rather they form one complex reality which coalesces from a divine and a human element (*sed unam realitatem complexam efformant, quae humano et divino coalescit elemento*). For this reason, by no weak analogy, it is compared to the mystery of the incarnate Word. As the assumed nature inseparably united to Him, serves the divine Word as a living organ of salvation, so, in a similar way, does the visible social structure of the Church serve the Spirit of Christ, who vivifies it, in the building up of the body."

22. Schillebeeckx, *Christ the Sacrament*, 54: "Each sacrament is the personal saving act of the risen Christ himself, but realized in the visible form of an official act of the Church.... The essential reality that in one or other of seven possible ways is outwardly expressed in the reception of each of the sacraments is consequently the entry into living contact with the visible Church as the earthly mystery of Christ in heaven. To receive the sacraments of the Church in faith is therefore the same thing as to encounter Christ himself. In this light the sacramentality of the seven sacraments is the same as the sacramentality of the whole Church." For a recent and fuller discussion of this theme see de La Soujeole, *Introduction*, 122ff. and 473ff. De La Soujeole, along with a number of French writers, wishes to accord the Church the status of "person" in and of itself (see *Introduction*, 497ff.). While this theologoumenon finds some warrant in *Mystici Corporis* 53, I confess to finding it utterly unconvincing. The problem here is easily seen, for example, in the case of Maritain's account. See *On the Church of Christ*, trans. Joseph W. Evans (Notre Dame, Ind.: University of Notre Dame Press, 1973), 17, where Maritain quotes Thomas, *ST* II-II, q. 83, a. 16, ad 3, to bolster his account. Attention to q. 83 shows that when Thomas speaks of the "person of the Church" he does so because the Church *as the body of Christ* has been taken up into unity with the person of its head.

23. This, of course, runs the danger of confusion with the phenomenon of the sacramentals instituted by the Church—for a definition of which see *CCC* 1667–1679.

24. Jean-Philippe Revel, *Traité des sacraments* I.1.

> This does not exclude the possibility that the sacrament may make known the inner nature and meaning of the mystery.... It is only the essence of the supernatural mystery that may not become visible in the sacrament. This essence must ever remain the object of faith which, penetrating beneath the surface of the sacrament, lays hold of that which can be reached neither by the outer senses, nor by the intellect groping about in the realm of sensory perception.[25]

The character of a sacrament as mystery rests in its peculiar character as sign and in its relationship to faith. Only in faith can the complexity of what lies before our eyes be approached. As I have already noted, the mysterious character of the Church as sacrament stems from the fact that in the Church and through it Christ acts. And, just as the mode of the hypostatic union remains incomprehensible because the agent of that unity is the Word and the nature of divine power is *a priori* beyond us, so too the Church is sacrament because in his divine power Christ chooses us to be united to him. For the purpose of my argument, it is important to note that such a resolutely Christological vision of the sacramental economy demands a necessary complexity in our perception and discernment of reality.

Unity and Eschatology

As we have also seen, the sacramental act that is the Church, both is *and builds* the unity of Christ's body, the kingdom of God.[26] This is a unity between the members of that body founded on and encompassed within the unity that obtains between Father and Son. And this unity, in turn, is founded on the Father's gift to the Son of all that the Father is, and the Son's loving return in the Spirit to the Father. This unity is already ours in Christ through baptism, and is that toward which we strive and are drawn. And, thus the visible, institutional Church serves the goal of purifying and unifying that draws souls more closely into the body of Christ.

But it is souls who are drawn, and souls still in the process of transformation—souls who rarely grasp the unity toward which they head, and souls whose receptiveness to the Spirit develops and matures in a schedule known to and guided by God. And because of this fact, Christians experience the Church both as a sign of the community that it mystically is and

25. Scheeben, *Mysteries of Christianity*, 560.

26. See also *GS* §4.42, quoting *LG* §1: "The promotion of unity belongs to the innermost nature of the Church, for she is, 'thanks to her relationship with Christ, a sacramental sign and an instrument of intimate union with God, and of the unity of the whole human race.' Thus she shows the world that an authentic union, social and external, results from a union of minds and hearts, namely from that faith and charity by which her own unity is unbreakably rooted in the Holy Spirit."

will be, and yet as wounded by the presence of sin, confusion, and injustice among and between its members. This injustice can of course be so visibly present that some experience the Church only as alienating; even if, by the grace of God, we are not among their number, we may easily acknowledge that the Church *in via* has both a beautiful and a tragic guise.

The complexity of this situation is rendered all the greater because the head of the body uses his various limbs with respect to each other. We cannot speak only of individuals pursuing paths toward and on the basis of eschatological unity. Individuals are used as examples and warnings, they find themselves impelled together by providence for their mutual benefit, and all this in ways that escape certain knowledge and often the most basic understanding. Thus, the eschatological nature of Christian unity only enhances the mysterious character of the sacramental order.

None of this is to deny that there exist means for guidance in the dark. The same providential act that renders the sacramental nature of the Church mysterious also orders this community so that it may teach with authority. But rather than dwelling on the ways in which the community's teaching authority in some ways makes possible a true appreciation for the impenetrable nature of the individual members of the body, I would like to note that traditions of spiritual discernment and guidance have been the constant companion to accounts of the Christian community's nature *in via*. Such traditions exist because of the Church's eschatological nature. Finding ourselves mysteriously already in the end, and yet waiting for that end, traditions of discernment and guidance have been given us both for enduring that wait and to enable us to recognize ever better the impenetrable nature of the human person *in via*. This relationship between fundamental theological principles of ecclesiology and practices of discipline and discernment will find itself echoed in my treatment of tradition. But the question remains, how does the act of handing on also serve the formation of this unity, and contribute effectively to the salvation of souls as the council has it?

Unam Realitatem Complexam (*LG* §8.1)

And so, we come to tradition.[27] While the term most easily names that which is handed on and down in the community's life—and thus leads immediately

27. *LG* §8: "Societas autem organis hierarchicis instructa et mysticum Christi Corpus, coetus adspectabilis et communitas spiritualis, Ecclesia terrestris et Ecclesia coelestibus bonis ditata, non ut duae res considerandae sunt, sed unam realitatem complexam efformant, quae humano et divino coalescit elemento. Ideo ob non mediocrem analogiam incarnati Verbi mysterio assimilatur."

to questions concerning the relative authority of different beliefs and practices that have been handed down—"tradition" names also the *act* of handing on. The background against which I understand this act is the strain of reflection that runs from Möhler and Newman and Blondel to, in its most theologically sophisticated form, Congar. For this line of reflection, tradition is at root a handing on and a communication of Christian teaching dependent on the possession of the whole reality of Christian faith and life: dependent, that is, on something akin to a formed Christian conscience, but a conscience attentive to the living mystery of Christ made present in the Spirit. Congar speaks, for example, of the handing on of the faith in the early period as not only noetic, but also as a handing on of the Christian life as the context for that proclamation: "The noetic *traditio* of the faith was completed in a real *traditio* of the new life of Jesus Christ in the waters of which he is the source."[28] It is in this context that such authors insist on the unity of Scripture and tradition *in* Tradition; only within the life of faith is the meaning of Scripture grasped.[29]

But, at the same time, this same strain of reflection insists that this presence of the whole of Christian faith and life is a gift of God. The Spirit is, for Congar, the transcendent subject of tradition, the Church's "operative principle" of unity, strengthening faith, ensuring its transmission, drawing us into and toward unity in Christ.[30] Through the Spirit's work there may, then, be both a formation and handing on through human means, and the reliable presence of that whole in new generations. In this context the act of handing on, of *traditio*, may involve both repetition and a drawing on the gift of the whole in ways unknown to prior generations. Of course, whereas the union of human and divine in Christ is hypostatic, the Spirit is not incarnate in the Church. And thus the Spirit draws us into a unity in which Spirit and humanity retain their identities—and human beings retain their ability to fall away.[31]

28. Yves Congar, *Tradition and Traditions*, one volume edition, trans. Michael Naseby and T. Rainsborough (London: Burns and Oates, 1966): 279. It is interesting also to see Congar expanding on a discussion found at *ST* III, q. 42, a.4. Why is it, Thomas asks, that Christ did not write books? Because he taught in a manner that engraved his teaching on the hearts of his hearers, because his teaching could not all be expressed in writing, and so that his teaching might slowly unfold in the Church. See e.g. *The Meaning of Tradition*, trans. A. N. Woodrow (San Francisco: Ignatius, 2004), 23–24.

29. Cf. Maurice Blondel, *The Letter on Apologetics and History and Dogma*, trans. Alexander Dru and Iltyd Trethowan (Grand Rapids, Mich.: Eerdmans, 1995), 267: "[Tradition] preserves not so much the intellectual aspect of the past, as its living reality.... It relies, no doubt, on texts, but at the same time it relies primarily on something else, on an experience always in act which enables it to remain in some respects master of the texts, instead of being strictly subservient to them."

30. Yves Congar, *The Meaning of Tradition*, 51ff. See also *DV* §5's insistence on the necessity of grace for faith and on the constancy of the Spirit's work, enabling our growth in understanding of revelation. The same perspective is taken up in further detail in *DV* §8.

31. Congar, *The Meaning of Tradition*, 55–56.

In considering the act of tradition as sacramental I am not striking out into entirely unknown territory. Yves Congar's magisterial text *Tradition and Traditions* points the way, if in rather general terms. At one point he considers the character of the Church's time and writes as follows:

> Sacred history, where God's design is accomplished by his power, includes a threefold presence: first, a presence of saving acts, performed once for all, which are effective not just by the simple mental reference of memory but by a present operative power they keep; second, a presence of the end in view, not only as thought of or as desired but as the fruit virtually present in the seed; third, a presence of true union with God, as the fruit of what it brings about, as the seed of the final fulfillment, and at the same time a present lived reality. We may call this the sacramental nature of the time of the Church.[32]

Congar adapts his notion of a threefold presence from Thomas's own account of the threefold reference of the sacraments, in order to show that the history of the Church must be understood as a complex sphere of divine action within which we are drawn into the saving acts of Christ's earthly mission and prepared for the end.[33] The presence of union with God as a "lived reality" is that which makes the act of *traditio* possible.

Not surprisingly, the work of the Spirit is central for Congar; for it is the Spirit's role (as we saw earlier) to "effect a communication between realities" and ultimately to realize the eschatological kingdom of God. Hence, the history of the Church should be understood as a sphere of divine action within which the Spirit draws forth responses to the divine call, responses which build toward that eschatological unity:

> Sacred history, the history of the Church as the Church of God, is made out of the succession of God's "visitations" thanks to which men elicit those responses of faith and love by which the city of God is built up. In a theological analysis, this moment of the divine activity, which logically precedes our free decisions or reactions, is attributed simultaneously to God and to the sacred humanity of Christ, our head.[34]

A few paragraphs later Congar beautifully conveys the sheer diversity of realities that must be part of this history of visitations:

> [T]he history of the Church is ... that of the achievement or consolidation of [the covenant] relationship, already perfectly established, but not yet fully consummated. This history could be formulated as in Hebrews 11: "it was by faith, fulfilling the gos-

32. Yves Congar, *Tradition and Traditions*, 259.

33. Congar references *In IV sent*. d. 8, q. 1, a. 1, sol. 3; *ST* I-II, q. 101, a. 2; III, q. 60, a. 3; q. 73, a. 4.

34. Congar, *Tradition and Traditions*, 262–63. Cf. 406ff.

> pel and by a mission of the holy spirit that the Council of Nicaea . . . ; it was by faith . . . that Augustine . . . ; by faith . . . that Francis Xavier . . . that Therese Martin, and so on." This history recalls Christians' responses to the calls of God and of time; it is made up of councils, acts of the magisterium, missionary endeavours, and religious foundations, of conversions and of decisions taken for God; but also the more secret history, to be disclosed only at the last judgement, of all the movements of faith and love drawn from our human freedom by God's grace.[35]

These responses, these moments of renewed or intensified covenant relationship, are moments of *traditio* in which the faith is received and handed on in new and yet continuous form. And thus, this account of the sacramentality of the Church's time hints at the possibility of a more developed reflection on Tradition's sacramentality.

Acts of doctrinal definition, theological statement, and spiritual vision may be read as moments of response to the divine call, moments drawn out of the community and out of individuals to reveal for us all aspects of the love that builds the City of God. Such moments are transformative for their subjects because in such responses the intellect and the will are opened and formed, and the depths of the mystery of Christ more keenly felt. These moments provide, for those of us who dwell on them, opportunities for recognizing dimensions of Christian faith and life in action and thus opportunities for us to attend ever more closely to the gift and its life in all the baptized. It is important, I think, to note that many of the people and events Congar names are complex personalities and events. Even in the most fraught and politically complex of ecclesial events we may see the beauty and tragedy of the Church in microcosm. Particular individuals taken up into such events may, for example, present aspects inspiring or depressing in turn, but we may still grasp the beauty of the thought that results, and we may still acknowledge that in such moments of definition God is at work enabling human minds to articulate with deeper penetration and in appropriate order what it is to think in the light of revelation and with the gift of faith. As we learn, and always through God's grace, our intellects and wills are gradually better ordered toward their true ends, and, as *Dei Verbum* says, these events "[contribute] effectively toward the salvation of souls." However, already it may be apparent that my vision of such events parallels how we regard the life of the Church more broadly as both beautiful and tragic, and as consequently demanding of us complex habits of

35. Congar, *Tradition and Traditions*, 263.

discernment. There is more to be said here, and I would like to move forward by considering tradition as sacrament in the light of the two pairs of terms I introduced above when discussing the sacramentality of the Church more broadly.

Act and Unity. Let us think a little more about why I have accorded priority to tradition as act. In the first place, I have done so because the act of passing on is founded in Christ's own actions toward the apostles. He speaks and acts among them to reveal the Father, and he does so in a way that demands (and also elicits in the Spirit) their response. This emphasis on the manner in which Christ reveals through the entirety of his personal life with the very earliest Christian community is itself central to *Dei Verbum*. But in the second place, Christ's self-giving in revelation shows us who he is; it reveals the eternal relationship of Father and Son. The Son's handing of himself over to us—which he does by revealing himself, by giving himself up for us, and by incorporating us into his person—reveals and is founded in the Father's gift of being to the Son (and we find, once again, the same position is espoused *in nuce* by Congar). The Son's gift of himself to us is an incorporative act that enables our unity with him and with the Triune life. The act of *traditio* is an act that is a part of this gift at work; done faithfully it itself is an effective sign of Christ's incorporative restoration of human intellect and will. But, because that restoration is a restoration of the intellect in relationship to the unity of humanity under God, *traditio* is also a sign of that unity.[36]

The character of this act is, however, misunderstood unless we see how central interpretation, reimagining, and speculation are to the act of *traditio*. If we focus for the moment on the process by which expressed Christian thought gradually expands and is defined over the centuries, we can see that interpretation is intrinsic to the activity of handing on. In, for example, the work of basic catechesis and preaching, the activities of synthesizing, finding examples, adapting teaching to audience are always also works of interpretation even if conducted with a deep sense of faithfulness to what has been handed on. More obviously, perhaps, the work of definition and

36. This emphasis on the link between the very idea of tradition and the unity of humanity under God is an important undercurrent in Pieper's short *Tradition: Concept and Claim*, trans. E. Christian Kopff (South Bend, Ind.: St Augustine's Press, 2010). The very last sentence of the work states his claim boldly, p. 68: "real unity among human beings has its roots in nothing else but the common possession of tradition in the strictest sense—I mean, our sharing in common the sacred tradition that goes back to God's words."

achieving clarity (where faith allows!) has so often involved both new formulation and even the forgetting of older paths. This work occurs a myriad of times in the work of individual thinkers, and is seen most clearly under the guidance of the Spirit in the work of the great councils and definitions of the Church's magisterial history. So that we do not think that the presence of constant interpretation invalidates any claim to continuity in tradition, it is important to remember not only that the presence of Scripture and of the Church's magisterial tradition provide an anchor and focus for such interpretation, but also (as I earlier drew on Congar to emphasize) that tradition is a gift, constantly sustained by the Spirit's work in the Body of Christ. It is through the Spirit's work in Christians that encounter with the mystery of Christ is sustained.[37] Continuity within sometimes radical renewal can thus be understood only when we see both human and divine agency at work.

We could, at this point, devote much time, with profit, to slowly defining the character of the newness that enters the world in such moments of definition and interpretation. But I do not want to take us there. Rather, I want to explore briefly how recognizing the necessity of interpretation to the work of faithful handing on helps us to see a little more clearly the sacramental character of the act of *traditio* itself. Tradition is an act, I suggest, through which Christ reveals to us, and shapes, the vocation of intellect and will, a vocation of aiding and ordering the eschatological unity of Christ's body. It is *the* act that lies at the heart of the very enterprise of Christian thinking, revealing to us the combination of submission and active speculation to which we are called during the time between ascension and the end. And thus this act is sacramental because it is an effective sign of the death and resurrection of the mind, which is the restoration of the mind—within the unity of the human race—that we encounter in Christ. The acts of handing on that we see in the Church's history—acts marked by both beauty and tragedy—may, through grace, enable us better to grasp the character of the reformation of intellect and will that has begun in us through our baptism. As we grow in understanding of the act of tradition, following as far as we may the work of grace in such acts, we also come to see the manner in which Christ draws out from his body a diverse unity of flourishing intellects; we

37. Attention to Henri de Lubac's "The Problem of the Development of Dogma," in *Theology in History*, trans. Anne Englund Nash (San Francisco: Ignatius Press, 1996), 248–80, esp. 267–78, is rarely a bad thing when this problem is under consideration. De Lubac's understanding of how expressed faith relates to the mystery of faith and his account of how one may sustain something like the vision I have expressed while still believing that revelation may be said to have ended with the death of the apostles are both of great importance.

should come to see that the performance of true theological diversity is an education in reason's flourishing—even as we must also recognize the tragedy of mere self-assertion.

As should have been clear from my consideration of the sacramentality of the Church in general, the Church is an effective sign of our eschatological unity. The act of tradition necessarily partakes of the same quality: through this act performed in good and mixed faith, the Spirit draws out for us a series of interrelated monuments of tradition, giving structure to the rule of faith and showing us the possible boundaries and nodal points of Christian life and practice. As we properly attend to these moments of response we too may come to grasp the shape of the restored human intellect not only as individuals, but as part of a conversation that will reach its fullness only at the end.

Mystery and Eschatology. *Traditio* is also an eschatological act. Consider how tradition, as both act and content, seems designed both to elevate and to defeat the mind. It elevates the mind, showing us paths down which reason may be restored; it defeats because of the sheer difficulty of proceeding without a constant reliance on grace in the face of impenetrable mystery.[38] But this mystery attends because of the manner in which the ultimate agent and object of tradition presents himself to us. This is so because the Father presents himself to us in Christ, through the sacramental economy of Christ's body, in an economy that slowly but providentially draws intellect and will toward their supernatural end in contemplation.

Learning from Tradition

My account of tradition as a sacramental act is partly intended to render more perspicacious the central place of attention to tradition in dogmatic theology. In a recent essay in the *Thomist* I have argued that a robust theology of tradition helps us to view fundamental moments of definition as the ever-present and exemplary objects of theological attention.[39] We should,

38. Pieper, *Tradition*, 18: "There is already at the earliest stage an important difference [between 'teaching' and 'handing on a tradition'], which is that the teacher from the beginning already knows and recognizes of himself what he is teaching,whereas the person who hand down tradition can see through the *tradita* just as little as the recipient of tradition. No 'older generation' knows any more about the Judgment after Death [for example] than the last in line, to whom this *traditum* is handed down."

39. "The Memory of Tradition: Post-Conciliar Renewal and One Recent Thomism," *The Thomist* 79, no. 4 (2015): 511–50.

I suggested, conceive of dogmas not only as propositions expressing the truths of revelation, but also as memorializing of the situations that gave them birth, injunctions to attend to particular historical moments of response to the divine call. This account is, I would hope, further bolstered by an account of tradition as sacramental; those historical moments to which our attention is summoned may be further viewed as grace-filled moments in which the vocation of thought is actualized for us, and through which Christ's transformation of our intellects and wills is made present.

Earlier I claimed that from awareness of the Church as an eschatological reality flow disciplines for spiritual discernment and guidance. Good ecclesiological reflection, I suggested, must sustain both robust notions of divine providential guidance and awareness of the irreducible complexity of our knowledge of providence. Disciplines that enable attention to both of these necessarily follow. It should not surprise, then, that describing the act of tradition as sacramental within the context of the Church's sacramentality *per se* has the consequence of demanding from us an account of the habits of attention and discernment that are appropriate when we think in the light of tradition. There is much that might be said here about the possibilities and challenges of reading the debates that led to the formed expressions of tradition in the light of that tradition, but to get to the heart of what I have particularly in view allow me to focus on just one concern. My exaltation of theological principles and perspectives may have seemed to militate against an account of attention to tradition that can take seriously careful historical investigation. I suggest that, in fact, the opposite is the case.

A properly theological account of tradition demands of us a vision of handing on that occurs under the aegis of Son and Spirit and as part of the divine economy of revelation and graceful sanctification. Such a *theological* emphasis demands that we hold before us a number of perduring philosophical and theological questions when we engage modern historical scholarship. For example, one who operates with a robustly theological account of tradition will need of necessity to be attentive to the problems involved in accounts of human or societal action that exclude divine action. Such a conception of tradition will also demand a close engagement with those hermeneutics of suspicion that read acts of handing on as always betrayal, or as always involving rupture with the past. While these accounts have much to suggest to a theological poetics, there is obviously much that we are pushed to resist on theological grounds. It is striking that while the past few decades have seen some excellent deconstructive work focused on the assumptions of modern sociological and hermeneutical analyses of human action, they have nevertheless seen little work on the *theological* underpinnings of a vision of theological attention that takes them seriously even as it questions.

Such a theological articulation—attentive to the reality of the Spirit working among us to preserve as well as aid human freedom—must sustain a robust notion of double agency. Adopting Congar's language, tradition understood sacramentally is a series of responses and encounters in which human agency as we know it between ascension and the end is fully operative. Those human agents are also *in the process of* sanctification and transformation, their own intellectual vision not yet perfected, their ability to articulate the knowledge that the gift of faith has infused still weak, their love for God still in many cases faltering, however intense. And thus there is need for constant attention to the mysteriousness of the interplay between divine and human action in such moments.

Drawing further on an analogy I offered earlier, the one who investigates must become almost akin to the confessor or spiritual director of his or her subjects, ever attentive to the complexities of discerning the penitent's moral state, generous in attributing motive and yet recognizing always that insight easily fails and that human beings are easily seduced. The faithful and well-intentioned theological thinker, impelled to work by the Spirit, drawn by the Spirit to state that which may become dogma, nevertheless frequently errs in motive and reasons falsely and weakly. In such a context we can and must be robust in our historical investigation, unflinching in our willingness to explore and admit contradiction and uncertainty in those held up before us as theological exemplars; attentive to the sheer mysteriousness of understanding the course of theological development, and willing to feel the pull of all methodologies that proffer the possibility of a denser location of moments and individuals in their historical contexts.

Of course, the analogy breaks down in at least one fundamental way; we investigate texts and monuments of tradition, and do not question living subjects; we see their struggles at even further remove than does the confessor listening to the words of the penitent and trying to discern the mind's state. However, when we see that a sacramental account of tradition demands of us this twofold attention, then it should be apparent that it is precisely the robustness of the theology that allows a truly rigorous account of historical investigation. Again, none of this militates against the possibility that there is a defined course of magisterial teaching within the

Church. Rather, the divine provision of these points of intellectual light in the darkness not only enables the mind to grasp through faith, as Thomists would say, the first truth. This divine provision creates a space within which we may take our time, breathe freely and attend to the complexity of the tradition itself, knowing that here we find divinely ordered materials that will aid us in the development of intellect and love and thus draw us toward realizing that unity which is ours in Christ.

Interlude: On Scripture

I have already hinted at the argument, deeply embedded in chapter II of *Dei Verbum*, that Scripture flows from the act of *traditio*. The status of Scripture now needs direct (if brief) comment, if only to show what sort of defense against the charge that so much emphasis on tradition displaces Scripture emerges from my argument so far.

In the recent *Festschrift* for the late John Webster, I offered a sketch of ways in which we might draw on an early essay by Joseph Ratzinger to envision Scripture as constituted by a series of creative and inspired interpretations of Scripture's earlier layers.[40] These interpretations culminate in the New Testament, which includes both Jesus's own radical interpretation of the "Old" *and* the earliest community's own radical interpretation of Christ in the light of the resurrection and ascension. But this latter includes also the promise that the Church will continue to be guided in continued interpretation through the presence of Christ and his Spirit. Christian thought and worship are thus centrally scriptural, and yet are so under the aegis of its Lord who guides us in interpretation. The young Ratzinger's perspective here enfolds the status of Scripture within a vision of a *traditio* that occurs under divine aegis. Scripture is thus not relativized over against a distinct source of knowledge; rather, *traditio* characterizes Scripture itself and lays a foundation for appropriate attention to it. The argument flows from Ratzinger's insistence that the incarnate Word of God is revelation in its fullness, an insistence found also in the final text of *Dei Verbum* itself.[41] As the second chapter of that text has it:

40. "The Word Answering the Word: Opening the Space of Catholic Biblical Interpretation," in *Theological Theology: Essays in Honor of John B. Webster*, ed. R. David Nelson, Darren Sarisky, and Justin Stratis (London: Bloomsbury), 37–53.

41. See Joseph Ratzinger in *Commentary on the Documents of Vatican II.* Vol. III, ed. Herbert Vorgrimler, trans. William Glen-Doepel et al. (London Burns & Oates, 1969), 170–72.

> Sacred Scripture is the speech of God as it is put down in writing under the breath of the Holy Spirit. And tradition transmits in its entirety the Word of God which has been entrusted to the apostles by Christ the Lord and the Holy Spirit.[42]

Scripture's status is here founded in an account of the incarnate Word *as* revelation and then in an account of Christ and the Spirit's encompassing and shaping of our response to Scripture. Within such an account, its text is "the speech of God" set down "under the breath of the Spirit" but it is such intended to be interpreted in the light of the ever-present Word's speech. But even this is too simplistic, as it is Scripture, understood as that divine speech, which has also formed our attention and stands as a constant referent in the process of attention to the incarnate Christ's presence.

One way in which unhappiness with my account of *traditio* might take form is to ask how Scripture acts as a corrective voice of its own. Of course, there is a certain Romanticism about the idea of a text speaking for itself; Stanley Fish will be turning over in his retirement. But the metaphorical language may be allowed, in part for theological reasons, since the Word most certainly uses Scripture to voice the gospel among us. And it may be allowed also in order to conceptualize the way in which, throughout the history of the Church, Scripture's literal sense has stimulated reform or has been the foundation for a critique of (failing) conceptions of Christian practice. In such contexts Scripture may be said to speak.

And yet there is a balance to maintain; Scripture's "voice" must be reified with care. We fail to exercise sufficient care, I suggest, when we treat that "voice" as equivalent to reconstructions of the meaning of the text by modern biblical criticism. My point here is not to offer a rash condemnation *in toto* of a tradition as multifarious as "modern biblical criticism," but to draw attention to the multiplicity of ways in which this voice may speak. It is certainly the case, for example, that for many of those who fought (rightly or wrongly) against the perceived aridity of Neo-Thomism many aspects of modern biblical study were foundational in bringing to consciousness the reality of Christ's historical location and cultural consciousness. But the text of Scripture, as I have also argued in the *Festschrift* essay mentioned above, may be conceived as open to a multiplicity of readings. We should struggle mightily to see the contexts of textual production—and how those texts may have been heard by their original audience—*and* we should struggle to trace how the Church was led under the Spirit's guidance to read those texts in the tradition. Offering a fuller argument for how this might be so, and how

42. *DV* §9.

such a conception of multiple readings is a theologically coherent way to take forward *Dei Verbum*'s emphases, is a grand task that must await another occasion.

Conclusion: Returning to "Development"

If the act of tradition may be read sacramentally, then the natural complement of so doing is reflection on the growth in understanding of the gospel that comes over time. *Dei Verbum* again, providentially alludes to this theme but seems to demand from us further reflection. The relevant text runs as follows:

> This tradition which comes from the Apostles develops (*proficit*) in the Church with the help of the Holy Spirit. For there is a growth in the understanding (*crescit perceptio*) of the realities and the words which have been handed down. This happens through the contemplation and study made by believers, who treasure these things in their hearts (see Luke 2:19, 51) through a penetrating understanding of the spiritual realities which they experience, and through the preaching of those who have received through Episcopal succession the sure gift of truth. For as the centuries succeed one another, the Church constantly moves forward toward the fullness of divine truth until the words of God reach their complete fulfillment in her.[43]

This text is interesting, in part, for what it does not say. While we find clear statements that tradition develops, and that the Church grows in understanding over time (statements which must be read together),[44] we find no invocation of any of the various analogies or metaphors used to capture the notion development that had been in the air since the early nineteenth century. This absence reflects a careful decision to insist on the idea of development, while not taking sides in an ongoing scholarly debate about how one could best describe this process. Oddly, the debate that the document bypasses here has not been pursued with sufficient vigor in the decades that

43. *DV* §8: "Haec quae est ab Apostolis Traditio sub assistentia Spiritus Sancti in Ecclesia proficit: crescit enim tam rerum quam verborum traditorum perceptio, tum ex contemplatione et studio credentium, qui ea conferunt in corde suo (cf. Lc 2,19 et 51), tum ex intima spiritualium rerum quam experiuntur intelligentia, tum ex praeconio eorum qui cum episcopatus successione charisma veritatis certum acceperunt. Ecclesia scilicet, volventibus saeculis, ad plenitudinem divinae veritatis iugiter tendit, donec in ipsa consummentur verba Dei."

44. See Ratzinger in *Commentary on the Documents of Vatican II*, Vol III, ed. Vorgrimler, 186–88. Ratzinger notes that in debate Cardinal Léger found the idea of tradition itself developing unhelpful. In its own debate the Theological Commission decided not to change this wording, noting that the clause asserting development in the understanding of revelation should be read as qualifying the statement that tradition itself develops. In the same context Ratzinger notes that, unlike Trent and Vatican I, this text does not cite Vincent of Lérins's famous statement at *comm.* 23.3 that a growth in understanding occurs "with the same sense and the same understanding (*eodem sensu eademque sententia*)."

have followed. In a manner that parallels the broader fate of the theology of tradition, theological reflection on the notion of doctrinal development has been halting in recent decades. Penetrating and often accurate critique of some of Newman's own language—especially concerning the manner in which he deploys analogies concerning the development of the mind to suggest the inevitable and organic development of ideas—has seemed to render his vision incompatible with the decidedly nonlinear complexities that modern historical work frequently delivers us.[45] Parallel critiques have seemed to undermine the accounts of virtually all who have thought in his wake (or in the parallel wake of the Tübingen school). Elsewhere I have tried to exempt de Lubac from these critiques, but here I want to turn back briefly to Newman himself.[46]

The fifteenth of the *University Sermons* is unfairly neglected in treatments of his account of development, being treated for the most part as merely a sketch of the work he would soon go on to produce in the *Essay on Development*. I suggest that, in fact, we should read the sermon as offering us the foundations for an account of "development" that offers rather different paths for exploration than those found in the *Essay* (whether or not Newman himself would have taken the path I want to mark out). I will reflect on two themes that are fundamental to this text: first, the variety of ways in which Newman describes the "idea" of Christianity, and second, the manner in which he combines an account of the divine action—the gifting of that idea—with a sensitive account of the human mind's failure to articulate what it knows. Taken together, what he suggests opens for us a possible conversation complementary to those that, through the paper's earlier sections, I have suggested we should pursue.

First, then, we should note Newman's use of a variety of different terminologies to speak of "an idea" of Christianity. He speaks somewhat tentatively of an inward idea or belief in the singular, but he speaks also of a collection of "ideas." These ideas are also a "living impression" or "a collection of judgments and impressions." This phenomenon is the result of the mind's reception of and initial attempts to comprehend divine activity, although Newman speaks of this in different persons as both inchoate, as

45. The literature here is extensive. A *locus classicus*, however, is Nicholas Lash, *Newman on Development. The Search for an Exploration in History* (London: Sheed and Ward, 1975). In recent literature one of the most extensive attempts at retrieving aspects of Newman's account in dialogue with that of Congar is Andrew Meszaros, *The Prophetic Church: History and Doctrinal Development in John Henry Newman and Yves Congar* (Oxford: Oxford University Press, 2016).

46. Lewis Ayres, *Nicaea and Its Legacy: An Approach to Fourth-Century Theology* (Oxford: Oxford University Press, 2004): 425–29.

conscious and as unconscious.[47] In any case, it is a reception of and reflection on that which is received as divine gift. This collection of judgments or living impressions is also "what Scripture calls knowledge."[48] The sheer variety of terminology here opens the possibility of our stepping back from the singular idea and its unfolding, toward a more hesitant sense of the mind's engagement with the divine impress, the divine infusion of faith. I use the phrase "divine infusion of faith" carefully; just after Newman speaks of this collection of judgments as "what Scripture calls knowledge," he writes:

> This awful vision is what Scripture seems to designate by the phrases "Christ in us," "Christ dwelling in us by faith," "Christ formed in us," and "Christ manifesting Himself unto us." And though it is faint and doubtful in some minds, and distinct in others, as some remote object in the twilight or in the day, this arises from the circumstances of the particular mind, and does not interfere with the perfection of the gift itself.[49]

Newman thus sees the idea or collection of ideas as the result of Christ's impress on the soul. He does not explicitly develop here a fully Catholic account of theological faith; he focuses on the theological framework within which we may speak about such a gift, Christ's effective presence to the soul.[50]

This focus, however, combines with his account of the mind's natural and "spontaneous" desire to explore, analyze and describe that which impresses itself through divine action.[51] The ideas of which he speaks have "a life in them which shows itself in progress." This is so because of the depth of truth that they contain, because they stem from the active work of Christ drawing us on, because they have "a depth, which extends into mystery."[52] This "life" flows from the character of revelation, both in the sense that Christ himself gives us this faith and uses it for our salvation, and in

47. John Henry Newman, *Fifteen Sermons Preached Before the University of Oxford*, ed. J. D. Earnest and G. Tracey (Oxford: Oxford University Press, 2006), 216ff.

48. Newman, *Fifteen Sermons*, 223.

49. Newman, *Fifteen Sermons*, 223–4.

50. See Newman, *Fifteen Sermons* 228: "it is difficult to determine what divine grace may not do for us, if not immediately in implanting new ideas, yet in refining and elevating those which we gain through natural informants. If, as we all acknowledge, grace renews our moral feelings… it does not appear why, in a certain sense, it may not impart ideas concerning the nature of God." It is also worth noting that in the rough notes that Newman prepared for a proposed preface to the French translation of the sermons he asserts laconically that through grace a divine certainty of faith is infused (see p. 238), but that his main concern in the sermons is with the human side of faith (available at Newman, *Fifteen Sermons*, 236–251). This is not, I think, defensive, merely Newman being clear that his account is compatible with and perhaps presupposes such an infusion, but that he will not focus on it here.

51. Newman, *Fifteen Sermons*, 216.

52. Newman, *Fifteen Sermons*, 214.

the sense that this revealed knowledge draws and entices the human mind by its joint character of truth and mystery. Already it should be apparent that Newman's account can be developed alongside an account of *traditio* as the fundamental theological act, flowing from the very nature of revelation, and as an act through which Christ and the Spirit may reform and restore the soul.[53]

Second, I would like to note Newman's account of the difficulty that fallen human beings naturally experience in articulating what they know. Newman comments:

> But, further, if the ideas may be latent in the Christian mind, by which it is animated and formed, it is less wonderful that they should be difficult to elicit and define; and of this difficulty we have abundant proof in the history whether of the Church, or of individuals. Surely it is not at all wonderful, that, when individuals attempt to analyze their own belief, they should find the task arduous in the extreme, if not altogether beyond them; or, again, a work of many years; or, again, that they should shrink from the developments, if offered to them, as foreign to their thoughts.[54]

A little later he insists in quite a striking passage that a "characteristic" of dogmatic statements is "the difficulty of recognizing them." Dogmatic statements, reasoned out by the Christian community and under the guidance of Son and Spirit may be correct, yet our weak grasp of the unitary living idea within us makes recognizing the correspondence of the piecemeal differentiated statements of dogma to the living idea extremely difficult.[55] Similarly, when we look back it may be difficult for us to grasp the reasoning that led to a particular dogmatic formulation, because such reasoning always has a unique character, since those who reason have recourse both to deductive argument and to the living idea within them.[56] The difficulty that we have

53. In this regard note also the concluding sentence about the salvific character of revealed knowledge: Newman, *Fifteen Sermons*, 233–34: "All is dreary till we believe, what our hearts tell us, that we are subjects of His Governance; nothing is dreary, all inspires hope and trust, directly we understand that we are under His hand, and that whatever comes to us is from Him. What is it to us whether the knowledge He gives us be greater or less, if it be He who gives it? What is it us whether it be exact or vague, if He bids us trust it? What have we to care whether we are or are not given to divide substance from shadow, if He is training us heavenwards by means of either?"

54. Newman, *Fifteen Sermons*, 218.

55. Newman, *Fifteen Sermons*, 219.

56. Newman, *Fifteen Sermons*, 224–25. We should note especially this passage: "[T]hough the Christian mind reasons out a series of dogmatic statements, one from another, this it has ever done, and always must do, not from those statements taken in themselves, as logical propositions, but as being itself enlightened and (as if) inhabited by that sacred impression which is prior to them, which acts as a regulating principle, ever present, upon the reason.... For though the development of an idea is a deduction of proposition from proposition, these propositions are ever formed in and round the idea itself (so to speak), and are in fact one and all only aspects of it." Here Newman hints at the sort of notion of radical newness in interpretation (even as it remains *interpretation*) that is explored by such

in presenting doctrinal "development" as a logical and organic process is simply a consequence of the manner in which human and divine interact here. Newman adds as a proviso—as I have done myself more than once in this paper—that recognition of this difficulty in comprehension in no way militates against the idea of God's provision of clear teaching in both Scripture and the Church's tradition. Nor is recognition of this difficulty license for presenting Christian teaching as an ever-changing and discontinuous series.[57] His emphasis on the sheer difficulty of comprehending deepens Newman's account of the space opened up by the interaction of divine and human agency in the Christian community's growth in understanding of revelation. But recognizing the space in which *traditio* occurs as one of divine and human agency is that which I have argued to be central in understanding why the act of *traditio* may be understood as sacramental (a step that is, of course, beyond Newman's own formulations). This account of development, then, may form an integral part of a theology of tradition which takes *traditio* as the fundamental theological act, and which takes the unfolding of our understanding of revelation through the proclamation and speculation of truly human agents, through human sub-creation, as simultaneously nurtured by Son and Spirit.[58]

I hope, then, that taking forward some of the main emphases of *Dei Verbum*'s second chapter—and taking some of its ambiguities and conscious omissions as charges for our own reflection—may prove a fruitful way of thinking theologically about the character of revelation and theological reflection. Emphasis on the manner in which the act of tradition is a sacramental part of the divine economy may provide, I suggest, a unifying theme, one that will enable us to shape an account of theology that will realize

---

thinkers as Congar and Ratzinger in the mid-twentieth century. For discussion see the brief comments in the previous section of the essay and, more extensively, my "The Word Answering the Word."

57. It is, in part, this recognition that leads Newman to offer his famous "notes" of appropriate development in the *Essay*. Read today those "notes" can seem somewhat circular, but if they were to be read as removing the difficulty we have in understanding the interpretive leaps and moves that Newman reflects upon here so candidly, that would be an important loss.

58. I use "sub-creation" in the sense given the term by J. R. R. Tolkien in his "On Fairy-Stories," in *Tree and Leaf* (London: George Allen and Unwin, 1964), 11–70. The term there describes the giving of internal consistency and coherence to a "secondary" world in that type of tale he describes as fantasy. Of importance, however, is the insistence that sub-creative activity, if it is successful, speaks to fundamental human and fallen experiences of recovery, escape, and consolation (especially the consolation that follows from acceptance of the inevitability and even the benefits of death). In the essay's epilogue Tolkien sees the possibility of this activity, the activity of "the effoliation and multiple enrichment of creation," as now hallowed by the character of the divine economy. Tolkien's perspective may, perhaps, be used also to approach the character of the Christian doctrinal enterprise: an act of "sub-creation" (using all the tools of human sub-creative activity), but one that is not only hallowed by but *demanded* by the Creator's redemptive work, an activity taken up into that work.

some of the untapped potential of the Council's work. As I indicated at the beginning of this essay, although my approach is a clearly Catholic one, I have tried to draw my central themes from the wellspring at the gospel's core. And I have done so as an opening to particular sorts of ecumenical conversation: only by our attending to and even arguing (reasonably politely) over the very contents of the gospel do we grow in ecumenical understanding.

Chapter 4

"The Kingdom of Christ Now Present in Mystery" and the Question of the "Distance between Christ as Lord, King, and Judge and His Church"

Christoph Schwöbel

Remembering through the Lenses of One Swiss Theologian

The many events held to commemorate the end of the Second Vatican Council on December 8, 1965, the day of the Feast of the Immaculate Conception, had just come to an end when, on October 31, 2017, the preparations for celebrating the 500-year anniversary of the Reformation entered their final phase. Both Vatican II and the quincentennial of the Reformation have occasioned much debate in and between the churches. Remembering Vatican II is for many in the Roman Catholic Church, especially among Roman Catholic theologians in Europe, a look back on a promise that has not yet been fulfilled in the history of the Church since the Council. Many see the pontificate of Pope Francis as a recovery of the forward-pointing initiatives of Vatican II and hope that the Church will find occasion to go back to the foundations for the future that, in their interpretation, were laid in Vatican II.[1] For oth-

1. This was also the focus of the 2015 Conference of the Ecclesiological Investigations Research Network at Georgetown University, under the title "Remembering the Future."

ers in the Roman Catholic Church, the legacy of Vatican II is by no means unproblematic. Has the celebrated *aggiornamento* led to forgetfulness with regard to the theological and philosophical resources that would be needed to respond in a theologically responsible and intellectually rigorous way to the challenges of the twenty-first century? Has too much of neo-scholastic theology been discarded and ignored in the aftermath of the Council, a resource that for many seems rich and fruitful for meeting the challenges of our late modern situation? Is a new phase of *ressourcement* needed to retrieve the intellectual potential of the tradition in order to deal critically and constructively with the perplexities of our late modern situation?

The preparations for the anniversary of the Reformation led to passionate debates focusing on the differences between the views of historians and the views of theologians regarding the Lutheran Reformation as it related to other reformations and reform initiatives in the late medieval and early modern church. Was the Reformation a giant step in the modern history of freedom or is it at the root of all modern and postmodern evils?[2] Is Luther's insistence on the freedom of conscience, bound only by the evidence of biblical testimonies and evident reasons, famously exercised at the Diet of Worms, a precursor of modern views of autonomy? Or is Luther's view, with its emphasis that sinners need to be liberated in order to be free in the certainty of faith, rather a reminder that freedom is founded in relationship to the triune God, a relationship that the Enlightenment programmatically discarded? To what extent is the Reformation a modification of debates that had already been conducted in the medieval church, and to what extent does it have ecumenical potential for the reconciliation of the divided churches? Earlier hopes in some Protestant circles that the ban on Luther might be lifted by Rome on the occasion of the 500-year anniversary of the Reformation in 2017 not having been fulfilled, the most sensitive question is now, after the anniversary, whether and how the Roman Catholic and the Protestant churches can together discover the heritage of the Reformation as a stimulus for further ecumenical exploration.

Ecclesiological concerns are in many ways at the heart of the debates in our churches and among the theologians. This raises the question: Does *Lumen Gentium*, the Second Vatican Council's constitution on the Church, offer resources and inspirations for clarifying the theological understanding

2. For a sharply critical assessment of the effects of the Reformation see Brad S. Gregory, *The Unintended Reformation: How a Religious Revolution Secularized Society* (Cambridge, Mass.: Harvard University Press, 2012).

of our respective ecclesiological traditions and of the nature and calling of the one Church of Jesus Christ? Are there ways in which the understanding of the Church could lead to ways of mutual recognition, of the acknowledgment that the Roman Catholic Church and the Protestant Churches both belong to one Church of Jesus Christ, and perhaps, in their different theological traditions and forms of church order, even point to a complementarity and an ongoing interdependence such that one ecclesial tradition cannot be understood without the other? After all, the Roman Catholic Church as we know it now owes much of its self-understanding to the Council of Trent, which started as an attempt at finding a new form of unity and ended in emphasizing differences.

In this situation it is a promising prospect to look again at the central tenets and problems of the ecclesiology of the Second Vatican Council through the lenses of one Swiss theologian who could be equally critical with regard to a Roman Catholic or a Lutheran understanding of the Church. Karl Barth was forced, because of ill health, to decline the invitation to take part as an observer in the last sessions of the Council in 1963; he later contacted Cardinal Bea, the first president of the Secretariat for Promoting Christian Unity, in order to inquire about possibilities of learning about the significance of the Council in Rome. Receiving then an invitation to visit Rome, Barth embarked on what he called his "peregrinatio ad limina Apostolorum" from September 22 to 29, 1966, accompanied by his wife, Nelly, and his Catholic friend and physician Dr. Alfred Briellmann.[3] On his return to Basel, Barth continued his engagement with the topics of the conversations in Rome with a theological colloquium in the winter semester 1966/67. For the last session of the colloquium, focused on the *Dogmatic Constitution on Divine Revelation*, Barth engaged the then Tübingen professor Joseph Ratzinger as a conversation partner in an attempt to clarify open questions.[4]

For the discussions in Rome, which were conducted in French, Barth had prepared sets of questions on the different conciliar documents. They had grown out of a careful study of the Latin text of the documents over the summer in 1966. In these questions Barth presents first "questions for clarification" and then raises "critical questions." Barth's brief questions are both

3. Barth himself gave an account of the journey in "Account of the Trip to Rome," printed as the introduction to Karl Barth, *Ad Limina Apostolorum. An Appraisal of Vatican II,* trans. Keith R. Crim (Eugene, Ore.: Wipf and Stock; reprint of John Knox Press, 1968), 9–18. (Hereafter, *ALA*.) On the circumstances of Barth's journey to Rome see Eberhard Busch, *Karl Barths Lebenslauf. Nach seinen Briefen und autobiographischen Texten* (Munich: Chr. Kaiser, 1975), 497–503, especially 500.

4. Cf. Busch, *Karl Barths Lebenslauf*, 502.

theologically weighty and witty, sometimes ironic in tone, but offered in an irenic spirit. They still provide a useful guide to the most central questions of theological conversations between the Roman Catholic Church and the Protestant churches. After decades of ecumenical dialogue, starting shortly after Vatican II, they have lost nothing of their perceptive poignancy.

In order to offer some clarification on what Barth's questions concerning the Dogmatic Constitution on the Church, *Lumen Gentium,* refer to, I shall first offer a brief overview of the main theses of the Council document and its systematic structure. This is, of course, not a neutral reading of the ecclesiology of Vatican II but a reading, undertaken from a Lutheran perspective, that tries to follow the way in which the constitution presents the reality of the Church. I shall concentrate first on chapters 1 to 3 of the Council document, leaving aside Barth's mariological question, because that would require a special treatment. After that we can turn to Barth's questions and then try to contextualize them in his own ecclesiology as it developed from the early twenties of the last century. This should provide the groundwork for a brief assessment of the theological point and the ecumenical possibilities of Barth's ecclesiological reflections in the context of his journey to the threshold of the apostles.

Lumen Gentium: The Foundation, the Shape, and the Mission of the Church

The title of the dogmatic constitution refers to what the first sentence of the document tersely states in the assertion: "Christ is the Light of the nations."[5] Both, the Christological focus and the universal outlook, permeate the whole document. The light that is Christ shall become visible on the face of the Church in order to proclaim Christ as the light of the nations. How are the focus on the particularity of Christ and the universality of the vision that Christ opens up related in the being, shape, and mission of the Church? In chapter I of *Lumen Gentium* (*LG*) with the heading "The Mystery of the Church," the Church is described as being "in Christ like a sacrament or as a sign and instrument both of a very closely knit union with God and of the unity of the whole human race" (§1). The unity of the whole human race and the closely knit union with God are related in such a way that the union with God is the presupposition of envisioning the unity of humankind. What follows is a Trinitarian account of the foundation of the Church. It has its

5. *Lumen Gentium* (*LG*) §1. Hereafter, citations to *LG* will be given parenthetically in the text.

origin in the work of the Father, who created the world "to raise men to a participation of the divine life." (§2). The destiny of the world as created by God "by a free and hidden plan of His own wisdom and goodness" (§2) consists in raising humans to participation in the divine life. Creation is from the beginning destined to find its fulfilment in communion with God. After the Fall, God "did not leave men to themselves, but ceaselessly offered helps to salvation" (§2), in order to achieve the preordained destiny of humans to be conformed to Christ. The "foreshadowing of the Church" takes place in Israel and the Old Covenant and is aimed at glorious completion of the communion of God and creation at the end of time, when "all the just . . . will be gathered together with the Father in the universal Church" (§2).

This gathering together is accomplished through the sending of the Son, who "inaugurated the Kingdom of heaven on earth and revealed to us the mystery of that Kingdom" (§3). "It was in Him, before the foundation of the world, that the Father chose us and predestined us to become adopted sons" (§3). The Church can therefore be defined as the "Kingdom of Christ now present in mystery" (§3), guided in the way of all truth by the Spirit, thereby "unified in communion" (§4) as well as equipped and directed "with hierarchical and charismatic gifts" (§4). The mystery of its foundation is made manifest by Christ's preaching of the gospel in word and deed, and by his cross and resurrection. The different biblical images which are used to characterise this community (§6), the flock of sheep, the vineyard, the household of God, and the New Jerusalem, are drawn together in the image of the body of Christ: "In that Body the life of Christ is poured into the believers who, through the sacraments, are united in a hidden and real way to Christ who suffered and was glorified" (§7). In this body the many "form one body" (§7) by being "formed in the likeness of Christ" in Baptism and by being "taken into communion with Him and with one another" (§7). in the Eucharist. In the Church that is constituted in Baptism and in the Eucharist, Christ continually distributes "gifts of ministries in which, by His own power, we serve each other unto salvation so that carrying out the truth in love, we might through all things grow unto Him who is our Head" (§7). Described in this way, the Church has Christ as the Head of the body, the principle of unity. However, this unity is *both* relational, since the Church is a body of many members, brought into union by the Holy Spirit, *and* dynamic, in that in its pilgrimage on earth, "as pilgrims in a strange land, tracing in trial and in oppression the paths He trod" (§7), it is on the way toward its perfected communion with Christ, its Head. Difference, understood as personal encounter and union with Christ in a nuptial communion of persons, is expressed in the last of the images, the image of the Church as the bride of Christ. The Church is "subject to its Head" and yet in union with Christ is destined "to expand and reach all the fullness of God." Whereas the image of the body and its members emphasizes the relational unity of the members of the Church with Christ and so with one another, the image of the Church as the bride emphasizes that in this community, there remains a distinction between Christ and the Church within this communion, which is the presupposition for stating: "He fills the Church, which is His body and His fullness, with His divine gifts so that it may expand and reach all the fullness of God" (§7).

While the foundation of the Church is consistently expressed in *Trinitarian* terms, mediating the oneness in Christ and the plurality of the members, brought together by the one Spirit, the structure of the Church on earth is expressed in more specifically *Christological* terms "as an entity with visible delineation (*ut compaginem visibilem*) through which He communicated truth and grace to all" (§8). Where the visible reality of the Church is concerned, we find a complementarity of talking about the Church in successive sentences, on the one hand, as a community, "the community of faith, hope and charity" (§8), and, on the other hand, as "a society structured with hierarchical organs" (§8). The two "sides" of the Church, a society structured with hierarchical organs and the "Mystical Body of Christ" (§8), however, "are not to be considered two realities, nor are the visible assembly and the spiritual community, nor the earthly Church and the Church enriched with heavenly things." Following the pattern of the unity of the person of Christ in two natures, these two sides "form one complex reality which coalesces from a divine and a human element" (§8).

The historical quasi-incarnational reality of the Church "subsists in the Catholic Church, which is governed by the successor of Peter and by the Bishops in communion with him although many elements of sanctification and of truth are found outside of its visible structure" (§8). Here we have the famous "*subsistit in*," which has been at the heart of much controversy. It seems to be most appropriate to interpret this formula, not in the sense of an antecedent metaphysics, but as a summary of the relationship that exists between the Church that is confessed in the Creed and the concrete reality of the Catholic Church. The main emphasis consists in rejecting any kind of ecclesiological docetism and in underlining the incarnational reality of the Church. Therefore it is emphasized that the Catholic Church is governed by the successor of Peter and the communion of Bishops and not by the *Romanus Pontifex*, as the first draft of the constitution formulated it. The Roman Church is part of the Catholic Church.

Furthermore, the phrase *subsistit in* was consciously chosen to avoid an exclusive identity statement asserting that the Church of Christ *is* the Catholic Church. The *subsistit in* was applied (instead of the simple *est* of a straightward identity statement or the *adest* of a statement of inclusion, restricted to the Roman Catholic Church) in order to acknowledge what the constitution itself says, that "many elements of sanctification and truth are found outside of its visible structure" (§8). In this way the constitution states that these elements, the word of revelation, the sacraments, even the priesthood, must be seen as "gifts belonging to the Church of Christ"; they exist in genuine participation in the Church instituted by Christ and therefore "are forces impelling toward catholic unity" (§8). In contrast to an exclusive *est* (or a slightly weaker *adest* which was also under consideration), the phrase *subsistit in* opens up the possibility of including the "elements" outside the Catholic Church as belonging to the Church of Christ and thus seeing them as forces "impelling toward catholic unity."[6] In this sense it is also stressed that the phrase does not talk about the Roman Catholic Church but about the "the Catholic Church, which is governed by the successor of Peter and by the Bishops in communion with him" (§8).

LG develops the view of the shape, the social body of the Church, in chapter 2, "On the People of God," by taking up the image of the wandering people of God from the Letter to the Hebrews (Heb 3:7–4:11). This is the social shape, the form of sociality, which is grounded in God's will not to sanctify and save people individually (*singulatim*) but to constitute them in one people, called to recognize God in truth and to serve him in holiness.[7] The

6. *LG* §8. In his commentary on the dogmatic constitution on the church in the official German documentation of the Council, Cardinal Aloys Grillmeier has emphasized that the careful Christological phrases of *LG* consciously avoid interpreting the Church as the "extension of the Incarnation" in the sense of Johann Adam Möhler's idea of a "continuing Incarnation" in the Church. In his famous *Symbolik* Möhler writes: "So ist denn die sichtbare Kirche . . . der unter den Menschen in menschlicher Form fortwährend erscheinende, stets sich erneuernde, ewig sich verjüngende Sohn Gottes, die andauernde Fleischwerdung desselben, so wie den auch die Gläubigen in der heiligen Schrift der Leib Christi genannt werden." (*Symbolik* §36, 6th ed. 1895, 332f.) Grillmeier points out that the references to the encyclicals *Sapientiae christianae* and *Satis cogitum* by Leo XIII, as well as to the encyclical *Mystici corporis* by Pius XII. underline the point that the Son of God who assumed in Incarnation one individual body also assumes only one mystical body. The idea of an extension of the Incarnation is in Grillmayer's view explicitly refuted in *Mystici Corporis* (DH 3806). Cf. *Das Zweite Vatikanische Konzil. Konstitutionen, Dekrete und Erklärungen*, new edition, ed. Peter Hünermann (Darmstadt: Wissenschaftliche Buchgesellschaft, 2014), 171–75.

7. Cf. *LG* §9.

people of God, which is actualized in the Church in virtue of its constitution in the work of the triune God, is the social shape which the Church must take if it is the "Kingdom of Christ now present in mystery" (§3). Whatever has to be said about the structures of the Church, must refer back to the foundation of the Church and must point forward to the consummation of the Church in the Kingdom of God. *LG* expresses that by relating the dimensions of the life of the Church to the royal (§9), the priestly (§§10, 11), and the prophetic offices of Christ (§12). Interpreting the work of Christ systematically under these three headings was first introduced by Eusebius and it was in its systematic form made popular by John Calvin. His ordering of the threefold ministry of Christ has found an almost universal, indeed Catholic, reception in the Church.[8] What *LG* emphasizes is that these offices which Christ exercises through the witness of the Church as "the Kingdom of Christ now present in mystery," must be shared in an ordered way by all members of the Church. We are all members of Christ's Kingdom, dignified as members of that society which has Christ as its head. The Council emphasizes here again the universal mission of the church in its participation in Christ's royal office that makes the Church "a lasting and sure seed of unity, hope and salvation for the whole human race" (§9). The participation in the royal office of Christ makes the Church "a communion of life, charity and truth" and as such it is Christ's "instrument for the redemption of all" (§9). This connection between the character of the people of God as *communion* and its instrumentality for the redemption that Christ brings, seems to suggest that the very character of the communion of life, charity, and truth plays a role in its mission as an instrument of Christ's mission to redeem humankind. Redemption has the concrete form of inclusion into this communion. Similarly, it is emphasized that because of the priesthood of Christ, all who are baptised and share in the priesthood of Christ "by regeneration and the anointing of the Holy Spirit" (§10) are thereby "consecrated as a spiritual house and a holy priesthood" (§10).

This section of the constitution emphasizes that although there is a difference between the common priesthood of believers (*sacerdotium commune fidelium*) and the "ministerial or hierarchical Priesthood" (§10), which has to be seen as a difference "in essence and not only in degree" (§10), they are nevertheless constitutively interrelated. It is to be emphasized that their difference and interrelation are described not simply by relating them externally to one another but in terms of their participation, each in its peculiar

8. Cf. Eusebius, *Historia ecclesiastica 1.3.8*, and John Calvin, *Institutes of the Christian Religion* 2.15.

mode, in the priesthood of Christ (*unum enim et alterum suo peculiari modo de uno Christo sacerdotio participant* [§10]). In virtue of their shared participation in Christ's priesthood, the common ground on which they rest, one does not have to be seen as lesser or higher than the other. Their difference and interrelation depends on the *mode* of their participation in Christ's priestly office, "each in that way which is proper to himself" (§11). Whereas the ministerial priest "acting in the person of Christ ... makes present the Eucharistic sacrifice, and offers to God in the name of all people," the faithful "join in the offering of the Eucharist" in virtue of their royal priesthood. The Council goes on to stress that because of their common participation in the priesthood of Christ one cannot be without the other. Although in different ways, both are necessary for the celebration of the sacraments, because only jointly they are the "priestly community (*communitas sacerdotalis*)" (§11).

All believers also participate in Christ's prophetic office by sharing "the whole people's supernatural discernment in matters of faith," "from the Bishops down to the last of the lay faithful" (§12). The Church "spreads abroad a living witness" (§12) to Christ in his prophetic office which comprises all the dimensions of the life of the Church. It is here that the Council places the teaching of the indefectibility of the Church so that the universal community of believers (*universitas fidelium*) in virtue of the *sensus fidei* (in the official English translation: "discernment in matters of faith") cannot err in matters of belief (*in credendo falli nequit*)."[9] This *sensus fidei*, however is not simply the agreement, the consensus of the faithful, but it is "aroused and sustained by the Spirit of truth" and is in this way the ground of consensus in the Church.

In the following paragraphs the Council goes on to relate the Church that is in this way defined by its participation in the threefold office of Christ to humanity in its entirety. The true catholicity, the calling of all people into the Church ("All men are called to belong to the new people of God" [*LG* §12]), is achieved through the work of the Holy Spirit, who "brings together the whole Church and each and every one of those who believe" (§13) by relating them in their particularity and diversity to Christ as the Head of the Church so that "within the Church particular Churches hold a rightful place" (§13).

The special task of the Holy Spirit in relating particularity and univer-

9. *LG* §12. It is important to keep in mind that this is also according to the Reformers a fundamental characteristic of faith as the certainty constituted by the Holy Spirit: "Quia fidei non est falli," Martin Luther asserts in his dispute with Erasmus of Rotterdam in *On the Bondage of the Will*, translated in the Philadelphia edition: "because it is in the nature of faith not to be deceived" (LW 33, 88; WA 18, 652).

sality is the basis for the following picture of concentric circles in which the Catholic Church is seen as related to the other Churches and religions. The first circle are the "Catholic faithful" (§14). "They are fully incorporated in the society of the Church who possessing the Spirit of Christ accept her entire system and all the means of salvation given to her, and are united with her as part of her visible bodily structure and through her with Christ, who rules her through the Supreme pontiff and the bishops" (§14). The second circle comprises those "who being baptized are honored with the name of Christian, though they do not profess the faith in its entirety or do not preserve unity of communion with the successor of Peter" (§15). The marks of those included in this circle are that they who "honor Sacred Scripture, taking it as a norm of belief and a pattern of life," believe in God the Father Almighty and in Christ, the Son of God. Baptism is of special significance here: "They are consecrated by baptism, in which they are united with Christ." The shared union with Christ is further strengthened by the way in which these Christians "are joined with us in the Holy Spirit, for to them too He gives His gifts and graces whereby He is operative among them with His sanctifying power" (§15). The further concentric circles comprise the Jews, "the people to whom the testament and the promises were given and from whom Christ was born according to the flesh" (§16). God's faithfulness to Israel is expressed in allusion to Romans 11:1–2 in the statement: "On account of their fathers this people remains most dear to God, for God does not repent of the gifts He makes nor of the calls He issues" (§16). There is a further circle for the Muslims, "who, professing to hold the faith of Abraham, along with us adore the one and merciful God" (§16). A further circle includes those "who in images and shadows seek the unknown God" (§16) and then those "who, without blame on their part, have not yet arrived at an explicit knowledge of God and with His grace strive to live a good life" (§16). It is to be noted that with regard to those "who, being baptized, are honored with the name of Christian" (§15), the link that exists is to be recognized by the Church, so that we have here an ecclesiological justification for this recognition.

With regard to the wider circles of the Jewish people, the Muslims, and those of other faiths, the justification for their relationship to the Church becomes explicitly theological: "for it is He who gives all men life and breath and all things, and as Saviour wills all men to be saved" (§16). It is God's plan "to raise men to the participation of the divine life" (§2) and therefore "[h]e planned to assemble in the holy Church all those who would believe in

Christ" (§2). Within this plan the Church has a particular mission: "For the Church is compelled by the Holy Spirit to do her part that God's plan may be fully realized, whereby He has constituted Christ as the source of salvation for the whole world. By the proclamation of the Gospel she prepares her hearers to receive and profess the faith" (§17). In this divine "plan," covering the whole divine economy from the creation to the eschatological consummation, the Church has its particular function in being a witness to and instrument of God's universal will to be in communion with his reconciled creation. Within the dynamic of the divine economy the differences between the ways of being related to the Church and to the will of God are not permanent, but are to be transcended. The Trinitarian account of the function of the Church points already to its perfect realization in the *eschaton*. "In this way the Church both prays and labors in order that the entire world may become the People of God, the Body of the Lord and the Temple of the Holy Spirit, and that in Christ, the Head of all, all honor and glory may be rendered to the Creator and Father of the Universe" (§17).

The relationship between chapter 2, "On the People of God," and chapter 3, "On the Hierarchical Structure of the Church and in Particular in the Episcopate," and the relationship of both to the first chapter, on the mystery of the Church, have been the subject of lively discussions since the Council. Are these two perspectives on the Church, one focusing on the community of the wandering people of God, the other on the hierarchically structured society? Does one of these perspectives have a clear and substantive priority over the other? It seems to me, as a Lutheran reader of the constitution, that the foundation in the Trinitarian work of God the Father, the Son and the Spirit in chapter I determines the social shape of the church as the people of God. Within this framework, the different orders and different tasks within the one church are then specified. They all are related to one another in such a way that they are mutually related in the one people of God, the body of Christ and the temple of the Holy Spirit. The offices and orders of the church are there to support the people of God on its way through history. This seems to be indicated by the first sentence in the third chapter: "For the nurturing and constant growth of the People of God, Christ the Lord instituted in His Church a variety of ministries, which work for the good of the whole body" (§18). As such the different ministries work toward a "common goal," that all of the people of God "may arrive at salvation" (§18). The *institutio dominica* of the apostolic office is then described as a stepped process, beginning with calling of the Twelve, their appointment in order to be sent "to preach the Kingdom of God" (§19). The pre-Easter calling is then completed as the Council states with reference to John 21:14–17 by "a college or a stable group," with Peter as the one presiding. It is to be noted that the formation of the college of apostles with Peter placed in a special position presupposes the Easter revelation. The dominical institution is then confirmed at Pentecost with the promise of the outpouring of the Spirit. The gift of the Spirit enables witnessing to the gospel of Christ. "That divine mission, entrusted by Christ to the apostles, will last until the end of the world, since the Gospel they are to teach is for all time the source of all life for the Church" (§20).

It is for this purpose that the apostles appointed successors so that the proclamation of the gospel can continue throughout the generations. Somehow it seems to be assumed that with the appointment of successors by the apostles, the divine institution of the office of apostle and the formation of a college of apostles is also handed on in the succession of bishops, whose task is described on the basis of the threefold office of Christ as "teachers for doctrine, priests for sacred worship, and ministers for governing" (§20), again following the pattern of the threefold office of Christ. In this sense the teaching of the Council is summarized in the following way:

> Therefore, the Sacred Council teaches that bishops by divine institution have succeeded to the place of the apostles, as shepherds of the Church, and he who hears them hears Christ, and he who rejects them, rejects Christ and Him who sent Christ. (§20)

This strong statement, bearing the special emphasis "the Sacred Council teaches," is in the following paragraphs explicated in two ways. On the one hand, it is emphasized that Christ is present in the bishops and in this sense the instrumentality of the bishops for Christ's action is underlined:

> In the bishops, therefore, for whom priests are assistants, Our Lord Jesus Christ, the Supreme High Priest, is present in the midst of those who believe. For sitting at the right hand of God the Father, He is not absent from the gathering of His high priests, but above all through their excellent service He is preaching the word of God to all nations, and constantly administering the sacraments of faith to those who believe, by their paternal functioning. He incorporates new members in His Body by a heavenly regeneration, and finally by their wisdom and prudence He directs and guides the People of the New Testament in their pilgrimage toward eternal happiness. (§21)

Whereas here Christ is the subject of the actions described, although he acts through the instrumentality of the bishops, there are also statements that refer to the actions of the bishops once they have received the "special outpouring of the Holy Spirit" that is handed on in episcopal consecration. In those acts, "the grace of the Holy Spirit is conferred and the sacred character so impressed that bishops in an eminent and visible way sustain the roles of Christ Himself as Teacher, Shepherd and High Priest, and that they act in His person" (§21). The paragraphs that follow §21 explain the collegiality of the bishops and their being assembled under one head, the Roman Pontiff, in terms of the horizontal and vertical relations that converge in the office of the bishop. "This college, insofar as it is composed of many, expresses the variety and universality of God's people, but insofar as it is assembled under one head, it expresses the unity of the flock of Christ" (§22).

These are not simply provisions for the organization of the church, combining a hierarchical element of subordination with a collegial element of cooperation. Ecclesiologically, this combination of a horizontal collegiate structure and the assembly of the college of bishops under the pope makes it clear that there is no simple direct vertical and unitary correlation between Christ, the vicar of Christ, and an individual bishop, but this relationship is mediated through the horizontal element of collegiality, giving the particular local churches a significant status within the one church. The ecclesiological effect is that through the relationships with other churches that are sustained by the mutual relationships of the bishops, the diversity of the many churches becomes an important element in the one church. In terms of the constitution of the church, the one foundation in the *regnum Christi iam praesens in mysterio* is in this way relationally diversified in the action of the Holy Spirit so that "[t]his variety of local churches with one common aspiration is splendid evidence of the catholicity of the undivided Church" (§23). The representation of Christ is bound to this relational structure.

The specific tasks of the bishops are summarized according to the threefold office of Christ as the preaching of the gospel (§25), the administration of the sacraments, especially the Eucharist, and the task of government. The priests participate in these tasks as "partakers of the function of Christ the sole Mediator, on their level of ministry" (§28), and the deacons assist them in these tasks.

In the exposition of the threefold ministry of the bishops, the prophetic office is described as the proclamation of the gospel; they exercise this office as "teachers endowed with the authority of Christ, who preach to the people committed to them the faith they must believe and put into practice." More specifically, this task is described as a bringing forth "from the treasury of Revelation new things and old, making it bear fruit and vigilantly warding off any errors that threaten their flock.... In matters of faith and morals, "the bishops speak in the name of Christ and the faithful are to accept their teaching and adhere to it with a religious assent" (§25).

For a theologian from the tradition of the Reformation, here the problem arises of how the faithful are enabled to accept the teaching of their bishops. At this point of the exposition in *LG*, it seems to be presupposed that because the bishops speak "in the name of Christ," the acceptance of their teaching is a matter of "religious submission of mind and will." But how is this submission of mind and will made possible? Does it not have to be understood as being enabled by God the Holy Spirit who awakens in believers the recognition of the truth that the gospel of Christ, communicated by the preaching of the Church, is indeed the truth about God's relationship to his creation?

The bishops exercise the priestly office, as *LG* states, "especially in the Eucharist, which he offers or causes to be offered and by which the Church continually lives and grows" (§26). When *LG* turns here to small churches, especially in the Diaspora, it stresses that in these communities "Christ is present, and in virtue of His presence there is brought together one, holy, catholic and apostolic Church." The connection between the tasks of the bishop seems to be indicated in the next sentence: "Every legitimate celebration of the Eucharist is regulated by the bishop." The celebration of the Eucharist must wherever it occurs be conducted under the oversight of a bishop. Again, the question arises, how the presence of Christ and the oversight of the bishop are precisely related. The office of king which the bishops exercise with a power (*potestas*) that is "proper, ordinary and immediate, although its exercise is ultimately regulated by the supreme authority of the Church" (§27) is described almost entirely in pastoral terms. The bishop is called to follow "the example of the Good Shepherd" and so his flock, "the faithful must cling to their bishop, as the Church does to Christ, and Jesus Christ to the Father, so that all may be of one mind through unity and abound to the glory of God" (§27).

This brief overview of the first three chapters of *LG* must suffice here to present the text which provides the context for the questions Karl Barth raises with regard to matters of ecclesiology. Even this short exposition documents the careful way, based on the witness of Scripture and supported by a wealth of references to the tradition, in which *Lumen Gentium* attempts to relate the foundation of the Church in the being and will of the Triune God, the special character of its sociality, and the tasks entrusted to specific groups in the church as the wandering people of God. Everything hangs on the relationship between Christ—prophet, priest, and king, who in the power of the Holy Spirit calls the Church into being, thereby fulfilling the will of the Father from the beginning of creation—and the specific character, attributes, and mission entrusted to the Church on earth as the "Kingdom of Christ already present in mystery."

Karl Barth's Questions

In the questions he submitted for discussion, Barth distinguished between "questions for clarification" and "critical questions." If we omit the fifth (the mariological) question in each group, there remain four questions in each group. The first question for clarification asks: "In the relationship of chapters I and II is the 'Body of Christ' subordinated to the 'People of God,' or vice versa?"[10] What is the clarification this question demands? If we look back on our presentation of *LG* we would have to say that the emphasis in chapter 1, with its exposition of the understanding of the Body of Christ, is on the constitution of the Church, whereas in chapter 2 the understanding of the people of God as the social shape of the Church and the dynamics of the history of the Church on its way toward the Kingdom are emphasized. Furthermore, one would have to say that in the imagery of the body of Christ, the "closely knit union with God," the "vertical" dimension of the Church, is underlined. In the imagery of the people of God, leading to the concentric circles comprising the whole of humanity, the "unity of the whole human race" (§1), the "horizontal" dimension of the Church in the process of history, carries the main accent. It seems that Barth seeks clarification about the relationship between the constitution and the social shape of the Church.

The second question for clarification focuses on the relationship between the "separated brethren" and the "entirety" of the Roman Catholic Church in sections 14 and 15: According to *LG* §§14–15, what are the "separated brethren"? What does the "entirety" of the faith which is reserved to the Roman Catholic Church consist in? It is interesting that the term *fratres sejuncti* or *fratres separate,* for which Barth seems to have had a special affection, for he uses it also as a self-description, is not mentioned in *LG* §§14–15 but does appear in *Unitatis Redintegratio* 3.4. Barth's question presupposes the view of the constitution that there is only one Church, and this is the form, or the sign and instrument, by means of which the unity of

10. Barth, *ALA*, 23.

humankind is actualized. However, Barth has spotted that there are different ways in which human persons are related to this one Church. According to *LG* §§14 and 15, those who belong to the Roman Catholic Church are fully incorporated (*incorporantur* [§14]) into the society of the Church. Christians who do not belong to Roman Catholic Church are conjoint to the church (*conjuncti* [§15]), whereas those who are not Christians are somehow related to or ordered toward the Roman Catholic Church (*ordinantur* [§16]). Barth then asks in what does the "entirety" of the faith of the Catholic Church consist. The reason for this question is the statement that non-Roman Catholic Christians (like Barth himself), according to *LG* §15, "do not profess the Catholic faith in its entirety (integram autem fidem non profitentur)." In what, then, does the entirety consist? *LG*'s answer is this:

> They are fully incorporated in the society of the Church who, possessing the Spirit of Christ, accept her entire system and all the means of salvation given to her, and are united with her as part of her visible bodily structure and through her with Christ, who rules her through the Supreme Pontiff and the bishops. The bonds which bind men to the Church in a visible way are profession of faith, the sacraments, and ecclesiastical government and communion. (§14)

The profession of faith includes in the Catholic understanding accepting the "entire system" and "all the means of salvation," that is, the seven sacraments, as well as being united with the Church and with Christ through the hierarchical structure of the Church. Conversely, Christ rules the Church, *LG* §14 claims, "through the Supreme Pontiff and his bishops." If we consider for a moment that, according to the traditions of the Reformation, it is sufficient for the Church that the gospel is preached and the sacraments of baptism and Holy Communion are administered in a way appropriate to the gospel, because these are the means for Christ's self-presentation, the point of Barth's question is whether faith in its "entirety" does not comprise too much: not only God's work in Christ but also the human institutions in which the Church witnesses to Christ.

The third question may sound quixotic but uncovers a very real problem: "Did Paul belong to the 'college' of the apostles, over which Peter presided (19–26)?" Barth asks for clarification with regard to the answer to the question: Who is an apostle? If the appointment of the twelve and their being formed in a college with Peter as its head is a pre-Easter event, then, clearly Paul is not an apostle. However, is that in keeping with the New Testament understanding of an apostle as a witness of the risen Lord? Is it right to say, as *LG* does, that the apostles chosen before Easter were "confirmed" in their mission at Pentecost, or is the sending of the Spirit an event that does not confirm an already-given reality but rather constitutes that reality? This seemingly innocent and somewhat whimsical question raises the issue of the relationship between continuity and actuality in the constitution of the Church. Has the Church once been constituted in history in the gathering and commissioning of the Twelve and is it continued through history by the acts of transmitting the historical constitution, or is the church constituted again and again by Christ in the Spirit through God's self-revelation in Christ, a disclosure experience like the one that Paul had on the road to Damascus? This question overlaps with the question, often raised by Eastern Orthodoxy with regard to "Western" ecclesiology, whether the role of Christ and the role of the Spirit are sufficiently and clearly related. Once this question is raised it becomes clear that what is at stake is the correct relationship between the doctrine of the Trinity and the doctrine of the Church.

The fourth question points to an eternal tension in the picture that is presented in *LG* of the hierarchical structure of the Church: "Are only the pope, bishops, priests, and deacons 'partakers of the function of Christ' (28)? If so, then the laity (30–42) are not part of the hierarachy, are they? But why not, since they share in all three offices of Christ, and in the apostolate of the church?"

Here Barth lays his finger on the question of the role of the sacrament of Orders, as it is presented in *LG* §28, as making those who are consecrated "partakers of the function of Christ." If all believers, including the laity, share in the threefold office of Christ, how can the conferral of the function of Christ be restricted to those who receive the sacrament of orders? This, again, raises the question: Who is the agent in granting participation in the three offices of Christ? If it is Christ who lets those who believe in him participate in his threefold office, how can the Church in the form of the ecclesial hierarchy consecrate only some to be "partakers in the function of Christ"?

If one looks closely at all four requests for clarification they have a common focus. How can the agency of Christ and the agency of the Church be properly distinguished and related? It is exactly this issue to which Barth turns in his "critical questions."

The first of these critical questions serves as a framework for all the further ones:

Wherein lies the difference between Christ as Lord, King and Judge and his church? Are only the laity his witnesses in the world? Are the hierarchy more than that? Is not the whole church a witnessing people? Is it revelation and the continuation of the incarnation.[11]

The reference to the "distance" between Christ and His Church seems almost like a conscious reminder of the mantra of Barth's early dialectical theology, the Kierkegaardian expression of the "infinitive qualitative difference of time and eternity."[12] What is at stake here is the proper distinction and the appropriate relationship between God and humanity in the constitution and in the ongoing life of the Church. This is the distinctive emphasis in the understanding of the Church as the "creature of the Word" or the "creature of the Gospel." When one follows Barth and his emphasis on the character of the whole Church as a "witnessing people," it is clear that the constitution of the Church is a divine act through Christ in the Spirit; as such it is a reality that can only be witnessed. The Church does not incorporate its own constitution. Its divine constitution can only be pointed to as the reality which incorporates the act of witness and so conditions the credibility of the visible Church as a "witnessing people." This is for Barth an essential character of the whole Church, with regard both to the hierarchy and to the laity. In effect, it relativizes any difference between hierarchy and laity. In contrast to this understanding of the creative constitution of the Church, Barth asks whether the Church is "revelation and a continuation of the incarnation."

If one looks closely, one finds in *LG* phrases emphasizing the divine constitution of the Church and expressions talking about the continuation of the revelation in the Church as the body of Christ. Is the Church in spite of all qualifications the continuation of the revelation in Christ and so the extension of the Incarnation?[13] In the last resort, this is both a Christological question about the distinction of the two natures and the unity of the person in Christ and a question about the way in which this Christological pattern is seen as constitutive for the being of the Church, as in the famous

11. *ALA*, 23. In the German original the term that is rendered as "difference" in the English translation is expressed as "Distanz": "Wo bleibt die Distanz zwischen Christus las dem Herrn, König und Richter und seiner Kirche?" (*ALA*, 27)

12. Cf. the famous expression in Karl Barth, *Der Römerbrief*, 2nd edition 1922 (11th reprint Zürich: Theologischer Verlag Zürich, 1976), XIII: "Wenn ich ein 'System' habe, so besteht es darin, daß ich das, was Kierkegaard den 'unendlichen qualitativen Unterschied' von Zeit und Ewigkeit genannt hat, in seiner negative und positive Bedeutung möglichst beharrlich im Auge behalte. 'Gott ist im Himmel und du auf Erden.'" On the interpretation cf. Bruce L. McCormack, *Karl Barth's Critically Realistic Dialectical Theology* (Oxford: Clarendon Press, 1995), 224–26.

13. Barth refers here to *LG* §52, the introduction to the section on Mariology where the Council states: "Quod salutis divinum mysterium nobis revelatur et continuatur in Ecclesia, quam Dominus ut corpus suum constituit, et in qua fideles Christo Capiti adhaerentes atque cum omnibus sanctis Eius communicantes." The expression "salutis divinum mysterium" refers here to the Christological statement of the Nicene Creed, where the subject of the statement is Christ.

statement in *LG* §8 where the Church is described as "one complex reality which coalesces from a divine and a human element."

Barth's second critical question focuses on what appears to be a privileging of the Eucharist in the theological description of the Church, for example, in *LG* §11 where the Eucharist is described as the "fount and apex of the whole Christian life": "Why is it among the four marks of the church in Acts 2:42 (devotion to the apostles' teaching, fellowship, breaking of the bread, and prayers) it is the third (Eucharist) that is designated as constitutive for the life of Church?" In a way that reads like an echo of the popular prejudices that the churches of the Reformation are Churches of the Word whereas the Roman Catholic Church is a Church of the Sacraments, a perception apparently supported by Pope John Paul II's pontifical encyclical *Ecclesia de eucharistia* (2003). Ecumenically, it seems that this emphasis on the Eucharist as the source from which the Church lives poses severe obstacles to fellowship at the Lord's Table. For Barth the question seems to be how the Eucharist is related to the apostles' teaching, to fellowship, and to prayers as is witnessed in Scripture. For *LG*, as *LG* §11 shows, this relationship is developed in the context of the seven sacraments. And again, one has to keep in mind that the statement in *LG* §11 is the exposition of the priestly office, which is followed by the exposition of the prophetic office in *LG* §12 and that of the royal office in *LG* §13, all of this following after the introduction of the common priesthood of believers (§10).[14]

The relationship to the other sacraments is also addressed in Barth's third critical question: "Does the church 'beget' the faithful? (28; 64) Does it do this through baptism?" Barth refers here to a passage in the section on the "Blessed Virgin and the Church." There the Council states:

> The Church indeed, contemplating her hidden sanctity, imitating her charity and faithfully fulfilling the Father's will, by receiving the word of God in faith becomes herself a mother. By her preaching she brings forth to a new and immortal life the sons who are born to her in baptism, conceived of the Holy Spirit and born of God. She herself is a virgin, who keeps the faith given to her by her Spouse whole and entire. Imitating the mother of her Lord, and by the power of the Holy Spirit, she keeps with virginal purity an entire faith, a firm hope and a sincere charity. (§64)

This passage echoes another passage Barth refers to on the role of priests in the chapter on the hierarchical structure of the church: "Let them, as father in Christ, take care of the faithful whom they have begotten by baptism and their teaching" (§28). The biblical foundation of this expression is probably

14. *LG* §10.

found in Galatians 4:26, where Paul talks about the heavenly Jerusalem as our mother. In the tradition of the Reformation both Luther and Calvin used the expression of the Church as the mother of the faithful.[15] However, it is always clear that this refers to the visible Church and that what is expressed in this way figuratively is the constitution of the believer through God's word communicated by the pastors. Particularly in Calvin's exposition, the stress on God as the agent and the instrumentality of the preaching of the gospel is strongly emphasized. It seems that Barth is again raising the question about who is the subject in constituting the Church, and, like Calvin, he seems to have in mind that the constitution of the Church and the constitution of faith are one and the same act.

The fourth critical question Barth raises points in a similar direction, the emphasis on the "difference between Christ as Lord, King, and Judge and his church." Therefore the last judgment with Christ as judge and the "coming down" of the new Jerusalem from God is underlined:

> Where in the allusions to the eschatological dimension of the church (e.g. 48–50; 65) do we find the return of Christ as the judge? Where do we find the "new Jerusalem," the holy city that comes down from God (Rev. 21:2), and does not ascend to him? Where indeed is the new creation (Teilhard de Chardin)?[16]

This question appears, if one scrutinizes the text of *LG*, slightly puzzling, because indeed there are not only allusions to "restoration" and "renovation" but also passages like *LG* §48, in which the judgment scene in Matthew 25:17–34 as well as 2 Corinthians 5:10 ("we shall all be made manifest before the judgment seat of Christ") are explicitly quoted. What Barth's question seems to aim at is a certain dominance of a realized eschatology which sees the eschatological perfection in terms of the elevation of the Church to heavenly glory. Is there enough emphasis on Christ returning as judge, the coming down of the New Jerusalem from God over against the perfecting of the Church? There is for Barth not only continuity between ecclesiology and eschatology but also a pronounced discontinuity, in which is included that the Church will also be made manifest before the judgment seat of Christ. Again, we find another modulation of the question about the "distance" between Christ and his Church.

Barth's brief critical questions do not in themselves completely disclose the theological standpoint from which these questions are asked. We

15. Cf. Martin Luther's hymn "Sie ist mir lieb, die werte Magd," with its allusion to Rev 12:1–17. For Calvin, see his *Institutes* IV, 1,4.

16 *ALA* 27.

have tried to develop their theological impact as much as possible from the phrases Barth uses and from the passages in *LG* to which he refers. However, the full weight of Barth's questions can become clear only if we look, albeit very briefly, at the background of the questions, which can be found in some aspects of Barth's own teaching about the Church.

The Background of Barth's Questions in Barth's Own Ecclesiology

In the early stages of the development of his thinking, the Church was not one of the central topics of Barth's theology. After the farewell to his theological teachers in autumn 1914, the new departure in Barth's theology was very much focused on his tasks as a pastor in a local church. The challenge of being a *verbum divini minister*, a servant of the word of God, was central to Barth's self-understanding. The orientation of theology toward the witness of Scripture—which, after a period of searching for new foundations, became the basis for the theology of Barth and his friend Eduard Thurneysen—did not lend itself to the practical engagement for church reform as it was put on the agenda by many theologians in Germany after the breakup of the old church structures after the First World War. If one reads Barth's correspondence during the years immediately after the end of the First World War, one gets the impression of his conscious withdrawal from dealing with the crisis of theology by engaging in church reform and the development of new church structures. The awareness that God and God's word are the crisis of all worldly structures, including those of the Church, is from that time onward a persistent feature of Barth's theology—and it is not a crisis that could be overcome by strategies of church reform.

In his 1923 lecture "The Church and the Revelation," Barth asks whether the Church can really be a community in truth, and whether it can really be the bearer of a prophetic word in the circumstances of the time. If we follow his argument, presented in the lecture with a host rhetorical flourishes, it boils down to a series of statements that Barth wrote down as a "table of contents" for the lecture.[17] To answer these questions negatively

17. Karl Barth, "Die Kirche und die Offenbarung (1923), in Karl Barth, *Gesamtausgabe*, vol. III.1, *Vorträge und kleinere Arbeiten 1922–1925*, ed. Holger Finze (Zürich: Theologischer Verlag Zürich 1990), 307–48. The "table of contents" (loc. cit. 313) comprises seven points. Barth asks whether the church understood as the product of human religious experience can be truly community, i.e., Community in truth (1). This means for him whether it can be the bearer of a prophetic word in time (2). Responding negatively to these questions means for Barth that a religious persons subject themselves "as such" under God's judgment (3). Responding negatively to these questions means shifting the focus on the

would mean for Barth that the church, just as every religious person, put itself under the judgment of God. For those who stand under the judgment of God the only starting point is to consider the Church as a community that is constituted in baptism. The true Christian church is the community of those who have been pardoned in God's judgment. The foundation of this Church is God's word of revelation. This is the definite eclipse of all Christian subjectivism and, at the same time, the presupposition of all real Christian prophecy. The acknowledgment of the judgment, of baptism, and of the divine word of revelation is faith. Faith however is the work of the Holy Spirit. We have here the dialectical movement of the negation of the possibility of the Church based on human religious experience or on human action—the judgment—as the condition for recognizing the positive actuality of the Church as it is given in baptism and addresses us in God's word of revelation. The dialectic, which also characterizes Barth's lecture "The Word of God as the Task of Theology," is here applied to the existence of the Church.

With the *Göttingen Dogmatics* (the first two parts of which Barth presented to his students at Göttingen in 1924/25, while the final part was delivered after he had moved to Münster in 1925), we have a radical transition in both style and content. When Barth had moved to the extraordinary professorship in Reformed Theology at Göttingen in 1921 he had had to brush up quickly on the history of Christian doctrine, especially on Reformed confessions of faith and the confessional Reformed theology of the seventeenth century; he also had to relate the theological dialectic he had developed in sermons, in the theological interpretation of Scripture in *Romans*, and in his highly rhetorical lectures, to the formal teaching of dogmatics. The outcome of his first systematic exposition of dogmatics is nothing less than staggering: learned, precisely structured, and conceptually both concise and adventurous.

The paragraph on the Church (34) is the final paragraph of the section on the doctrine of reconciliation, which starts with God's faithfulness (27), discusses the person (28) and work (29) of Christ, and then goes on to offer an exposition of the so-called means of salvation. Between baptism, voca-

consideration of the Church as it is constituted by baptism (4). This true Christian church is "the community of those who have been pardoned in [God's] judgment." Its ground is not human religious experience but "the divine word of revelation addressed to humans" (5). "6. This ground of the true Christian church is as a matter of principle the *end* of all Christian subjectivism and the *presupposition* of a truly Christian prophecy. However, knowledge of judgment, of baptism and of the divine word of revelation is faith. And faith is the work of the Holy Spirit."

tion (30), and Holy Communion (33) Barth discusses justification (31) and sanctification (32). The paragraph on the church is preceded by a paragraph in which Barth discusses the preservation and perseverance of faith, as they are grounded in God's perseverance, and Holy Communion (33).

The main thesis of paragraph 34, on the Church, reads:

> God has chosen all his children to *one grace* and therefore he has not selected them individually, but from eternity as the *one body* of which Christ is the head. The Lord knows who are his [2 Tim 2:19]. They believe in the invisible community of all those who are called with one another, in the one only, holy, catholic, imperishable church, the mother of them all, but [they] also [believe] that precisely this Church is visible amidst the ambiguity of history in the form of the particular Christian churches. They are true, pure Christian Church to the extent that they, under the rule of Christ by means of the service of those specially called for that task and by means of the power associated with that service, live for the proclamation of the word of God through pure preaching, but also through the right sacrament and true penitential discipline, and in this way glorify God and not themselves and are witnesses of the Kingdom of his grace.[18]

This carefully crafted paragraph revolves around the dialectical relationship between the invisible and the visible Church. The invisible Church is the Church of a gracious God. "It is constituted by eternal election, becomes actual through vocation and lives and moves in faith and obedience of those who, in spite of all their misery, are filled and driven by the Holy Spirit."[19] Barth's description of the invisible Church is firmly theocentric. If God can be known only by God, so that God can be known only in God's free and sovereign self-revelation, one has to say of the Church that "the eternal ground of her reality is also the ground of the knowledge of her."[20] Because it is constituted by God, the Church can be known only by God and so can be known only in that knowledge that is created by God in God's self-revelation—faith. The fact that the invisible Church can exclusively be believed and not be known in any other way is for Barth an indication that it is an "unambiguously divine reality."[21]

With his theocentric approach, focusing everything on the constitution of the Church by God, it is no surprise that Barth explains the essential attributes of the Church in a consistently theological fashion. The Church is one

18. Karl Barth, "*Unterricht in der christlichen Religion*," in Karl Barth, *Gesamtausgabe*, vol. II, *Die Lehre von der Versöhnung/Die Lehre von der Erlösung 1925/1926*, ed. Hinrich Stoevesandt (Zürich: Theologischer Verlag Zürich, 2003), 349–50.

19. Barth, "*Unterricht in der christlichen Religion*," 352.

20. Barth, "*Unterricht in der christlichen Religion*," 354.

21. Barth, "*Unterricht in der christlichen Religion*," 354.

because God is one in a sense that transcends any kind of created unity. The Church is holy because it consists of those who are justified and sanctified by Christ and she is infallible because, even when she is in error, she cannot lose her ground in God and God's truth. For Barth the limit of criticizing the Church is precisely at that point where one starts criticizing Christ as the ground of the Church. That the Church is catholic implies for Barth that those who separate from the church can do so only if they believe that the catholicity of the Church resides, because of its being rooted in the truth of God, in those who part company with the majority. Barth adds here that, in virtue of its ground in God and its being rooted in the royal office of Christ, the Church has perpetual existence. Like Calvin before him, Barth adopts the formula of the church as the "mater fidelium" in order to emphasize, against all Protestant tendencies of religious individualism, that one cannot be a Christian outside the Church. The argument for this is one that refers back to election. Election occurs in Christ, and Christ is the reconciler not of individuals but of his body. It is interesting that Barth here deviates from the traditional wording of believing the one, holy catholic and apostolic Church. The theme of apostolicity is taken up when he characterizes the ministry as the ministry of the divine word.

For Barth, the visible Church is also an article of faith. The church is believed both as invisible and visible Church. "Visible" and "invisible" are not two species of the same genus, he emphasizes, but one and the same subject in two respects. In order to explain the dialectic, Barth points to a parallel in his doctrine of the Word of God. Just as God's revelation is the Word becoming flesh in Christ, this Word becoming Scripture and Scripture becoming a human word in proclamation, so the invisible Church is where the visible Church is. However, the visible church can never by itself be an object of faith; the visible Church belongs to faith as pointing to its ground in God. By itself, it is a creature in which one cannot believe, because one can only believe in the creator. Everything else is idolatry. Therefore Barth can say: "One believes in God when one believes in the visibility of the Church that falls from above into history—because that is He, that is His work of reconciliation—just as an individual human person believes in God by believing in the grace falling from above into his boundless unholiness."[22] Believing in the Church means to believe in God as God creates, preserves, and perfects the Church. For Barth it is therefore clear that the visible church wit-

22. Barth, "*Unterricht in der christlichen Religion,*" 364.

nesses to the invisible church and in doing so witnesses to God as the only object of faith: "The glory of the church is to give all glory to God."[23]

On this foundation, the marks of the Church which Barth develops in the Reformed tradition are the purity of its proclamation, interpreted as proclamation according to Scripture, and as the right administration of the sacraments, also according to Scripture, and as the penitential discipline in the Church; all have the character of pointing to the church's foundation in God's eternal election, in the vocation of the believers, and in the way in which God, in the Holy Spirit, creates, preserves, and supports the faith of the believers.

Barth's description of the shape of the Church, based on Christian worship in which the word is proclaimed, the sacraments are administered, and discipline is practiced as penitence, interprets the sociality of the church, that is, the structure of its ordered ministry, consistently as a different aspect of witnessing to its ground and foundation. The mission of the church is therefore one which comprises the whole people of God. Barth approvingly quotes the thesis of the Reformed scholastic theologian Francis Turretin: "*Discrimen inter clericos et laicos figmentum papale est.*"[24] Denying an essential difference between clerics and the laity is for Barth only one way of emphasizing that the ministry of the divine word is in principle conferred on the whole church as the people of God. Wherever it is adequately practiced that ministry has the character of service. In serving the divine Word the church as the people of God does, in principle, the same that Christ does in heaven.[25]

When one tries to survey the development of Barth's ecclesiology as it developed from the mid-nineteen twenties to its final form in his *Church Dogmatics*, one is struck by the fact that the main tenets of Barth's understanding of the church stay firmly in place. The church is consistently interpreted from its ground and foundation in Christ. God's action in Christ the human witness of the church within itself, but there is no way in which the human action of the Church could in any way include God's action within itself. God's action envelops human action in the church according to the pattern of enhypostatic Christology and so that the action of the Church remain essentially Christ's actions to which the church can only witness. However, by witnessing to God's electing, reconciling, and saving act in Christ, which

23. Barth, "*Unterricht in der christlichen Religion*," 364.

24. Barth, "*Unterricht in der christlichen Religion*," 373.

25. Barth, "*Unterricht in der christlichen Religion*," 373: "Ihr *ministerium* (i.e. der Gemeinde), in dem sie auf Erden prinzipiell dasselbe tut, was Christus im Himmel tut, ist also '*ministerium verbi divini*'. Dieser Dienst ist prinzipiell der Kirche als solcher übertragen."

is never at its own disposal or under its own control, the church puts itself as a witness at the disposal of—and, in a liberating sense, under—Christ's control.

What does change over the years is Barth's view of Roman Catholicism. Beginning shortly after the *Göttingen Dogmatics* (1924/25) there begins a process in which Barth increasingly sees Roman Catholicism as being closer to the original intentions and character of the Protestant Reformation than is neo-Protestantism. In this sense, Roman Catholicism becomes a question for Protestant theology and Protestant churches. Barth writes: "Catholicism becomes this question to us because in its presuppositions for the Church, in spite of all contradictions, it is closer to the Reformers than is the Church of the Reformation insofar as it has actually and finally become the new Protestantism."[26] This is indeed a radical question, and a question well worth contemplating in the aftermath of the 500-year anniversary of the Reformation: Is Roman Catholicism (and Barth refers here to his contemporary Roman Catholicism) closer to the original insights of the Reformation than what he perceived as the dominant neo-Protestantism of his day? The original critical stance of the Reformation against late medieval teaching—that it had obscured the difference between God's action and human action by subjecting the word of God to human institutions and theological opinions—is here leveled by Barth against what he saw as the neo-Protestantism of his day: that it obscures the subjectivity of God by subjecting it to the confines of human subjectivity. In his criticism of that tendency Barth saw Roman Catholicism as an indispensable ally.

In the *Church Dogmatics*, Barth's ecclesiology is consistently developed on the basis of his Christology.[27] It can be presented in four steps. The first step places the constitution of the Church in the election of Jesus Christ and, in him, of the whole community of God. "The election of grace, as the election of Jesus Christ, is simultaneously the eternal election of the one community of God by the existence of which Jesus Christ is to be attested to the whole world and the whole world summoned to faith in Jesus Christ."[28] For

26. Karl Barth, "Der römische Katholizismus als Frage an die protestantische Kirche," in idem, *Die Theologie und die Kirche* (Munich: Kaiser, 1928), 329–63, 338. English trans.: "Roman Catholicism: A Question for the Protestant Church," *Theology and Church*, trans. Louise Pettitbone Smith (London: SCM, 1962), 297–333, 314.

27. Cf. for a comprehensive treatment of Barth's ecclesiology, cf. Ernst-Wilhelm Wendebourg, *Die Christusgemeinde und ihre Herr: Eine kritische Studie zur Ekklesiologie Karl Barths* (Berlin: Luthersches Verlagshaus. 1967), and Kimlyn J. Bender, *Karl Barth's Christological Ecclesiology* (Aldershot: Ashgate, 2005).

28. *CD* II/2, §34, 195.

Barth, as well as for *LG*, the Church is not an accident in the history of creation but was intended from eternity. In the Trinitarian account of *LG*, this is more closely associated with the being, will, and work of God the Father. However, the election also already occurs in Christ. "All the elect, before time began, the Father 'foreknew and pre-destined to become conformed to the image of His Son, that he should be the firstborn among many brethren.' He planned to assemble in the holy Church all those who would believe in Christ."[29] Like Barth, *LG* §2 also posits its theology of Israel in this context.

Barth presents the full exposition of his ecclesiology in the context of the systematic development of his Christology in *Church Dogmatics* volume IV/1–3. The intricate structure of these three part-volumes is one the most daring and impressively original achievements in modern theology. The complex chiastic structure combines the discussion of the two natures of Christ, of the two states of humiliation and exaltation, the person and the work of Christ with an exposition of the doctrine of sin, and of the salvation of the individual person (justification, sanctification, vocation). This is developed into a fully fledged ecclesiology and a tri-partite account of the doctrine of the Holy Spirit structured by the triad of Faith, Love, and Hope. With respect to the understanding of the church the systematic arrangement contains the thesis. We can speak about the church in a strict sense only as the church of Jesus Christ. If we want to say anything at all in ecclesiological matters we have to speak of the church as the creature and instrument of Christ. And so the different dimensions all present the church as the self-actualization of Christ as the Lord as Servant, as the Servant as Lord, and as The Witness, as the power of Christ becomes present, actual and effective in the church. It would be difficult to think of a more radically focused Christological ecclesiology. In a way, Karl Barth's first question he presented in Rome contains it all: "Wherein lies the difference between Christ as Lord, King and Judge and his church?" Only if this difference or distance is secured can every aspect of the church be understood as a mode of the unity of Christ's being and act, as God in Christ creates, reconciles, and perfects the world by gathering, building up, and sending the community of the church through the Holy Spirit. In this way God's gracious self-presentation in the particular form of the offices of Lord, King, and Judge can be understood as the way in which Barth fulfils the promise that *LG* expresses in its own language as the gathering, upbuilding, and sending "of a very closely knit

29. *LG* §2 with reference to Rom 8:29.

union with God and of the unity of the whole human race."[30] In a way, the first critical question contains the whole of Barth's constructive programme.

Here it must suffice simply to quote the three perspectives of God's self-revelation in Christ which structure the constitution, being, and mission of the church—its foundation, shape, and mission. There is, first of all, the gathering of the community through the Holy Spirit: "The Holy Spirit is the awakening power in which Jesus Christ has formed and continually renews His body, i.e. His own earthly-historical form of existence, the one holy catholic and apostolic Church.... It is therefore the provisional representation of the whole world of humankind, justified in Him [Jesus Christ]."[31] This condensed phrase contains both the way in which Barth interprets the language of the Body of Christ and the way in which he links the church as a "provisional representation" to the whole world of humankind, relating the doctrine of justification to the priestly office of Christ. The second perspective, the building up of the community, refers to the exercise of the royal office of Christ and relates the "provisional representation," the particular example of the universal reality, to the sanctification of the whole world of humankind: "The Holy Spirit is the quickening power with which Jesus the Lord builds up Christianity in the world as His body, i.e., as the earthly-historical form of His own existence, causing it to grow, sustaining and ordering it as the communion of His saints, and thus fitting it to give a provisional representation of the sanctification of all humanity and human life as it has taken place in Him."[32] The third perspective—in which the dialectical unity of the two preceding Christological movements, "The Lord as Servant" and the "Servant as Lord," is elaborated in the exposition of Jesus Christ as the "True Witness" and "The Mediator"—presents the ecclesiological dimension as the sending of the community: "The Holy Spirit is the enlightening power of the living Lord Jesus Christ in which He confesses the community called by Him as His body, i.e., as His own earthly-historical form of existence, by entrusting to it the ministry of His prophetic Word and therefore the provisional representation of the calling of all humanity and indeed of all creatures as it has taken place in Him."[33] The constitution, shape, and mission of the church can theologically be expressed only in

30. *LG* §1.

31. Karl Barth, *The Church Dogmatics* IV/1 (§§57–63), ed. G. W. Bromiley and T. F. Torrance, trans. G. W. Bromiley (Edinburgh: T&T Clark, 1956), 643.

32. Karl Barth, *The Church Dogmatics* IV/2 (§§64–68), ed. by G.W. Bromiley and T. F. Torrance, trans. G. W. Bromiley (Edinburgh: T&T Clark, 1958), 614.

33. Karl Barth, *The Church Dogmatics* IV/3 (§§69–73), ed. G. W. Bromiley and T. F. Torrance, trans. G. W. Bromiley (Edinburgh: T&T Clark, 1961), 681.

the complex unity of these three Christological perspectives, and this gives a full view of what, for Barth, the language of Christ as the "Light of the World" comprises.

Lumen Gentium and Barth's Ecclesiology in Conversation

How did the Roman Catholic theologians whom Barth encountered in Rome respond to his questions? We do not know, but we can speculate on their responses and on what questions they themselves put to Barth. Instead of emphasizing the difference or distance between Jesus Christ and the Church, they would, I believe, have pointed to the relationship between Christ and the Church by pointing out that Christ created the Church as the instrument of his presence in the world as the "kingdom of Christ now present in mystery." They would have insisted that there remains a difference between Christ and those acting *in persona Christi* because the church is the *instrument* by means of which Christ wants to become present. There remains a difference, but this difference comes to expression only in the intimate relationship that is rooted in the unity of Christ's person. The Catholic theologians might have questioned whether Barth, in the systematic construction of his Christology, is right to put the prophetic office of Christ last as the integration of the two aspects of the priestly and the royal office of Christ. They would certainly have had reason to ask Barth whether his sacramental theology is truly incarnational so that the embodied character of the visible words of the sacraments is fully acknowledged. One can imagine that they would have asked Barth in which sense the representation is provisional. Is not one of the core points of the theology of the Reformation that God's justification offered in the proclamation of the Word and the celebration of the sacraments is God's eschatological judgment—ultimate and not provisional, and therefore the basis for the assurance of salvation.

One may suspect that Barth would not have given in easily. He could have asked whether the "regnum Christi iam praesens in mysterio" with theological necessity includes the whole hierarchical order and the system of the seven sacraments and, indeed, the rule of canon law in the church. Can these be theologically justified as forms of the "kingdom of Christ" in whatever mysterious fashion? Barth would have insisted, I believe, that the church is *not* the extension of the incarnation but the creature and instrument of Christ's *own* presence. There *must* be difference in representation; otherwise the church represents itself. The life of the people of God as well as the order of the ministries in the church must be considered as modes of God's *self-presentation* through Christ in the Spirit. In this way, Barth would have pointed out that at times there seems to be ambiguity in the theological terminology of *LG*. The most important statements have the triune God as their subject in propositions about the constitution, the preservation, and the consummation of the Church. The strength of the theological conception of *LG* is precisely in its consistent attempt to relate all ontological descriptions of the church to narratives about the action of God the Father, the Son, and the Spirit. God's creative action precedes everything that can be said about the created existence and agency of the church. This is especially clear where the church is depicted as the instrument of the actualization of God's will in the history of salvation. Here human action appears as the means through which God achieves his goal for his creation. However, there are a number of sentences where humans appear as the subject of saving actions. Barth picks out a number of them. Can it be said, even with reference to 1 Corinthians 4:15, that the priests "have begotten [believers] by baptism and their teaching" (§28)? Is not the categorical distinction between the agency of the triune God and the agency of all created beings, even ordained bishops and priests, the presupposition for talking about their relationship? Is it not that which Paul expressed by saying that he had begotten the members of the congregation in Corinth "in Christ Jesus through the Gospel" (1 Cor 4:15)? And is not the gospel to be understood here not as Paul's teaching, but as "the power of God for salvation to everyone who has faith" (Rom 1:17)? Can one speak with theological responsibility about the church as the continuation of the revelation (*salutis divinum mysterium nobis revelatur et continuatur in Ecclesia*) (§52)? Is not Christ himself in his self-presentation the continuation of the revelation? This question echoes Barth's lifelong concern that God remains the Lord over God's relation to his creation in all its aspects, also in the constitution of human faith and witness. For Barth, the danger of the conflation of creative divine agency and created human agency is also apparent in the fact that in the eschatological dimension it is not sufficiently emphasized that the consummation of everything—Christ's coming for the last judgment and the coming down of the New Jerusalem—is a divine act which is not simply the end of the progression of the church through history. Conversely, the Roman Catholic theologians could ask Barth whether he has sufficiently done justice to the incarnational mode of God's action in Christ and the inspirational presence of God the Holy Spirit? Perhaps those of the Roman Catholic theologians who had experience of Eastern Orthodox theology—and here we are completely in the realm of speculation—would like to point out perceived difficulties of Barth's Christological ecclesiology. Does it give enough space to the operation of the Holy Spirit, who at times appears as the efficacy of the self-revelation of Christ, as "the awakening power" and the "illuminating power," but not as person in the Trinity who is not only consecutive upon the revelation in Christ but also constitutive for it?

We can continue this imaginary conversation, backed up by our account of *LG* and the brief sketch of Barth's ecclesiology for some time. However, the most interesting question has not yet been touched on in this exchange. Does Barth's visit to Rome *ad limina apostolorum* contain a promise for our contemporary ecumenical endeavors?

The Promise of a Theological Conversation

If we see the ecclesiology of *LG* and Barth's questions with regard to the document in the context of the whole Council, it is clear that the ecumenical movement is seen as grounded in the action of the triune God. Just as the Church is grounded in God's Trinitarian action, so the fellowship between the churches is a divine work. The only ecumenism that Barth and the Council can meaningfully envisage is God's ecumenism.[34] All human attempts at working for the visible unity of the Church must be based on God's being, will, and action; they must be grounded in the gift of unity that is already given in Christ. While this theological understanding of ecumenism is clearly implied in *LG*, it is expressly declared in *Unitatis Redintegratio*, the Council's decree on ecumenism: "the Lord of Ages wisely and patiently follows out the plan of grace on our behalf, sinners that we are. In recent times, more than ever before, He has been rousing divided Christians to remorse over their divisions and to a longing for unity."[35] Awakening Christians to repentance over their divisions is part of God's plan "to raise men to a participation of the divine life."[36] That ecumenism is in this way God's ecumenism is most clearly emphasized in the concluding statement of *UR* §2, which is in full agreement with the theological exposition of the

34. Cf. Christoph Schwöbel, "Gottes Ökumene. Über das Verhältnis von Kirchengemeinschaft und Gottesverständnis," in *Befreiende Wahrheit. Festschrift Eilert Herms* , ed. W. Härle, M. Heesch, and R. Preul (Marburg: N. G. Elwert, 2000), 449–66; also in Christoph Schwöbel, *Christlicher Glaube im Pluralismus, Studien zu einer Theologie der Kultur* (Tübingen: Mohr Siebeck 2003), 107–32.

35. *UR* §1.

36. *UR* §2.

Church in *LG*: "This is the sacred mystery of the unity of the Church, in Christ and through Christ, the Holy Spirit energizing its various functions. It is a mystery that finds its highest exemplar and source in the unity of the Persons of the Trinity: the Father and the Son in the Holy Spirit, one God."[37] This vision for ecumenism is offered with a clear view of the methods of ecumenical theological dialogue that follow from it. Catholic doctrine should be presented "lucidly" (*lucide*), "profoundly and precisely" (*et profundius et rectius*), free of all "false irenicism": "The Catholic faith must be explained more profoundly and precisely, in such a way and in such terms as our separated brethren can also really understand."[38] What is meant by "profoundly and precisely" and how can it be possible that the separated brethren "can also really understand"? *UR* §11 presents a clear rule for this: "Moreover, in ecumenical dialogue, Catholic theologians standing fast by the teaching of the Church and investigating the divine mysteries with the separated brethren must proceed with love for the truth, with charity, and with humility. When comparing doctrines with one another, they should remember that in Catholic doctrine there exists a 'hierarchy' of truths, since they vary in their relation to the fundamental Christian faith. Thus the way will be opened by which through fraternal rivalry all will be stirred to a deeper understanding and a clearer presentation (*ad profundiorem cognitionem et clariorem manifestationem*) of the unfathomable riches of Christ."

It appears that Barth's conversations at Rome are a promising early example of such a dialogue. In raising his questions, Barth seems to have acted not in the role of the celebrated theological teacher but more in the role of listener, providing through his questions the occasions for learning "more profoundly and precisely" the truth of Catholic doctrines as they are anchored in the "hierarchy of truths." The dialogue should be aimed at uncovering the relation of the different teachings to the "fundamental Christian faith." If we have a look at the Latin wording, we find that this rule of method is phrased a little differently: "In comparandis doctrinis meminerint existere ordinem seu 'hierarchiam' veritatum doctrinae catholicae, cum diversus sit earum nexus cum fundamento fidei christianae."[39] The task is thus to understand the hierarchical ordering of the different doctrines in

37. *UR* §2.

38. *UR* §11.

39. *UR* §11. The official English translation reads: "When comparing doctrines with one another, they should remember that in Catholic doctrine there exists a 'hierarchy' of truths, since they vary in their relation to the fundamental Christian faith." The last part of the sentence should be translated "profoundly and precisely" as: "since they vary in their relation with the foundation of Christian faith."

their relation to the *fundamentum fidei christianae*. What then is the foundation of Christian faith? If one follows both the logic of the exposition of *LG* and Karl Barth's critical questions, then that foundation could not be a fundamental dogmatic statement, but only the self-revelation of God through Christ in the Spirit, precisely the process that enables *LG* to call the Church "the kingdom of Christ already present in mystery" (*LG* §3). If one surveys the questions Barth raised in Rome, both the questions for clarification and the critical questions, one forms the impression that they refer precisely to the *nexus cum fundamento fidei christianae*, to the relation with the foundation of Christian faith. This is what he seeks to understand more profoundly and precisely, how the statements in the conciliar documents relate to the foundation of Christian faith, the foundation that is given to Christian faith in the revelation of the triune God.

Paying careful attention to these recommendations for the method of ecumenism raises a number of critical questions with regard to the method that the ecumenical dialogues followed after the Second Vatican Council. If the relation of the doctrines to the foundation of faith matters, would the most promising way of seeking common expressions of the Christian faith be through a differentiated consensus? Is it right to seek an agreement between doctrinal propositions? Or would the task not more likely consist in relating the different propositions to the foundation of Christian faith so that one would not seek a propositional consensus, an agreement of doctrinal expressions, but rather a consensus concerning the way in which these different doctrines of different ecclesial traditions refer to the foundation of faith?[40] Would such a referential consensus not be more appropriate to the task of a truly theological ecumenism that is grounded in God's ecumenism, the way in which "the Lord of Ages wisely and patiently follows out the plan of grace on our behalf, sinners that we are"?[41] And might the "separated brethren," the *fratres sejuncti*, discover in such a theological exploration in dialogical conversation, that although they might disagree in doctrinal

40. A research group of Lutheran theologians from Tübingen and Heidelberg and Roman Catholic theologians from the Lateran University have followed such a method of ecumenical conversation, in which the Roman Catholic theologians interpret the authoritative Roman Catholic *and* the Lutheran doctrinal texts, and the Lutheran theologians interpret the Lutheran *and* the Roman Catholic texts. The results of this endeavor, which was established in 2001 with the support of the then Prefect of the Congregation for the Doctrine of the Faith, have so far been published by Mohr Siebeck (Tübingen) and Lateran University Press (Rome) in three volumes, each volume edited by Eilert Herms and Lubomir Žak: *Grund und Gegenstand des Glaubens nach römisch-katholischer und evangelisch-lutherischer Lehre* (2008); *Wort und Sakrament im Grund und Gegenstand des Glaubens* (2012); and *Taufe und Abendmahl im Grund und Gegenstand des Glaubens* (2017). Two more volumes are in preparation.

41. *UR* §1.

propositions, they are nevertheless in agreement about the foundation of Christian faith, and the way Christian teaching should be rooted in and should witness to that foundation? And could it be that in this process of exploring the relation of theological teaching to the foundation of Christian faith the *fratres sejuncti* would discover that, in virtue of this foundation, they are already, in Christ, *fratres conjuncti*, in a fundamentally inclusive sense that would include the sisters in communion?

Chapter 5

The Humanity of God and the Mediation of the Church

Lumen Gentium as Christocentric Ecclesiology

Thomas Joseph White, OP

The Principle of Christological Instrumentality

In the third part of the *Summa theologiae*, q. 42, a. 4, Thomas Aquinas asks the question "why did Jesus Christ not write a book." The answers that he gives are threefold, each of which has consequences for thinking rightly about a Christocentric ecclesiology. The first is that Christ is different from other teachers because his teaching inscribes truth directly into the soul of the human person by grace, illuminating the mind and enflaming the heart with charity. There are outward words of Christ, but these must not be mistaken for the inward effect of those words, which is of a higher and different order than that produced by all other teachers. Second, were Christ to have composed a book, one written by a man who is God, the Church might risk promoting the study of the book as something superior to the knowledge of Christ as a person. This point is meant evidently to underscore that the modes of mediation that render Christ present are not to be exalted above the one true mediator himself (1 Tim 2:5), who is the Lord made manifest by these mediations. Finally, Aquinas notes that there is wisdom in the fact that the knowledge of Jesus is transmitted through the apostolic Church, in her preaching and writing, so that we should cooperate actively and depend mutually upon one another for the knowledge and grace of Christ. The tradition of the primitive Church gives formal determination and measure, even now, to the knowledge of Christ we receive by his actual grace. We do not live with Christ alone, but only ever in the Church, in social, sacramental, and epistemological interdependence, in a common life of instruction, repentance, forgiveness, and charity.

Aquinas is speaking about the mediation of the knowledge of Christ in a hierarchical, and nuanced way. The sacred humanity of Christ is that of the eternal Word of God, the second person of the Trinity. He renders himself personally present as God by his human life among us.[1] If we point to the man Jesus, we might rightly say, "This concrete individual here is the God of Israel."[2] The human words, actions, and sufferings of Jesus are the human words, actions, and sufferings of the second person of the Trinity.[3] Furthermore, in all this, the humanity of Jesus is the conjoined instrument of the person of the Word, so that Jesus may express his divine identity *in a distinctly human way*, by human thoughts and words, actions, and sufferings. In a like manner, his individual human nature is not something that subsists outside the Word, but is the Word himself individually subsistent among us as a man.[4]

The Church is enlivened by the grace of the God-man present among us, the resurrected and exalted Lord who continues to act in history, through a shared life of grace with members of his mystical body.[5] The Church lives especially through the ecclesial mediations established by the historical Jesus and by the apostolic community: the sacraments, apostolic tradition, the Scriptures. These mediations, however, are genuinely subordinate to and perpetually in the service of the perennial presence and agency of the Lord, the self-communication of his truth, and the work of his grace in the life of the Church. They are meant to manifest him in his reality, and to preserve among us a physical and sensible mode of expression of his living form as the Son of God, while engendering in us by grace an active response to, and cooperation with, his uniquely saving mystery.[6]

When Aquinas speaks about the mediating agency of the sacred human-

1. Aquinas, *Summa theologiae* (*ST*) III, q. 2.

2. *ST* III, q. 16, aa. 9–10.

3. *ST* III, q. 16, a. 4.

4. *ST* III, q. 2, a. 3.

5. *ST* III, q. 8, aa. 1 and 3.

6. See Aquinas, *ST* III, qq. 61–65, on the limited but real sacramental efficacy of the sacraments of the New Testament, and the seminal study of Aquinas' original contribution to the idea of sacraments as "instruments" by Theophil Tschipke, *Die Menschheit Christi als Heilsorgan der Gottheit* (Freiburg im Breisgau: Herder, 1940); French Translation: *L'humanité du Christ comme instrument de salut de la divinité*, trans. P. Secrétan (Fribourg: Academic Press Fribourg, 2003); and more recently regarding the development of the sacramental theory of the later Thomistic school, Reginald Lynch, *The Cleansing of the Heart: Sacraments as Instrumental Causes in the Thomistic Tradition* (Washington, D.C.: The Catholic University of America Press, 2017).

ity of Jesus, he characterizes this agency in part by reference to the classical orthodox teaching regarding dyotheletism. There are two "activities" or operations in Christ, divine and human, just as there are two natures, and two wills.[7] These exist in a symphonic harmony that is hierarchical and noncompetitive. Christ acts simultaneously as God and as human, and his human intentions, free decisions, and sensate actions are subordinate to and expressive of his divine wisdom and will, which he shares eternally with the Father and the Holy Spirit.[8] This symphonic concord is meant to manifest who Jesus is. So, for example, when the incarnate Lord stands at the tomb of Lazarus and weeps in the Gospel of John, chapter 11, it is God the Son who humanly mourns in sadness and longing the loss of his friend. The suffering of sadness and desire here is human but simultaneously expressive in a human way of the transcendent and immanent divine love of Christ. When the Lord then turns to raise Lazarus from the dead, he calls out "rise" in a human voice, motivated by a human decision. But this action is the human expression of a deeper transcendent intention that he shares with the Father and the Holy Spirit, the divine desire to restore Lazarus to life, as a sign of the authority of Christ and of the mystery of the resurrection that is to come.[9]

Three related features of biblical, Christological ontology arise here that are seminal for a right understanding not only of Christ but also of the Church. The three features are interrelated by a movement from the more specific to the more general and so are progressively inclusive of one another conceptually, like Russian dolls. First there is a principle originally underscored by the Prologue of the Gospel of St. John, and then emphasized thematically by both St. Irenaeus of Lyon and St. Cyril of Alexandria. God works through the matter of human flesh to redeem the world. It is the body of Christ that saves us, both by virtue of Christ's physical actions and by virtue of his sufferings.[10] Matter is in no way in a relationship of antithesis to our salvation by grace alone, but is at the core of the process by which

7. *ST* III, q. 18, a. 1; q. 19, a. 1.

8. *ST* III, q. 18, aa. 2–6.

9. Aquinas, *Commentary on St. John's Gospel* XI, lec. 6, nos. 1557–58: "He cried out ... saying, Lazarus, come out.... Then (v. 44), the effect of this voice is given.... For such was the power of Christ's voice that it gave life without any delay, as will happen at the general resurrection when the dead will rise in the twinkling of an eye when they hear the sound of the trumpet: 'And the dead in Christ will rise first' (1 Thess. 4:16). For Christ's mission was already being anticipated, as it was stated above: 'The hour is coming, and now is, when the dead will hear the voice of the Son of God, and those who hear will live' (John 5:25). In this way what our Lord said was fulfilled: 'I go to awake him' (John 11:11)."

10. Consider Irenaeus, *Against Heresies* III, chap. 22, and Cyril of Alexandria, *Second Letter to Nestorius*, where the soteriological argument is enunciated that Christ took human flesh in order to communicate the saving effects of divine life to our human nature, in and through the life-giving flesh of Christ.

God gives grace, in and through the flesh of Jesus, his bodily incarnation, apostolic life, physical suffering and death, and corporeal resurrection.

Second, following St. John Damascene, we must say that God saves us by his divine activity in and through the human agency of Christ. The instrumentality of the sacred humanity of Jesus includes the actions and sufferings of his flesh, but also those of his soul, including his spiritual faculties of intellect and will.[11] When the Lord accepts in the Garden of Gethsemane to subject himself for our sake to physical torment and execution, as well as the experience of rejection and refusal by many, he actively conforms his human decisions and intentions to the divine prerogative that he bears within himself as God.[12] This not only is meritorious for our salvation by virtue of the plentitude of charity that inhabits the human heart of Christ but also is rendered effective in our lives, since the mystery that Christ lived as man is itself communicated to us by the grace of the Holy Spirit.[13]

Finally, and most generally, God saves us not only through the medium of the human flesh of Christ and his human actions in that flesh, but more fundamentally through the medium of his created human nature.[14] In other words, God can be present in and work through created realities in order to convey to the world the grace of salvation. There is no rivalry then between the primary cause (the Creator) and the secondary causes (creatures of God considered as being themselves true ontological causes). Because God is the author of all that is, he is present in the heart of all that is and can act in and through it, not only in proportion to the natural causal activities of creatures, as in ordinary divine providence, but also in disproportion, employing the world of creaturely reality in view of the ends of divine grace.[15]

11. John Damascene, *On the Orthodox Faith* III, c. 6 and 18: "When it is allowed by that which is more excellent [the divine will of Christ], the mind of Christ gives proof of its own authority [over his body], but it is under the dominion of and obedient to that which is more excellent, and does those things which the divine will purposes.... So, then, He had by nature, both as God and as man, the power of will. But His human will was obedient and subordinate to His divine will, not being guided by its own inclination, but willing those things which the divine will willed.... For when He prayed that He might escape death, it was with His divine will naturally willing and permitting it that He did so pray and agonize and fear, and again when His divine will willed that His human will should choose death, the passion became [humanly] voluntary to Him" [trans. S. D. F. Salmond, Nicene and Post-Nicene Fathers, vol. 9 (Oxford: James Parker, 1899)]. Clearly Damascene is indebted in these passages to the theological perspective of Maximus the Confessor.

12. See the study of this theme in eastern Christology by Demetrios Bathrellos, *The Byzantine Christ: Person, Nature, and Will in the Christology of Saint Maximus the Confessor* (Oxford: Oxford University Press, 2004).

13. The idea is presented by Aquinas in *ST* III, q. 48, a. 6; q. 56, a. 1, and q. 19, a. 1, ad 1.

14. Aquinas notes that the human nature of Christ is created but that Christ is not a creature in *ST* III, q. 16, a. 8.

15. See the argument to this effect in Thomas Joseph White, *The Incarnate Lord: A Thomistic Study*

The life of God is now present and active in the ordinary world in an extraordinary way, always originating from the incarnation. The created humanity of Christ is forever the instrumental source of grace for the whole Church.[16]

What does this Thomistic prologue have to do with the ecclesiology of *Lumen Gentium* and with its relationship to the future of Catholic-Protestant ecumenism? What we are seeking is what Gottlieb Söhngen, following nineteenth-century Catholic theologians, termed the analogy of faith: the likeness that emerges between distinct mysteries of Christianity.[17] The analogy in question is one of proportionality that reveals to us the fitting internal wisdom and beauty of God's revelation. If Christ can save us through the instrumentality of his sacred humanity, in its created nature, its human agency, and its physical materiality, then God can work through such features of reality more generally, in different ways that are subordinate to Christ, within the life of the Church. We might call these Christological harmonies of an ecclesiological variation. The apostolic mediation of the faith is threefold in this respect. God communicates the life of Christian grace to us through, first, the apostolic preaching of the Church, second, her sacramental mysteries, and third, the prudential governance of her ministers. (God works for the sanctification of the faithful both through the governmental wisdom of those ministers and through their divinely permitted, sometimes serious defects.) In each of these cases we are speaking about human agency, and physical things (including the human body), and most generally of the use of created natural substances employed to communicate the life of God. Neither the ministers of the Church nor the sacraments are themselves God or Christ, with the important exception of the validly confected Eucharist, which Catholics confess to be the real presence of the body and blood of Christ (and which remains a point of dispute with and within the ecclesial communities issued from the Reformation). But creaturely realities—human ministerial agents and rightly celebrated sacraments—are genuine channels of grace through which the Son of God is made manifest and acts upon the world, according to the particular conditions of his own desire.

Thus far, we might presume a fair amount of consensus among Catholic and Protestant interlocutors, even if they might differ significantly about the

---

in Christology (Washington, D.C.: The Catholic University of America Press, 2015), chapter 3, which engages in particular with positions of Karl Barth.

16. *ST* III, q. 8, a. 5; q. 58, a. 3.

17. See Gottlieb Söhngen, "The Analogy of Faith: Likeness to God from Faith Alone?" *Pro Ecclesia* XXI:1 (2012): 56–76, and "The Analogy of Faith: Unity in the Science of Faith," *Pro Ecclesia* XXI:2 (2012): 169–74 [trans. K. Oakes].

modalities or concrete forms that these mediations take. Let us consider, then, some important features of the ecclesiology of *Lumen Gentium*, especially insofar as they address the historical controversies that characterize so deeply Catholic-Protestant relations.

Catholicity in Communion

In the first monograph of his career, *Chrétiens Désunis; Principes d'Un "Oecuménisme" Catholique*, Yves Congar set out what were to become a set of normative principles for Catholic ecumenism at the Second Vatican Council, formulated especially in the documents *Reintegratio Unitatis* and *Lumen Gentium*.[18] The Counterreformation theology of Robert Bellarmine sought to emphasize the continuity between the invisible and visible dimensions of the Church; it affirmed that ecclesial membership is constituted by or ratified within a visible structure of participation in the sevenfold sacramentary, the confession of the creed as interpreted by the Catholic hierarchy, and the visible governing of the Church by the apostolic episcopacy, in union with the Roman pontiff.[19] Congar does not reject this "visibility paradigm" for Catholicity but qualifies the understanding of it in various ways.

Most significantly, Congar distinguishes the *essence* of the Church from the instrumental *means* of the Church's sacramental sustenance and doctrinal instruction.[20] The Church at essence is the dynamic communion of the members of Christ's body in his life of grace. The Church lives "formally" by and in the theological virtues: faith, hope, and charity. It is these that constitute the inward sanctity and vitality of the Church. The Church is enlivened, however, by the means of her sanctification. These include in particular, the communication of divine revelation through the medium of the Scriptures as interpreted by the apostolic tradition and magisterial teaching, as well as the celebration of the sacraments. These "means" are instrumental efficient causes, one might say, subordinate to Christ and the Holy Spirit, by which God communicates his life to the Church.

From here one can speak about three features of ecclesial life in ecumenical context. First, Congar has identified the "formal cause" of the Church

18. Yves Congar, *Chrétiens Désunis; Principes d'Un "Oecuménisme" Catholique* (Paris: Cerf, 1937).

19. Robert Bellarmine, *Disputationes de Controversiis Christianae Fidei adversus hujus temporis Haereticos* (Naples: Giuliano, 1857) II, 3, "De Ecclesia Militante," c. 7. See the analysis of Bellarmine's theology by Benoît-Dominique de La Soujeole in *Introduction to the Mystery of the Church*, trans. Michael J. Miller (Washington, D.C.: The Catholic University of America Press, 2014), 361–76.

20. Congar, *Chrétiens Désunis*, 73–78, 88–95, 108–13.

as the communion established principally by the grace of the theological virtues, and communicated by baptism.[21] This understanding gives rise to an ecumenical possibility: that the life of the Church is found, at least in nucleus, not only within the Catholic Church, but also outside of her visible frontiers, at least if those frontiers are defined by recourse to the Bellarminian definition. The heart of Catholic ecumenical activity, then, is to seek to identify a *common life of supernatural faith* present not only in Catholic Christians but also in non-Catholic baptized Christians and communities, a life potentially animated by a shared supernatural, eschatological hope and love of charity for Jesus Christ, and for neighbor.[22]

Second, however, this life of grace shared among the baptized is communicated principally by the sacraments and in the union of divinely revealed truth maintained integrally within the Catholic tradition. Therefore, the genuine aims of a sound ecumenism require that Catholic Christians seek to identify revealed truths they hold in common with non-Catholics always with eventual reference to the plenary *sensus fidei* of the visible Catholic Church, and in view of a deepened participation in her sacramental life by all (the fullness of the sacraments of confirmation, reconciliation, and Eucharistic communion).[23]

Third, then, the final cause or term of the Church's inner life of grace is found in this communion of charity with God and with other human beings, brought to its eschatological fulfillment. This ultimate mystery of spiritual communion is especially anticipated and in a sense even effectuated in this life by common participation in the sacrament of the Eucharist.[24] We might say that if Congar's ecumenical theology takes its root in the grace common to all by virtue of baptism, it has its teleological fullness in the common visible life of communion that is Eucharistic. The means of the Church, her episcopal, sacramental, doctrinal, and liturgical apparatus, is meant to effectuate and instantiate the latter, as a precursor to the final reign of Christ, the eschatological Kingdom of God.[25]

Is Jesus Christ at the center of Congar's ecclesiological vision? We might analyze his portrayal of the Church by recourse to three of the four Aristotelian-Thomistic causes: the efficient, formal, and final causes. Is Christ the efficient source of all life in the Church? Following Aquinas, Congar identi-

21. Congar, *Chrétiens Désunis*, 116–48, esp. pp. 124–26.
22. Congar, *Chrétiens Désunis*, 278–308.
23. Congar, *Chrétiens Désunis*, 100–104.
24. Congar, *Chrétiens Désunis*, 80–85, 99–100
25. Congar, *Chrétiens Désunis*, 103–7.

fies the Son of God (by virtue of his deity, which he shares with the Father and the Spirit) as the unique principle and source of all grace and truth in the Church. The risen Lord works not only divinely but also humanly, through the instrumentality of his own humanity (conjoined to his divine person), willing both divinely and humanly to communicate his grace to the Church. The Lord also works through "separated instruments," the ordained ministers of the Church. These personnel are themselves morally imperfect and act as the participated agents of Christ's work only under specific conditions and in limited ways. In other words, their instrumental causality is subordinate to the causality of Christ, and is not to be confused or identified formally with the unique transcendent efficient causality of the Son of God, who is the sole principle of all our grace.[26]

The formal cause or essence of the Church is clearly not identical with Christ himself, according to Congar, since Christ alone is the God-man who remains distinct from and transcendent of the Church. There is no direct parallel between the ontology of the hypostatic union and the ontology of the Church, because only Christ is God, and the Church remains a perennially created entity.[27] The Church is constituted essentially, however, by the life of grace received from Christ in the Holy Spirit. This grace is assimilative of the faithful to Christ, and realizes a kind of participation in the life of God by way of divinization (2 Pet 1:3–4). Christ is also the final extrinsic terminus of the Church, the omega point toward which the communion of the Church tends in her Eucharistic union with the glorified body and blood of the Lord, and in her aspiration to know perfectly the truth of his divinity.[28]

The paradigm of ecclesial life identified by Congar was rearticulated in an alternative fashion by Henri de Lubac in his great mid-century work, *Catholicisme; Les aspect sociaux du dogme.*[29] De Lubac presents his notion of the Church as simultaneously personal and visible Eucharistic commu-

26. See the particularly clear statement of these ideas in *Chrétiens Désunis*, 93. The Christological origin of the Church and her grace, transmitted instrumentally by means of Christ through particular actions of the ecclesiastical hierarchy, is studied thematically by the Thomist ecclesiologist Charles Journet in *L'Église du Verbe Incarné; Vol. I: La hiérarchie apostolique* (Paris: Saint-Augustin, 1998), a volume that Congar cites frequently in his mature work.

27. See on this point the important study of Congar, "Dogme christologique et Ecclésiologie. Vérité et limites d'un parallèle," in *Sainte Église; Études et approaches ecclésiologique* (Paris: Cerf, 1963), 84–101, where he considers this topic in some depth. On page 96–101, after making several Thomistic distinctions, Congar demonstrates why it is not theologically balanced to speak in any strict sense of the Church of Christ as a "prolongation of the Incarnation."

28. Congar, "Dogme christologique et Ecclésiologie," 85–86.

29. Henri de Lubac, *Catholicisme; Les aspect sociaux du dogme*, 4th ed. (Paris: Cerf, 1947); *Catholicism: Christ and the Common Destiny of Man*, trans. L. Sheppard and E. Englund (San Francisco: Ignatius, 1988).

nion primarily in response to the social crisis of modern secular humanism, rather than to ecumenical questions. The secular modern person often finds himself trapped in a fragmented individualistic ethos, even as he eschews it and seeks deeper participation in something larger than himself, somehow transcendent and more meaningful. De Lubac argues that the Church embodies a supernatural response on the part of God to this innate, ineradicable desire of the human heart for social participation in an authentic, transcendent good. He demonstrates indisputably by reference to patristic evidence that the Church traditionally has conceived of salvation as having an irreducibly social dimension.[30] One is only ever saved in and with others, in and with the Church.[31] Salvation incorporates us into the life of spiritual, sacramental, and doctrinal communion that Congar sought to identify.[32] This ecclesial fullness of Eucharistic life in Christ marks out the true social destiny of the human race, one that finds its deepest concentration in the Church's Eucharistic communion, and her shared life of Christian truth. In the words of *Lumen Gentium*, the "Church is in Christ like a sacrament or as a sign and instrument both of a very closely knit union with God and of the unity of the whole human race."[33]

The communion ecclesiologies articulated by Congar and de Lubac each sought to depict accurately the Church as a simultaneously visible and invisible reality, as a communion of persons effectuated by both historical, sensate and internal, spiritual means of sanctification.[34] The balance they were seeking to maintain between means and ends seems to have had a great effect at the Council. A similar pattern of reflection is evident in the theological structure of *Lumen Gentium*. The document begins (chapter one) with a reflection on the Church as a "mystery," one that is both visible and invisible, grounded in the life and initiative of the Most Holy Trinity, established by Christ and maintained in communion through his grace, but also through the visible means of his ministers and sacraments. The second chapter of the document, then, treats of the whole "people of God" as the entirety of those incorporated into the mystery of Christ, laity as well as religious, and those in holy orders. Here in sections 14–16 one finds the famous

30. De Lubac, *Catholicisme*, chap. 1–2.

31. De Lubac, *Catholicisme*, chap. 7–8, on the collective character of salvation and predestination.

32. De Lubac, *Catholicisme*, chap. 3, on the sacramental life and the visible communion of the Church.

33. *LG* §1. (All translations of official Vatican documents are taken from www.vatican.va.)

34. See the helpful analysis of this theme in modern ecclesiology by Benoît-Dominique de La Soujeole in *Le sacrament de la communion; Essai d'ecclesiologie fondamentale* (Paris and Fribourg: Cerf and Éditions Universitaires Fribourg Suisse, 1998).

vision of the concentric circles of ecclesial incorporation, a core element of *Lumen Gentium* that suggests the influence of Congar and de Lubac, or at any rate of ideas that greatly resemble theirs. Catholic Christians are members of the Church of Christ and uniquely possess the fullness of the means of sanctification. Eastern Christian Churches stand in close proximity to the Catholic Church due to a shared sacramental and doctrinal patrimony, while ecclesial communities issued from the Reformation share a common baptism and reverence for the Word of God. The Jewish people are at a further remove from the fullness of communion but remain an elect people of God beloved for the sake of their fathers, while Muslims are monotheists who maintain some truths derived originally from the Christian revelation. Other religionists may be enlightened by partial truths about God, whose grace may sometimes be at work outside of the sacramental economy. Finally, even those who do not know God may be persons of good will whose consciences are enlightened by God when they seek to do good and avoid evil, as best they know how. At the same time, life outside of the visible means of the Church instituted by Christ is perilous, and there is no salvation outside of the Church.[35] Or stated otherwise, insofar as non-Catholics or non-Christians are moved by the grace of God, they are also inclined in however hidden a way toward the fullness of membership in the visible mystical body of Christ, and the fullness of sacramental life.[36]

35. *LG* §14: "This Sacred Council wishes to turn its attention firstly to the Catholic faithful. Basing itself upon Sacred Scripture and Tradition, it teaches that the Church, now sojourning on earth as an exile, is necessary for salvation. Christ, present to us in His Body, which is the Church, is the one Mediator and the unique way of salvation. In explicit terms He Himself affirmed the necessity of faith and baptism, and thereby affirmed also the necessity of the Church, for through baptism (Cf. Mk 16:16; Jn. 3.5) as through a door men enter the Church. Whosoever, therefore, knowing that the Catholic Church was made necessary by Christ, would refuse to enter or to remain in it, could not be saved.

"They are fully incorporated in the society of the Church who, possessing the Spirit of Christ accept her entire system and all the means of salvation given to her, and are united with her as part of her visible bodily structure and through her with Christ, who rules her through the Supreme Pontiff and the bishops. The bonds which bind men to the Church in a visible way are profession of faith, the sacraments, and ecclesiastical government and communion. He is not saved, however, who, though part of the body of the Church, does not persevere in charity. He remains indeed in the bosom of the Church, but, as it were, only in a 'bodily' manner and not 'in his heart.' All the Church's children should remember that their exalted status is to be attributed not to their own merits but to the special grace of Christ. If they fail moreover to respond to that grace in thought, word and deed, not only shall they not be saved but they will be the more severely judged."

36. For example, regarding non-Catholic Christians, *LG* §15 states: "The Church recognizes that in many ways she is linked with those who, being baptized, are honored with the name of Christian, though they do not profess the faith in its entirety or do not preserve unity of communion with the successor of Peter. For there are many who honor Sacred Scripture, taking it as a norm of belief and a pattern of life, and who show a sincere zeal. They lovingly believe in God the Father Almighty and in Christ, the Son of God and Saviour. They are consecrated by baptism, in which they are united with Christ. They also recognize and accept other sacraments within their own Churches or ecclesiastical

It is only after having spoken of these "essential" matters and their hidden but universal scope that the document goes on in chapter three to examine the instrumental *means* of sanctification: the apostolic hierarchy, the threefold hierarchy of holy orders, and the irreplaceable role of the Roman pontiff for the safeguarding of the universal communion of the Church. Clearly the document is tracing out a theological vision similar to that of Congar, in which holy orders are seen to derive from Christ, to be at the service of Christ, and to help effectuate the reality and perfection of the spiritual communion of the life of the Church.[37]

The document then transitions intentionally into a treatment of the differentiated states of life of the people of God. The laity form the subject of chapter four, which appeals to the theology of baptism as the wellspring for the consecration and sanctification of the lay faithful in all aspects of their Christian lives in the world. This anticipates chapter five, on the subject of the universal call to holiness. Clerics, laity, and religious are all called to sanctity by means of the diverse states of life through which they live the Christian life and participate in the sacramental economy. This central point about a symphony of diverse forms of membership in Christ forms a natural point of transition into the subject of religious life, which is a means or a form of Christian life derived from baptism, but which when lived integrally is proportioned more proximately to the final end of the Church: eschatological beatitude and the life of holiness. In other words, religious live in one particular state of life in the Church alongside the clergy and the laity but in so doing, they also help recall the finality of Christian life to all. Consequently, the document terminates with chapter seven on the eschatological nature of the Church in pilgrimage toward the state of beatitude. Here is where the Marian profile of the Church is presented. The Mother of God in her eschatological beatitude and in her bodily assumption manifests the

communities. Many of them rejoice in the episcopate, celebrate the Holy Eucharist and cultivate devotion toward the Virgin Mother of God. They also share with us in prayer and other spiritual benefits. Likewise we can say that in some real way they are joined with us in the Holy Spirit, for to them too He gives His gifts and graces whereby He is operative among them with His sanctifying power. Some indeed He has strengthened to the extent of the shedding of their blood. In all of Christ's disciples the Spirit arouses the desire to be peacefully united, in the manner determined by Christ, as one flock under one shepherd, and He prompts them to pursue this end. Mother Church never ceases to pray, hope and work that this may come about. She exhorts her children to purification and renewal so that the sign of Christ may shine more brightly over the face of the earth." On this positive interpretation of the dictum "extra ecclesiam nulla salus" in twentieth-century Catholic theology, see Bernard Sesboüe, *Hors de l'Église pas de salut: Histoire d'une formule et problèmes d'interprétation* (Paris: Desclée de Brouwer, 2004).

37. Consider *LG* §§26–29, in comparison with Congar in *Chrétiens Désunis*, 92–95, and "Dogme christologique et Ecclésiologie," 84–87.

plenitude of the life of Christ in his people. She is therefore an exemplar or archetype of human salvation for the whole Church.[38] The Virgin Mary is not the extrinsic term of the Church's life: The Church exists for God and for Christ alone. But she is the exemplar of the Church's immanent life of holiness, as the first among all those who are saved by Christ, and who are sanctified inwardly by the prompting and direction of the Holy Spirit.[39]

What has been accomplished in the ecclesiological presentation of *Lumen Gentium*? For the sake of our argument, the key point is that the instrumental means of sanctification form a key part of the visible life of the Church in this world, but they are ontologically relative, or relational, in a threefold way. First they are relative by their dependency upon Christ who is the unique mediator of salvation, and the primary source and origin of all grace.[40] He works through the ecclesial means of salvation and sanctification, but he is not bound by them. His work outside of the visible frontiers of the Church, however, inclines human beings toward the fullness of the visible means of salvation, and is ecclesiologically oriented.[41] Second, the ecclesial mediations are relative to the spiritual and visible communion of the mystical body of Christ that they help to effectuate. The word of God and the sacraments form and nourish the Church, in view of the life of grace and truth that is essential to the communion of the faithful, and that unifies the ecclesial body under the direction of the Holy Spirit.[42] Finally, the media-

38. *LG* §53: "The Virgin Mary, who at the message of the angel received the Word of God in her heart and in her body and gave Life to the world, is acknowledged and honored as being truly the Mother of God and Mother of the Redeemer. Redeemed by reason of the merits of her Son and united to Him by a close and indissoluble tie, she is endowed with the high office and dignity of being the Mother of the Son of God, by which account she is also the beloved daughter of the Father and the temple of the Holy Spirit. Because of this gift of sublime grace she far surpasses all creatures, both in heaven and on earth. At the same time, however, because she belongs to the offspring of Adam she is one with all those who are to be saved. She is 'the mother of the members of Christ . . . having cooperated by charity that faithful might be born in the Church, who are members of that Head.' (St. Augustine, *De S. Virginitate* 6) Wherefore she is hailed as a pre-eminent and singular member of the Church, and as its type and excellent exemplar in faith and charity. The Catholic Church, taught by the Holy Spirit, honors her with filial affection and piety as a most beloved mother."

39. On this theme of the Virgin Mary as the "eschatological icon" of the Church, see the *Catechism of the Catholic Church*, no. 972; Jean-Miguel Garrigues, *L'Epouse du Dieu Vivant: Marie plenitude trinitaire de l'Église* (Paris: Parole et Silence, 2000); Thomas Joseph White, "The Virgin Mary and the Church: The Marian Exemplarity of Ecclesial Faith," *Nova et Vetera* (English Edition) 11, no. 2 (2013): 375–405.

40. The document of the Congregation for the Doctrine of the Faith from the year 2000, *Dominus Jesus*, intensifies this vision of Christocentric ecclesiology. See para. 11, 12, 16.

41. See the argument to this effect by Charles Journet in *L'Église du Verbe Incarné; Vol. I: La hiérarchie apostolique*, 82–109; and *L'Église du Verbe Incarné; Vol. III: La structure interne de l'Eglise et son unite catholique* (Paris: Saint-Augustin, 2000), 1715–1802.

42. See especially *LG* §11 and 21. §11: "Incorporated in the Church through baptism, the faithful are destined by the baptismal character for the worship of the Christian religion; reborn as sons of God

tions in question exist in view of a higher state: that of the eschatological glory of God revealed fully in the resurrected Christ. In heaven, there are no sacraments and there is no Bible. There is the Word of God made flesh, the Lamb of God, who continues forever to enlighten the city of the saints, all those who see God face to face (Rev 21:23–24; 22:5).[43]

This vision of ecclesiology stands in fundamental continuity with the Tridentine doctrine of the sacraments, and with the First Vatican Council on papal authority, thus preserving important features of the classical Bellarminian understanding of the Church. However, it has reframed these features within a deeper vision of the unity of the Church as a spiritual communion in the charity of Christ. The Church is depicted first and foremost as centered in Christ and as derivative from his grace. The diversity of Christian states of life is treated positively, as the diversity of means of sanctification is understood in a unified fashion by reference to a single teleological end of sanctification to which all are called. The historical development of the Church is acknowledged, while a unity of essence across time is also affirmed. The centrality of membership in the Catholic Church is underscored in concord with a genuine openness to ecumenism, and a theological warrant is given to interreligious dialogue. Positive elements of political humanism are acknowledged within a framework that accentuates above all the unique mediation of Christ as the savior of all persons, and the Church as the visible sign and instrument of salvation in Christ. The Virgin Mary is understood as a unique exemplar of the life of the Christian faithful, but also fundamentally as a member of the larger Church of Christ.

Catholic and Protestant Disputes about Mediation

In 1950 Congar published his major work *Vraie et fausse réforme dans l'Église* in which he sought to characterize basic differences between Protestant ecclesiology and reform-oriented Catholic ecclesiology.[44] Interestingly, Congar engages in earnest with Luther's famous claim that "justification by faith

they must confess before men the faith which they have received from God through the Church. They are more perfectly bound to the Church by the sacrament of Confirmation, and the Holy Spirit endows them with special strength so that they are more strictly obliged to spread and defend the faith, both by word and by deed, as true witnesses of Christ. Taking part in the Eucharistic sacrifice, which is the fount and apex of the whole Christian life, they offer the Divine Victim to God, and offer themselves along with It."

43. *LG* §§48–51.

44. A second version was published in 1968 in the wake of the Second Vatican Council. However it was not greatly altered, as Congar notes in the preface. It is this edition that I am citing from below. Yves Congar, *Vraie et fausse réforme dans l'Église* (Paris: Cerf, 1968).

alone" is the foundational article upon which the Church stands or falls.[45] Students of Luther's thought, and Protestants more generally, have their own significant disputes about how to interpret this claim, and about whether it is significant ecclesiologically, or even theologically warranted. Congar argues, however, that the notion is integrally related to core Protestant ecclesiological theses, because it touches directly upon the key question of mediation and the role of the visible church in conveying (or not) the mystery of salvation.[46] As Congar interprets the thought of Luther, Christ is related first and foremost directly to individual persons, by election and by the extrinsic gift of righteousness, so that these gifts are conveyed only inwardly and without mediation, and not instrumentally through ecclesial mediations.[47] Consequently, the life of the Church is identified essentially not with the visible political society of the faithful, but with the invisible communion of the predestined as such. The visible Church is understood effectively, then, as a pure result and sign of the invisible work of grace in the life of each of the elect; the Church brings the elect together in this world in outward service of God.[48] Baptism serves as the outward evidence and seal of election, but need not be conceived of as an instrumental cause of the gift of grace.[49] Tradition and doctrine are understood to be always reformable in the light of the unique mediating authority of Scripture alone, to which each elect individual has access independently of the historically contingent ecclesial mediations of councils or papal teachings. Ecclesial traditions therefore may be expressions of scriptural faith but are not infallibly guaranteed to be so. There are no sacraments of holy orders or reconciliation for Luther as these are clas-

45. Congar, *Vraie et fausse réforme*, 341–85.

46. Congar, *Vraie et fausse réforme*, 344–53.

47. Congar, *Vraie et fausse réforme*, 350: "The Church is nothing other than the gathering of true believers in Christ; it is constituted through faith and by faith. It is therefore invisible with respect to its principle and even in its essential reality insofar as this reality stems from a divine principle, and adheres to him and is by this very fact, entirely pure. Luther says frequently that the Church is constituted by the adherence of faith to Christ hidden in God and therefore is invisible: it is the kingdom which is entirely spiritual and invisible, in our faith stemming from Christ who is spiritual and invisible." (Trans. by the author.)

48. Congar, *Vraie et fausse réforme*, 351–52.

49. Congar, *Vraie et fausse réforme*, 360: "In what concerns the sacraments, baptism and the eucharist, Luther sees in them not means intervening as such in the gift of grace, but the *signs* of God accompanying his [inner] action." 363: "If one wanted to penetrate further into the tenants and destinations of this thought, I believe that one would have to uphold a certain conception of grace. Grace is not seen by Luther and the other Protestant reformers as a certain created reality caused by God in the soul by the means of the sacred humanity of Christ and the sacraments of the Church in which the ordered power of the cross is operative. Rather, it is seen as an act of God: an act of God who is in heaven, carried out in virtue of the Passion of Christ, but without any physical-historical continuity with that event. Our relationship to God is reestablished in Christ, but in the Christ who is in heaven, who acts upon us from the heights of heaven, by his Spirit."

sically understood in the Catholic tradition, and so likewise there exists no episcopal and papal jurisdiction of the visible church as a condition for one's integration into the spiritual communion of the Church.[50]

What we see in each of these cases is that according to Luther, or for Congar's Luther, incorporation into the visible Church is understood principally as an effect of the life of Christ rather than as an instrumental means by which the believer enters into the mystical body. The visible Church is real and of course matters deeply, but the concrete mediations of preaching and sacramental agency, as well as the sociological functions of Church authority, are actualistic occasions of grace at most, but not stable mediums through which the life of Christ is at work in habitual, predictable, and assured fashions.

According to Congar, this focus on the movement from the inward spiritual activity of God to the visible sign and outward effect allows Protestant ecclesiology to integrate into itself a dialectical tension between the freedom of God and the creaturely limitations of the Church.[51] Human beings do not have a stable claim upon the transcendent freedom of God, who is always able to make himself known under the conditions he chooses, over and against the finite and fallible presumptions of human agents.[52] The revelatory actualism of God stands over against any creaturely attempt to fashion stable forms of containment or transmission of the divine gift. What follows dialectically then is blessed rage for purity against all complicities with a perceived idolatry, or danger thereof: Scripture against the corruptible traditions; justification by faith against a theology of sanctifying cooperation and of merits; the doctrine of *sola gratia* against an ecclesiology of sacerdotal mediation and the sevenfold sacramental organism. For Congar this theology rightly underscores the spiritual essence of ecclesial life but does so to the detriment of an authentic acknowledgment of the perennial necessity of the visible means of sanctification instituted by Christ himself.[53] Consequently,

50. Congar, *Vraie et fausse réforme*, 357–58.

51. Congar, *Vraie et fausse réforme*, 396–418.

52. See Congar, *Vraie et fausse réforme*, 410, where he clearly alludes to Barth in this respect.

53. Congar states the point polemically in regard to Barth in "Dogme christologique et Ecclésiologie," 85: "In the New Testament dispensation, the Church does not find herself, in her activity, in a purely prophetic condition, in the situation of being seized occasionally, like the prophets of the Old Testament, so as to announce a good or a salvation that is still far away. Instead, in her apostolic condition [the Church is] in the situation of an instrument that communicates a good or a salvation that has already been made manifest in Jesus Christ. In this respect, the Barthian philosophy of the '*Ereignis*,' that Barth projects even onto Jesus Christ, is profoundly erroneous and contrary to the whole movement of the economy of grace to which the Bible bears witness. This is why, even though the Church is nothing more than the visible conveyance of the action of God, she is a conveyance 'instituted,' disposed and deputed in a permanent fashion in her role of conveyance.... Concretely, the Church

it ignores the visible Eucharistic communion that is essential to the life of the Church in this world, and it eclipses key elements of the doctrinal patrimony received from the apostolic Church herself.[54] God does work through revelatory actualism in the Catholic Church, and in such a way as to reform and renew the life of the Church, even sometimes dialectically, but not in such a way as to rupture decisively with essential elements of the visible ecclesial communion, and with the perennial mediations that are of divine right and of apostolic origin.[55]

It is illuminating to compare Congar's characterizations of Protestant ecclesiology with Karl Barth's characterizations of Catholic ecclesiology written just some years before, in *Church Dogmatics* I, 2. Barth claimed conspicuously in the first volume of the *Church Dogmatics* that the *analogia entis* was the "anti-Christ," and that its use by Catholics was the only reason Barth could see not to become Catholic himself.[56] But what is this *analogia entis*? Seemingly it is something more than mere belief in the possibility of natural theology, however divisive this particular belief might be. Indeed, in *Church Dogmatics* I, 2 Barth engages in a nuanced and attentive discussion of Catholic Marian theology where he traces out what he takes to be a set of interrelated principles in Catholic ecclesiology, all of which are in some way problematic for a common reason.[57] Barth's critique begins with a consideration of the Catholic affirmation of the unique holiness of the Blessed Virgin Mary, manifest in her especial cooperation with grace and her privileged degree of holiness and merit. Marian theology, Barth notes, is integrally related to the broader Catholic understanding of the life of sanctification through cooperation with the grace of Christ, and therefore of the life of the Church.[58] He also associates these ideas with the Catholic belief in stable, mediating instruments of the transmission of revelation, by recourse to sacred tradition and the infallible exercise of the Petrine office.[59] How could such a diversity of Catholic doctrines be related by recourse to one principle? Barth notes that one might, as Erich Przywara does, draw a connection between these doctrines and the metaphysics of the *analogia entis*.

Institution is constituted by the deposit, in her, and the transmission (Tradition and apostolic succession) of three apostolic 'powers' of the priesthood, spiritual jurisdiction and the magisterium, the first of these 'powers' being linked to a sacramental consecration and a 'character'."

54. Congar, *Vraie et fausse réforme*, 418–46.

55. See the analysis in Congar, *Vraie et fausse réforme*, 241–76.

56. Karl Barth, *Church Dogmatics* [*CD*] I/1, p. xiii. (All citations of the *CD* are taken from the English translations by G. W. Bromiley and T. F. Torrance [London: T&T Clark, 2004].)

57. *CD* I/2, 138–47. See the related discussion of the *analogia entis* on pp. 35–44.

58. *CD* I/2, 144–45.

59. *CD* I/2, 146.

E. Przywara purports to give us final clarity in the matter when he writes that there are contained "in the Catholic doctrine of the *analogia entis* the possibilities of a true incarnational cosmos, including body and soul, community and individual, because in their totality . . . they are 'open' to God. From the standpoint of the Catholic doctrine of the *analogia entis* creation in its totality is the vision, mounting from likeness to likeness, of the God who is beyond every likeness. It is, therefore, a receptive readiness for Him. In its final essence it is, as it were, already Mary's 'Behold, the handmaid of the Lord. Be it unto me according to Thy word.'" (*Religionsphil. Kath. Theol.* 1926, p. 53).[60]

Barth is interested to clarify the content of Przywara's claim and to consider it critically in light of Protestant theological principles. According to Przywara, or for Barth's Przywara, God in his transcendent alterity is omnipresent to all creatures in as much as he is the very giver of their being, and so God can become present in the world in a new way in the incarnation, becoming truly human, and living an integrally human life among us, without doing violence to his own created human nature and ours. *So likewise*, mutatis mutandis, human beings are naturally disposed toward the pursuit of the knowledge of God and toward agency that takes place in light of the knowledge of God. Consequently, under the direction of God's grace, and sustained by the Holy Spirit, human beings are capable of stable forms of cooperation with God in view of their sanctification in habitual grace. Again, if God can sanctify the Church and the Virgin Mary in the order of charity, how much more easily might he maintain the truth of the teaching of the Gospel down through the ages, through a stable form of tradition and dogmatic interpretation of Scripture, as well as an inerrant teaching office.[61]

Barth perceives in this collection of ideas an inherently problematic "Catholic both-and" where both Christ and the creature are agents of revelation, both Christ and the creature are subject to sanctification, both Christ and the creature are able to mediate the presence of the holiness of God. Where the New Testament teaches that Christ alone is to be glorified, the creature has now entered in as a secondary but privileged, illegitimate claimant to what in reality belongs only to Christ and to God.

Utterly logical was the connexion in the life-work of Pius IX between the proclamation of the *immaculata conceptio* in 1854 and that of papal infallibility in 1870 (and the canonisation of natural theology in Thomas's sense, achieved at the same Vatican Council). The Church in which Mary is venerated is bound to regard itself as it has done in the Vatican decree; just as the same Church must be the Church of the

60. *CD* I/2, 144–45.
61. *CD* I/2, 146.

man who co-operates with grace on the basis of grace. The Evangelical statement of faith which we must set against Marian dogma is thus the very same as must be maintained against the Roman Catholic doctrine of grace and the Church. Jesus Christ, the Word of God, exists, reigns and rules in as sovereign a way within the created world as He does from eternity with the Father, no doubt over and in man, no doubt in His Church and by it, but in such a way that at every point He is always Himself the Lord, and man, like the Church, can give honour only to Him and never, however indirectly, to himself as well.... Revelation and reconciliation are irreversibly, indivisibly and exclusively God's work. Thus the problem to which the Roman Catholic doctrine of grace and the Church, to which Mariology in particular is the so-called answer, i.e., the problem of creaturely co-operation in God's revelation and reconciliation, is at once a spurious problem, the sole answer to which can be false doctrines.[62]

At base Barth is convinced that Catholic ecclesiology seeks to assimilate the revelation of God into a system of human contrivance, in which the human agent can control artificially the conditions in which revelation is dispensed and in which the Gospel is authentically lived. This system is based fundamentally in a Pelagian theory of human knowledge and action (the *analogia entis* as Barth understands it), such that creatures are understood to have a stable natural disposition to cooperation with the grace and revelatory activity of the uncreated God. What is seemingly eclipsed is the transcendent freedom of God to reveal himself only in and by the mystery of Christ, and in the terms directly specified by the apostolic revelation of Scripture itself.

It is interesting that Barth and Congar agree in key ways about where the disagreement lies, then, between Catholics and Protestants. The controversy is about the relationship between uncreated divine agency and created human agency, especially within the context of the post-apostolic Church. Did Christ institute stable ecclesial mediations, such as the episcopacy, that are meant to perdure down through time? What role does the juridical government of the ministers play in maintaining the supernatural unity of the Church? What is the place of stable forms of authoritative tradition in the interpretation of Scripture? Analogously, what is the active role of the co-operation of the human person with the revelation given in Christ? Is there a so-called habitual grace of sanctification that allows the sinner who has been justified to cooperate actively with the grace of Christ? What is the archetypal form of holiness that is traditionally ascribed by the Catholic Church to the Mother of God, and is it something real, truly revealed by

62. *CD* I/2, 146.

God, or something illusory and manmade? Do human beings have natural dispositions toward the knowledge and love of God? Does philosophy play an inevitable role in the articulation of any realistic form of Christian theology? These questions do have a common thread running through them: they all touch in some way upon the relation of the transcendent causality of God acting in the person of Jesus Christ, and created active causes that cooperate with the grace of Christ.

Christological *Analogia Entis*

Hans Urs von Balthasar in his great ecumenical work on Karl Barth's theology sought to reframe Barth's debates with Przywara in a distinctively Christological key.[63] Balthasar interprets Barth's work as having been subject to development, passing from his earlier dialectical themes (of God's work of grace over against human activity) to a mature vision of the analogy between creation and God that is revealed in Christ and discernable in the mystery of the Incarnation. The humanity of Christ manifests his Godhead and there exists a likeness in Christ between his humanity and his divinity.[64] Balthasar begins, as it were, from this *analogia entis Christi*, and then seeks to understand all other likenesses between creation and God in light of this most ultimate instance of similitude. Following Gottlieb Söhngen, he argues that the likeness between creatures and God that is discernable to the human mind philosophically (that of so-called natural theology) is intelligible only ever from within the ambit of Christological faith, and in subordination to the latter.[65] One may maintain a traditional Catholic vision of the metaphysics of creation as distinct from the knowledge of God made possible by Christ, but simultaneously maintain that the former is never existentially separable from the latter. In the concrete historical economy of fallen human beings, metaphysical understanding of creation is always integrally dependent upon and related to the Christological light of grace.[66]

One might dispute, on any number of fronts, whether Balthasar right-

63. Hans Urs von Balthasar, *Karl Barth. Darstellung und Deutung seiner Theologie* (Cologne: Verlag Jakob Hegner, 1951); English translation: *The Theology of Karl Barth*, trans. Edward Oakes (San Francisco: Ignatius Press, 1992).

64. Balthasar, *The Theology of Karl Barth*, 328–34. See also Hans Urs von Balthasar, *Theo-Drama: Theological Dramatic Theory*, vol. 3: *The Dramatis Personae: The Person in Christ*, trans. Graham Harrison (San Francisco: Ignatius Press, 1992), 220–29.

65. Balthasar, *The Theology of Karl Barth*, 311–19.

66. The idea is developed thematically in Balthasar, *The Theology of Karl Barth*, 302–25.

ly interprets Barth.[67] However, independently of the disputed accuracy of Balthasar's interpretations, there is also the question of the ecumenical promise of "Balthasar's Barth." Barth himself, of course, never presumed to serve as a living magisterium for the dogmatics of the Church, and even less as a criterion thinker for Catholic-Reformed unity. Precisely because he is not such an authority, then, perhaps Balthasar's reformation of Barth's perspective may be of greater help to the unity of the Church than Barth's own thinking was. Indeed, perhaps a Catholic interpretation of some of Barth's core ideas might be of greatest use not only to Protestants but also to Catholics.

Balthasar composed his interpretation of Barth prior to the publication of *Church Dogmatics* IV, which contains Barth's mature, substantive Christological reflections. However, one may observe in these latter, particularly in *CD* IV, 2, a set of references to the idea of an *analogia entis Christi*, at least with regard to the two essences and activities of Christ, which Barth depicts in Chalcedonian terms as hypostatically unified in a single subject, distinct in essence and mutually united in operative concord. The humanity of Christ is the "organ" or instrument of his divinity.

> In [Christ's] person there is given to human essence the human power fully to attest His divine power, to serve it in a way commensurate with it, effectively to execute its act and acts. All this is given to it as the human essence of the Son of God—not of itself, but as His organ, as the body of which He is the Head. But it is given to it as the human essence of the One who is Son of Man as well as Son of God.... We insist that [the] function [of the human essence of Christ] is that of an organ of the Son of Man who is also and primarily the Son of God. It is to Him and not this organ, to His human essence as such, that there is given 'all power in heaven and in earth' (Mt. 28:18). It does not possess, but it mediates and attests the divine power and authority. It bears and serves it. It is adapted in its function for what the incarnate Word, the Son of God and Son of Man, wills to do, and does actually do, for and to the world as He exists in it, in the human sphere.[68]

Clearly it would seem that there is present in Barth's mature Christological vision, then, a kind of instrumental subordination of the human essence of Christ to his divine essence, within the concrete economic event of salvation history. Is there room here for thinking more generally about how all of created reality might be understood in light of Christ's humanity, and

67. See the significant critique of Balthasar's reading of Barth by Bruce L. McCormack in *Karl Barth's Critically Realistic Dialectical Theology: Its Genesis and Development, 1909–1936* (Oxford: Clarendon, 1995); also McCormack's "Karl Barth's Version of an 'Analogy of Being': A Dialectical No and Yes to Roman Catholicism," in *The Analogy of Being: The Invention of the Antichrist or the Wisdom of God?* ed. Thomas Joseph White (Grand Rapids, Mich.: Eerdmans, 2010), 88–144.

68. *CD* IV/2, 97–98.

of how the mystery of the visible Catholic Church might be understood in instrumental and subordinate terms, within a distinctively Christocentric vision? If so, then one might envisage some form of deeper convergence between the Christology of Barth and that of the Second Vatican Council.

Here then we might return to our reflections on instrumentality that we began with using St. Thomas Aquinas. The argument could be formulated thus: Barth himself rightly acknowledges that the humanity of Christ is the "organ" or living instrument of his divine person, and is expressive of the very identity and life of the Word incarnate.[69] If, however, the humanity of Christ can be an instrument of his divine person, then created realities can be living instruments employed by God for the communication of grace and truth in the world. Furthermore, we do know that Christ as man instituted the Church (in some fashion), instituted sacraments, and chose apostolic minsters to preach the truths of the Gospel. Both the New Testament and the early post-apostolic writings bear witness to this fact. If this is the case, and if Christ's human nature is employed by God—even now in the resurrected life—in a stable fashion so as to communicate grace and truth, then why could God not now make use of minsters distinct from Christ to communicate the grace and truth of Christ to the world, in stable and enduring ways? If God can do this always in subordination to the truth of Christ, why should he not establish a collective body of *institutional kind* to safeguard and transmit the patrimony of the Gospel and to serve as a living instrument of its communication down through time?

One might object that such a structure is utterly unlike the humanity of Christ because the ecclesial hierarchy of the Catholic Church is composed of sinful, fallible human beings, utterly unlike the unique God-human precisely with regard to grace and truth.[70] To which one might respond: yes, but that is precisely why God might fittingly sustain an institutional Church in being, by way of the seven sacraments as channels of the grace of Christ, and the preservation of apostolic teaching free from error, so as to safeguard the Gospel of Christ and his grace from the effects of sinful human beings.[71] This is even necessary in some sense, given that the Gospel of grace is transmitted through history principally in and by a visible

69. See the broader considerations of *CD* IV/2, 36–115, especially pp. 96–108.

70. Congar considers this objection constructively in dialogue with Reformation objections in *Vraie et fausse réforme*, as does Journet in *L'Église du Verbe Incarné; Vol. I: La hiérarchie apostolique*.

71. The argument is of course initially made in pronounced biblical and theological terms by Augustine in his response to the Donatists with regard to the trustworthiness of Catholic baptism independently of the worthiness or unworthiness of the minister, as a principle of Christological stability in the Church.

community, which must be in some way sustained in being despite human fallibility and gracelessness. In fact, Catholic ecclesiology on this point insists on what we might call the purely extrinsic justification of the Church as an institutional body: the Church's means of truth and grace are preserved in being and employed habitually by God not because of the intrinsic merits of her ministers but because of the unique sanctity of Christ alone, and his fidelity to the Church.[72] Consequently, the continuing in being of the Catholic Church down through time is a testimony to the unique sufficiency of the grace of Christ, and to the glory of his wisdom and goodness. The Church bears witness to the preserving power of God in a theocentric and Christocentric testimony, not in one based upon the glory of her finite, fallible human ministers.

Analogously, by an analogy of faith (not recourse to the metaphysics of creation per se), if God can sanctify *the human nature* of Christ so that his ordinary human actions *habitually* bear witness to his divine identity as the Son, and to the mystery of his unity with the Father and the Spirit, then God can fittingly also bring human beings by grace into the ambit of habitual cooperation with Christ's sanctifying grace.[73] Only Christ is the Lord, and no Catholic saint is anything other than a redeemed human being, and, apart from the Virgin Mary, all are fundamentally sinners (ontologically and temporally) prior to being redeemed. Nevertheless, precisely because God has become human, God can also work through the instrumentality of human beings other than Christ, in their lives of habitual charity, sanctified by the Holy Spirit, so that they become stable agents who live in the grace of Christ. "It is no longer I who live, but Christ who lives in me," as St. Paul testifies (Gal. 2:20). At the perfective extreme end of this process is the example of the Virgin Mary, who is perfectly sanctified in the grace of Christ even from the first moment of her being. Such persons, the saints, do not diminish or detract from the uniquely salvific life of Christ. Rather, they magnify or manifest the reality of Christ's agency and its effective power at the heart of his Church.[74]

72. See the theological analysis to this effect by Journet, *L'Église du Verbe Incarné; Vol. I: La hiérarchie apostolique*, 21–195.

73. See on this point the treatment of habitual grace by Aquinas in *ST* I-II, qq. 111–114. Joseph Wawrykow in his study *God's Grace and Human Action: 'Merit' in the Theology of Thomas Aquinas* (Notre Dame, Ind.: Notre Dame University Press, 1996) has shown the thoroughly Augustinian provenance of this idea as anti-Pelagian. See the convergent perspective in Michael Root, "Aquinas, Merit, and Reformation Theology after the Joint Declaration on the Doctrine of Justification," *Modern Theology* 20, no. 1 (2004): 5–22.

74. I have made an argument to this effect regarding Mariology in Thomas Joseph White, "The Virgin Mary and the Church: The Marian Exemplarity of Ecclesial Faith," *Nova et Vetera*, 375–406.

Yet again, analogously, one might argue that being human simply entails the possibility of philosophical and religious activity and the capacity (however flawed or wounded by sin) of orienting one's self toward God by thought and by religious action.[75] If that is the case, then human beings simply must and always will interpret divine revelation and Scripture as active agents. They always will create rival systems of theological interpretation and elaborate alternative doctrinal and philosophical understandings of the mystery of Christ. They always will construe various religious ways of responding to and acting within the grace of Christ. There never will be simply an apostolic interpretation of Christ preserved from post-apostolic interpretation and life, but only ever also the interpretation and life of Luther or Bellarmine, of Calvin or the Fathers of the Council of Trent, of Karl Barth or Karol Wojtyla.[76] While these forms of life and interpretation may be more or less congruent or opposed, the deeper point is not that they must contradict, but that such phenomena are intrinsically unavoidable. Thus the claim that all particular interpretations are fallible and revisable leads inevitability in practice to the principle of private judgment, as John Henry Newman noted, and over the long term to the inevitability of ecclesiological factions.[77]

If such a feature of Christian culture is to be avoided, then there must exist a stable form of enduring cooperation with divine revelation, a magisterium, by which the authoritative teachings of Scripture and apostolic tradition might be rightfully discerned and adjudicated both in life and in teaching. To say that this is the case does not entail that we must detract from the unique dignity and truth of Christ, as God made human. On the contrary, precisely because God has become human, so analogously, all that is human in the Christian community can be placed at the service of the one and only man who is God. The active political, philosophical, and ritual religious life of humankind can be sanctified by Christ in stable and determinate ways, precisely so that the glory of his unique divinity may be

75. See Aquinas's arguments on the virtue of religion as a natural virtue, typically distorted by sin in its fallen exercise, in *ST* II-II, q. 81, a. 5; q. 85, a. 1; *ST* I-II, q. 109, a. 3.

76. See the argument to this effect by John Henry Newman in the *Apologia Pro Vita Sua* (New York: Penguin, 2004), 219: "The judgment, which experience passes whether on establishments or on education, as a means of maintaining religious truth in this anarchical world, must be extended even to Scripture, though Scripture be divine. Experience proves surely that the Bible does not answer a purpose for which it was never intended. It may be accidentally the means of the conversion of individuals; but a book, after all, cannot make a stand against the wild living intellect of man, and in this day it begins to testify, as regards its own structure and contents, to the power of that universal solvent, which is so successfully acting upon religious establishments."

77. On private judgment in matters of revealed doctrine, see, for example, Newman, *Discourses Addressed to Mixed Congregations* (London: Longmans, Green and Co., 1906), discourse 10: "Faith and Private Judgment," and *Apologia Pro Vita Sua*, "Note A: Liberalism," 252–62.

witnessed to in all facets of human life and in all human cultures, down through time, until the end of the ages. This is part of what it means to call the truth of Christ "catholic" or universal.

Of course the arguments I have given here are not intended to demonstrate that the ecclesiology of the Second Vatican Council must be believed simply in as much as or just because one believes in the true divinity and humanity of Christ. Rather, the argument is one from fittingness. God has truly become human, and the humanity of Christ is truly expressive instrumentally of the grace and truth of Christ as the eternal Son. Likewise, then, it is fitting that God should preserve a secure testimony to and sacramental mode of communication of the mystery of Christ down through the ages, despite human sinfulness and confusion, by the institutional actions of human beings. It is fitting that some human beings should become especially public witnesses to the life of grace and holiness that has been communicated to us in Christ. It is fitting that human beings who are members of Christ's mystical body might make full use of their philosophical, artistic, and political gifts in the service of the gospel, down through the ages, and that this might leave a deep mark upon the stable structures of Catholic dogmatic theology.

Note that this way of seeing things need not presume an absence of dialectic between the transcendent holiness of God and the disoriented sinfulness of human beings within the Church. Here we should consider Congar's answer to Barth's concerns. The dialectic of God and humanity, down through time, is resolved by the work of the Word made flesh *within the Church*, and not apart from it, by his grace sustaining, reforming, correcting, enlightening, and enlivening his Church, through his sacraments, and apostolic doctrine, his saints and his ordained ministers, and through the whole *sensus fidei* of the people of God, so as to arrive down through time, as if through fire and trial, at a plenary understanding of the Catholic truth of Christ.[78]

Ecclesiology after Vatican II: Conflicts and Convergences

Perhaps the principles affirmed here are largely acceptable to many Protestant theologians. If so, then the real question remains as to what structure the true church has in her apostolic origin, her early patristic maturation,

78. See the arguments made by Yves Congar in *Tradition and Traditions: An Historical and Theological Essay*, trans. M. Naseby and T. Rainborough (London: Burns and Oates, 1966), 314–45.

and in her historical development. Is this structure that of the Catholic Church (and in their own ways, the sister Churches of the eastern Orthodox tradition)? Or is the episcopal and sacramental life of the Catholic Church a historically accidental epiphenomenon and an artificial superstructure created by human beings, imposed problematically by them upon the Word of God? And perhaps most importantly, who can make such a discernment in a definitive way, since the making of such a discernment is itself an effect of grace? Are we left in the end to the resources of individual conscience alone? Appeal to one's individual conscience is surely a necessary condition for adherence to Christian truth, but perhaps it is not a sufficient condition. Can we not also appeal to a living authority that has received the assistance of God so as to help us discern actively what God has genuinely instituted in the life of the Church and sustained in being down through time? Of course a document like *Lumen Gentium* is intended to serve just this purpose. In the end, Catholics are those who believe themselves moved by grace so as to judge that the ecclesiological vision of the Catholic magisterium corresponds truly to reality and reflects a right understanding of sacred Scripture and apostolic tradition. Protestants do not make judgements of this kind, because they appeal to other ecclesiological criteria, other traditions of interpreting Scripture, by which they understand the Church differently as a historical entity existing down through time.

Where then might these reflections leave us as regards the future of Catholic-Protestant ecumenical relations, in the wake of the Second Vatican Council? Allow me to conclude with four ideas for future discussion between Catholic and Protestant ecclesiologists.

Divine Transcendence and Human Causality

What is our understanding of the freedom of God to transcend his mediations but also to sustain them in being, to commit to them in constancy for the salvation and sanctification of the Church? Can Protestants agree with Catholics about the possibility of a likeness between humanity and God revealed in Christ? If so, what about a likeness between creation and God more generally? If the latter exists, can human agency be taken up into the divine plan in such a way as to communicate and manifest Christ? Can stable ecclesial structures represent this form of cooperation in ways that do not rival divine activity but in fact serve that activity effectively?

Metaphysics of Secondary Causality and Inevitable Tradition

What theological ontology (and philosophical metaphysics) must we maintain in order to affirm and think responsibly about the mystery of the God-man, of the being, operations, work, kenosis, death, and glorification of Christ, as the revelation of God among us? If God can work through the humanity of Jesus, then he can work through a created human nature to reveal his divine identity, and transmit his life of grace. How does this take place in persons who are not Christ, but who are witnesses to Christ? The work of anyone who claims to be a teacher in the Church (including the author of the so-called *Church Dogmatics*) necessarily aspires at least implicitly to be instrumental to the communication of the grace and truth of Christ, and God does seemingly work through such transmission, in a manner similar to the way he works through preaching and sacraments. In this case, then, there is inevitably "ecclesial tradition" present in the heart of the Church and essential to her life. How do we identify the traditions that are authentic vehicles of the life of grace and measure them against rival claimants? If we wish to avoid charges of ecclesiological Pelagianism, then we must affirm that there is a grace of God at work within the transmission of the tradition in some way so as to assure the continuity of New Testament doctrine across time. What is the form that this grace takes when it manifests itself concretely in human history?

Physicality

The Word became flesh and saved us through his bodily passion, death, and resurrection. This reveals to us an anthropological truth embedded within Christology: that we are spiritual *animals*, physical creatures made to respond to God in the flesh, as corporeal beings. There is, therefore, a fitting correlate, that Christ should institute sacraments and a sacramental society touching various aspects of common human existence, so that we might turn our entire lives toward God effectively, both spiritually and physically, in the grace of Christ.[79] Mediations may function as temptations to impurity or idolatry, but they also may function as invitations to a concrete life of charity and forgiveness, a life the sacraments communicate visibly, inviting

79. See the arguments of Aquinas on the fittingness of visible sacraments for this reason, in *ST* III, q. 61.

us to live in communion with one another as embodied persons. Ultimately this is the only kind of life human persons are truly meant to pursue.

What role, then, should our physicality and animality play in our understanding of the life of the Church? How is our human sexuality, in its joy and its fruitfulness, truly subject to God within the life of the Church? How is the natural complementarity of male and female revealed in Genesis and articulated unambiguously by Christ (Gen 1:27; Matt 19:4–6) made to express the life of Christ in us in differentiated and complementary ways? And how do we account for, and embody in ecclesial forms of life, a realistic and rightly ordered acknowledgment of the irreducible complementarity of men and women, as well as the equality of men and women and their capacity for authentic relationships of justice and friendship?

Christocentricity

Karl Barth rightly focused the attention of modern theologians upon the centrality of Christ, or what might be termed the "Christological concentration" of the life of the Church. In related fashion, he rightly stressed the relativity of her mediations; the eschatological end toward which all is oriented in Christ; the centrality of Scripture; and the reality of revealed truth as the essential truth that is necessary for an integral understanding of reality in the light of God.

Today one might observe multiple limitations to the ecclesiological paradigm ushered in by the Second Vatican Council, at least in some of its interpreters. Christian humanism becomes liberalism; ecumenism becomes doctrinal indifferentism; and interreligious dialogue becomes Catholic syncretism. A Catholic Barthian answers in turn: "No." Christ is the unique mediator of salvation, and the unique one who is revealed; his Church is the concrete form that salvation takes in obedience to the Word of God; other religions are only anticipations of Christianity to the extent that they (somehow under grace) dispose human beings to the advent of the life of Christ in the Church, and do not impede that life.[80] Liberalism without Christ descends into a culture of economic management, technological consumerism, and sad hedonism.

For Catholic Christianity, life in Christ is wholly other than all this,

80. Consider in this respect the doctrinal teaching of the Catholic Church in the document *Dominus Jesus: On the Unicity and Salvific Universality of Jesus Christ and the Church* from the year 2000, available at www.vatican.va.

something from the strange new world of the Bible, alien and righteous, a line touching the circle of the world only at a tangent, the living voice of God among us. What is it calling us toward? The discovery of God, the Lord, and of his Church, and therein (and only therein) of ourselves, becoming the New Adam and the New Eve, in the likeness of grace, and in the analogy of being, as God's creation being redeemed in love. This occurs visibly and invisibly, socially and personally, in the Catholic life of sanctification by the unifying waters of baptism, and by the eating and drinking of the physical flesh and the blood of the crucified and risen Lord, Jesus Christ. Would that those who are baptized in the name of the Holy Trinity might agree on this, for in that case, the Church would indeed be universal, and the prayer of Christ fulfilled: "I do not pray for these only, but also for those who believe in me through their word, that they may all be one, even as you Father are in me, and I in you ... so that the world may believe that you have sent me" (John 17:20–21).[81]

81. RSV, translation slightly altered.

Chapter 6

The Same God?

The Voice of Karl Barth in the Maelstrom of Current Debates over the Relation of Islam to Christianity

Bruce L. McCormack

Nostra Aetate has been in the news of late as a result of the controversy at Wheaton College in December 2015 which led to the departure of Professor Larycia Hawkins from her tenured post on the faculty of that institution. The facts of that case, so far as they can be known, need not occupy us here. What is of interest for me as a Reformed and Protestant theologian is the fact that an eminent theologian like Miroslav Volf could claim in an op-ed piece for the *Washington Post*, "There isn't any theological justification for Hawkins' forced administrative leave. Her suspension is not about theology and orthodoxy. It is about enmity towards Muslims."[1] Now that is a strong statement, quite obviously; one which leaves no room for discussion. But lest it be thought that such rhetoric was inflated by the unjust treatment of Larycia Hawkins, consider what Volf wrote in his well-known book *Allah*:

> Since in monotheistic traditions convictions about God are repositories of ultimate values, if respective conceptions of God are radically different, then ultimate values are radically different. And if ultimate values are radically different, the people who espouse them *will not be able to negotiate their differences* successfully and will *inescapably* clash.... Muslims and Christians will be able to live in peace with one another *only if* (1) the identities of each religious group are respected and given

1. Miroslav Volf, "Wheaton Professor's Suspension is about Anti-Muslim Bigotry, not Theology," *The Washington Post*, December 17, 2015.

room for free expression, and (2) there are significant overlaps in the ultimate values that orient the lives of people in these communities. These two conditions *will be met only if* the God of the Bible and the God of the Qur'an turn out to embody overlapping ultimate values, that is, *if* Muslims and Christians … turn out to have "a common God."[2]

The absolute nature of this series of claims is noteworthy. Volf is clearly convinced that there can be no theological grounds whatsoever for Christians to live peaceably with Muslims other than a positive affirmation of what I will call the "same God" thesis. Those who fail to agree with this thesis make clashes between Christians and Muslims "inescapable." Their own role in fostering enmity is ensured, and the label "bigot" (employed in the title of Volf's op-ed piece) is hung around their necks without further ado.

The problem with Volf's blanket condemnation of any who have reservations with regard to the "same God" thesis is that it would have to apply not only to those conservative Evangelicals who use their "orthodoxy" to mask motivations which include racism and sexism but also to those modern Protestants who are convinced that the classical metaphysics which fed both classical Christian orthodoxy and Islam in their origins is no longer a live option—and who, as a consequence, do their thinking about Christology and Trinity "from below," on the basis of a starting point in the divine economy. To start "from below" (however that is defined) is to open the door wide to turning from consideration of the relation of the humanity of Christ to God into reflection upon the Trinitarian "persons" in their distinctiveness. Where this takes place, it is no longer possible to employ a "generic" concept of God, which is under-determined and improperly specified. Now the Trinitarian "persons" would need to be differentiated materially and not just formally (i.e., in terms of the so-called "modes of origination").

Volf makes his case much too easy by choosing "soft" targets for his polemic, like Pat Robertson and Albert Mohler Jr., whom he can safely assume his readers will want to see driven from the field. The truth is that the goal of living in peace with Muslims, of relating to them with love and respect, does not require acceptance of the "same God" thesis; other theological grounds—equally, if not more, compelling—can be adduced. And if that is the case, then the question of whether or not Christians and Muslims worship the same God ought to be one that can be reasonably and calmly discussed, without fear of fostering culture wars or furthering strife in the Middle East.

2. Miroslav Volf, *Allah: A Christian Response* (New York: Harper One, 2011), 8–9.

All of this is made amply clear through Karl Barth's friendly engagement with *Nostra Aetate*. It is to that engagement that I now turn.

Nostra Aetate and Karl Barth's Central Question

In its third section, *Nostra Aetate* takes up the knotty problem of the relation of the Catholic Church to Islam. The holy Council writes:

> The church has ... a high regard for Muslims. They worship God, who is one, living and subsistent, merciful and almighty, the Creator of heaven and earth, who has also spoken to humanity. They endeavor to submit themselves without reserve to the hidden decrees of God, just as Abraham submitted himself to God's plan, to whose faith Muslims eagerly link their own.... [T]hey await the day of judgment and the reward of God following the resurrection of the dead.[3]

Such claims are made against the background of a theological grounding of the relation of Christians to representatives of all other "non-Christian" religions back in section 1. "Humanity forms but one community. This is so because all stem from one stock which God created to people the entire earth (see Acts 17:26), and also because all share a common destiny, namely God."[4] We are also told in section 5: "We cannot truly pray to God the Father of all if we treat any people as other than sisters and brothers, for all are created in God's image."[5] On this showing, all human beings are "sisters and brothers" by virtue of their createdness. It is because this is so that the Council can say that all human beings form a single "community." Additionally, human beings are said to "share a common destiny, namely God." This would seem to be a somewhat vaguely expressed version of the more robust claim that all men and women are created with the same "supernatural end" in view, viz., the beatific vision. In any case, it suggests the unity of the human race at the beginning and at the end, albeit a unity that can be fractured by disobedience.

Karl Barth's central question to all of this is not surprising to anyone who knows his theology well:

> Would not the justifiable human concern of the declaration have been expressed better by adhering to the proven methods of Paul, the apostle to the Gentiles, in which he proclaimed nothing to Jews or Greeks but the One who had been crucified

3. "Nostra Aetate" in *The Basic Documents, Vatican Council II: Constitutions, Decrees and Declarations*, ed., by Austin Flannery, OP (Northport, N.Y./Dublin: Costello Publishing Company and Dominican Publications, 1996) §3.

4. *NA* §1.

5. *NA* §5.

for them—a stumbling block to the first and folly to the others—in order to address them as men [and women] from that point, and to call them to a realization of their common humanity?[6]

Notice that Barth does say that the Council has a justifiable concern. His question is whether that concern has been grounded theologically in an adequate way. Human beings, he is suggesting, are not "one" as created; they are made one, they become one, in the Christ who lived and died for all.

I call this question "central" to Barth's reflections on *Nostra Aetate* because in it one catches sight of the most fundamental disagreement between Barth and Roman Catholicism, which endured through the whole of his engagement with the latter: Does creation have an *independent* meaning or value (let's call it a "natural end") which is complete in itself without reference to the redeeming work of God in Christ? Or does creation exist for the sake of redemption—so that creation is wrongly understood where it is considered in abstraction from Christology? Where creation is thought to have an independent meaning or value that can be known naturally, it is usually the case that this meaning or value can be, and typically is, made to be the basis for some sort of natural theology. And so we arrive quite naturally at a "generic" conception of "deity," a conception available to anyone capable of drawing a few "correct" inferences with respect to God's being from the "nature" known by all.

But, then, Barth's protest against natural theology is itself a function of his belief that the speculative metaphysics of the pre-modern churches is no longer viable. And with the demise of classical metaphysics, there can no longer be any adequate ground for a "generic" conception of divine "oneness." Barth's starting point in the faith of the primitive churches as attested in the New Testament—above all, in the identity statement "Jesus is Lord" (Phil 2:9)—lays a new and different foundation for thinking about the being of God. This is seen clearly in Barth's doctrine of the Trinity.

At this point, it is necessary to look away from *Ad Limina Apostolorum* just a bit, to find in Barth's treatment of the Trinity the basis for the questions that he directed to *Nostra Aetate*.

6. Karl Barth, *Ad Limina Apostolorum* (Zurich: Evangelischer Verlag Zurich , 1967), 39; *Ad Limina Apostolorum* (Richmond: John Knox, 1968), 36. (Hereafter, *ALA*.)

Already in his first sketch of the doctrine of the Trinity, Barth makes it clear, by his decision to locate the doctrine within prolegomena, that this doctrine is the necessary presupposition of any responsible consideration of God's nature and attributes. For "it will not do to have God as a general concept within which the Christian God as he is basically known in the doctrine of the Trinity is only a special instance."[7] The debates that took place thirty years or so ago over whether it was best to begin consideration of the Trinity with the "three persons" or the "one" substance or Subject is a rather tame, in-house discussion in comparison with the ordering of the Trinity to the doctrine of the nature and attributes of God.

This prioritizing of the Trinity in Barth's dogmatics meant nothing less than that no talk of the Christian God can be responsible to its "object" which does not begin and end with the Self-disclosure of God in Jesus Christ. Barth's most basic conviction was this: only God can reveal God. The One who would reveal God must Himself be God.[8] Therefore, the "root" of the doctrine of the (immanent) Trinity is to be found in the "oldest Christian confession"—viz., that Jesus is "Lord,"[9] a name he shares with his Father.[10] The doctrine of the Trinity, historically, was a development of this basic belief.[11]

Barth then constructs his doctrine of the immanent Trinity on a foundation laid in the differentiation of economic "roles." Because God is present (complete, whole, and entire) in each of his "roles" as the acting Subject God is, we can justly say that when we have the differentiation of "roles" played by the divine "persons" in the self-revelation of God before us, we also have the differentiation of "persons" in themselves before us. The "roles" are the "modes of being" of the eternal God—and vice versa. That is the logic that drives Barth's construction of the doctrine of the Trinity from the earliest days of his dogmatic activity. This identification of the content of the economic Trinity and the content of the immanent Trinity is given axiomatic force in *Church Dogmatics* I/1 when Barth says, "Statements about the divine modes of being antecedently in themselves cannot be different in content from those that are made about their reality in revelation."[12]

7. Karl Barth, *The Göttingen Dogmatics: Instruction in the Christian Religion*, vol. 1 (Grand Rapids, Mich.: Eerdmans, 1991), 97–98.

8. Barth, *The Göttingen Dogmatics*, 117.

9. Barth, *The Göttingen Dogmatics*, 99.

10. Barth, *The Göttingen Dogmatics*, 117.

11. Barth, *The Göttingen Dogmatics*, 99.

12. Barth, *CD* I/1, 479.

And so it comes about that Barth's basic model of interpretation where the immanent or ontological Trinity is concerned is that of a single Subject in three modes of being; modes of being that are differentiated not simply by "modes of origination" but by differences in roles played in the realization of a shared "end" (i.e., the redemption of the world in Jesus Christ). An "eternal repetition in eternity" with a determinate telos in view; that is Barth's doctrine when viewed from the standpoint of its complete development.[13] To be sure, such a view allows him to find a grain of truth in the Trinitarian axiom of inseparable operations. If there is but a single divine Subject, then all that is done by God *ad extra* is done by this one Subject. But the modes of being are differentiated materially and not just formally. If the one Subject does something in his mode of being as Son, he is not doing it in his modes of being as Father and Spirit.

Lest it be thought that this rendering implies a God "behind" the modes (i.e., the Subject who acts in his modes), it has to be remembered that the life-act of God in which God has God's being is an eternal repetition of the Subject in his differing modes of being. The modes of being simply are what God is essentially. Essence and existence are one, but they are one in this specific sense.

Barth's preferred term for speaking of this state-of-affairs is *Dreieinigkeit*, "three in oneness."[14] The doctrine of the Trinity in his hands is not constructed by trying to think together a given concept of "oneness" with a given concept of "threeness." Rather, the concept of "three-in-oneness" has to arise out of a focus on the life-act of God, God's wholly necessary act of self-constitution as the God revealed in Jesus Christ. Numerical predication, like all human predication in relation to God, is at best analogical in nature.[15] It cannot be taken literally so as to imply that one already possesses a fixed concept of "oneness" in advance of acquiring a concept of "threeness" and then simply adds the latter to the former. Triunity in God goes all the way down, shaping and determining the idea of "oneness."

To put it this way is to suggest that the New Testament witness to the being of God in Christ requires—and, indeed, carries out—a reconstruction of the received idea of "oneness." This point has received strong confirmation in recent biblical theology. The name "Lord," "understood as God's own name" in the LXX rendering of Exodus 3:14, is transferred to Jesus Christ in

13. Barth, *CD* I/1, 350.
14. Barth, *CD* I/1, 369.
15. Barth, *CD* I/1, 354.

"the oldest texts in the New Testament, in terms of their transmission history, texts like Philippians 2:6–11."[16] Through the transfer of God's proper name to Jesus Christ, the very nature of God came quickly to be defined Christologically and God acquired a new proper name, that is, the name of "Father."[17] And so we find formulae like that in 1 Corinthians 8:6, "for us there is one God, the Father, from whom are all things and for whom we exist, and one Lord Jesus Christ, through whom are all things and through whom we exist." What is happening in such passages is that a relational metaphor, "Father," is now understood to be definitive of God's eternal nature and being. And the reason for this is that the giving of the name which is above all names to the exalted Jesus would have been unthinkable for those who continued to affirm faith in the God of Israel had they not also been convinced that Jesus Christ was proper to the identity of that God and had been "from the beginning." In other words, Jesus Christ does not first obtain a share in the identity of the God of Israel at the point of his exaltation. If he can be "given" this name, it is only because it is proper to him; it belongs to him and cannot be added. Richard Bauckham has argued that this "christological monotheism" became the instrument by means of which the earliest Christians reconciled the worship of Jesus with worship of the God of Israel.[18]

Through this process of Christological redefinition, the idea of the "oneness" of God is enriched and rendered complex, quite obviously. The "oneness" of God is now the "unity of Father and Son."[19] As a consequence, the center of gravity has shifted from an abstract (metaphysical) consideration of God's "unity" or "uniqueness" that could be found in the Hellenistic Judaism of the inter-testamental period to a relational conception of divine "oneness" with soteriological and ethical implications. As Reinhard Feldmeier and Hermann Spieckermann put it:

> In contradistinction to the "known" monotheism of the strong [in 1 Cor 8:4ff.], Paul formulates his understanding of God's uniqueness by not reducing it to the propositional truth of a singular divinity, a truth susceptible to misuse. God is one, instead,

16. Reinhard Feldmeier and Hermannn Spieckermann, *The God of the Living: A Biblical Theology* (Waco, Tex.: Baylor University Press, 2011), 43.

17. Feldmeier and Spieckermann, *The God of the Living*, 48: "The name 'Father,' employed of God over a hundred times in the Gospel of John, has now definitively become the new proper name of God." On the Christological redefining of God's nature, see ibid., 53.

18. Richard J. Bauckham, "The Worship of Jesus in Philippians 2:9–11," in *Where Christology Began: Essays on Philippians 2*, ed. Ralph P. Martin and Brian J. Dodd (Louisville, Ky.: Westminster John Knox, 1998), 128–39.

19. Feldmeier and Spieckermann, *The God of the Living*, 113.

as the one who is one with himself in relation to the other and [who] thus, as the power of love, also brings human beings together and makes them neighbors. God is thus the One to the extent that he is the One who, in unity with the Son, bestows unity.[20]

Returning then to Karl Barth, that Jesus Christ should be regarded as proper to the identity of the God of Israel was a long-held conviction of Barth's. The fact that he interpreted the concept of the Logos in John's prologue as already identified with "Jesus Christ" when it first appears in 1:1 is a strong indication that this is so. Indeed, he could go so far as to say that the "Logos" who appears in 1:1 is a "predicate" of Jesus rather than the other way around.[21] That is to say, Barth knows nothing of a "Logos *asarkos*" in and to whom is lacking a "determination" for incarnation; whose identity is complete in itself apart from and prior to election (since there is no "moment" prior to the divine election).

The conclusion toward which all of this presses is that the second person of the Trinity is a "compound person," not one of three (materially indistinguishable) instantiations of an abstract concept of unity and singularity. That such a conception stands at some distance from an instantiation of an Absolute (utterly simple, impassible and, in all likelihood, utterly ineffable) Trinitarian "person" is clear. The second person of the Trinity has a name—not just in time but in eternity-past. And that name is "Jesus Christ."

That conclusion is further strengthened by elements in Barth's later Christology in *Church Dogmatics* IV/1 and following. At a minimum, Barth posits in the "eternal Son" a humility and even an "obedience" to the Father's "command" as the ontological condition of the possibility in God of the humility and obedience of "Jesus Christ" in time. Even more likely, however, it was Barth's intention in claiming this much to suggest that the eternal Son's humility and obedience is only "real" in that it is rendered concrete in this world in the humility and obedience of the human Jesus. Put another way, the Trinitarian "person" we call the "Son" is God *as human*; a "compound person" whose humility and obedience in eternity and in time constitutes a singular history. God is the "Son" as human humility and obedience.

To say all of this is to press Barth to the very limits—and beyond—of

20. Feldmeier and Spieckermann, *The God of the Living*, 112.

21. Barth, *CD* II/2, 97. See on this point, Bruce L. McCormack, "The Identity of the Son: Karl Barth's Exegesis of Hebrews 1:1–4 (and Similar Passages)," in *Christology, Hermeneutics and Hebrews: Profiles from the History of Interpretation*, ed. Jon C. Laansma and Daniel J. Treier (London: T&T Clark, 2012), 155–72.

what he could himself say. I have written often enough about it and will say no more here. My point in this paper is that modern theologians who reacted to the onto-theologies of the past either through rejection or through attempts at reconstruction cannot easily return to the classical metaphysics presupposed in the "same God" thesis. Pragmatic arguments alone (no matter how laden with emotion they may be) will not effect conversions to ancient perspectives, especially when other grounds exist for living in peace with Muslims.

But I hope I have also made it amply clear that our taking up the challenge of the "same God" thesis has laid upon us the obligation to consider not only the doctrine of God but also the Trinity, Christology—and, had we time, atonement and theodicy (since divine suffering is the final outcome of Barth's later Christology). The calling of systematic theologians is to think organically across a range of doctrines when confronted by a challenge of the sort created by the "same God" thesis. Such a thesis cannot be treated atomistically without cost to the discipline itself.

Nostra Aetate Re-Visited: Extending Barth's Questions

Vatican II stopped short of saying that Christians and Muslims *worship* the same God. What is pointed to is, in fact, an overlap in the content assigned by both sides to "God" or "Allah." Muslims are said to believe in "one" God who is both merciful and almighty; the "Creator" of all that is not God ("heaven and earth"); the God who reveals God's self personally, by speaking to and through individuals (as was the case with the prophets of the Old Testament). They also believe in the divine predestination, the resurrection of the dead, and the final judgment. There is therefore "truth" to be found in Islam—something which the Council would have us look for in every religion. "The Catholic Church rejects nothing of what is true and holy in these religions."[22] The Council understands the presence of truth in religions other than Christianity as evidencing the presence of "a ray of that truth which enlightens all men and women" (which would seem to be an allusion to John 1:4).

What this adds up to, as Christoph Schwöbel has pointed out, is not the claim that Christians and Muslims worship the same God but the more modest proposal that they "have" the same God.[23] That means, I would

22. *NA* §2.
23. Christoph Schwöbel, "The Same God? The Perspective of Faith, the Identity of God, Tolerance

take it, that it is one and the same God to whom each is responsible. Now, that could mean no more than that there is only one God and no others. Everyone will have to contend with one and the same God in the final judgment. But it could also mean that the two religions have been addressed and engaged by the same God. The degree of conceptual overlap affirmed by the Council in their respective God-concepts suggests the latter. But the Council does not explicitly draw this conclusion. It leaves the question open and does so, I would say, in a spirit of generosity and humility.

It is of interest here to pay close attention to what Barth says about John 1:4 (which reads, "In him was life, and the life was the light of men"). He does not understand "the life" as "the general life of creation" (looking back at 1:3) but as the "light" of revelation.[24] Barth's exegetical decision here is based on the observation that elsewhere in John's Gospel, the word "life" is consistently given a "soteriological-eschatological" meaning. It is the "life" which the Son has received from the Father (5:26), which is offered to all those who believe in him (6:33, 51), and which he himself is (14:6).[25] And so it comes as no surprise that Barth does not understand "light" as "given in and with the life of creation"[26] (i.e., as a natural light) but rather as coming with that redemption in which a share in eternal life is promised and received by faith. "God's self-revealing is a separate action that goes beyond creation. In relation to what was made, to its life and to the knowledge that may be gained from it, *phōs* [in 1:4] is a new and different light which is only arising. It is the light of dawn, not the full light of eternity already present."[27] Just as the "life" is the "life which overcomes death" and not natural life, so also the "light" spoken of in John 1:5 refers to the in-breaking of the eschatological light which Jesus Christ himself is in his appearing. And so, wherever there is light, it is his "light;" the "light" which he himself is.

It would be strange to try to understand this "light" as portioned out, divided or partial. The "light" shines in the darkness wherever Jesus Christ is in the fullness of his reality, where he gives himself to be known. Talk of a "ray of that truth which enlightens all men and women" as occurs in *Nostra Aetate* would seem to entail an identification of "light" with the so-called "light of reason" or some such thing, a sharing by nature in the divine light.

---

and Dialogue," in *Do We Worship the Same God? Jews, Christians, and Muslims in Dialogue*, ed. Miroslav Volf (Grand Rapids, Mich.: Eerdmans, 2012), 1–17 at 17.

24. Karl Barth, *Witness to the Word: A Commentary on John 1*, trans. Geoffrey W. Bromiley (Grand Rapids, Mich.: Eerdmans, 1986), 37.

25. Barth, *Witness to the Word*, 39.

26. Barth, *Witness to the Word*, 39.

27. Barth, *Witness to the Word*, 40.

And that, from Barth's perspective, would mean the evacuation of the New Testament witness of the eschatology that is basic to it.

The difficulties surrounding the talk of "brothers and sisters" stand in parallel to those difficulties just considered. In Paul's writings, especially, it is quite clear that the status of "brothers and sisters" is something that is bestowed by the "Spirit of adoption" (Rom 8:15) in that a sinner is justified and regenerated. To be "adopted" is to be given a share in Christ's natural sonship (since he alone is Son by nature). And it is to be made an heir to all the gifts that are bestowed upon him by the Spirit (Rom 8:17). It is a status that is realized individual by individual, as persons are awakened to faith and obedience. But even the word "status" is incorrect. Being a son or daughter of God is a lived relation, not a state of "being." And so Paul can also say that creation still awaits *with longing* "the revealing of the children of God" (Rom 8:19) and that "we wait for adoption" (Rom 8:23). "Adoption," like justification and regeneration, is an eschatological event which is complete in the here and now not "in" us but "for" us in Christ. It is Barth's great merit, I think, to have captured the eschatological element in Paul's thinking about "sons and daughters" of God.

Thus far, the theological grounding of Barth's questions to *Nostra Aetate*. We have not yet even mentioned, however, the questions that Barth regarded as most pressing in his own day where an engagement of Judaism and Islam are concerned. And our presentation of Barth's response to *Nostra Aetate* would be not only incomplete but distorted if these questions were not raised.

On "Religions" and the Question of Guilt

In his meeting in Rome with Cardinal Bea—who was a principle architect of *Nostra Aetate* and the person responsible for his invitation—Barth pointed to the temptation that immediately arises where Christianity is placed on a common field of comparison with the other "religions." There had never been a question for Barth as to whether Christianity was a religion. But, as he pointed out to Bea, in words reminiscent of his early critiques of religion in the second decade of the twentieth century, "Religion is the most dangerous form of human pride; on the Tower of Babel there stood, crowning all, an altar!"[28] The temptation that lies ready to hand is that the

28. This statement has been lifted from Eberhard Busch's diary, kept while he was personal secretary to Karl Barth in the final three years of the latter's life. There is no guarantee that the words are

"religions" under comparison will be arranged in some sort of taxonomy in which some "religions" are considered "high religions" while others are treated as "primitive," and Christianity will be regarded as the "highest" of the high religions, as their completion. Where this happens, it becomes very hard for adherents of the "highest" religion to acknowledge their sins, to confess their guilt. In saying this much, Barth was only preparing the ground to suggest that, if Christianity were truly the "highest religion," then it would show itself to be such through a confession of guilt for its behavior in relation to both Judaism and Islam. For his part, Bea thought that a confession of guilt in relation to the Jews was unnecessary. *Nostra Aetate* had repudiated persecution of the Jews; what more was needed? Barth's answer, obviously, was an admission on the part of the Church that it had failed to live up to this standard throughout its history, with devastating consequences. As far as a confession of guilt in relation to Islam was concerned, Bea thought Barth must be joking.[29]

And so we come to the last three of Barth's critical questions raised in response to the Council. He asks in question 6, "On what basis does the Declaration (4,1ff.) speak of the past and present history of Israel in the same breath with Hinduism, Buddhism, and Islam as a 'non-Christian' religion, while . . . the Old Testament does not present a religion at all but the original form of the one revelation of God?" In question 7 he inquires, "Would it not be more appropriate, in view of the anti-Semitism of the ancient, medieval, and to a large degree the modern church, to set forth an explicit confession of guilt here . . . ? And, in 3,2, where Islam is mentioned, would not such a confession be appropriate in view of the deplorable role of the Church in the so-called Crusades?"[30]

I think that any fair-minded person would have to admit that Barth was way ahead of his time in calling for a confession of guilt in relation not only to the Jews but also to Muslims. And it is striking that he did not need to find a basis for doing so in the "same God" thesis. He found it instead in the obligations laid upon Christians by the fact that the redemptive activity of God in Christ was meant for Christians too—though not only for them!

Barth's, clearly. But the diary entry which records Barth's "report" of his experiences in Rome was written on the evening of their conversation—and just six days after Barth's return. There is little if any reason to question the general accuracy of what is recorded here. And Barth's comments do mesh, as we shall see, quite nicely with the critical questions he had prepared for his Roman interlocutors. See Busch, *Meine Zeit mit Karl Barth: Tagebuch 1965–68* (Göttingen: Vandenhoeck & Ruprecht, 2011), 87 (for the entry dated October 5, 1966).

29. Busch, *Meine Zeit mit Karl Barth*, 87.

30. Barth, *ALA*, 36–37.

I conclude then with a few historical observations and one or two constructive thoughts of my own.

An Important Challenge for Those Hesitant with Regard to the "Same God" Thesis

It is common for those who defend the thesis that Christians and Muslims worship the same God to assert that rejection of that thesis would have a necessarily negative impact on the relation of Christians to Jews. The basic claim is that if the triune God of Christians is not the "God of Abraham, Isaac, and Jacob" worshiped by Muslims, then the triune God cannot be the same God as is worshiped by Jews either. But is it really so simple as that?

It should go without saying that, in a Protestant dogmatics, it is Holy Scripture which provides *the* source and norm of what can and should be said. The relation of Islam to Christianity is, self-evidently, not a topic that could have come in for consideration in the Christian canon, inasmuch as the origins of the two faiths are separated by centuries. What is said in the New Testament, however, about the relation of Christian faith to the faith of Israel is considerable—and on close inspection, does not admit of addition or diminution. The reason is as follows.

The incarnation of God in Jesus Christ attested in a wide range of passages in the New Testament is the ultimate ground of the belief held by the earliest Christians that he is the fulfilment of the covenant promises of God and the culmination of God's missionary work in the world through the history of Israel. That Islam also claims for itself the status of fulfilment and culmination is not to be denied, of course. But to accept that claim is not only to set aside the Christian claim (and the theological grounding of it in the Incarnation), it is also to set aside the basis of the Christian understanding of the relation of Christians to Jews—which makes a conversation about Christians and Jews to unfold on a basis other than that provided in the New Testament witness.

The most significant passage in this regard is Romans 9–11. In 9:4–5, Paul writes: "They are Israelites, and to them belong the adoption, the glory, the covenants, the giving of the law, the worship, and the promises; to them belong the patriarchs, and from them, according to the flesh, comes the Messiah, who is over all, God blessed forever. Amen." And, even more significantly, in Romans 11:29, "the gifts and the calling of God are irrevocable." Commenting upon the first of these passages, Karl Barth had this to say:

> [T]he existence of the Synagogue side by side with the Church is an ontological impossibility, a wound, a gaping hole in the body of Christ, something which is quite intolerable. For what does the Church have which the Synagogue does not also have, and long before it (Rom 9:4–5)—especially Jesus Christ Himself, who is of the Jews, who is the Jewish Messiah, and only as such the Lord of the Church. The decisive question is not what the Jewish Synagogue can be without Him, but what the Church is as long as it confronts an alien and hostile Israel? "Jewish missions" is not the right word for the call to remove this breach, a call which must go out unceasingly from the Church to these brethren who do not yet know either unity with it—a unity which does not have to be established but is already there ontologically, who will not accept what they already are, and what they were long before us poor Gentiles.[31]

That God is not finished with Israel "according to the flesh" is made amply clear in Romans 11:25–32. The "end of history" which will take place when the Redeemer comes from Zion will mean a final joining of Jews and Christians in a single body of those made fit to offer God eternal praise in his kingdom. And this is not treated by Paul as an "accident," as an *ad hoc* solution to a spiritual catastrophe which God had somehow not anticipated before creating and "permitting" the Fall. It was in accordance with the divine election in which the end of history was contained "from the beginning."

It is because all of this is so that Karl Barth could describe the Church and the Synagogue as two forms of the one community of faith. The root of this description is to be found in the Pauline affirmation in Ephesians 1:4 that those who will finally believe were "chosen" in Christ "before the foundation of the world." What we do not find in the New Testament is any sufficient reason to think that the elect of God constitute a community in three forms (the Church, the Synagogue and the Mosque). We are, of course, free to hope that is the case, just as we may hope for universal salvation. But on what basis could we teach it as dogma?

The bottom line is this: Christians find ample reason in their scriptures to understand that the Church is bound to the Synagogue in a relation of ontological oneness, regardless of what decision they make with regard to their relation to Islam. But it is interesting to turn the question around. Would the defenders of the "same God" thesis be willing to declare that the elect of God form one community in three forms? Even to raise such a question brings clearly into the light of day the limitations of the work done up to this point in defending it. No attempt has been made to explore the ecclesiological and Christological implications of the thesis, all of which testifies

31. Barth, *CD* IV/1, 671.

to the fact that it finds its home more nearly in the realm of comparative religions (and the pragmatics of politics) than it does in theology.

Where Do We Now Stand?

Nothing that has been said constitutes a dogmatic rejection of the "same God" thesis. Not in the least. From a Barthian perspective, the question of whether Christians and Muslims worship the same God has to be left open. It stands just outside of the limits of what can be said in the sphere of dogmatics and belongs more nearly to hope than to the knowledge of faith. The holy Council showed great wisdom, I think, in neither affirming nor denying such a thesis. It ought never to be made the stuff of dogmatic proclamation.

But ample reason for hope does exist. And it is here that we return to where I started. There are theological grounds for peace and cooperation between Christians and Muslims—even in the absence of dogmatic affirmation of the "same God" thesis. Barth's understanding of election is, as is well-known, universal in scope. All human beings are elect in Jesus Christ from the foundations of the world. All have a determination for fellowship with God in Christ. Barth also—again rather famously—maintains that it is possible for an individual to resist her/his determination for fellowship and to do so without end. It is for this reason that a universal salvation at the end of history can only be a matter of hope and not a matter of knowledge. All human beings are given in Christ a determination for redemptive fellowship with the triune God. But Barth maintains that it is possible to continue to live in contradiction to one's true being; an impossible possibility to be sure, but a real possibility. And so we can only hope. But this much we can say with certainty. Christ died in the place of all human beings who were chosen in Him. The atoning work of Christ is for all. And that is reason enough to treat every person we meet as, in Barth's phrase, a brother or sister "*in spe*."[32] That is reason enough to want to live in peace with Muslims, to want to honor in them the *exalted* humanity that is theirs too in Christ.

Conclusion

In his book *Allah*, Miroslav Volf says that there are three criteria of material overlap in their respective concepts of God that are sufficient to guarantee that Christians and Muslims worship the "same God." They are: (1) belief

32. Barth, *CD* IV/3, 885.

that "there is only one God"; (2) belief that "God created everything that is not God"; and (3) belief that "God is different from everything that is not God."[33] It is not obvious, however, that any of the three beliefs in question is material in nature as they stand. Even the concept of "one-ness" remains a formal concept of numerical identity unless and until it is combined in some way with lived existence—and with that, an answer to the question of how this concept of one-ness can arise out of a logically prior concept of a unified, fully self-conscious subject.

Beyond that reservation, however, there is this. Surely, Plotinus could have met all of these criteria, formal as they are. Are we then to say that Plotinus too worshiped the "same God" as Christians and Muslims? Can we really say this with conviction, as belonging to the knowledge of faith? It would seem to me that the discussion to this point has been carried out from a perspective with the lowest possible degree of visual resolution. What is needed is for the discussion to become genuinely theological; that would mean thinking carefully across a range of doctrines in their organic relatedness. Until that should happen, the better part of wisdom is to exercise the charity as well as the restraint of *Nostra Aetate*—neither affirming nor denying the "same God" thesis but leaving the question open as one does with all questions belonging to eschatology.

33. Volf, *Allah*, 97–98.

Chapter 7

The Diversity of Religions and the Paschal Mystery

Bruce D. Marshall

Anniversaries, Celebrated and Overlooked

By the fall of 2015 fifty years had passed since the ratification of *Nostra Aetate* during the last months of the Second Vatican Council. The anniversary was widely noted. My own diocese of Dallas took the step of sponsoring a conference devoted specifically to reflection on and celebration of *Nostra Aetate*, and events of this kind were not uncommon throughout the Catholic Church in Europe and North America. December 2015 marked, of course, the fiftieth anniversary of the conclusion of Vatican II, by any measure an event of epoch-making importance not only in the Catholic world but in the world at large. Among Catholics the achievement of the Council that seemed most worth celebrating fifty years later was evidently *Nostra Aetate*. Of all that was said and done at Vatican II, it was the Council's declaration of openness to all that "is true and holy"[1] in the world's religions that Catholics especially wanted to remember and declare once again to the world, together with the Council's emphatic repudiation of antisemitism and its plea for a new beginning in the Church's relationship with the Jewish people, "the stock of Abraham."[2]

Less frequently remembered in celebrations of Vatican II's fiftieth anniversary was the Council's decree on missions, *Ad Gentes*, ratified on the last working day of the Council in December 1965. This inattention to the decree

I am grateful to Paul Griffiths for his comments on a preliminary version of this chapter.

1. *NA* §2.
2. *NA* §4.

on the Church's missionary activity during the anniversary year was nothing new. Though it is one of the longest documents the Council produced (exceeded in this respect only by *Lumen Gentium* and *Gaudium et Spes*), and though it has the status of a decree, whose teaching binds the Church's members, rather than (as with *NA*) the lower status of a declaration, which chiefly concerns those outside the Church, interest in *Ad Gentes* over the last fifty years has lagged far behind the enthusiasm that has greeted *Nostra Aetate* in the reception of the Council. In fact it seems fair to say that *Ad Gentes*, while it has not been treated so lightly as, say, the decree on the media or "social communication" (*Inter Mirifica*), is among the least deeply received texts of the Council.

The reason for this neglect is perhaps not difficult to discern. *Nostra Aetate* §2 signals the Church's embrace of all that is true and holy in the religious traditions of humanity, her "high regard" for the beliefs and practices of other religious traditions, even though they differ "in many ways from her own teaching."[3] By contrast *Ad Gentes* §9 teaches that the missionary activity of the Catholic Church "purges of evil associations those elements of truth and grace which are found among peoples"—including those elements of truth and grace (or holiness) bound up with their religious traditions, which "need to be enlightened and corrected" by the missionary Church.[4] The Church's mission in the world "restores," moreover, these elements of truth and grace "to Christ their source who overthrows the rule of the devil and limits the manifold malice of evil."[5] The Church's missionary activity frees the world, including its religions, from the grip of demons in which it is otherwise held. If we follow the lead of *Ad Gentes* §9, it seems that the Church can fully embrace truth and holiness in the religions of the world only as a *result* of her own successful mission to the world, when the mis-

3. "High regard" is the rendering of the Latin original's "sincera cum observantia" in Austin Flannery, OP, ed., *Vatican Council II*, vol. 1: *The Conciliar and Post-Conciliar Documents* (rev. ed., Northport, N.Y.: Costello Publishing, 1996), 739. The Vatican website (http://www.vatican.va/archive/hist_councils/ii_vatican_council/documents/vat-ii_decl_19651028_nostra-aetate_en.html) has "regards with sincere reverence," but "with sincere respect" would probably be closer to the mark. In any case it is clear that *NA* §2 is not neutral about the phenomenon of religious diversity, but sees it as a good. If the text were neutral on this score it would simply observe that there are religious ways "of life and conduct ... precepts and doctrines" that differ from those of the Catholic Church. But it prefixes to this observation a positive evaluation: "Ecclesia catholica ... Sincera cum observantia considerat illos modos agendi et vivendi, illa praecepta et doctrinas" ("The Catholic Church regards these ways of life and conduct, these precepts and doctrines, with sincere respect").

All translations are my own. I will draw on both the Flannery and Vatican website translations of Vatican II, but have also freely modified them in light of the Latin originals, as found in *Acta Apostolicae Sedis* (for *NA*, *AAS* 58 [1966], 740–44; for *AG*, ibid., 947–90).

4. *AG* §3.

5. *AG* §9.

sionary Church has, by the working of divine power, purged those extra-ecclesial traces of truth and holiness of the demonic distortions introduced by sin. Properly appreciating what is true and holy in non-Christian religions is, if we follow this line of conciliar thought, not the presupposition, but the outcome, of fruitful missionary activity—of conversion to Christ.

We can put the contrast between the two texts, *Nostra Aetate* and *Ad Gentes*, more broadly. Whereas *Nostra Aetate* seems like a license for Catholics to celebrate religious diversity, *Ad Gentes* plainly and unsparingly teaches that God calls every human being to life in the Roman Catholic Church. The Catholic Church, *Ad Gentes* says at the outset (to Karl Barth's manifest annoyance), is "called upon to save and renew every creature."[6] The Church does this, of course, not as an independent agent, but by a caused causation, acting as Christ's "sacrament,"[7] servant, and instrument,[8] and in particular as his body, in which all are offered and called to divine life in baptism.[9] The Catholic Church has the "obligation"[10] and, indeed, the "sacred right"[11] to evangelize the whole world ("all men"), to send out preachers of the gospel for the express purpose of "implanting the Church among people who do not yet believe in Christ."[12]

Essentially the same point about the reach of the Church's mission had been made, if more briefly, in *Lumen Gentium*, ratified by the Council a year before *Ad Gentes*. That document, which can certainly not be said to have lacked a significant reception, begins by taking as its subject matter the Catholic Church's "nature and *universal* mission."[13] *Lumen Gentium* goes on to say that "[a]ll men are called to belong to the new People of God"[14]—a definite description whose referent *Nostra Aetate* itself strikingly equates with that of the term "Church": "it is true that the Church is the new People

6. *AG* §1. Karl Barth, *Ad Limina Apostolorum*, 2nd ed. (Zürich: EVZ Verlag, 1967), 37: "Wieder und wieder: ist es die *Kirche*, die die Welt *errettet* und *erneuert* ([*AG*]1, 1)? Ist ihre Aufgabe, zwischen dem ersten und letzten Advent Jesu Christi ([*AG*] 9, 1) durch die Verkündigung des Evangeliums von ihm *Zeugnis* zu geben, nicht groß und herrlich genug?" (Barth's emphasis). "Again and again: is it the *Church* that *saves* and *renews* the world? Is its task of bearing *witness* to Jesus Christ between his first and last advent by the proclamation of the gospel not great and glorious enough?" An English version of the whole is *Ad Limina Apostolorum: An Appraisal of Vatican II*, trans. Keith R. Crim (Richmond, Va.: John Knox Press, 1968); for this passage, see 34. (Hereafter, *ALA*.)

7. *AG* §§1, 5.

8. Cf. *LG* §13.

9. *AG* §7.

10. *AG* §1.

11. *AG* §7.

12. *AG* §6.

13. *LG* §1, my emphasis. The text is in *AAS* 57 (1965), 5–75.

14. *LG* §13.

of God."[15] An insistence on the Catholic Church's mission to bring every human being within her own fold is thus deep-laid in the teaching of Vatican II, at least as much as the better known and more widely celebrated teaching that the Church "rejects nothing that is true and holy" outside her own visible boundaries, especially in the teaching and practice of other religions.[16]

The teaching of Vatican II on the Catholic Church's relation with non-Christian religions thus presents us with a perplexity. On the one hand the Council seems to present the diversity of religions not simply as a fact, but as a good, one that is, as such, to be welcomed by the Church. On the other hand the Council seems to present non-Christian religions as an obstacle to her own divinely given mandate to evangelize the whole world, an obstacle that must be overcome so that the light of Christ may shine clearly, and be seen for what it is, namely the one light of the world. To that extent, the diversity of religions is not a good to be embraced, but a barrier to be surmounted, if not an evil to be opposed.

At first glance it may seem as though we do not yet have a genuinely theological perplexity here, but only a practical problem, albeit a big one. It's not obvious, in other words, that there is actually a contradiction or antinomy between the claim that there is truth and goodness in non-Christian religions for the Church to embrace, and the imperative to seek out every human being for the Catholic fold. As *Nostra Aetate* §2 urges, Christians need to see all truth and holiness, including that present in the religions of the world, as "a ray of that truth which enlightens all men," the truth that is Christ himself. The missionary imperative thus coheres straightforwardly, it would seem, with the recognition of truth and goodness in the religions whose adherents we seek to evangelize. We need only help them open their eyes to the fact that the light they already see, more or less clearly, in their own religion is in truth the light of Christ. We need to do this in a way that does not seem to disparage or discredit their religion in the process. To the extent that they are attached to their religion, and committed to following it, disregard for that religion on the part of the missionary Church may discourage them from seeing that its true purpose is to point them to our religion—that is, to Christ and his Church. Thus the often great practical delicacy and difficulty of the task. But there is no reason in principle, one might argue,

15. *NA* §4. "Church" refers, in turn, to "the Roman Catholic Church"; that is always the primary and, as it were, sole indisputable referent of the term "Church" (cf. *LG* §8).

16. *NA* §2.

why the Catholic Church cannot appreciate truth and holiness wherever she finds them, and at the same time seek to attract all who are touched by this extra-ecclesial truth and holiness into the Catholic Church, whose head is the true light who enlightens every human being (cf. Jn. 1:9). There is no theological problem here.

I think the teaching of Vatican II on the Church and non-Christian religions actually does pose a deeper and more difficult theological problem than this sort of argument suggests. In order see how, it will be useful to think a bit about *Nostra Aetate* §4, and its much-discussed teaching on the Church and the Jewish people.

The Purposes of *Nostra Aetate*

Nostra Aetate began not as a statement on the Catholic Church's relation to non-Christian religions but as a conciliar text on the Jewish people. That the Council would work on a text specifically on the Jews and Judaism was the result of an express directive of John XXIII, who had signaled in many ways his desire for better relations between the Church and the Jewish people, perhaps most publicly by his revision of the Good Friday prayer for the Jews in 1959. In September 1960 the Pope charged Cardinal Bea that the new Secretariat for Promoting Christian Unity prepare a declaration on the Jewish people for consideration by the Council. The path from the Pope's initiative to the final approval of *Nostra Aetate* in October 1965 was, in Bea's own words, "notable because of great difficulties, not all of which were theological, for some were partly due to the unhappy political circumstances of our time."[17] In fact public opposition in the Arab world to any positive gesture toward the Jews on the part of the Council was so vehement, not least among Arab Catholics, that the statement on the Jews was for a time withdrawn from the Council's agenda. It was later reintroduced (again at the

17. Augustin Cardinal Bea, SJ, *The Church and the Jewish People: A Commentary on the Second Vatican Council's Declaration on the Relation of the Church to Non-Christian Religions*, trans. Philip Loretz, SJ (New York: Harper and Row, 1966), 22–23. Bea's reading of *Nostra Aetate* has special significance, since he was chiefly responsible for the preparation of the text and for shepherding it through the Council. His account of the text's history is, however, very brief. There are numerous detailed histories of the events leading up to the promulgation of *NA*, which do not, however, always avoid being tendentious, particularly by reducing theological questions to political or moral positions (and failings). See John M. Oesterreicher (himself a significant figure in the genesis of the text), "Introduction and Commentary," in Herbert Vorgrimler, ed., *Commentary on the Documents of Vatican II*, vol. 3 (New York: Herder and Herder, 1969), 1–136; *History of Vatican II*, 5 vols., ed. Giuseppe Alberigo and Joseph A. Komonchak (Maryknoll, N.Y./Leuven: Orbis/Peeters: 1995–2006), with relevant material spread across all five volumes.

insistence of John XXIII) as part of a broader treatment of the Church and non-Christian religions. The text on non-Christian religions initially took shape as an awkward addendum to the decree on ecumenism but eventually became a separate document. The virtually unanimous final vote in favor on *Nostra Aetate* is particularly remarkable when one considers how difficult it was to bring such a document before the Council in the first place.

That a text originally designed as a statement on the Jewish people came to be included in a declaration on non-Christian religions as a whole, and that "as a matter of prudence" rather than for reasons of doctrinal or theological principle, no doubt explains why *Nostra Aetate* cannot plausibly be said to give a balanced treatment of its alleged subject matter, namely non-Christian religions.[18] As a colleague has put it, the staple marks remain visible in the final text. The obvious joint lies between §§1–3, which treat of the human religious quest and comment briefly on Hinduism, Buddhism, and Islam, and §4, which treats the Jews and Judaism and makes up close to half of the total length of the document.

This manifest disparity makes it odd on its face for Karl Barth to complain that *Nostra Aetate* treats Judaism merely as one among many religions of the world, "in the same breath" with other "non-Christian religion[s]."[19] *Nostra Aetate* is obviously far more concerned about the Jews than it is about the adherents of any other religion, and it treats both the Jewish people and their religion quite differently than it treats any others. This is based, among other things, on the shared acceptance in Judaism and Christianity of what *Nostra Aetate* §4 calls "the revelation of the Old Testament," coupled with Christianity's dependence on the Jewish people for the reception of this revelation.[20] Still, Judaism is clearly a "non-Christian religion," at least in the sense that the Jewish community has traditionally regarded it as apostasy from Judaism for a Jew to become a Christian. From the Jewish point of view, in other words, and probably also from the Christian, the two religions can share no adherents, and so as religious communities they can share no members.[21] Yet for Catholics, so *Nostra Aetate* 4 teaches, the Jewish people

18. The quoted phrase is from Bea, *Church and the Jewish People*, 23.

19. Barth, *ALA*, 39 (ET: 36).

20. Barth seems to have forgotten the quoted passage when he observes, as though it were an objection to *NA* §4, that "in the Old Testament it is not a matter of a 'religion' but of the primal form of the one revelation of God" (*ALA*, 40 [ET: 36]).

21. Today Messianic Jews, who often understand themselves to be at once Jews and Christians (the latter in belief if not always in name), pose an obvious challenge to traditional ways of distinguishing church and synagogue. The Christian, and even more the Jewish, community has so far greeted Messianic Jewish claims with notable reserve.

and their religion occupy a position of intimacy with the Church and her faith that can, in the nature of the case, be held by no other people, and no other religion.

Of the Jewish people, alone among "those who have not yet received the Gospel,"[22] the Church claims to know something quite definite about their place in the saving plan of God. As the Scripture shared by Jews and Christians teaches at its heart, and as the apostle Paul deliberately reaffirms even in the face of Israel's rejection of her Messiah, God has chosen this people from among the nations to be his own. He has done so, as the New Testament also clearly teaches, to prepare for and prefigure "that new and perfect covenant which was to be ratified in Christ."[23] That God's choice of the Jewish people, his decision to mark them off from the nations, is part of his larger purpose of salvation in Christ does not mean that the election of the Jews is temporary. Paraphrasing Rom 11:29, *Nostra Aetate* §4 teaches that "the Jews remain very dear to God, for the sake of the patriarchs, for God does not take back the gifts he bestowed or the choice he made."[24] Note that the text says "the Jews" remain dear to God, not simply those who practice the Jewish religion; the subject of *Nostra Aetate* §4 is explicitly "the stock of Abraham," the Jewish people as such. To this extent *Nostra Aetate* seems congruent with Jewish law and Jewish self-understanding, where being a descendent of Abraham according to the flesh is what makes one a Jew, prior to, and even apart from, the practice of Judaism (however lamentable the failure to lead a halakhic life is in Jewish self-understanding).

Nostra Aetate evidently teaches the abiding and permanent character of Jewish election, of God's decision to separate from the nations Israel according to the flesh, and to reserve for her a relationship of special intimacy with himself. With the authority of an ecumenical council Vatican II insists, we could say, that the scriptural witness to the election of Israel be read in this way. It not only reaffirms the scriptural teaching that the Jews remain dear to God but discovers in that teaching an irrevocable element of Catholic faith itself. This way of understanding the special place of the Jewish people in the purposes of God has often been reasserted by the subsequent magisterium, particularly in the teaching of John Paul II, who spoke to the Jewish community in Rome of the Church's faith that "the Jews are beloved of God,

22. *LG* §16.
23. *LG* §9.
24. See, similarly, *LG* §16.

who has called them with an irrevocable calling," and elsewhere insisted that "the Old Covenant" was "never revoked by God."[25]

Granted Catholic faith in Jewish election, are the Jews nonetheless included in the missionary mandate of the Catholic Church? If we take our cues from *Ad Gentes*, the answer would clearly seem to be yes. "All have need of Christ, who is the model, master, liberator, savior, and giver of life."[26] As *Nostra Aetate* §4 also does not fail to insist, "Christ out of infinite love freely underwent suffering and death because of the sins of all men, so that all might attain salvation." Consequently "everyone ... ought to be converted to Christ, who is made known through the preaching of the Church, and they ought, by baptism, to become incorporated into him, and into the Church, which is his body."[27] The mandate is divine and universal; it makes present God's own call to life in Christ, and it excludes no human being. God's covenant with the Jewish people has never been revoked, the stock of Abraham remains very dear to God, and just for that reason, it would seem, the Church must reach out in mission to the Jewish people, inviting them to share the life of what *Lumen Gentium* 9 calls "the new Israel, which ... is the Church of Christ," or what *Nostra Aetate* §4 itself calls "the new people of God."

If we pursue the question further, however, the answer becomes much less clear. The election of Israel is basic to God's saving purposes in the world, but it is not an end in itself. Israel, we could say, is elected *as* the fleshly descendants of Abraham, Isaac, and Jacob, but the Jewish people is elected *for* a distinctive holiness, a communal way of life in the world unique to them, consisting in obedience to the commandments God gave to them alone. The Jewish people is even now chosen by God (if the election of Israel is irrevocable) to be a sign to all the nations not chosen. By their Torah-observant life the elect people is, indeed, a kind of sacrament of God's presence and saving purposes in the world—from a Christian point of view, of course, saving purposes fully realized in Jesus Christ. For any individual, having a Jewish mother (or being ritually converted to Judaism) is, according to rabbinic norms, enough to make him or her a Jew. But for the Jewish people as a whole, the commandments of the Torah, and a visible degree of communal commitment

25. John Paul II, *Spiritual Pilgrimage: Texts on Jews and Judaism 1979–1995*, ed. Eugene J. Fisher and Leon Klenicki (New York: Crossroad, 1995), 63, 15. On John Paul II and the Jews see my essay, "Elder Brothers: John Paul II's Teaching on the Jewish People as a Question to the Church," in *John Paul II and the Jewish People: A Christian-Jewish Dialogue*, ed. David Dahlin and Matthew Levering (Lanham, Md.: Rowman and Littlefield, 2008), 113–29.

26. *AG* §8.

27. *AG* §7; cf. *NA* §4, last sentence.

to observing them, is necessary in order for this people to remain distinct from the mass of gentiles, from the nations. Without the commandments God gave to the elect people as binding on their life until the end of time, they would cease to be distinct from the nations, and their election itself would be void. It would, in other words, have been "revoked."

So according to Catholic faith, Israel remains God's elect people, now and forever. In order for the Jewish people to carry out the mission for which they were elected, however, and in order to secure the distinction from the nations on which that mission depends, God gives the Jewish people the Torah, and bids them to keep it, now and forever. And this is simply to say that God bids the Jewish people to practice the Jewish religion, until the end of time. "God does not take back the gifts he bestowed or the choice he made."[28] The choice is to single out Abraham's descendants so that they may be a sign to all the gentiles, and God's chief gift, a condition *sine qua non* for effectively carrying out his choice, is the Torah, the Jewish religion.

We thus find ourselves confronted with a problem, the solution to which is not immediately evident. According to Catholic teaching, God bids every human being to enter the Church and to live her sacramental life, that is, to practice the Catholic religion. Also according to Catholic teaching, God elects the Jewish people irrevocably, and as a result bids at least some human beings, the descendants of Abraham, Isaac, and Jacob, not to practice the Catholic religion, but to practice Judaism. According to Catholic teaching, therefore, the Church's missionary mandate both is, and is not, universal.[29]

A Providential Diversity of Religions?

At least when it comes to Judaism, therefore, *Nostra Aetate* §2's teaching on the presence of truth and holiness in non-Christian religions seems to cut quite deep. The election of Israel appears to count as very strong evidence,

28. *NA* §4.

29. My purpose here is not to treat the Church's relationship with the Jews and Judaism (the subject of *NA* §4), but her relationship with other non-Christian religions (the subject of *NA* §§1–3). I introduce the perplexity evident in juxtaposing *NA* §4 on the election of Israel with *AG* §§1–9 on the Church's universal missionary vocation only to exhibit, in its most acute form, a tension visible throughout the Council's teaching on the Church and non-Christian religions (as I will argue in the next section). Elsewhere I have spelled out more precisely the apparent contradiction involved in believing both that Israel is forever God's elect and that the Church has a universal saving mission, and have puzzled over the considerable difficulty of untying this knot. See "Christ and Israel: An Unsolved Problem in Catholic Theology," in *The Call of Abraham: Essays on the Election of Israel in Honor of Jon D. Levenson*, ed. Gary A. Anderson and Joel S. Kaminsky (Notre Dame, Ind.: University of Notre Dame Press, 2013), 330–50, and, from a different angle, "Religion and Election: Aquinas on Natural Law, Judaism, and Salvation in Christ," *Nova et Vetera* (English edition) 14, no. 1 (2016): 61–125.

precisely on the basis of Catholic faith, for a divinely willed diversity of religions, or what is sometimes called a "providential diversity of religions." At the same time the Council teaches with remarkable clarity that every human being is called to be "converted to Christ"[30] in a public and communal way, to share by baptism and faith in the ecclesial life that pours forth from Christ himself. In this way Vatican II evidently rejects the idea that the diversity of religions should be seen as a providential gift, at least to the extent that the divinely willed character of a religion might be taken as a reason to remain in some other religious community rather than leave it to enter the Catholic Church. In the case of Judaism, as we have observed, how to square these teachings of Vatican II with one another is less than obvious.

It might seem as though this problem is confined to the Catholic Church's understanding of Judaism. Alone among non-Christian religious communities, the Catholic Church understands herself to be in possession of divinely revealed truths regarding the Jewish people and God's purposes for them, truths which seem to militate against any mandate on the part of the Church to convert Jews to Catholicism. The Church does not have such divine teaching regarding any other religious community or tradition (in particular, for *NA*, Hinduism, Buddhism, and Islam), and so must seek her own understanding of other traditions on the basis of the empirical knowledge she is able to obtain of them, in light of the revelation communicated in Scripture and tradition but not directly informed by it. So it might be argued that no other religious tradition poses the kind of perplexity for Catholic theology that arises when we juxtapose the Council's teaching on the Church's universal mission with that on the election of Israel. If there is a providential diversity of religions, it is limited to Judaism.

Here too, however, the matter turns out to be less clear than initially it might seem. *Nostra Aetate* §2 implies that there is truth and holiness in other non-Christian religions besides Judaism; the immediate reference is to Hinduism and Buddhism, but what is said about them can no doubt be generalized. *Nostra Aetate* here teaches, significantly, not only that rays of Christ's own truth and holiness are in some way accessible to adherents of other religious traditions, but that "these religions" themselves have in them, to some degree, "what is true and holy." Pre-conciliar Catholic theology was on the whole much more concerned with the salvation of non-Christians than with the revelatory or salvific value of non-Christian religions.[31]

30. *AG* §7.

31. See, e.g., Louis Capéran, *Le problème du salut des infidèles*, 2 vols, 3rd ed. (Toulouse: Grand

Nostra Aetate §2 thus takes a striking step when it affirms, against the background of that pre-conciliar discussion, the presence of truth and holiness not simply in the hearts and minds of non-Christians, but in their religions as such. Not only is it possible for individual *persons* outside the visible bounds of the Catholic Church to have some share in the truth and holiness that shines forth from Christ, and thus in some sense to belong to the Catholic Church; it is also possible for non-Christian *religions* to provide access of a kind to this same truth and holiness. And *Nostra Aetate* §2 goes on to say, again significantly, that the Catholic Church urges her children not only to "acknowledge," but to "preserve and encourage the spiritual and moral truths found among non-Christians, also their social life and culture," even—perhaps precisely—when she finds them "differing in many ways from her own teaching."

From here it has proven to be a short step to the thought that a great many religions, certainly including Hinduism, Buddhism, and Islam, are willed by God as the providential means by which their adherents will have the access they need to the religious truth and holiness that is the goal of every human life. Catholics should not, therefore, seek to convert the adherents of other religions to Christianity, unless perhaps their religion proves to be utterly devoid of what is true and holy. They should instead find ways of encouraging Hindus to be better adherents of Hinduism, Muslims of Islam, and so forth. Read in this way, Vatican II teaches, in effect, that the Church has a genuine missionary mandate only to wholly secularized cultures, cultures indwelt by people who adhere to no religion at all.[32]

Whether or not inspired by *Nostra Aetate* itself, the inferential steps just outlined have proven practically irresistible to Catholic (and much Protestant) theology of religions over the last fifty years. They are embraced by both pluralists and inclusivists, that is, by those who hold that the truth and holiness at which all religions aim is beyond all of them, and not known to any of them in a privileged way, and those who hold that this truth and holiness is most fully known to and present in the Catholic Church, perhaps unsurpassably so, but is in varying degrees also known to and present in many other religions.

John Hick is the best-known example of the pluralist view, but there are

Séminare, 1934); Riccardo Lombardi, SJ, *The Salvation of the Unbeliever*, trans. Dorothy M. White (Westminster, Md.: Newman Press, 1956).

32. Of course Vatican II is much concerned with the Church's mission in an increasingly secularized Western culture, especially in Europe, though whether in just this sense is, as we shall see, another matter.

Catholic versions as well.[33] Karl Rahner remains probably the most influential source for the many Catholic versions of the inclusivist view. Rahner himself had little interest in non-Christian religions as such, in their actual practices and beliefs. He was motivated mainly by the hope of seeing the inhabitants of secularized Western societies, who may be avowed atheists, as implicit or "anonymous" Christians in the interior depths of their conscious life, and theorized about the adherents of non-Christian religions in much the same terms.[34] His ideas have proven quite amenable to inclusivist theologies of religious diversity, according to which avowed Buddhists or Shiites (for example) may actually, if anonymously, be Christians in the interior depths.

Even a theologian like George Lindbeck, who is sharply critical not only of pluralism but of inclusivism (especially in the "experiential expressivist" versions popularized by Rahner and others), reads *Nostra Aetate*, if with a certain characteristic hesitation, as limiting the Church's missionary mandate. "The missionary task of Christians may at times be to encourage Marxists to become better Marxists, Jews and Muslims to become better Jews and Muslims, and Buddhists to become better Buddhists.... The Declaration on Non-Christian Religions at the Second Vatican Council, for example, makes it quite clear that the purpose of dialogue need not be to convert, but may be rather to benefit other religions."[35]

Ilaria Morali points out, rightly enough, that *Nostra Aetate* §2 is the only text of Vatican II that attributes the possession of truth and holiness to other religious traditions as such, and not only to the persons (or some of the persons) who adhere to them.[36] But there it is, in black and white, and one

33. See, inter alia, John Hick, *An Interpretation of Religion: Human Responses to the Transcendent*, 2nd ed. (New Haven, Conn.: Yale University Press, 2004).

34. See, e.g., Karl Rahner, "Anonymous Christians," in *Theological Investigations*, vol. 6 (New York: Crossroad, 1982), 390–98; for Rahner's application of the idea of "anonymous Christianity" to other religions, see "Christianity and the Non-Christian Religions," in *Theological Investigations*, vol. 5 (Baltimore: Helicon Press, 1966), 115–34.

35. George A. Lindbeck, *The Nature of Doctrine: Religion and Theology in a Postliberal Age*, 2nd ed. (Louisville, Ky.: Westminster John Knox, 2009), 40, citing *NA* §2 (p. 54 in the original edition of 1984; the reference to Marxism brings to mind that the book was originally published while the Cold War was still on, and Marxism seemed like a potent, if now sclerotic, quasi-religious historical force). Picking up on a strain in *NA* §2, Lindbeck inclines strongly to a "providential diversity of religions" in which non-Christian religions are willed by God precisely in their differences from Christianity, rather than, as in the more standard inclusivist view, merely "objectifying poorly what Christianity objectifies well (as Karl Rahner proposes)": in "these faiths ... potentialities can be actualized and realities explored that are not within the direct purview of the peoples of Messianic witness, but that are nevertheless God-willed and God-approved anticipations of aspects of the coming kingdom" (40–41 [1984: 54–55]).

36. "Salvation, Religions, and Dialogue in the Roman Magisterium: From Pius IX to Vatican II and Postconciliar Popes," in *Catholic Engagement with World Religions* , ed. Karl J. Becker and Ilaria Morali (Maryknoll, N.Y.: Orbis, 2010), 122–42; here: 130a.

can't handle the difficulties this creates simply by saying that there are many other texts that seem to speak otherwise. Indeed *Nostra Aetate* §2 emphasizes that Catholics should "acknowledge, preserve, and encourage" the spiritual and moral goods possessed by non-Christian traditions precisely "while witnessing to their own faith and way of life." This, of course, does not remove the apparent opposition between Vatican II's teaching on the Church's universal missionary vocation and the Council's way of appreciating non-Christian religions. It simply makes the opposition more obvious. Is there a way to ease this tension?

Salvation in Christ Is Ecclesial and Intentional

In order to answer this question, we need to think a bit about salvation in Christ, that is, about the goal at which the Church's universal mission aims. If salvation in Christ is such that non-Christian religions can in some way genuinely mediate it, or provide access to it, then other religions could accomplish in their own way what the Church's mission also aims to achieve. This would make the tension between the Council's teaching on the universality of that mission and the value it ascribes to non-Christian religions very difficult to overcome. If, on the other hand, the truth and goodness present in other religions does not include access to salvation in Christ, then the tension largely goes away.

Like the election of Israel, the mission of the Catholic Church to invite every human being to share in her own life is not an end it itself. Its ultimate end or purpose is to bring about the union in love of every human being with Jesus Christ. In the language of *Ad Gentes* §7, "everyone . . . ought to be converted to Christ." Conversion to Christ is the end at which the Church's mission aims. At the same time the Church, especially in her preaching and sacramental life, is the means Christ himself uses to unite human beings to himself in charity, or, we could say, to bring about direct and intimate contact with him. By faith in the Church's proclamation of him and baptism at her hands, he joins each of us to the very events of the paschal mystery, to his suffering, death, and resurrection. Uniting us with Christ in the saving events of the paschal mystery, the faith elicited by the Church's proclamation and the sacrament of baptism that perfects this faith unite us by their very nature with Christ's Church, the body of which he is the head. Faith and baptism are, in other words, inherently ecclesial. "Christ himself, 'by explicitly insisting on the necessity of faith and baptism (Mk 16:16, Jn 3:5), at the same time confirmed the necessity of the Church, into which human beings enter through baptism as through a door.'"[37] The irreducibly ecclesial character of salvation in Christ is not a result of sin or a concession to human weakness, but belongs to God's primordial decision to share his own life with creatures. "It pleased God to call human beings to share his life not merely singly, without any mutual bond, but rather to form them into a people, in which his children once scattered abroad might be gathered into one."[38]

In thinking about Christian salvation there is no need to play off Christ against his Church, and no point in doing so; the faith and baptism that unite us to him truly unite us to her, and conversely. Thus to the objection that we don't need the sacraments, and therefore don't need the Church, because we are saved by the grace and passion of Christ, Thomas Aquinas succinctly replies, "The sacraments have their effect on account of the power of Christ's passion, and the passion of Christ is in a certain way applied to human beings by the sacraments, according to Rom 6:[3] ... 'We have been baptized into his death.'"[39]

Seen in this Catholic way, union with the Church is not external or adventitious to union with Christ. Union with Christ is, in turn, not simply the means or the way to salvation, ultimately extrinsic to it. Union with Christ *is* human salvation, realized truly yet through a glass darkly here and now, and in its full glory when we see face to face. "Christ not only took our nature; he became one of our flesh and blood with a frail and mortal body subject to suffering ... so that he might make his brothers according to the flesh sharers in the divine nature [II Pet. 1:4], both now in our earthly exile through sanctifying grace, and then in our heavenly homeland through the attainment of eternal blessedness."[40]

No one can be a spectator to his own salvation so understood. This is basic to understanding both the significance of the Church's universal mission and the extent of the truth and goodness available through non-Christian religions.

Theologians sometimes suggest that Christ saves us in such a way that his cross has, and need have, no effect in our own life. In this view Jesus' saving work is wholly complete within the confines of his own individual human history as it unfolds from Bethlehem to Golgotha (or, perhaps, from

37. *AG* §7, quoting *LG* §14.
38. *AG* §2; cf. *LG* §9.
39. *ST* III, q. 61, a. 1 ad 3.
40. Pius XII, *Mystici corporis Christi*, §46 (*Acta Apostolicae Sedis* 35 [1943], 214.

his willing subjection to the Father in eternity, down to the depths of Golgotha, and back). Then and there everything that will ever be included in our salvation, anything in which our salvation actually consists, has already come to pass. This saving work of Christ, co-extensive with his individual human history, need never impinge on our own history. In fact strictly speaking, Jesus' work, insofar as it is genuinely saving for us, *cannot* impinge on our own history. If it could, then some act or event within our own history—such as love for the crucified, on the model of Mary and John at the foot of the cross (Jn 19:25–27)—would be included in, and in some way constitutive of, our salvation. And this would mean that the total reality of our salvation has not taken place in the acts and events of Jesus' own individual life. We are "already" saved by the cross, as it is sometimes put, before we know it, and indeed before we or any other human being even existed, saved in the eternal self-determination of God, his decision to be the God who makes his way from the crib to the cross.

We may, of course, come to know this truth about ourselves—that we have been saved by the cross—but knowing this truth brings us no closer to Christ, conforms us no more truly to his cross, and so brings us no closer to our salvation, than we already were when we were ignorant of it. Still less, on this understanding, can any act of our will, any act we undertake in light of the knowledge of our salvation in Christ, bring us closer to Christ and our salvation in him. So regarded, salvation in Christ becomes something like a mathematical truth as classically conceived (and as still conceived by those who accept a "platonist" understanding of mathematics). Such a truth is quite independent of us, of our beliefs and attitudes. Knowing it may change the knower, but not the truth itself. One of the greatly reassuring features of mathematical truths so understood is precisely that they cannot be affected by us, that we can do nothing to change their truth value. Whether our own salvation, a truth *about* us, and not simply about numbers or other mathematical entities, can be a truth of this sort is, however, a rather different matter.[41]

To be sure, understanding salvation in Christ along the lines of a mathematical truth would allow us to do more than simply ease the tension between Vatican II's insistence on the missionary vocation of the Church and its discernment of Christ's truth and holiness in non-Christian religions. We could make the whole question go away.

41. Whether the theology of Karl Barth embodies such a spectator's understanding of Christ's saving work I will not try to decide here.

If we are at most onlookers to our salvation in Christ, then no non-Christian religion can bring us any closer to salvation in him than we would be without it. Of course this goes for the Christian religion as well. If the human acts necessary for our salvation are solely those of Jesus himself, considered simply as his own and as constitutive of his individual history, then no acts of the Church or the individuals within her, sacramental or otherwise, can be necessary for our salvation, or bring us closer to it. The most the Church can do is make it possible for us to become genuine onlookers to salvation in Christ, who remain, however, equidistant from it with those who are not yet onlookers, having yet to join the spectators' ranks. There is no need to square truth and holiness in non-Christian religions with the Church's missionary imperative, since no religion, Christian or otherwise, actually mediates salvation in Christ to its adherents. This is not simply a contingent failure of the religions themselves but is in the nature of the case. According to this spectatorial theology, salvation in Christ is not mediated at all. Identical with the actions and undergoings of Jesus' individual history, it simply occurs, as they occur.

The actions and events that make up Jesus' individual history are not, however, of such a sort as to leave us only spectators to their saving power. Jesus Christ does not simply invite us to look upon his cross from afar, at a safe distance. He bids us to take it up, to be united with him in his death—his suffering and cross—so that we may share in his life, his resurrection (Rom 6:5; 8). Each of us is to take up his cross in our own way, in our own place and time, so that it genuinely becomes our cross. According to the interpretation he himself places upon it (Mk 8:34), Jesus does not go to the cross so that his passion and death may remain events confined to his own individual history. He accepts his saving cross in such a way as to give us a share in it. So Paul explains to the Philippians: "For Christ's sake it has been granted to you not only that you may believe in him, but also that you may suffer for him" (Phil 1:29).

The paschal mystery is not imprisoned in Jesus' own history, as the events that make up the identity of a fictional character are locked up in the narrative that speaks of him. The actions and events of a fictional narrative allow us to locate its characters in a world that we can know and look upon, perhaps with deep longing, but cannot enter. Unlike a fictional character, indeed unlike any merely human agent, Jesus draws us into his history, making us even now real sharers in the once-for-all events of the paschal mystery. Our salvation does not consist only in the unique and unrepeatable sequence of actions and events that take place on the way from Bethlehem to Golgotha. It includes a share in those actions and events, in the paschal mystery itself. Salvation is union with Christ. So again Paul, who insists that he wants to be found *in* Christ (cf. Phil 3:9), "having the righteousness of God that comes through faith in Christ, in order that I may know him," to be sure, but also "the power of his resurrection and the sharing of his sufferings, conforming me to his death, if in some way I may attain the resurrection from the dead" (Phil 3:10–11).

This participatory, and in that sense typically Catholic, understanding of salvation in Christ might seem to threaten the biblical teaching that we are saved by Christ alone. In fact, though, seeing salvation as union with Christ does not conflict with the *sola Christi* rightly emphasized by historic Protestantism, the teaching that the cross of Jesus is itself sufficient, indeed more than sufficient, for our salvation.

A genuine conflict would arise if the union with Christ that takes place in our own history through baptismal faith were rightly numbered as a second saving event alongside the paschal mystery, added to the paschal mystery in order to yield salvation. In that case both the passion of Christ and the sacrament of baptism would be necessary for our salvation, while neither would, of itself, be sufficient. But baptism is not a second saving event next to the cross, as if the cross and the sacrament of baptism were two tokens of the same type, or two species of the same genus. Rather baptism, including the faith that inherently belongs to it, is the very death and resurrection of the Lord, *as* participated by us. Baptism is not a saving event that must be added to the uniquely saving action and passion of Jesus; it is Jesus' own way of uniting us with his saving action and passion (and so for all of the other sacraments, each in its own way). Or as Aquinas puts the point, the sacraments do not increase, or make any addition to, the saving power of the cross. They "apply" the cross, in all its sufficiency and uniqueness, to us. Our salvation does not take place in Christ's own history as opposed to ours, but in his own history as participated and shared by ours, when ours becomes joined, sacramentally, to his.

Aquinas develops this point when he asks whether the grace that belongs to Jesus as an individual human being, the supreme fullness of grace that belongs uniquely to him, is the same as the grace by which he is the head of the Church. The relation by which Christ is the head of the Church has as its counterpart from our side (or seen from the point of view of the Church) the relation of being united to Christ, that is, of being saved in him, at least potentially, and so being a member of his mystical body.[42] If the perfection of grace that belongs to Jesus himself is not one and the same as the grace by which he is head of his mystical body, it follows that his own fullness of grace is not sufficient for our salvation. Some further grace would have to be added, beyond Christ's own, for us to attain salvation. This further grace could not belong personally to Christ himself, since the grace he possesses as an individual human being cannot be increased. His human soul is already the subject of the fullest and most perfect grace that could be received by a creature. Any further grace would have to be discrete from his, and belong to someone else rather than to Christ himself (perhaps to the individual human being who was saved by it).

Aquinas rejects this view. "From his fullness we have all received," the apostle John teaches (Jn 1:16), his fullness, that is, of grace and truth (Jn 1:14, 17). Following the Church Fathers, Aquinas sees in these texts Christ's headship over the Church, which consists most basically in the fact that all the goods of grace and truth present in the members of the mystical body are received from the head, from Christ himself as an individual human being. The grace by which we belong to Christ's body and so are saved in him is the same as the grace that already belongs to him personally, the perfection of grace that fills his human soul. The grace in virtue of which he is the head of the Church is simply the grace that belongs to him as an individual human being, now seen not only as possessed by him, but as participated by us. As Aquinas puts the point, "The personal grace by which the soul of Christ is perfectly just is the same in its essence as his grace insofar as he is head of the Church, justifying others; they differ only in concept."[43] The one grace of Christ, that is, we conceive as personal when we think of it simply as possessed by Jesus himself, and as capital, the saving grace of headship, when we think of it as shared with and received by others

The man Christ Jesus is thus not simply the cause of grace in us, that is, the primary agent or efficient cause of our being in grace. In a sense he is also the formal or exemplar cause of sanctifying grace in the members of

42. See *ST* III, q. 8, a. 3, c, which also includes a discussion of degrees of membership in the "mystical body of the Church (*corpus Ecclesiae mysticum*)," from the perfect union of those in glory to the still potential union of those living in this world outside faith and the sacraments. That Jesus is the savior of the world requires, as Aquinas sees it, that he is the head of a mystical body: "To save human beings [I Tim 4:10] and to be the one who makes propitiation for their sins [I Jn 2:2] belong to Christ insofar as he is head" (*ST* III, q. 8, a. 3, sc).

43. *ST* III, q. 8, a. 5, c: "[E]adem est secundum essentiam gratia personalis qua anima Christi est iustificata, et gratia eius secundum quam est caput Ecclesiae iustificans alios, differt tamen secundum rationem." On the use of Jn 1:16 in this context, see *ST* III, q. 8, a. 5, sc; q. 7, a. 1, c.

his mystical body, since grace in us is simply a participation in the personal plenitude of grace and truth that belongs to him alone. As Aquinas notes in his commentary on Jn 1:16, "The fullness of grace that is in Christ is the cause of all the graces that are in all intellectual creatures ... by participation in his sufficient plenitude."[44] The paschal mystery is sufficient for our salvation not only efficiently but formally; what Jesus Christ causes in making us members of his body is, in the first place, a share in his own personal holiness and justice.

The grace that saves us is thus not our own, but his—not only in the sense that he causes it, but in the sense that he alone possesses it inherently, in an original rather than a derivative way. The grace in us by which we become pleasing to God is not ours as discrete from his, still less our own as opposed to his. It is ours, it belongs to us, only as a sharing, wholly dependent on him, in his singular fullness of grace. The human soul of Christ, Aquinas argues, is the source of infinite grace for others, "since it has the Word united to it, who is the infinite and inexhaustible source of the whole of the emanation of creatures." As head of the Church, Christ's grace "is infinite with respect to its influence." Not only can Christ cause an unlimited number of creatures to receive his grace; an unlimited number of creatures can share in his fullness. He is the measureless fountain of grace that can never be diminished no matter how many creatures drink their fill of it. "The grace of Christ is sufficient not only for the salvation of some human beings, but of every human being in the whole world, according to I Jn. 2:2 ... and even of a multitude of worlds, if they exist."[45]

One final point. That we are participants in our own salvation rather than simply spectators to it follows, in the last analysis, from the way Jesus mediates to us a saving participation in his own plenitude of grace. He does so by his own personal act, which calls forth and is received by a personal act on our part. Our salvation in Christ is personal from both sides, his and ours, and it consists in a relationship between persons.

It is sometimes proposed that God saves us in Christ simply by being incarnate, by uniting our nature with his own in the person of the Son. This union transforms and perfects our human nature as such, and thereby imparts saving transformation to all who share in this nature, that is, to every human being. Because of the incarnation we are, as it were, already heirs

44. *S. Thomae Aquinatis Super Evangelium S. Ioannis Lectura*, ed. Raphael Cai, OP (5th ed., Turin: Marietti, 1952), (caput) 1, (lectio) 10 (no. 202).

45. The quoted passages are from *Super Ioannem* 3, 6 (no. 544).

to salvation, simply by being human. Our salvation requires no human act of Jesus himself, certainly no act personal to the one who receives salvation from him. It requires only the act of the Logos in assuming our nature.

This cannot be right, since our salvation does depend on Jesus' human acts, on what Aquinas calls "the things the incarnate Son of God did and suffered in the human nature united to him."[46] The action and passion of Jesus is of course the action and passion of God the Son, but these are the *human* acts and sufferings of the Logos, what God the Son does and suffers *secundum quod homo*, in virtue of the human nature he has freely assumed. This includes the personal act of offering to each of us, individually, a saving share in his fullness of grace. Jesus imparts salvation to us, Aquinas rightly observes, not by his mere possession of our human nature, but by his deliberate personal act. "Grace does not flow from Christ into us by means of human nature, but solely by the personal action of Christ himself."[47] The doctrine of the incarnation cannot be taken as warrant for the claim that we are spectators to our own salvation.

We are, then, participants in our salvation in Christ, not bystanders to it. As a result no human being who has the use of reason, to use the traditional phrase, can be the merely passive recipient of union with Christ in the saving mystery of his passion, innocent and unaware of what she or he has undergone. If we are to become sharers in the paschal mystery and so be joined to Christ, our own minds and wills have to be involved. Our union with Christ in his passion will not come to pass unless we ourselves intend it, and this requires that we be aware of his saving passion and resurrection, with at least enough definiteness that we can intend to be joined with him crucified and risen. No one, moreover, can enter into saving union with Christ without also being drawn into his Church, normally entering the Church "as through a door," crossing the visible threshold marked by the sacrament of baptism.

Mediating a Share in the Paschal Mystery

Salvation in Christ, then, has two basic features that we must account for in any theological understanding of non-Christian religions and their possible

46. *ST* III, q. 27, prooem. "The summit of the whole enterprise of theology (*ad consummationem totius theologici negotii*)," Aquinas observes, lies in the knowledge of "the very Savior of all (*de ipso omnium Salvatore*)," which has two irreducibly distinct facets: "first, the mystery of the incarnation itself, by which God became man for our salvation; second, those things which have been done and suffered by our Savior, that is, by God incarnate" (*ST* III, Prologus).

47. *ST* III, q. 8, a. 5, ad 1: "[G]ratia non derivatur a Christo in nos mediante natura humana, sed per solam personalem actionem ipsius Christi."

saving significance. Salvation, precisely on the part of those who receive it, is (1) inherently ecclesial and (2) both voluntary and intentional.

So much seems clear from the normal pattern of union with Christ visible in faith and baptism. Here we are sure that human beings really are joined to Christ, by explicit confession of the Church's faith and the sacramental act by which Christ's cross and resurrection truly touch us, truly lay hold of us, and we him. Anything we might want to say about how human beings may find saving union with Christ apart from these ecclesial acts will have to conform to the paradigm consisting of explicit faith and baptism.

It is well known that Vatican II does want to say something on this last point, most forcefully and influentially in *Gaudium et Spes* §22, but also in *Lumen Gentium* §16 and *Ad Gentes* §7. In so doing the Council says nothing wholly new, but it does lay down some very clear teaching on a matter that had troubled and preoccupied Catholic theology since the sixteenth century: what to say about the possibility of salvation for those without faith and baptism.[48]

According to *Gaudium et Spes* §22, "The Son of God has, by his incarnation, united himself in some fashion (*quodammodo*) with every human being."[49] By faith and baptism Christ has united "the Christian man" to himself in such a way as to make the Christian "a sharer (*consociatus*) in the paschal mystery, as one who has been configured to the death of Christ." However, *Gaudium et Spes* §22 goes on to say, this union with Christ in the saving mystery of his cross and resurrection is not only for Christians "but for all men of good will in whose hearts grace works in an invisible way. For, since Christ died for all men, and since the ultimate vocation of man is in fact one, and divine, we ought to believe that the Holy Spirit, in a way known to God, offers to all the possibility of sharing in this paschal mystery."[50]

48. The discovery of the New World at the end of the fifteenth century made "the salvation of the unbeliever" an urgent problem, as it had not been in the Middle Ages. That there were human beings with no access to baptism and no opportunity to confess faith in Christ—in fact a countless number, over untold generations—was now a reality that had to be faced, and not simply a hypothetical possibility that might be considered in passing. We should therefore not expect St. Thomas, or any other medieval theologian, to offer an adequately developed treatment of the problem.

49. Original text in *AAS* 58 (1966): 1025–1120. *GS* §22 makes here a quite traditional point, that by the incarnation itself "human nature has been exalted to a sublime dignity, even in us." No one who has the nature assumed by God the Son can remain untouched by the fact that this nature has now become God's own; "in some fashion" every human being, every subject of human nature, is brought into contact with the Son of God when he becomes flesh. This should not be confused with the claim we have just set aside, viz., that the incarnation is saving for us all by itself, apart from any personal act of Jesus or any personal response by us. *GS* §22 in fact goes out of its way to oppose such a view. God the incarnate Son "acted with a human will, and with a human heart he loved.... The innocent lamb, he merited life for us by his blood freely outpoured ... in such a way that each one of us can say with the Apostle: the Son of God 'loved me and gave himself up for me' (Gal 2:20)."

50. Vatican translation, modified. "Quod non tantum pro christifidelibus valet, sed et pro omnibus

As *Ad Gentes* §7 emphasizes, in graciously bringing about this hidden union of non-Christians with the paschal mystery, the Holy Spirit works in them, "in ways known to God himself," that very faith in Christ without which it is impossible to please God (Heb 11:6), the faith visibly professed by Christians. Saving union with Christ, in other words, always involves the act of faith in him. This act finds its fullest and most perfect form in the explicit adult profession of baptismal faith, but the same act, so *Ad Gentes* §7 teaches, is present in some fashion wherever Christ takes hold of a human life in a saving way, even among those who "through no fault of their own are ignorant of the Gospel."[51]

In light of these texts we can now pose a precise question. Depending on how we answer it, this question may help us ease the tension between Vatican II's teaching on the Church's universal missionary mandate and the positive value the Council ascribes to non-Christian religions. Are the beliefs and practices of other religions themselves a means by which the adherents of those religions may enter by faith into union with the paschal mystery?

When the question is posed in this way, there are excellent reasons to think that the answer is simply no. Adherence to the beliefs and practices of other religions is not itself able to mediate (be a means for) the act of faith that invisibly unites non-Christians to Christ in the saving mysteries of his death and resurrection. *Nostra Aetate* §2's embrace of all that is true and holy in the religious traditions of the world should not be mistaken for the claim that what is true and holy in these traditions enables their adherents to enter into saving union with Christ in the paschal mystery. The most obvious reason for this is simply that reading *Nostra Aetate* §2 this way generates a conflict with the Council's teaching on the Church's mission which is otherwise needless.

What is true and holy in other religions will in the first place be shared with the Church, though *Nostra Aetate* §2 also seems to say that there may be truth and holiness among non-Christians that differs from that possessed

hominibus bonae voluntatis in quorum corde gratia invisibili modo operatur [cf. *LG* §16]. Cum enim pro omnibus mortuus sit Christus [Rom 8:32] cumque vocatio hominis ultima revera una sit, scilicet divina, tenere debemus Spiritum Sanctum cunctis possibilitatem offerre ut, modo Deo cognito, huic paschali mysterio consocientur."

51. It would therefore be a mistake to read *LG* §16 and *GS* §22, when they speak of the availability of salvation to those outside the visible bounds of the Church, as though this can take place without the act of faith in Christ, indeed what was traditionally called the act of supernatural and divine faith, worked by the Holy Spirit. God brings about the salvation of non-Christians "in ways known to himself" (*AG* §7; cf. *GS* §22), but this is to say that God somehow brings about in non-Christians the faith in Christ "without which it is impossible to please" him, not that he saves Christians by faith in Christ, and non-Christians without it.

by the Church.[52] In any case the paschal mystery, and the divinely willed sacramental means of being united with it, cannot be among those elements of truth and holiness present in the beliefs and practices of non-Christian religions. If they were, then the Church's missionary activity might be useful or beneficial to non-Christians. But it would not be necessary. Still less would it be necessary "for all men and nations,"[53] that is, genuinely universal. The Church's proclamation of Jesus crucified and risen and her offer of union with him in baptism might at most, as Rahner argues, be a more vivid or reliable way of entering into the paschal mystery than, say, the disciplined practices of Buddhist meditation. Should Buddhist meditation not only be a good in its own right, but a way of entering into union with Christ crucified and risen, then those practices would be the effective equivalents of faith and baptism. They would themselves mediate the supreme good for the sake of which the Church's mission itself exists; they would themselves be "a free and secure way to participate fully in the mystery of Christ."[54] There would thus be no need, no necessity, for the Church to call adherents of Buddhism (for example) to faith in Christ and to offer them baptism into him.

Nostra Aetate §2 itself, though, is clear that the Church's missionary imperative is universal, that is, necessarily directed to all who have not yet professed faith in Christ and received the sacrament of baptism. Precisely while embracing what is true and holy in the religious traditions of humanity, "she proclaims, and is in duty bound to proclaim without fail, Christ who is the way, the truth, and the life" (Jn 14:6).[55] The necessity of the Church's mission, however, is not only that of obedience to a divine command. The Church's missionary action is necessary also for the salvation of human beings, at which the mission aims. Mission is necessary not only with reference to its source (the triune God who commands it), but with reference to its goal, salvation as participation in the paschal mystery. Thus the teaching of *Ad Gentes* §1, which particularly irritated Karl Barth.[56] God gives *the Church* the task of saving the world, a vocation that has not been entrusted to any other religious community, and could not be, since the salvation mediated by faith and baptism, which the Church is charged with making present to the world, by nature unites us to the Church herself. "The Church, the salt of the earth and the light of the world (Mt 5:13–14), is [today] even

52. See the section above on the "providential diversity of religions."

53. *AG* §5.

54. In the language of *AG* §5.

55. See also *AG* §6: the Church has "an obligation to preach the gospel to all who are still outside."

56. See above, note 6.

more urgently called to save and renew every creature, so that all things may be restored in Christ [cf. Eph 1:10], and in him human beings may form one family and one people of God."[57]

Ad Gentes §7 adds that the Church's missionary obligation is inseparable from God's basic will for the salvation of all (1 Tim 2:4). Just because God desires the salvation of every human being—that is, because God excludes no human being from the possibility of sharing in the paschal mystery—"today, as always, missionary activity retains its full force and necessity." In just this sense "the Church, in Christ, is like a sacrament."[58] Jesus Christ "founded his Church as the sacrament of salvation," that is, the effective sign and instrument by which he carries out his saving work in the world.[59]

This insistence on the necessity of proclaiming the gospel to every creature would be senseless if what is true and holy in other religions were sufficient to unite us to the saving mystery of Christ's passion and resurrection. There are no effective equivalents to the proclamation of Christ crucified and to his sacraments, whose saving power is, as Aquinas points out, that of Christ's passion itself, which they make present in the world. These the Church alone offers, and can offer, to the world. "Obedient to the command of Christ and moved by the grace and charity of the Holy Spirit, the Church makes herself fully present to all men and nations in order to lead them to the faith, freedom, and peace of Christ"; the Church, and she alone, "opens up for all men a free and secure way to participate fully in the mystery of Christ."[60] A providential diversity of religions there may indeed be; God may will the presence of these traditions in the world for any number of reasons, known or unknown to us. But he does not will them as means of salvation in Christ.[61]

An obvious question arises, though. The Council clearly says that the act of saving faith in Christ is possible for non-Christians. Human beings, that is, can come to faith in Christ even without the Church's missionary presentation of him. If their own religious traditions don't mediate this act of faith to them, enable them to have the faith that unites them to Christ in his passion, what does?

The question underlines a puzzling feature of the teaching of *Gaudi-*

57. *AG* §1.

58. *LG* §1.

59. *AG* §5; cf. *AG* §1; *LG* §§9, 48.

60. *AG* §5.

61. This doesn't rule out taking other religions, or features of them, for a *praeparatio evangelica*, as in *LG* §16 and *AG* §3. It does mean, though, that these features cannot suffice to mediate saving faith in Christ. Otherwise the *praeparatio* would *be* the *evangelium*.

um et Spes §22, and also of *Ad Gentes* §7. In those who "through no fault of their own"[62] are unable to respond to the proclamation of the gospel, the Holy Spirit is able to work faith in Christ and thereby a share in the paschal mystery. To have faith, as we have observed, is to *intend* union with Christ crucified; no one is an unwitting participant in the paschal mystery. So these texts evidently attribute to the Holy Spirit a capacity to bring about the formation, even in the hearts of those who have never heard the gospel, the intention to be united to Christ in his passion.

How this can happen is difficult to understand. The texts seem to propose that with divine assistance human beings can form a definite intention, the intention to be united to Christ crucified and risen, in the absence of all of the social and linguistic conditions normally necessary for the formation of that intention. A person can, it seems, form the intention of believing in Jesus Christ without ever having heard of him, and without having any term in his natural language that refers to him. If this is right, then a person can have saving faith in Christ without being able to form the sentence (in whatever language he speaks), "I believe in Christ," or "Christ, I believe in you," let alone being able to assent to it. As I read these texts, in fact, they propose that human beings can form this intention of being united to Christ in the absence of *any* adequate social and linguistic means, since they are held to do so without the means that are alone sufficient for this, namely baptism and the Church's missionary proclamation.

Gaudium et Spes senses the difficulty posed by its teaching, taking the unusual step of saying that when the Holy Spirit works invisibly to offer all "men of good will" a share in the paschal mystery, he does so "in a way known to God" (*modo Deo cognito*). This seems to say that we should not be surprised if we cannot offer a satisfying theological account of how the Holy Spirit brings about the human intention to be conformed to Christ in those who, for example, have never heard his name. It's obvious that how God brings about this saving intention must be known to God himself. The qualification has to mean that while God knows how he does this, it's quite possible that we won't, and we may have to grant that God here does something that we simply cannot understand.[63]

62. *AG* §7, *LG* §16.

63. In fact the English translation of *GS* §22 on the Vatican website actually says that the Spirit's saving work takes place "in a manner known *only* to God" (my emphasis). If the Council actually said that it would be teaching that the knowledge of how salvation takes place "invisibly," apart from baptism and the public profession of faith, is definitely unknowable to us. Like the *quid est* or essence of God as classically conceived, it could be known only by the blessed, and not by us in this present life. This is not, however, what *GS* §22 says. There is nothing in the Latin text corresponding to "only"; it

It might be objected that the problem is not so grave as I make it seem, as long as one accepts the traditional view that thought has priority over (natural) language, making the capacity to form an intention dependent on the interior contents of our mind as opposed to the linguistic stock contingently provided by our social environment. On this view, which goes back at least as far as Plato and takes many different forms, we human beings think in a universal and shared mental language, made up of purely mental words or concepts generated by the impact of the objective world upon the mind. The diverse natural languages we speak are just a series of conventional signs or markers of this shared interior discourse. The words we actually utter or write are signs of these mental concepts or interior words we all have in common, and the sentences we form correspond to judgments we can all make by combining our interior words. Given this basic picture of the way mind and language are related, it does not seem especially shocking that we should be able to form the intention to believe in Christ, even if we lacked the ability to form or utter the sentence, "I believe in Christ."[64]

This way of looking at the relationship between thought and language obviously has a long history in Christian theology as well as in Western philosophy.[65] St. Augustine and St. Thomas Aquinas both articulate influential (though different) versions of it, and it may very well have been among the background assumptions of most of the bishops and *periti* at Vatican II. There are nonetheless good reasons for thinking it not to be true. As a result it would be best not to burden the Council with it, that is, not to treat the Council's teaching on non-Christian religions as though it logically presupposed a highly questionable picture of thought and language, such that the teaching could be true only if the traditional picture is true.

Among the reasons why this view of the relationship of mind, natural or spoken language, and reality won't work we can briefly mention two: first, it doesn't explain anything, and second, if it were true, human communication by means of natural language would be impossible.

---

simply says "in a way known to God." The French, German, and Italian translations on the Vatican website get this right, though the Spanish translation, like the English, does not (*en la forma de sólo Dios conocida*).

64. Claude Panaccio gives a philosophically perceptive account of the idea of mental language, its history, and its problems in *Le discours intérieur: De Platon à Guillaume d'Ockham* (Paris: Seuil, 1999).

65. For an early and influential statement of the view, see Aristotle, *De interpretatione* 1 (16a3–8). For some observations on what the medieval Latin commentary tradition made of this much-discussed passage and others like it, see E. Jennifer Ashworth, "Aquinas, Scotus and Others on Naming, Knowing, and the Origin of Language," *Logic and Language in the Middle Ages: A Volume in Honor of Sten Ebbesen*, ed. Jakob Leth Fink, Heine Hansen, and Ana María Mora-Márquez (Leiden: Brill, 2013), 257–72.

In this traditional picture the spoken and written words of a natural language don't refer directly to objects. They refer to or signify thoughts or mental words, and they get their meaning entirely from the thoughts to which they're connected. The mind can't link up spoken and written words with objects except by recourse to its own interior language, which tells it what objects the user of a natural language is himself thinking about. For some while, though, most philosophers of language have argued that positing a mental language so conceived is at best unnecessary. We can account for the mind's ability to put words consistently in relation to objects, and so for our ability to assign meaning to utterances in a natural language and thereby correctly understand one another, without invoking a shadow language which holds mind, word, and object together. This isn't reductionism, as defenders of the traditional view sometimes suppose, but needed explanatory simplicity. Mental language as traditionally conceived has come to seem, in the manner of planetary epicycles or the interstellar ether, like an occult entity which does no useful explanatory work.

Not only is there no need to invoke mental language for explanatory purposes; the traditional picture invokes it in ways that create what look like insuperable difficulties. If spoken and written words really do get their meaning and reference from mental language, then it will be impossible to use natural language as a means of communication between human beings. And since natural language is the only means we've got, the traditional picture rules out the possibility of human communication altogether.

The difficulty, in brief, is that we have no way to tell what other people are thinking except by understanding what their words mean. That's the point of saying that we need natural language as a means of interpersonal communication. But in the traditional picture, what people's words mean, the content of what they say and write in their natural languages, depends on what they're thinking. External words get their meaning and reference from the language of thought, from the mental words to which they're conventionally connected. We are, however, unable to read other people's minds. We have no direct access to their thoughts. But given the traditional picture, that's what we would need in order to understand their words. We could communicate with another person only if we could read his mind, but if we could do that we wouldn't need natural language as a means of communication in the first place.

Thus when the Frenchman says "le papillon" I may associate his French syllables with a certain item of my own mental furniture, and so conjecture that "le papillon" means "eel." But there is no guarantee that *he* associates his syllables with the same item in his own interior stock, inaccessible to me, and that "eel" is therefore what he means by his utterance. He may insist (if he is bilingual) that no, when he says "le papillon" he has in mind the thought of a diurnal insect of the order Lepidoptera, a thought which (let us assume) is part of my mental stock as well as his, so that he actually means "butterfly" by these syllables, not "eel." But this just relocates the problem. How can I tell that when he says "diurnal," "insect," "Lepidoptera," and so forth, he has in mind the same mental words *these* sounds suggest to me? To say that it's a convention of English that these syllables refer to just the mental words for diurnal, insect, and so forth doesn't help, any more than saying that it's a convention of French that "le papillon" refers to the mental word for butterfly. How, after all, am I supposed to learn the conventions? Mama can gesture at butterflies and say "le papillon" all day long, but in the traditional picture "le papillon" doesn't refer to butterflies, which I can see. It refers to a mental word, a thought in her mind to which I have no access. On this picture, not only do I lack the means for understanding what other people are saying, I thereby lack the means to learn a natural language in the first place.[66]

The traditional view of the priority of thought over language thus faces the challenge of explaining how the conventions that connect public utterances in a natural language to the inner language of thought actually obtain, and how they can be known to obtain. Advocates of the traditional view naturally suppose that this challenge can be met. Thereby they hold, it is important to note, not only that the conventions actually obtain, but that they have to be observed. The traditional view grants that the possibility of linguistic communication depends on reliable connections between the spoken words of the various natural languages and the mental words belonging to the language of thought. This, however, rules out attributing thoughts to people who lack the words to express them. As Thomas Aquinas, certainly a proponent of the traditional view, puts the point, "insofar as something can be known by us in the intellect, it can be named [spoken of] by us."[67] From this it follows, of course, that if we cannot speak of something in the words of a natural language, we cannot know it.

66. For a more detailed discussion of the theses in the philosophy of language briefly touched on here and their application to theological problems, see Bruce D. Marshall, *Trinity and Truth* (Cambridge: Cambridge University Press, 2000), especially chapter 4.

67. *ST* I, q. 13, a. 1, c ("Secundum igitur quod aliquid a nobis intellectu cognosci potest, sic a nobis potest nominari").

Even if the traditional view works, therefore, it does not help explain how a person who has, for example, never heard Jesus Christ spoken of in a natural language can form the intention of believing in Christ, or of being united to him. He cannot form a sentence like "Christ, I believe in you" (or its equivalent in his own natural language), and so he cannot form the inward or mental intention of believing in Christ.[68] It is surely no accident that the ancient and medieval theologians who took more or less for granted the traditional picture of thought and language did not have the generous view of the saving value of non-Christian religions, their capacity to mediate the goods ordinarily communicated by baptism and faith, that has come to seem normal (or at least been common) after Vatican II. The views they held of thought and language were part of the reason, in fact, why the very possibility of salvation for those without baptism (or at least the well-formed desire for it) and some degree of explicit faith could be affirmed by Catholic theologians before the sixteenth century only in a marginal way, without much explanation.[69]

Even traditional views of the priority of thought over language held that we cannot attribute to human beings thoughts and intentions they lack the words to express. By contrast post-conciliar theology of religions regularly posits a capacity for just such thoughts and intentions, as a way of accounting for the presence of saving faith in Christ and a share in the paschal mystery among non-Christians. In principle any public discourse or social practice can serve as an adequate means for human beings to have faith in Christ. This surely includes the beliefs and practices of the great religions of the world, and may include explicit and persistent atheism as well.[70]

68. To be sure, the Church does attribute faith in Christ (the virtue, not the act) to some human beings who have no capacity to speak a natural language, in particular to baptized infants. This does not, however, require attributing to the infant an ability to form the intention of believing in Christ, to which she is just temporarily unable to give outward linguistic expression. For the traditional view of thought and language, the baptismal faith of infants is not an exception to the rule that what we can think of, we can speak of. The infant's faith is not, as in an adult, a disposition consequent upon the formation (under the impact of grace) of an intention to believe in Christ, but a saving gift of the Holy Spirit beyond the reach of nature, in that there can be no preparation for it in the infant herself. There is an intention to believe, and thus a kind of preparation, but it lies in the Church, and in particular those who profess the Church's faith on the infant's behalf at her baptism. As unifying soul of the Church the Spirit freely shares the faith professed by the infant's baptismal sponsors with the one being baptized. Aquinas comments: "The faith of one [member], indeed of the whole Church, benefits the infant by the operation of the Holy Spirit, who unites the Church and shares the goods of one with another" (*ST* III, q. 68, a. 9 ad 2).

69. There were also other factors in play; cf. my paper, "Perplexities Of Grace: Efficacy, Failure, and The Universal Saving Will of God," *The Thomist* (forthcoming). Especially in the Western Middle Ages there was, moreover, limited motivation to consider the matter in detail; cf. above, note 48.

70. For a defense of the idea of an open and lifelong but nonculpable atheism, which as such

Some human language and practice has to mediate the "wordless" interior experience of saving intimacy with Christ to those who have it.[71] But no specific discourse or practice is necessary, in particular the Church's missionary proclamation of Christ and her offer of a sacramental share in the paschal mystery. "[N]o matter what one states in his conceptual and theoretical-religious reflection, anyone who does not say in his *heart*, 'there is no God' (like the 'fool' in the psalm) but bears witness to him by the radical acceptance of his existence, is a believer" (Rahner's emphasis)—that is, a Christian believer, whose acceptance of his own being stems from the ever-present grace of the triune God: "In the acceptance of himself man is accepting Christ."[72] An "inclusivist" view along these lines assumes that explicit Christian faith and sacramental practice are the best and most secure way of expressing this interior or anonymous Christianity. But the saving intimacy with Christ normally granted by baptism and expressed in the communal profession of faith may be, and no doubt often is, present without them. As a result the Church's missionary project should expect that in many cases, "the proclamation of the gospel" simply "turns an anonymous Christian into someone who now also knows about his Christianity ... in an objectively reflective way and in a socially constituted confession, in the Church."[73]

Catholic theology of religions since Vatican II has most often followed this inclusivist pattern, undeterred by the difficulties involved in supposing that human beings can have definite beliefs and intentions they lack the linguistic resources to express. In fact inclusivist views usually betray no awareness of the possible difficulties facing this idea already recognized

---

can mediate "anonymous" saving faith in Christ, see Karl Rahner, "Atheism and Implicit Christianity," *Theological Investigations*, vol. 9 (London: Darton, Longman and Todd, n.d.), 145–64.

71. Literally "sentenceless" (*satzlose*), existing apart from any statement, proposition, or judgment. Karl Rahner, "Zur Frage der Dogmenentwicklung," *Schriften zur Theologie*, vol. 1, (Einsiedeln: Benziger Verlag, 1954–84), 77; *Theological Investigations*, vol. 1 (London: Darton, Longman and Todd, 1961), 64.

72. The quoted passages are from Rahner, "Anonymous Christians," 395, 394 (*Theological Investigations*, vol. 6; above, note 34). I have slightly modified the translation; cf. Karl Rahner, *Schriften zur Theologie*, vol. 6 (2nd ed., Einsiedeln: Benziger Verlag, 1968), 550. Similarly, the "innermost attitude and act of faith which grounds existence ... can in some circumstances take place in such a way that the conceptually objective content of this consciousness draws very little or almost nothing (or nothing at all?) from the explicit or anonymous stream of divine verbal communications within the official history of salvation." "Dogmatic Notes on 'Ecclesiological Piety,'" *Theological Investigations*, vol. 5, 336–65 (here: 353–54); translation slightly modified in light of *Schriften zur Theologie*, vol. 5 (2nd ed., Einsiedeln: Benziger Verlag, 1964), 399–400.

73. "Christianity and the Non-Christian Religions" (above, note 34), *Theological Investigations*, vol. 5, 132 (translation altered; see *Schriften zur Theologie*, vol. 5, 155).

by traditional accounts of thought and language, let alone those identified by modern analytic philosophers of language. For the most part they offer no arguments against these objections, but simply help themselves, in the manner of Rahner, to the claim that intentions and beliefs with definite content (for example, the intention to share in the paschal mystery, or the belief that the paschal mystery is saving for me) can be, in their innermost nature, "wordless." Or, though it comes to the same thing, they hold that virtually any utterance, regardless of its content, suffices to "mediate" definite intentions and beliefs to me, or for me to have them, granted that some utterances may do so more readily or more reliably than others. By such devices the inclusivist theologian of religions wants to hold that by committed adherence to the beliefs and practices of another religion, a person untouched by the Church's proclamation of Christ, perhaps even one who explicitly rejects it, can form the intention to share in the paschal mystery.

The main motive for inclusivism, and the plainest explanation of its popularity, lies in this claim to offer a robust answer to an important question left open, as we have seen, by the Council: how are saving faith in Christ and a share in the paschal mystery possible for non-Christians? Inclusivism answers by proposing that, for example, the statement, "Nirvana is the aim of human life" can rightly be taken to express the interior belief that participation in the life of the triune God is the aim of human life. The statement, "The dharma is the way to nirvana" can likewise be taken to express the "wordless" belief that Jesus Christ is the way to participation in the life of the triune God. How human communication is possible if we are free to take "nirvana" to refer not to the state of enlightenment that recognizes the non-entity of all things, but instead to participation in the life of the Trinity, or "the dharma" to refer to Jesus Christ, inclusivist theologians of religion typically do not say. In a similar way the inclusivist wants to say that the committed practice of Buddhist mindfulness forms the intention not of attaining nirvana, but of being united to Christ crucified. This is roughly like saying that assiduous practice at throwing crabapples against the side of a barn prepares one for playing the violin. Better to offer no answer at all than one as implausible as that.[74]

74 For a more detailed argument that religions propose different final aims rather than different paths to a common aim, see J. A. DiNoia, OP, *The Diversity of Religions: A Christian Perspective* (Washington, D.C.: The Catholic University of America Press, 1992).

Saving Action at a Distance

How we can attribute saving faith in Christ to those who lack the social and practical means to receive it, and the linguistic means to express it, so far remains unclear. The same goes *a fortiori* for the attribution of saving faith to those who have contact with the Church but remain outside her visible reality—the "men of good will"[75] who "through no fault of their own" remain adherents of other religions, or of no religion at all, yet who also "may attain eternal salvation."[76] We may offer one or another account of how saving faith can arise under these circumstances, or, prompted by *Gaudium et Spes* §22's apparent tolerance of agnosticism on this score, we may offer no account at all, leaving the matter to be known by God and not by us. Either way, it remains the clear teaching of the Council that any human being can have such faith. And this raises perhaps the most basic question stemming from Vatican II when it comes to the Church and non-Christian religions. According to *Ad Gentes* §7, the Church's missionary activity is necessary for the salvation of the world. How can this be, since according to *Gaudium et Spes* §22, and indeed *Ad Gentes* §7 itself, the missionary Church should expect to encounter those who have already become sharers in the saving mystery of the cross by faith?

Here Charles Journet introduces a useful distinction absent from more familiar ways of handling this question. Jesus Christ undertakes his saving action, Journet proposes, both by contact and at a distance. His action by contact, whether by way of his own human flesh or of the Church's preaching and sacramental ministry, always engages the senses. This sensible contact need not be tactile, as with baptism or the Eucharist; it can also be aural, as with the Church's proclamation of the gospel. In the nature of the case this action by contact is more direct and intimate than his action at a distance, which is purely interior and does not (yet) engage the senses. In either case saving grace in us is always a participation in Jesus' own personal fullness of grace. His grace can flow to us at a distance, when Jesus by the working of his Spirit teaches the mind and converts the heart without a response to the public proclamation of the Church and his sensible presence in her sacraments. When through the gift of his Spirit he teaches and converts by way of that proclamation and sensible sacramental presence, he acts in the more intimate manner of touch, of personal contact.

The language of action "by contact" and "at a distance" is familiar from

75. *GS* §22.
76. *LG* §16.

Newtonian physics, but in Journet's hands it is not simply a theological metaphor borrowed from early modern science. It correctly describes the way Jesus himself acts in the gospels, first of all in his acts of healing. Sometimes these acts take place from afar, as in the case of the centurion's servant (Mt 8:5–13), at other times (and more often) by contact, by word, touch, or both, as in the raising of Lazarus (Jn 11:28–44). "When Christ appeared it was through him, by *derivation* from his fullness (Jn 1:16), that grace flowed out into the world. This derivation can take place in two ways: by contact or from a distance, in the way in which Jesus healed bodies sometimes by contact and sometimes from a distance."[77] Jesus' delay in coming to Lazarus, Journet observes, can teach us that action by contact is the paradigm by contrast with which action at a distance may rightly be understood. "Why did he will to prolong his absence, apart from which Lazarus would not have died (Jn 11:21 and 32), if not to allow us to glimpse the privileged efficacy of his corporeal presence?"[78]

This stands to reason, especially if the body is not adventitious to our intimacy with God, if even the most sublime gifts of grace (including the gifts pertaining to knowledge, but not only those) must come to us embodied creatures through the senses. Christ founded his Church so that even now the saving action he "exercises from heaven could be channeled to us in a sensible way and continue to reach us in the manner that is best adapted to us—by way of direct contact."[79] Whether from the particular flesh of Jesus between his birth and his ascension, or from the Church and the sacraments that he willed her to enact until the end of time, "our nature ... has need of a sensible shock in order to be connaturally awakened to the life of grace."[80]

Only by this sensible contact does the grace of Christ reach us in its completeness and perfection. This means, in the present state of things between Christ's ascension and his return in glory, that he extends his grace to us in its fullness only through the public visible reality of the Church and her sacraments. Here alone Christ fully unites us to himself, by a grace that is,

77. Charles Journet, *Théologie de l'Église*, in *Œuvres complètes de Charles Journet*, vol. 15 (Paris: Éditions Lethielleux, 2017), 387 (originally published 1958). For an English version see Charles Cardinal Journet, *Theology of the Church*, trans. Victor Szczurek, O.Praem. (San Francisco: Ignatius Press, 2004), 322. In *L'Église du Verbe incarné*, the large work to which he devoted much of his life, Journet regularly uses this distinction between what Christ does "by contact" and "at a distance" to handle questions in ecclesiology broadly considered. See *Œuvres completes*, vol. 1, 30–51, 810–11; vol. 3, 1047–50, 1101, 1796–1802. *Théologie de l'Église* is, in Journet's term, an "abridgment" of the first two volumes of *L'Église du Verbe incarné* (*Œuvres completes*, vol. 15, 23; *Theology of the Church*, xxxi).

78. Journet, *Œuvres completes*, vol. 15, 142 (*Theology of the Church*, 103).

79. Journet, *Œuvres completes*, vol. 15, 143 (*Theology of the Church*, 104).

80. Journet, *Œuvres completes*, vol. 15, 142 (*Theology of the Church*, 104).

as Journet puts it, "fully Christic, fully Christ-conformed, and therefore fully Christ-conforming."[81] Christ's saving grace is, to be sure, offered to all, and his Spirit is at work in the heart of every human being to save each one of them. Among those untouched by the Church's proclamation and her sacraments, however, the saving grace of Christ is present in an as yet incomplete and imperfect way. Outside the visible bounds of the Catholic Church and of the explicit profession of Christian faith there are those who truly belong to Christ, and so also belong to his Church, if in a hidden way. Christ's Church is here truly present, though in an "initial," "tendential," and (Journet does not hesitate to say) "mutilated" way, which as such seeks out full visible union with Christ and his Church, urged on by his action at a distance—even if "through no fault of their own" those who belong to the Church in a hidden way are unable to attain this union in the present life. "[T]he unbaptized just [that is, justified] belong to the Church, which is the Mystical Body, in a salutary, but nevertheless initial—or mutilated—manner."[82]

So developed, the distinction between Christ's action at a distance and his action by contact helps ease the obvious tension between the Council's teaching that salvation in Christ is truly possible outside the visible boundaries of the Church,[83] and the teaching that the Church's mission to present Christ to the world is nonetheless necessary for salvation.[84] The Spirit's work of eliciting faith in those who cannot respond to the proclamation of the gospel or accept baptism imparts to them a genuine share in the paschal mystery, and so the promise of final salvation in Christ, but it does so at a distance, and thus in an imperfect and incomplete way. In just this way the Spirit's work as described in *Gaudium et Spes* §22 creates a craving for Christ's more intimate action by contact. This contact happens only in the Church, and through her sacraments. There alone Christ crucified and risen gives himself to us fully and immediately, to be touched and tasted by us.

When the Spirit invisibly works faith in the hearts of the unbaptized, he brings into being a "rough draft" (*ébauche*) of the Church, as Journet puts it, and so inclines those who have received this faith to seek out the full re-

81. Journet, *Œuvres completes*, vol. 15, 95; cf. 221 (*Theology of the Church*, 62; 175).

82. Journet, *Œuvres completes*, vol. 15, 218 (*Theology of the Church*, 172–73). Note that Journet here sees the Church and the Mystical Body of Christ as "co-extensive" (following the pattern of *Mystici Corporis Christi*), and just for this reason allows for a genuine, if imperfect, "belonging to" the Church for those who have inwardly embraced Christ's saving action at a distance, but remain outside the visible boundaries of the Church marked by baptism and the public profession of faith. See his description of "three distinct regimes" of belonging (which is not exactly "membership" in the strict or canonical sense), *Œuvres completes*, vol. 15, 384–91 (*Theology of the Church*, 319–24).

83. *GS* §22.

84. *AG* §7.

ality of the Church they presently sense, and belong to, only initially and in outline.[85] The saving faith Christ elicits at a distance just is, we could say, the tendency to seek out immediate contact with Christ proclaimed, present in the host, dwelling in the tabernacle. The missionary Church will reach many who do not yet have faith, and the mission will call them to it. And it will reach some, perhaps many, who already have faith, and offer to them the one true home their faith has always sought.

Conceived in this way, the availability of salvation to non-Christians does not compete with the public missionary activity of the Church, but anticipates and prepares for it. The Church's divine mandate "to save and renew every creature"[86] is precisely her mission to bring every human being into contact with the paschal mystery, or with the person of Christ himself in the saving mystery of his death and resurrection. That a share in the paschal mystery, and thereby final salvation, is available to those who do not yet enjoy contact with the Crucified cannot diminish the Church's missionary imperative. It could hardly do so, since saving faith at a distance, outside the visible boundaries of the Catholic Church, is simply an initial and incomplete version, or form, of the contact with the paschal mystery that is the aim of the Church's mission. Faith awakened at a distance just is a longing for contact with Jesus himself, even though the person to whom such faith has been given may as yet have no clear awareness that it is just this one whom she seeks.

To suppose that this faith could be content to remain at a distance is a bit like saying that a violinist who after long practice in private had mastered the most difficult parts of the Beethoven Violin Concerto could be satisfied not to play the whole concerto in public—even when an orchestra came to him and offered him the opportunity to perform it. The concerto is meant to be performed, as the paschal mystery is meant to be touched, and tasted. As *Ad Gentes* teaches, the Church must continue the saving mission with which she has been entrusted, until every human being has this contact with the paschal mystery—or until the close of the age (Mt 28:20), whichever comes first. In the process she will not only convert to Christ those who have not

85. "The Holy Spirit passes in a way beyond the frontiers of his Church (the Church in completed act), going to awaken those outside who sleep in the shadow death, and, if they accept the offers of his love, to begin among them, as a rough draft, a Church that is already his own (the Church in initiated act)" (*Œuvres completes*, vol. 15, 108 [*Theology of the Church*, 73]). Cf. 221 (175): "Christ pours out the graces of salvation on human beings in two ways: *from and distance and imperfectly* on those who are far off, and this grace ... can prepare only an indication, only an outline of the Church; but *by contact and fully* on those who immediately surround him" (Journet's emphasis).

86. *AG* §1.

believed in him, but be greeted with joy by those who, as *Gaudium et Spes* teaches, have from a distance longed for her coming.

It is often claimed that Rahner's inclusivism, or something like it, is required by the teaching of Vatican II on the universal availability of salvation in Christ. But an outlook like Journet's captures the teaching of the Council more effectively than standard inclusivism, since it not only embraces the universal offer of salvation but provides a lucid rationale for the Church's mission to "save every creature."

Rahner becomes noticeably irate at the suggestion that "anonymous" Christianity fails to uphold the universality and necessity of the Church's mission.[87] It is a bit hard to see why, at least as far as the logic of his position is concerned. On his view and others like it, the Church's mission to proclaim the gospel and share her sacramental life can bring about no union with Christ that the anonymous Christian does not already enjoy. The Church's missionary activity simply enables those who are already united with Christ in their hearts to become aware of this relationship in a more explicit way; in Rahner's jargon, it allows for a more adequate "categorial mediation" of one's "pre-thematic" union with Christ. Explicit faith so understood is not, to be sure, soteriologically trivial. It can, he says, enable those who attain it to get a firmer grip on the union with Christ they already experience inwardly, and this can make their salvation more certain and secure.[88] The Church's mission, moreover, will no doubt encounter those who are not yet Christians even anonymously. In their case the public proclamation of the gospel can be an occasion for the needed interior conversion to, and union with, Christ. But this proclamation is not necessary to that end, any more than it was necessary for those who came to that interior union without it, by way of whatever religion they already inhabit or, as the case may be, of no religion at all.

On Journet's account, by contrast, the Church's sacramental and verbal mission imparts a reality that is available in no other way: contact with Christ crucified and risen, an intimacy of taste and touch with the paschal mystery. The significance of the Church's mission is thus, if you like, straightforwardly ontological rather than merely epistemological. It does not simply bring about clearer knowledge of a relationship with Christ that

87. To be concerned about this, he says, would be "quite foolish." *Theological Investigations*, vol. 6, 397.

88. "A clearer and purer reflective grasp of Christianity offers, as such, a greater opportunity for salvation to the individual human being than if he were only an anonymous Christian" (*Theological Investigations*, vol. 5, 132, modified; see *Schriften zur Theologie*, vol. 5, 156).

already obtains. Rather, it brings about a relationship that did not previously obtain, the supreme and most intimate relationship normally available in this life. Apart from the Church's public mission, and thus outside her visible boundaries, the Holy Spirit is surely at work for the salvation of every human being. The supernatural grace the Spirit gives suffices for salvation; in those who inwardly accept this grace, it is the beginning of salvation in Christ. In this initial form, though, supernatural grace opens up—in fact, it just is—an interior space that longs to be filled by the contact with Christ that it does not yet possess. The Church's mission alone meets this need, with the sacramental presence of Christ.

It is, of course, standard Catholic teaching that grace and charity can grow, or be "augmented."[89] Catholic doctrine thus allows that human beings without baptism or publicly professed faith can live in sanctifying grace, or be among the just, as it is traditionally put, yet still be in need of the immeasurably greater perfection of grace and charity that only sacramental contact with Christ can provide. There is no need to suppose, as positions like Rahner's apparently do, that sanctifying grace in the "anonymous" Christian already brings about the same contact with Christ that the baptized enjoy, so that the Church's mission only meets the need of human nature, under the impact of this interior grace, for a more adequate verbal mediation of what it has already undergone. Journet remarks: "To the question of the *necessity of missions*, it is not enough to respond, as some have done, that they are necessary only *relatively*, in order that the divine plan of salvation be better accomplished. One must reply that they are necessary *absolutely*, in order that the final plan of salvation be truly accomplished ... so that human beings may be snatched from an abnormal condition where the salvation of Christ is accessible to them only 'by desire,' in a merely inchoate, imperfect, and perilous fashion."[90]

Lastly, making a distinction between Christ's action by contact and his action at a distance helps us to make progress, at least up to a point, on a question that has so far proven puzzling: how, if at all, salvation in Christ can be mediated outside the public sacramental life of the Church, and in particular by non-Christian religions.

89. See the Council of Trent's Decree on Justification, chs. 10 and 16, together with canons 24 and 32; DH 1535, 1548, 1574, 1582 (= Heinrich Denzinger, *Enchiridion Symbolorum: A Compendium of Creeds, Definitions, and Declarations of the Catholic Church* [Latin-English], 43rd ed., ed. Peter Hünermann [San Francisco: Ignatius Press, 2012]). Behind these texts lies a long theological discussion centering on the interpretation of Peter Lombard's *Sentences*, bk. I, dist. 17; medieval theologians differed on how growth in grace and charity should be explained, but not on the reality of such growth.

90. Journet, *Œuvres completes*, vol. 15, 410 (Journet's emphasis; *Theology of the Church*, 340).

We were faced with two problems on this score, one theological, the other philosophical. Theologically, we found no way to understand the beliefs and practices of other religions as ways of mediating, or giving access to, saving faith in Christ. This seemed to require treating what other religious communities say and do as effective equivalents of publicly professing the Church's faith and receiving her sacraments of initiation. But if, as Vatican II teaches, the Church's mission is truly universal and her sacraments uniquely efficacious, there can be no such equivalents. Philosophically, we found no way to make sense of the idea that people can have beliefs and intentions, specifically belief in Jesus Christ as universal savior and the intention to be united with him, when they lack the linguistic means to express that belief and form that intention, or even more, when they have available the linguistic means the Church's mission provides, yet do not express that belief or intention (continuing, for example, to adhere to another religion rather than Christianity).

An outlook like Journet's not only ameliorates the theological problem but eliminates it. As it is normally available to human beings in this life, salvation in Christ has its fullest and most complete form in the intimacy of contact with him. It is just this intimacy by contact at which the Church's mission aims, and which her proclamation and sacraments can alone provide, or mediate. Apart from baptism and the profession of the Church's faith, and thus at a greater or lesser distance from the Church's universal mission, salvation in Christ is genuinely available, precisely in the form of a graced desire for that contact with him offered only by the missionary Church. We can thus maintain that the Church's mission is truly universal and her sacraments without effective substitutes, and at the same time that salvation in Christ is truly possible for every human being.

When the matter is understood in this way, there is no theological or doctrinal obstacle to reading the high estimate of non-Christian religions in *Nostra Aetate* (and in LG §16) as including some capacity to mediate salvation in Christ. Christ's saving action at a distance can, in other words, make use of the beliefs and practices of non-Christian religions, to the extent that those religions "reflect a ray of that truth that enlightens all men."[91] It is not, I think, strictly necessary to read *Nostra Aetate* §2 as ascribing this mediating potential to what is "true and holy" in non-Christian religions. One might hold that, apart from explicit Christian faith, the truth and holiness present in non-Christian religions does not suffice to connect the adherents

91. *NA* §2.

of those religions to "the truth that enlightens all men" in a saving way. For the most part, ancient and medieval Christian theology saw the matter in this way, affirming the presence of truth and moral goodness, in greater or lesser degree, outside the visible borders of the Church, but denying that these could be means of salvation. Reading *Nostra Aetate* §2 and *Lumen Gentium* §16 in this way does, however, seem to go against the drift, if not the precise letter, of these texts. The same could be said for typical post-conciliar teaching on non-Christian religions.[92]

A view along Journet's lines creates the logical space for both the unique saving significance of the Church's sacramental life and the genuine potential of non-Christian religions to mediate salvation in Christ. Any particular human being either is baptized or she is not, and (normally in baptism) has either professed publicly the Christian faith, or she has not. It is impossible to be sort of baptized, or baptized up to a point. Baptism thus needs a toggle concept to capture its saving significance, an "on/off" concept, one that either applies or it does not. "Contact" is just such a concept. A and B are either touching or they are not, in contact or not. Understood as contact with the realities of the paschal mystery, baptism brings about a relationship with Christ that either obtains or it does not. This is just how Catholic doctrine understands baptism and the faith it professes: a gift for which there is, and in the nature of the case can be, no substitute.

Mediation, by contrast, can be more or less effective, more or less complete; it admits of degrees. It therefore needs a scalar concept to capture the way it works, one that applies more or less. "Distance" is such a concept. A and B can be close, or far apart, less or more distant from one another. The panoply of human religious practices and beliefs can be relatively close to those by which Christ creates contact with himself in his Church, or relatively far off, less or more distant. While nothing can prevent Christ's saving action, those practices and beliefs that are close will, on the whole, be more effective in mediating his action at a distance than those that are far off (granted that what makes for proximity among religions and what inhibits it is a complex matter about which it will be difficult to warrant clear judgments, and impossible in the case of an individual adherent of this or that religion). The vanishing point of distance is contact. Non-Christian religions can be understood as, on the whole, more or less likely to foster a yearn-

92. See, e.g., John Paul II, *Tertio Millennio Adveniente*, 6: "*The Incarnate Word is the fulfilment of the yearning present in all the religions of mankind*: this fulfilment is the work of God that exceeds every human expectation" (emphasis in the original).

ing for contact with the incarnate Word, the yearning that Christ's saving action at a distance aims to produce. We can thus appreciate the diverse religions, in the way Vatican II seems to urge, as instruments serviceable to Jesus Christ in the salvation of human beings, without taking them as substitutes for the sacraments of the Church, or supposing that they offer the contact with him that the Church and her sacraments alone can bring about. Affirming that non-Christian religions can to some extent mediate salvation in Christ need not, as we initially worried, contradict the Council's teaching on the Church's universal missionary imperative.

Distinguishing between contact and distance has two further theological advantages over the way Rahnerian inclusivism thinks about the Church and non-Christian religions. It properly makes the relationship between Christianity and other religions an empirical question, and it captures elements in Vatican II's teaching on non-Christian religions that inclusivism is deeply inclined to overlook.

Non-Christian religions can in fact mediate salvation in Christ, we have argued, but they do so at a distance, and distance comes in amounts, in more and less. In order to find out whether a particular set of religious practices and beliefs actually succeeds in mediating salvation in Christ, and with roughly what degree of success, we need to gauge, to the extent that we can, the distance between those practices and beliefs and the sacramental life of the Church. This is an empirical matter. So far as it can be discerned by us, the distance between the practices and beliefs of the Church and those of other religions will have to be measured by actually looking at those religions, becoming acquainted as best we can with their manifold particularities, and entering into patient dialogue with their adherents. The mediation of salvation in Christ outside the public life of the Church has to be discovered. It is not, as a view like Rahner's seems to suppose, an a priori truth about all religions. Seeing the matter Rahner's way actually encourages indifference to the knowledge of other religions, by fostering the empirically vacuous conviction that we already know what is most important in any particular religion (its capacity to mediate salvation, as understood by Christians) without having to look. It is not an accident that Journet, unlike Rahner, took an interest in the actual history and beliefs of non-Christian religions, and wrote extensively about the salvation-historical significance of those religions—especially Judaism—and their relationship to the faith of the Church.[93]

93. On Judaism, see *Destinées d'Israël: A propos du salut par les Juifs*, in *Œuvres completes*, vol. 11 (formerly vol. 9), 17–431 (originally published 1945), and the detailed treatment of "L'économie de la loi

From a greater or lesser distance, non-Christian religions can mediate the salvation that is in Christ, but they will also, to use Journet's term, "deviate" from the truth and goodness that are in Christ, in rough equivalence to their distance from the Church's faith and practice. He can put this quite sharply. Where they are present in non-Christian religions, "rays" of Christ's goodness and truth will tend to undermine those very religions, prompting an awareness of the inadequacy of other religions on the part of their own adherents. "Even at the heart of religious deviations, God raises up for himself true disciples who, without knowing it and perhaps even against their conscious design, work to rectify those deviations and tend, by separating the true and the false in them, to dissolve them from within."[94]

It is not usual in post-conciliar theology to talk about other religions this way, in part on the assumption that acknowledging religious disagreement inevitably inspires violence against those with whom one disagrees. Surely not. When they encounter people who disagree with their teaching, Christ's faithful will respond "without spilling anyone's blood but their own."[95] Religious disagreement is in any case empirically obvious; likewise, the great many degrees of which it admits. The disagreement between Christians and others who "worship a single God" (*unicum Deum adorant*, as *NA* §3 says of Islam) is, on its face, less than that between Christians and those who practice child sacrifice.[96] A religion that worships a single God and abominates child sacrifice is correspondingly more apt to mediate salvation in Christ than one that worships multiple gods and practices child sacrifice. By looking at non-Christian religions as, in essence, no more than so many different, but equally effective, ways of mediating the grace of Christ, Rahnerian inclusivism encourages disregard for the distance between other religions and the Church, and for how much that distance can vary. As a result inclusivism tends to overlook, or ignore, the clear acknowledgments of this distance in the teaching of Vatican II. By the light and grace of Christ, the Council clearly teaches, salvation is available to every human being. Yet we cannot assume, *Lumen Gentium* warns in the same breath, that other religions will generally succeed in leading their adherents to salvation

mosaïque" in Tome III of *L'Église du Verbe incarné*, *Œuvres completes*, vol. 4, 654–816 (originally published 1969); the latter includes, among other things, theological discussions of post-biblical Judaism and the establishment of the modern state of Israel. Regarding Journet's approach to non-Christian religions more generally, see Michel Cagin, OSB, "La théologie des religions chez Charles Journet," *Revue thomiste* 106 (2006): 173–203.

94. Journet, *Œuvres completes*, vol. 15, 389 (*Theology of the Church*, 323).

95. Journet, *Œuvres completes*, vol. 15, 411 (*Theology of the Church*, 341).

96. On some questions posed by "unicum Deum adorant," see below.

in Christ, still less that non- or anti-religious ways of life will do so. "More often (*saepius*) human beings, deceived by the evil one, have become vain in their thoughts and have exchanged the truth of God for a lie, serving the creature rather than the Creator (Rom 1:21 & 25).... Therefore to promote the glory of God and procure the salvation of all of these, the Church, mindful of the command of the Lord, 'Proclaim the gospel to every creature' (Mk 16:6), takes care zealously to foster missions."[97]

Journet's distinction between action by contact and at a distance also offers some help with the philosophical question we have confronted. Granted that non-Christian religions could mediate salvation in Christ without compromising the Church's universal missionary imperative, how can this actually happen? Sharing in the paschal mystery is by nature intentional, and it seems that only the missionary Church can provide the cognitive (and in particular, the linguistic) resources needed for forming the intention to share in it. Yet the Council clearly teaches that salvation in Christ is genuinely offered to all, including those untouched by, or (through no fault of their own) unresponsive to, the Church's mission.

Since distance comes in less and more, we don't have to see the linguistic and conceptual resources for mediating salvation in Christ as simply either present or absent. It seems obvious that some formations of religious practice and belief are closer to Christianity in their linguistic and conceptual resources than others, as Islam is manifestly closer than the cult of Molech. It therefore seems plausible that the religions which are closer would, on the whole, offer the means necessary for forming the intention to be united with Christ more effectively than those which are farther away.

Measuring the "distance" between Christianity and other religions is at best an uncertain and tentative enterprise. There are no bright lines, certainly no lines readily discernable by us, that separate religious formations adequate for forming the intention to be united with Christ from those that are simply inadequate. We know that the Church's proclamation of the gospel is alone fully sufficient for the formation of this intention, and can see other religions as more or less adequate to its formation. We need not choose between the philosophical implausibility of inclusivism and what looks, on doctrinal grounds, like the excessive stringency of denying to other religions conceptual and linguistic resources even minimally sufficient for mediating salvation in Christ. By viewing all religions as more or less equally useful means for giving human beings a share in the paschal mystery, inclusivism

97. *LG* §16. In the same vein see the passages from *AG* §§3 and 9, cited above at notes 4 and 5.

turns every tosser of crabapples into a would-be violinist. By teaching not only that truth and goodness are found in religions outside the Church, but that all such truth and goodness is a ray of Christ's own light, Vatican II surely encourages us to find a way of understanding how the linguistic and conceptual resources for union with Christ can likewise be present outside the Church.

All this seems right as far as it goes, but on closer inspection some difficult problems arise. Take the case of Islam. Christians now often hold that Muslims worship the same God that they do. Like Judaism, Christianity and Islam are "Abrahamic religions," believing in, worshipping, and following one and the same God in their different ways—they share "the faith of Abraham."[98] It seems likely, though, that Muslims actually intend *not* to worship the same God as Christians. According to their creedally codified faith, the "one God" in whom Christians believe is "the Father almighty" who, just because he is the Father, has an "only Son," a Son who is himself "true God," yet is not the Father. The Son is "true God *from* true God," and so is not simply identical with the Father from whom he is. Yet Christians profess to believe in "one God." As Christian theology, articulating this creedal faith, has put the matter since the late fourth century, the Son is another *person* from the Father, but not another *God*; so also the Holy Spirit is another person from the Father and the Son, but not another God. Appreciating that this is the belief of Christians, Islamic tradition has generally held that Christianity fails to locate a single God for worship, and thereby fails to worship the one God known to Muslims. Islam itself evidently rejects the "same God thesis," in Bruce McCormack's term, now commonly proposed by Christians.[99]

In its brief discussions of Islam, Vatican II is interestingly cautious on this score. As we have noted, it says of Muslims, "*unicum Deum adorant*"—"they worship a single God."[100] *Lumen Gentium* §16 uses the same language: "*nobiscum Deum adorant unicum*" ("with us, they worship a single God"). Evidently taking it for granted that Christians and Muslims do worship one and the same God, standard translations overlook this caution, and read the Council as asserting the "same God thesis." Thus Flannery: "They worship God, who is one"; "together with us, they adore the one ... God."[101]

98. For an acute problematizing of the notion of an "Abrahamic religion," see Jon D. Levenson, *Inheriting Abraham: The Legacy of the Patriarch in Judaism, Christianity, and Islam* (Princeton, N.J.: Princeton University Press, 2012).

99. See his contribution to this volume.

100. *NA* §3.

101. *NA* §3 and *LG* §16. Flannery, 739, 367.

By twice using the term *unicum* ("single," "sole") rather than *unum* ("one," hence "the one . . . "), however, the Council can be read as deliberately leaving this question open. *Lumen Gentium* §16's use of *nobiscum* ("with us") is the strongest evidence to the contrary. But this passage can be taken simply to say that Christians and Muslims have something important in common, namely that they worship only one God, a single God, not necessarily that this is the same God.

At this point a host of questions arise that we will not be able to pursue further here. Christians and Muslims (to continue with our example) clearly hold different, and indeed contradictory, beliefs about God. Christians believe that God is the Father, the Son, and the Holy Spirit; Muslims believe that God is not the Son or the Holy Spirit, and so is "Father," if at all, in some sense other than Christians propose (viz., by actually having a Son). Sometimes, though, we can locate or identify one and the same thing while using opposed descriptions of it; moreover we may know that we are doing this, or be unaware that we are doing it. Thus "the evening star" and "the morning star" both locate the planet Venus; we know this, while the ancients, or at least some of them, apparently did not. Are Christian and Muslim descriptions of God (triune; not triune) like this? Perhaps, but they might also be like another familiar case where two people see a figure approaching, and correctly share the belief that it is a single human being. One forms the belief that this single human being is Barack Obama, and the other that it is Donald Trump. Each prepares an effusive welcome for a single human being they both rightly believe is coming their way, but at most only one of them can be correct about who this human being actually is, and can be correspondingly disposed to offer his planned embrace.

The question, to generalize, is how much our descriptions of God have to have in common, and what precise sort of common description we need, in order for us to say intelligibly that we are talking about, and thus intending or believing in, the same thing. We might then ask whether intention is really necessary for worship. Could Christians and Muslims not worship the same God, even though one of them (or both) did not intend this? Inclusivists often talk as if they could. For this to happen, though, not only would particular intentions need to float free (implausibly, I have argued) of any particular beliefs about the world; human acts with a definite purpose (worship) and a definite content or object (God) would have to take place without any intention on the part of the agent to perform them. This seems, in an especially unlikely way, to make of the crabapple thrower a prospective violinist. It also undercuts the respect for other religions that usually motivates inclusivism: "You think your intention is to worship Allah as he commands, but actually your purpose is to find a share in the paschal mystery." Between Christianity and Islam, as also between Christianity and Judaism, the logic and psychology of worshipping "the same God" proves difficult to work out in a convincing way.[102]

The teaching of Vatican II on the possibility of a share in the paschal mystery for every human being confronts us with some philosophical problems that remain unsolved. Nevertheless the conflict between this teaching and the Council's insistence on the Church's universal missionary mandate is, I have argued, apparent rather than real. To be sure, the arguments by which I have sought to make the tension go away don't work for Judaism, or they work only in a limited way. But this should not surprise. Vatican II does not treat Judaism as simply one among many non-Christian religions. It sees the Church's relation to the Jewish people and their religion as *sui generis*. So we should not expect the categories we use to understand the Church's relation to non-Christian religions to apply without remainder to Judaism. We should, on the contrary, look for that relationship to pose theological challenges unique to it, challenges that will have to be met, if they can be, in their own way.

102. For a more detailed approach to some of these questions, focused not on Islam but on the Christian claim to worship the same God as the Jews, see my article, "Do Christians Worship the God of Israel?" in *Knowing the Triune God*, ed. James J. Buckley and David S. Yeago (Grand Rapids, Mich.: Eerdmans, 2001), 231–64. Rémi Brague offers a brief but wide-ranging and provocative treatment of the relationship of the Christian "image" of God to those of other religions, especially Islam, in *On the God of the Christians (and on one or two others)*, trans. Paul Seaton (South Bend, Ind.: St Augustine's Press, 2013); on difficulties inherent in claiming that Christians worship the same God as adherents of other religions, see especially chapters 1–3.

Chapter 8

Dignity and Domination

A Thomistic Sketch

John R. Bowlin

My topic is basic human dignity as a source of fundamental human rights, in particular the right not to be dominated. By domination, I refer to a feature of certain human relationships, relationships that leave some persons vulnerable to the arbitrary power of others, to power that need not give due account of itself.[1]

My inspiration comes from four mid-twentieth-century documents on the relationship between the church and the modern world. They are, in many ways, siblings, these four. I want to look at the time line and concerns that connect them, and I want to reflect on their different responses to the question of human dignity and the problem of domination. Along the way, I will consider how human dignity might be regarded theologically, how Aquinas's treatment of the natural law might contribute to that regard, and how a right not to be dominated might emerge from Thomas's contribution. Toward the end, I will consider how this account of dignity and domination might contribute to Christianity's civic project.

Four Documents

On April 11, 1963, Pope John XXIII promulgated *Pacem in Terris*. It was, according to Russell Hittinger, the high point in the effort initiated by Pope

1. Freedom from domination is the republican ideal of liberty. See Philip Pettit, *Republicanism: A Theory of Freedom and Government* (Oxford: Oxford University Press, 1997), 51–109.

Leo XIII to integrate the modern human rights project with the Catholic natural law tradition.[2]

The central concerns of *Pacem in Terris*—the equal dignity of every human person, the rights and duties that "flow as a direct consequence" from this feature of our shared humanity, the common good that emerges as rights are recognized and duties fulfilled, and the freedom from domination, from the arbitrary will of others, that "safeguards" this dignity[3]—each of these themes appears in Dr. Martin Luther King Jr.'s famous *Letter* from that same year.[4]

Writing just five days later from a city jail in Birmingham, Alabama, Dr. King quotes Augustine's famous remark from book I of *De Libero Arbitrio* (I.v.11). "An unjust law is no law at all." The claim, he says, should be "put in the terms of St. Thomas Aquinas: an unjust law is a human law that is not rooted in eternal and natural law."[5] His examples were close at hand: the conditions of legally enforced racial domination and segregation that he and others were contesting. There were some laws that forced black Americans to suffer undue losses to their persons, property, and dignity, while enabling their white fellow citizens to use the public offices of the state to secure private gain. There were other laws that imposed burdens on a minority without their consent and that guaranteed unchecked power to a majority. And there were otherwise just laws applied unjustly, with the aim of bringing benefit to some and undue harm to others.

Promulgated roughly two and a half years later, on the final day of the Second Vatican Council, *Gaudium et Spes* picks up these same themes. Human beings are created "to the image of God" (*GS* §12). All have a share "in the light of the divine mind" (*GS* §15), all have a law in their hearts "written by God" (*GS* §16). Their dignity comes by virtue of obedience to this law (*GS* §16), in actions that emerge from knowledge and free choice, not "blind impulse" or "external pressure" (*GS* §17). A collection of basic rights and duties, "universal and inviolable," follows from this "equal dignity of persons" (*GS* §§26, 29, 41), and justice is done and the common good secured when this equal dignity is recognized and when these rights and duties find expression in every social and political relationship (*GS* §26). Concretely, this

2. F. Russell Hittinger, "Natural Law and Public Discourse: The Legacies of Joseph Ratzinger," *Loyola Law Review* 60, no. 4 (2014): 241–71, here 271.

3. *Pacem in Terris*, 9, 14, 27, 40, 43, 44, 60, 87, 88.

4. Martin Luther King Jr., "Letter from a Birmingham Jail," in *I Have a Dream: Writings and Speeches That Changed the World*, ed. James Melvin Washington (San Francisco: HarperCollins, 1986), 83–100.

5. Martin Luther King Jr., "Letter from a Birmingham Jail," 89.

means that no relationship can be called just and good that "insults human dignity" (*GS* §27), that includes "domination by an individual or a political party" (*GS* §§75, 50), that is structured by unaccountable power and undue authority, leaving one party literally at the mercy of another. The Council mentions "subhuman living conditions, arbitrary imprisonment, deportation, slavery, prostitution, the selling of women and children; as well as disgraceful working conditions, where men are treated as mere tools for profit, rather than as free and responsible persons" (*GS* §27).

Finally, in May of that same year, 1965, a first draft of what eventually became *The Confession of 1967* was presented at the General Assembly of the United Presbyterian Church in the USA.[6] Among these four mid-twentieth-century documents on the relationship between the church and the modern world, the *Confession of 1967* (hereafter, *C'67*) is the outlier with respect to the themes of dignity and domination. Offered as "a present witness of God's grace in Jesus Christ" and addressing the issues of the day—racial discrimination, war, poverty, and the sexual revolution—*C'67* speaks in entirely different terms. It does not refer to a natural human dignity or a universal regime of human rights and correlative obligations. It speaks infrequently and, at times, ambivalently about justice and not at all about the good shared in common by those who participate in rightly ordered social and political relationships.[7] Most significantly, it does not identify domination as a central feature of social sin or speak of the need to hold power accountable to the norms of justice.

Instead it refers to God's "love for all humankind," to God's desire for a covenant relationship with all people.[8] It speaks of human sin and of the need for "God's reconciling act in Jesus Christ."[9] And it accents the effects of this act: a community of faithful people set right with God,[10] reconciled with one another, and enabled by the Holy Spirit to give and receive forgiveness.[11] In faith, this covenant people knows that "God loves and accepts them in spite of what they are," and they bear witness to the object of their

6. The chair of the drafting committee was Prof. Edward Dowey Jr. of Princeton Theological Seminary.

7. We are free to "work for justice and peace in society" in accord with God's purposes (9.17). We have to "fight against pretentions and injustices" of temporal power (9.25), and we must concede that "God's reconciliation in Jesus Christ is the ground" of whatever justice is actually achieved (9.45b). At the same time, our devotion to justice should be regarded with suspicion, as a mask for sin. We must confess that all human virtue is "infected by self-interest and hostility" (9.13).

8. *C'67*, 9.18–19.

9. *C'67*, 9.12–9.14; 9.10.

10. *C'67*, 9.10.

11. *C'67*, 9.20.

faith by reproducing this reconciling love, as the Spirit allows, in each of their social and political relationships.[12]

My point in drawing our attention to this distinction between *C'67* and the other three is not to disparage this talk of reconciliation and love, of relationships forged anew by God's redeeming grace. By no means! Indeed, the other documents speak in roughly these terms as well, *Gaudium et Spes* in particular. Its justly famous paragraph 22 refers to the fact that in Christ's sacrifice "God reconciled us to Himself." God delivered us from the bondage of sin, gathered us up into the household of God according "to the likeness of that Son Who is the firstborn of many brothers," and so enabled us to receive "the first-fruits of the Spirit" (Rom 8:23) and discharge "the new law of love" (*GS* §22). Whatever it is that we must say about human nature as the root of human dignity, for *Gaudium et Spes* it is "only in the mystery of the incarnate Word" that human nature comes fully to light and so too our special dignity (*GS* §§19, 22).

No, my point is that, unlike the other three, *C'67* does not pair its talk of a covenant relationship created on Divine initiative with the discourses of justice. It gives no attention to the thought that a covenant relationship with the God of Israel might have something to do with human dignity and human rights or with the need to oppose relationships structured by arbitrary power, power that need not give an account of itself by referring to the norms of justice.

The sources of this inattention, the reasons that account for *C'67*'s outlier status, are not immediately apparent in its paragraphs, but I think we can identify two. The first regards justice as an object of desire, and it follows from a suspicion: that the desire for any good, even the good of a rightly ordered social or political relationship, is, in the words of *C'67*, "infected by self-interest, . . . [by] hostility" to God and neighbor.[13]

By these lights, the desire for justice invariably comes with the dear self's desire for its own good, and this makes our commitment to the ideals of justice invariably self-consuming, self-defeating. Justice should regard the person we are obliged to treat justly. It should regard the good *they* are due and the benefit that comes to *them* by virtue of the just treatment they receive. This is its basic requirement. And yet if it's justice that I want, if the good its act achieves prompts my will and elicits my choice, then in the last analysis what I really want is something for myself—this good that I

12. *C'67*, 9.22; 9.44a–9.47d.
13. *C'67*, 9.13.

desire. In some way, it's my own welfare, my own happiness, that ultimately concerns me, not the good of the person I treat justly. Since sin invariably deforms my desires, my commitment to the just welfare of others, no matter its sincerity, will always arrive as a hoodwink and a swindle, as an instance of self-interested self-deception. Or better, in the language of *C'67*, it will always bears witness to our subtle capacity to "claim mastery of [our] own lives, turn against God and each other, and become exploiters and despoilers of the world."[14]

The suspicion is confirmed and amplified by the modern habit of speaking of justice in terms of subjective rights—something that *Pacem in Terris*, *Gaudium et Spes*, and Dr. King all deliberately do. A right, by *these* lights, is a claim that one party makes *against* another for the performance of some action or the delivery of some good. The person who makes the claim wants this performance, she desires this good, and not for the person who delivers it, not principally, but rather for herself. What other reason could possibly motivate a claim for her own right? If these suspicions are sound, then the church should obviously express its witness to the world by referring to selfless love and the work of reconciliation, while keeping quiet (or mostly quiet) about justice and its norms.

So goes the first reason that accounts for *C'67's* outlier status. The second regards human dignity and follows from a worry linked to a different suspicion. Both can be inferred from but not exactly found *in* the *Confession of 1967*—inferred from its silences and from the influence that Karl Barth's views had on its content and spirit.[15]

The worry is this: an account of human dignity and human rights that begins with our shared humanity, with our rational capacities and our basic grasp of the natural law, in effect begins in the wrong place. At the very least, it shifts our attention, right at the start, away from the reconciling work of God in Jesus Christ and toward something else, toward our own rational powers and moral capacities, powers and capacities that can be specified and known—perhaps imperfectly, but known nevertheless—apart from what God has done for us in Jesus Christ, apart from the relationship God has cre-

14. *C'67*, 9.12.

15. For an account of that influence see James H. Moorhead, "Redefining Confessionalism: American Presbyterians in the Twentieth Century," in *The Confessional Mosaic: Presbyterian and Twentieth-Century Theology*, ed. Milton J. Coalter, John M. Mulder, and Louis B. Meeks (Louisville, Ky.: Westminster/John Knox, 1990), 59–83, and "Beyond the Battle for the Bible: What Evangelicals Missed in Van Til's Critique of Barth," in *Karl Barth and American Evangelicalism*, ed. Bruce L. McCormack and Clifford B. Anderson (Grand Rapids, Mich.: Eerdmans, 2011), 42–72.

ated with us through the sacrifice of the Lamb, apart from the role we now occupy in the household of God.[16]

This worry is a variation on Barth's concern with natural theology and it comes with the following suspicion: that an account of human dignity and human rights derived in some way from our shared humanity in fact naturalizes the contingent. It makes necessary and universal what in fact is not, presumably in order to valorize some local set of norms and commitments. The thought is that those norms and commitments cannot be both determinate enough to specify concrete action and yet natural in the sense that they are recognized by all human beings and (more or less) embodied in their lives. The suspicion is that an appeal to our shared humanity cannot, on its own, do the work of making human dignity determinate enough in terms of content to identify the fundamental rights and specific duties that are said to follow from it.

When we make this appeal nevertheless, the dignity we describe and the rights and duties we identify will not be deliverances of our shared humanity but projected longings. Offered as harmless narcissism, they will express our desire to have some collection of home truths—our own "arbitrary ethic" as Barth would put it—valorized and justified through reference to human nature, created and shared.[17] Offered by those with cultural power and economic might, our talk of dignity and rights can express a desire to determine the conditions of the social and political relationships in which we stand, to have our home truths regulate the lives of others. Since these benefits are obvious and since home truths are many, this appeal to human dignity will be commonly and unhelpfully made, quite often on both sides of the most contentious moral and political debates.[18]

So goes the suspicion.[19] It's widely shared among the many secular

16. Thus Barth: "The order of obligation built on the order of being cannot as such be a real order of obligation, or at any rate of a divinely imperative obligation, as introduced by Jesus Christ, in the divine act of the world's reconciliation with God as the act of His pure goodness. If obligation is grounded in being, this undoubtedly means that it is not grounded in itself, but ontically subordinate to another, and noetically to be derived from this other. It is imperative only in virtue of that which is over it; and it becomes imperative for us only in virtue of its derivation from it. But if what is over it is the being in which man participates in his way as God does in His, how can it be and become imperative except with the assistance and co-operation of man, except on the presupposition of his agreement?" Throughout, all citations from the *CD* are from *Church Dogmatics*, 4 vols, in 13 parts, ed. G. W. Bromiley and T. F. Torrance (Edinburgh: T&T Clark, 1936–75). Here, *CD* II/2, 532.

17. *CD* II/2, 515.

18. The point is well made by Christopher McCrudden, "In Pursuit of Human Dignity: An Introduction to Current Debates," in *Understanding Human Dignity*, Proceedings of the British Academy, 192, ed. Christopher McCrudden (Oxford: Oxford University Press, 2013), 1–58, here 1; Michael Rosen, "Dignity: The Case Against," in *Understanding Human Dignity*, 143–54, here 149.

19. It's a variation on the Sellarsian critique of givenness. The determinate demands that we

critics of the discourses of human dignity; to this critique they tend to add the charge of speciesism and worries about disability, about persons who lack the aspect of our shared humanity that is said to confer dignity upon us.[20]

In what follows, I take up four tasks that will put these four documents in conversation around these themes of dignity and domination. First, I consider what *C'67* can learn about justice and desire from *Pacem in Terris*, *Gaudium et Spes*, and the traditions of Catholic moral theology in which they stand. Second, I draw on Thomas's treatment of human beings as subject to divine rule in order to recast the account of human dignity presented in *Pacem in Terris*, *Gaudium et Spes*, and Dr. King's letter in light of the concerns expressed in the *Confession of 1967*. Third, I offer three qualifications that distinguish my own understanding of citizenship, divine jurisdiction, and human dignity from Thomas's. And finally, I consider how Dr. King's light touch with natural law theory addresses a problem created for the church and its public witness by the theological recasting of human dignity and human rights that I propose. In his willingness to pair Thomas with Augustine, all the pieces come together: justice and the common good, dignity and role, domination and human rights.

Justice and Its Common Good

The relative inattention to justice in the *Confession of 1967* is, in large measure, a consequence of Kantian doubts about the moral status of any human action done for the sake of some good that is known and desired—desired by and for the agent who acts. In mid-twentieth-century Protestant theology, these doubts found prominent expression in Anders Nygren's famous work *Agape and Eros* (1930, 1936) and in Karl Barth's Christological reworking of the "concept and actuality of obligation."[21] In our own day, these doubts

endorse on appeal to created nature and human dignity—the particular catalogue of rights and duties—are simply *given*, given without drawing on the capacities, powers, and commitments, the social and political relationships, the roles and offices, that would in fact account for them, that would make them determinate in this particular way. See Wilfrid Sellars, "Empiricism and the Philosophy of Mind," in *Science, Perception, and Reality* (London: Routledge and Kegan Paul, 1963), 127–96, and John McDowell, "Avoiding the Myth of the Given," in *Having the World in View: Essays on Kant, Hegel and Sellars* (Cambridge, Mass.: Harvard University Press, 2009), 256–72.

20. Peter Singer, *Animal Liberation* (New York: HarperCollins, 1990), 6, 9; David Gushee, "A Christian Theological Account of Human Worth," in *Understanding Human Dignity*, 279; and Nicholas Wolterstorff, *Justice: Rights and Wrongs* (Princeton, N.J.: Princeton University Press, 2008), 323–41.

21. Nygren's work was published in two parts, in 1930 and 1936. An English translation was eventually published in one volume: *Agape and Eros: The Christian Idea of Love*, trans. Philip S Watson, (London: SCM Press, 1956).

have motivated prominent efforts to disentangle justice and desire for one's own good. One thinks of John Rawls on fairness, Nicholas Wolterstorff on rights, and John Hare on the will's two affections.[22]

And note, even when justice and desire *are* disentangled, we still confront that other source of doubt—the modern habit of referring to justice in terms of subjective rights and obligations. For Stanley Hauerwas, Christians who speak in these terms violate the Pauline injunction against conformity to the world. They speak as the world does in order to secure power in it.[23] For Oliver O'Donovan, rights that are said to adhere to particular subjects by virtue of their shared humanity too easily multiply into competing and irreconcilable claims, claims that pit one individual against another.[24] For Timothy Jackson, it is precisely this competition, this collection of irreconcilable claims and sources of power, that is incompatible with the Christian law of love.[25]

It's in the context of these doubts and suspicions, mid-twentieth-century and contemporary, that benefit comes from attending to what *Pacem in Terris* and *Gaudium et Spes* say about justice and desire. Crucial here is their insistence on a tight coordination, both conceptual and actual, between justice and the common good, whereby a good held in common is an effect of right action and (as a result) a proper object of just desire.

Thus *Pacem in Terris* observes that "one of the principal imperatives of the common good is the recognition of the moral order and the unfailing observance of its precepts."[26] *Gaudium et Spes* concurs. It refers to the com-

---

For Barth, "Kant ... expressed the essential concern of Christian Ethics by pointing out that of itself the concept of what is pleasing and useful and valuable does not give us the concept of what is obligatory" (*CD* II/2, 650). Even so, Barth doubts that a Kantian ethic can get to the idea of obligation without a Christological ground. He writes: "We do not seriously ask what we ought to do except when we see our duty as the content of a decision which confronts our own will—even when it is supremely free in form—in absolute and inflexible sovereignty, so that, even when we give it our wholehearted, spontaneous approval, it is never the result of our decision, and therefore it never owes its authority and power to our decisions but always to itself. That this is the case is unequivocally clear, and safeguarded against all relapses into eudaimonistic distortions, only when we keep plainly in view—as Kantian ethics very obvious failed to do—the Christological foundations of the concept and actuality of obligation" (*CD* II/2, 651).

For Nygren's influence on Barth's treatment of love see *CD* IV/2, 727–840.

22. John Rawls, *A Theory of Justice* (Cambridge, Mass.: Harvard University Press, 1971); Wolterstorff, *Justice*, 149–226; John E. Hare, *God's Command* (Oxford: Oxford University Press, 2015), 1–141.

23. Stanley Hauerwas, "The Politics of Justice: Why Justice Is a Bad Idea for Christians," in *After Christendom? How the Church Is to Behave If Freedom, Justice, and a Christian Nation Are Bad Ideas* (Nashville, Tenn.: Abingdon Press, 1991), 45–68.

24. Oliver O'Donovan, *The Desire of the Nations: Rediscovering the Roots of Political Theology* (Cambridge: Cambridge University Press, 1996), 248.

25. Timothy P. Jackson, *The Priority of Love: Christian Charity and Social Justice* (Princeton, N.J.: Princeton University Press, 2003), 28–69.

26. *Pacem in Terris*, 85.

mon good as "the sum of those conditions of social life which allow social groups and their individual members relatively thorough and ready access to their own fulfillment." It speaks of social groupings of all kinds, from the smallest to "the entire human family," and it insists that the right ordering of these groupings necessarily "involves rights and duties" (*GS* §26). Securing that order, and the peace that follows from it, is, according to *Gaudium et Spes*, "rightly and appropriately called an enterprise of justice" (*GS* §78).

Thomas puts the point this way. Justice regards human actions that mediate our social and political relationships—friendships, families, citizen's organizations, ecclesial communities, and political societies. This is its proper matter, its *propriam materiam*.[27] The person who cares about justice cares about the condition of these relationships. She wants to perform just actions, because, of course, these actions are right and due, but also (and crucially) because she wants to set her various relationships right. This is her most basic concern. When, in a particular case, she succeeds in this—when she acts justly, when her action is recognized and received, and when a relationship is (as a result) set right—the good that emerges, the good shared in common, is the relationship itself, now set right. This rightly ordered relationship is a good she desires *for* the person she treats justly, a good she hopes to secure by means of her right action.[28] Crucially, it is a good she hopes to enjoy *with* the other person. Indeed, she *must* proceed with this hope. There is no erasing herself, no refusing this good, without denying it for the other, without failing to provide *the other person* with the rightly ordered relationship that is their just due. In fact, a relationship set right by justice is a common good *par excellence*: it is had and enjoyed in common or not at all. On Thomas's rendering, the competition between my good and yours, your welfare and mine, so prominent a source of anxiety among the critics of rational desire, is ruled out by necessity in genuine desire for justice.

No doubt, many of our social and political relationships are divided by disagreement about the final ends of human life and the ultimate condition of human flourishing. Some of our fellow citizens may even doubt that human beings have a shared final end, and, among those who think we do, there is disagreement about what it is and how best to conceive it. (The

27. *ST* II-II, q. 58, a. 1. Throughout, I resort to the translation of Thomas's greater *Summa* made by the Fathers of the English Dominican Province, *Summa Theologica*, 5 vols. (Westminster, Md.: Christian Classics, 1981).

28. *ST* II-II, q. 58, a. 5 (common good of the political community); *ST* II-II, q. 47, a. 11 (the common good of other kinds of communities).

various schools of natural law theory bear witness to this!) And of course, Christians will insist that a shared conception of our final end is one thing, a shared participation in it quite another. The first is a consequence of wise teaching; the second a deliverance of grace, and grace comes as grace will. None of this can be denied, and yet none of it prevents us (Christians and non-Christians alike) from caring about the condition of our relationships or tending to the good shared in common that just is a relationship set right by just conduct.

Once again Thomas helps bring the matter into focus. Temporal justice, he tells us, regards proximate not final ends. It regards the right order of those social and political relationships in which we stand, not the final end to which we might refer them. The first regards the specific reality of justice, the second, its possible perfection by charity.[29]

As for doubts about the merit of subjective rights, neither *Pacem in Terris* nor *Gaudium et Spes* seems troubled by them, and the reason is simple. In neither document do we find rights reduced to claims that persons make against each other or regarded as essentially competitive, individualistic, or aggressive. Rather, in both documents—in *Gaudium et Spes* in particular—a subjective right is a normative status that comes with membership in a social or political relationship. One *has* a right, one *becomes* a rights-holder, one *acquires* this status precisely because one *is* a member of the relevant social or political relationship.[30]

It might be the kind of political relationship that we find in liberal democracies, where talk of rights is common, but it need not be. It could be a relationship of any kind, and so long as it is a good one—so long as it is not structured by arbitrary power, for example—the rights that accrue to members, rights they have by virtue of *being* members, are likely to be good as well.

A subjective right is like any other normative status that emerges in a

29. Regarding the specification and individuation of the moral virtues, Thomas writes: "Moral matters do not receive their species from the last end, but from their proximate ends, and these, though they be infinite in number, are not infinite in species" (*ST* I-II, q. 60, a. 1 ad 3). The claim that charity heals acquired justice and elevates its act beyond its own proximate ends to union with God and neighbor has been caught up in the recent exegetical debates about the place of the acquired virtues in graced life. For doubts about their place in that life see William Mattison, "Can Christians Possess the Acquired Cardinal Virtues?" *Theological Studies* 72, no. 3 (2011): 558–85, and Angela McKay Knobel, "Can Aquinas's Infused and Acquired Virtues Coexist in the Christian Life," *Studies in Christian Ethics* 23, no. 4 (2010): 381–96. For a response to those doubts see John Bowlin, "Elevating and Healing: Reflections on *Summa Theologiae* I-II q. 109, a. 2," *Journal of Moral Theology* 3, no. 1 (2014): 39–53.

30. To be fair to O'Donovan, this is the account of subjective rights that he is willing to endorse: subjective rights as normative statuses within a relationship. What he resists are accounts of subjective rights that float free of this social-practical base, that are not derived from the roles we might occupy in a relationship or their place within a regime of law. See O'Donovan, *Desire of the Nations*, 248.

good relationship and that survives critical scrutiny. Examples include: being baptized, bankrupt, or tenured; being a felon, an infant, or a king; being a married person, a student, or a stranger. In each instance, the normative status deserves recognition from the relevant persons in the social or political relationship.[31] The person who is baptized, bankrupt, or tenured deserves to be recognized for having this particular status—in church, in court, or among the faculty. In the same way, the person who has a subjective right should be recognized for having it, for being a rights-holder, for having this particular status within some particular relationship, and the other persons in that relationship should respond to her in accord with the normative demands of her status.

A rights-holder is a person who is due some good from another, and quite often it's by virtue of the role each party plays within the relationship they share. Thus students are entitled to certain goods from their professors by virtue of the role each occupies in the student-teacher relationship: competence with the subject, papers read in a timely fashion and returned with useful commentary, respect in exchanges, grades distributed according to appropriate criteria, and so on.[32] Consistent failure to deliver any one of these goods may well generate a claim for them, and this claim is certainly authorized by the right, but the two are not identical. The rights that a student has by virtue of *being* a student are one thing. The actions and claims that accord with that normative status are quite another.

Nor is the claim made simply to secure the transfer of goods and the private welfare of the rights-holder. At the very least, there is no necessity in this. If the claim is justly made, with just aims in mind, then, in part, what the claimant wants is to set the relationship right. When rights are recognized, when a due response is offered, this is precisely the outcome. And, as I said, following Thomas, one cannot want this outcome, this rightly ordered relationship, without wanting it *for* and *with* the person who shares in it. This is what it means to say that rights belong to justice and that justice regards the common good.

31. Referring to the power differential between the modern state and its citizens and to the need to coordinate rights and duties at different social levels, *Gaudium et Spes* puts the point in precisely these terms. "If the citizens' responsible cooperation is to produce the good results which may be expected in the normal course of political life, there must be a statute of positive law providing for a suitable division of the functions and bodies of authority and an efficient and independent system for the protection of rights. The rights of all persons, families and groups, and their practical application, must be recognized, respected and furthered, together with the duties binding on all citizens" (§75).

32. The relationship and its roles explain why, for example, I am not required to bring my students fresh coffee each morning before lecture. They are not due this good from me. They have no right to it. The relationship we share and the roles we occupy do not generate this requirement.

And note, we speak of rights here, of a normative status that the students carry with them wherever they go, and not simply of the just treatment they deserve in accord with the norms of the student-teacher relationship, because, as we know, too many professors refuse to act in accord with these norms. They take advantage of the power differential in the relationship and ignore its requirements. They fail to deliver the goods that their students are due by virtue of being students, by virtue of being *their* students. We speak of rights that students have, in other words, because of the importance and fragility of this particular relationship, because setting it right is so crucial, and because securing this common good is so often so difficult. We speak of a normative status that requires right responses from professors because students deserve recognition as persons who have specific rights in this particular relationship.

Citizenship and Dignity

So goes my reply to *C'67*'s worries about the self-regarding character of just desire and subjective rights. It's no more than a sketch, but I do think it gives us one example of what Protestant theologians can learn from *Pacem in Terris* and *Gaudium et Spes*. It also provides some of the terms we need for interpreting these documents in light of *C'67*'s unstated but implicit worry—that accounts of human dignity and human rights derived in some way from our shared humanity and its various capacities can be either determinate or shared but not both. If they are determinate enough to specify concrete action, it's unlikely that they are shared deliverances of our common humanity. If they are derived from our common humanity and shared across time and place, they might be vague moral generalities—do no injustice and the like—but nothing that can specify concrete action without further determination from something else—from local custom, positive law, acquired virtue, or a gift of grace.

But suppose we think of dignity in the terms I have used to discuss subjective rights. Suppose we think of it as a normative status within a social or political relationship. Suppose, as before, we consider how certain roles or offices within certain relationships can generate this particular normative status, how they can dignify the persons who occupy them. And suppose, once again, we distinguish good relationships from bad in order to set apart the normative statuses we are willing to endorse from those that we are not. The slave-master might have certain rights that come by virtue of the role he plays in the master-slave relationship, but insofar as that relationship is itself unjust, then so is that role and so too are the putative rights associated with it.

The same applies to dignity, and the point is crucial. As Jeremy Waldron has pointed out, to think of dignity in this way, as a normative status within a relationship, is to think in terms of rank and privilege, of nobility and hierarchy.[33] We are suddenly in an aristocratic world where "dignity is displayed in bearing and self-presentation" and where its unequal distribution makes some of its privileges false, perhaps even repulsive.[34] In this world, some are dignified by a superior rank or role. *They* are immune from degradation. Others might be stigmatized by their lower position in the social hierarchy. *They* are literally at the mercy of those who outrank them. The higher-ups need not give an account of themselves or of their conduct to their inferiors. This would be beneath their dignity. And their inferiors cannot expect mutual accountability. *This* requires status and power, precisely what they do not have.[35]

Relationships that are in some way equivalent to these, that are structured by a similar inequality of status and power and by the absence of due accountability between ranks—these will be similarly deformed. The normative statuses that emerge within them will be false, unjust semblances of the real coin. If we nevertheless find it useful to think of dignity in terms of a certain bearing, nobility, and immunity from degradation that persons possess simply by virtue of occupying a role within a social or political relationship, then we had better identify a different collection of roles and relationships.[36] This is Waldron's strategy, and he concentrates on the role that citizens occupy in a just political order. In a moment, I will too, but we could just as well refer to the dignity that comes by way of occupying the role of parent, child, priest, worker, or some other lofty human vocation (*GS* §§21, 47). Or we could speak, as both *Pacem in Terris* and *Gaudium et Spes* do, of the special dignity that comes to those who, by grace, have been made "sons and friends of God, and heirs to eternal glory."[37]

The fact that both documents speak of the dignity that comes to graced

33. Jeremy Waldron, "Citizenship and Dignity," in *Understanding Human Dignity*, 327–43, here 327.

34. Jeremy Waldron, *Dignity, Rank, and Rights*, ed. Meir Dan-Cohen (Oxford: Oxford University Press, 2012), 28.

35. Don Herzog, "Aristocratic Dignity?" in *Dignity, Rank, and Rights*, 99–118.

36. Waldron, *Dignity, Rank and Rights*, 22

37. *Pacem in Terris*, 10. *Gaudium et Spes* speaks in similar terms of a human dignity that is "perfected by God" insofar as "man . . . is called as a son to commune with God and share in His happiness" (§21). "To the sons of Adam He restores the divine likeness which had been disfigured from the first sin onward. Since human nature as He assumed it was not annulled, by that very fact it has been raised up to a divine dignity in our respect too" (§22).

humanity, to those who occupy the role of son or daughter within the household of God, brings the interpretive challenge I am trying to address into focus. According to Waldron, accounts of human dignity have to coordinate two different senses of the idea. There is the sense I have been considering: the dignity that comes by virtue of occupying an important role in a good relationship. And there is the idea of human dignity "invested in every human person" regardless of role or rank "from the highest to the lowest."[38] In the modern period, theorists of human dignity have concentrated on the second sense. They have developed egalitarian accounts grounded in human nature and its capacities, and they have dismissed accounts grounded in roles and relationships as relicts of an aristocratic age now past. *Pacem in Terris* and *Gaudium et Spes* offer modern accounts of precisely this kind, where a shared human dignity has its ground in a shared human nature, and yet, as I noted, both retain the role-based conception in order to speak of the change in normative status that grace effects, whereby our natural human dignity is "perfected in God" (*GS* §21), not "annulled" by grace but "raised up to a divine dignity" (*GS* §22).

This may be the best way to coordinate these two different senses of dignity within the economy of salvation—an egalitarian human dignity that refers to created nature and a graced human dignity that refers to roles and relationships. But for this way to work, the challenges posed by *C'67*'s implicit doubts about human dignity and human rights rooted in our shared humanity, in our rational capacities and our basic grasp of the natural law, will have to be addressed. Perhaps this can be done, I don't discount this possibility, but I will leave that task to others. Instead, with those challenges in mind, I want to sketch an account of natural human dignity that draws, not on our shared rational capacities, not directly at least, but rather on the role of citizen that we occupy by virtue of being persons subject to divine rule.

The key distinction in this account is ordinary and well known. The role one occupies as citizen of a commonwealth is one thing; the activities that one can perform by virtue of occupying that role are quite another. Dignity attaches to the role, to the fact that one *is* a citizen under the laws, not to the activities authorized by the role, and certainly not to excellence in the performance of them. Ideally, one does not lose the nobility and immunity from degrading treatment that one shares with one's fellow citizens simply because one is incapable of performing the activities of citizenship or because one performs them poorly or viciously. The Alzheimer's patient may

38. Waldron, "Citizenship and Dignity," 327.

not caucus or vote, she may not hold elites accountable or make sacrifices for the common good, and yet she remains a citizen nevertheless and she retains the dignity and privileges of this role. The abolitionists and Freedom Riders exhibited excellence in the activities of citizenship that few of us can match. They deserve recognition and honor for this excellence, and this excellence bears witness to the importance of the role they occupy as citizens and to the dignity offered by that role. They put that dignity on display in the care they had for the role and in the excellence they exhibited in it. But neither their care nor their excellence bestows greater measures of that dignity upon them. That status remains unchanged and shared with the rest of us who are also citizens, who play this role, but with far less excellence.[39] The same applies to those who violate the laws of the commonwealth. Correction might be required, punishment might be due, but citizens they remain, and by virtue of this role, so too their dignity, so too the rights and protections that due recognition of this status requires. This, anyway, is the ideal.

The images here are not only aristocratic but also theatrical and legal, and, as I read him, Thomas accents each while trying to coordinate the parts through the idea of rational nature. He writes:

> For because famous men were represented in comedies and tragedies, the name "person" was given to signify those who have dignity. Hence, in the church, it was customary to use the name 'person' for those who had some sort of dignity. For this reason the definition of person is given as "hypostasis distinct by reason of dignity." And because subsistence in a rational nature is of high dignity, it follows that every individual of a rational nature is called a "person."
>
> Quia enim in comoediis et tragoediis repraesentabantur aliqui homines famosi, impositum est hoc nomen persona ad significandum aliquos dignitatem habentes. Unde consueverunt dici personae in Ecclesiis, quae habent aliquam dignitatem. Propter quod quidam definiunt personam, dicentes quod persona est hypostasis proprietate distincta ad dignitatem pertinente. Et quia magnae dignitatis est in rationali natura subsistere, ideo omne individuum rationalis naturae dicitur persona, ut dictum est.[40]

39. For me, at least, this account of dignity and excellence helps bring Presidents Obama and Trump into focus. The office occupied dignifies both, and so too the role played, and yet, so far at least, Trump has played it with far less excellence. Often enough, Obama played it quite well. This difference bears on our recognition of the dignity that comes with the role. In Trump's presidency, that dignity has been difficult to see. In Obama's, it was quite often on vivid display. This relationship between excellence displayed and dignity recognized is an important aspect of our response to persons who occupy offices or roles dismissed by established custom or elite opinion. The dignity of work, for example, of manual labor, comes with the role and is put on display when the work is done well. The excellence enables recognition of the dignity, and this recognition can be used in social criticism, in resistance to an established rank ordering of roles.

40. *ST* I, q. 29, a. 3 ad 2. Translation modified. The remarks come in Thomas's discussion of divine persons. The implication is that the Trinity, a collection of *personae*, is in fact a collection of roles

A person is someone who plays a role, who has a persona in a drama, in the relationships it depicts. She has a certain dignity that comes with that role and by virtue of those relationships, and this dignity comes with certain rights and requirements, and these often drive the drama. Dignity demands due recognition. When recognition is denied, rights might be claimed.[41] When rights are claimed, a drama unfolds.

Notice the fallout. If we wish to say, as Thomas does, that we are persons by virtue of our rational human nature, then dignity comes to us by virtue of that persona. The claim is that our rational humanity, our personhood, is a role we occupy, a role that bestows dignity upon us simply by virtue of the fact that we have been given it and now occupy it.

Notice as well how Thomas's remarks on the natural law bring this claim into focus and make this dignity determinate. Whatever else we want to say about those remarks, one thing is certain. They are designed to spell out how rational human agency is created and governed by God, how it falls under divine jurisdiction, how it emerges by divine command and is ruled by God's eternal law. This is where dignity becomes determinate. We are not subject to God's eternal law as slaves to a tyrant's arbitrary whim but rather as citizens to a sovereign. The sovereign is not a *tyrant*, because He rules with a perfect orientation to the common good. His rule is not *arbitrary*, because His citizens share in it, because they know the demands of His law and are inclined to its ends as a result of their knowledge. For Thomas, reference to the natural law is just shorthand for this relationship between Creator and creature, Sovereign and subject. "The natural law" he writes, "is nothing else than the rational creature's participation in the eternal law" whereby we share in God's judgment about our good and so act as human beings do.[42]

---

and statuses that are distinct subsisting relations (*ST* I, q. 29, a. 4). For lovely discussion of this point see, Robert Jenson, *A Theology in Outline: Can These Bones Live?* (New York: Oxford University Press, 2016), 40–51.

41. Of course, they might not be. In fact, in many contexts, rights are denied due recognition and yet they are not claimed. Sometimes this is because of fear—as in Hegel's lordship and bondage story, which remains a drama nonetheless, because of the changes the characters undergo in the relationship. Sometimes the rights are not claimed because of misrecognition on the part of the dominated—as in the case of Uncle Tom. Sometimes fear and misrecognition are intermingled in the collective or personal subconscious, the reasons for the former giving rise to the latter. I am grateful to Jeffrey Stout for this qualification.

42. *ST* I-II, q. 91, a. 2. God gives an account of God's self to us through our participation in God's eternal law, a participation made possible by our creation through God's Word and our redemption through Christ's sacrifice. This much is plain. But in what sense is this account-giving *necessary* rather than arbitrary, *required* not a matter of whim? The question goes to the heart of contemporary debates about necessity and will in the divine nature. I will leave it to others to determine with whether creation is a necessary consequence of the fact that God is love. But once rational creatures appear, they can

It is because our participation in God's eternal law is rational, whereby we know and endorse its demands and so share in God's rule over our agency, that we are persons, persons who play the role of citizen subject to God's rule, citizens with a special dignity that comes by way of that role. And it is because our dignity is determinate in this special way that due recognition of it has a certain determinate character. At the very least, we can say that our dignity is denied the recognition it is due when, contrary to our role as citizens who know and endorse the demands of the law, we are subject to arbitrary rule, to power that need not give due account of itself. Since domination's lust is common this side of Adam's fall, we can expect this failure of due recognition. We know it will happen. And thus we can say that the special dignity we have as citizens subject to divine rule arrives with the right not to be dominated. Created as citizens with dignity, we have a right not be treated as slaves who have none.[43]

Crucially, this dignity and so too this immunity from domination, this right not to be subject to the undue power and authority of another, come with the *role*, with the fact that we are *citizens* subject to God's rule, *not* with the exercise of our rational agency that this role makes possible, *not* with excellence with respect to that exercise. Persons with dignity we remain so long as we are citizens of this commonwealth, regardless of whether we act in accord with the role we have been given or whether we do so well or ill. The Alzheimer's patient retains the dignity of her role, of her rational persona, even as she cannot act fully in accord with it. The same applies to the sinner. "*Every* act of reason and will ... must needs be in virtue of the natural law," says Thomas, in virtue of our status as citizens subject to God's rule, and we retain that status even when we perform vile or wicked actions.[44] So long as we remain *reasonably* vicious, we will act in conformity with the laws of this commonwealth, and, by virtue of that conformity, bear witness to our citizenship and thus to our dignity.

---

be subject to God's law *as* rational only as participants in God's law and thus only as subjects who receive (and endorse) an account of God's purposes for them. So too, I will leave it to others to decide whether a God who is love is required by His nature to save fallen humanity, whether salvation comes as necessity. But regardless, if we think of salvation (at least in part) as ever more perfect participation *in* and obedience *to* God's eternal law, then, again, God can save rational creatures only as God gives an account of God's eternal purpose for them and only as they know and endorse its demands. We might refer to this divine account-giving as revelation, and we see its effect upon social status in Jesus' remarks to his disciples in John 15:15. They are now friends, he says, not slaves, and the difference is what they know by virtue of what he has revealed. "I have called you friends, because I have made known to you everything that I have heard from my Father."

43. The slave exhibits the dignity that comes by virtue of being subject to divine rule in all that he does even as the role he plays in a temporal relationship denies him that very dignity.

44. *ST* I-II, q. 91, a. 2.

Notice too how this natural human dignity that refers to roles and relationships, to our participation in God's eternal law and our immunity from domination, comes fully into focus—as the *Confession of 1967* would surely insist that it must—only on analogy with the covenant of grace. For Thomas, the dignity that comes with our created, natural persona is conceived on analogy with the dignity that comes with our recreated, gracious persona. By grace, we are offered a new citizenship, a new role, and, in the language of *Pacem in Terris* and *Gaudium et Spes*, a dignity made perfect, raised up to a divine dignity. We are dignified by our status as citizens subject to the New Law, as persons (individuals of a rational nature) who know and endorse its demands and who are thus, in Thomas's words, ruled and ordered by its precepts sweetly, *suaviter*.[45] The analogy is obviously formal, but it is also actual, at least in hope. It enables us to say that we were made for this higher dignity, whereby nature's grace is recapitulated as grace. It authorizes the hope that this formality will become fully actual. This, anyway, is the content of faith's confession.

And notice, finally, how this Thomistic sketch can account for the personhood, and so too the basic human dignity, of all human beings on appeal to precisely this same faith and hope. For Thomas, our citizenship under the New Law bears witness to a heavenly citizenship among the blessed, and our hope for that first citizenship includes a hope for the second.[46] The argument, in brief outline, goes like this.

Citizenship under the New Law requires, not only the elevation of our humanity, but also its healing. The soul must be healed of sin's effects if its agency is to be elevated by God's love and governed by Love's Law.[47] For Thomas, this work of grace, this healing, makes this new citizenship possible and so too its elevated dignity. If we hope that this same grace will one day further elevate all human beings to a *heavenly* citizenship, then we must assume that it will effect a healing proportionate to this role and its dignity. This healing must make possible the beatific vision, the knowing and loving of God that distinguishes life in this city, and this hope must regard even those with the severest cognitive disabilities. Here I have in mind human beings who cannot in any way fall under divine jurisdiction by knowing and endorsing the demands of the law, not the natural law, not the New Law. If they are to become citizens of this eternal city, if they are to share

45. *ST* II-II, q. 23, a. 2; q. 29, aa. 1–3.
46. *ST* I-II, q. 106, a. 4.
47. *ST* I-II, q. 109, a. 2.

in the dignity that comes with this role, if they are to know and love God as the blessed do, then they must be healed of these very infirmities.[48] At the very least, this must be our hope, the content of our faith, and by virtue of each, we can regard them, even now, as occupying that role and sharing in its dignity.

This might seem odd, this dignity predicated on a hoped-for-citizenship, but in fact it is not. In fact, by virtue of a similar faith and hope we credit newborns with citizenship under the natural law, with the dignity that accords with that citizenship, and with the rights that accord with that dignity. Newborns do not know and love the human good. In Thomas's terms, they are not ruled by God's law by virtue of sharing in God's judgment about that good. They are not citizens in this jurisdiction, at least not yet. Still, we hope and expect that one day they will act in accord with this law and share in this citizenship, and by virtue of this hope we acknowledge their basic human dignity even now, and so too the protection from domination that it affords.

Crucially, each regime of law in this succession—natural law, New Law, and that law of the eternal city—depends on what came before, on the role that was played and the dignity that comes in each jurisdiction. This is what it means to say that grace perfects nature but does not overcome it. The dignity of those with the severest cognitive disabilities, a dignity that comes with their promised heavenly citizenship, cannot be acknowledged without assuming the basic human dignity that precedes it and that distinguishes their role as citizens subject to the natural law. Both of these normative statuses are acknowledged proleptically, acknowledged in hope, a hope that regards the grace of another, a grace that heals as it elevates and restores as it heals. Indeed, Thomas says that human nature is congruent (*congruentia*) for assumption by the Word "according to its dignity (*dignitatem*)."[49] "Human nature, as being rational and intellectual, was made for attaining to the Word to some extent by its operation, viz. by knowing and loving him," by hearing the New Law that has been promulgated and acting in accord with its demands.[50] We might say that, for Thomas, the dignity that being a human "person" signifies is christologically oriented.[51] Ultimately, our dignity,

48. See the discussion of the healed and restored bodies and intellects of the blessed in questions 79–83 of the *Summa theologiae's* supplement. The supplement was gathered from St. Thomas's commentary on the Fourth Book of the *Sentences* of Peter Lombard, written in the years 1252–56.

49. *ST* III, q. 4, a. 1.

50. *ST* III, q. 4, a. 1.

51. *ST* I, q. 29, a. 3 ad 2.

and so too our personhood, comes as a promise to be assumed by the Word, a capacity to be subject to Christ's Law and made a citizen in God's eternal commonwealth. It is a promise made to all, a capacity that all have.[52]

Of course, one can become a person with dignity, one can acquire this status, by virtue of the role one might play in other sorts of relationships—by virtue of being a child, parent, faculty member, citizen in a temporal political community, and so on. It will not be *human* dignity, but it may be the dignity one needs in order to be treated justly in one of those relationships. Thus a newborn will have the dignity that comes by virtue of being a daughter, a member of the family, and a citizen of a temporal political community. The same applies to the person with severest cognitive deficits. His *human* dignity might be established proleptically in hope, even as he is also recognized for the dignity he has by virtue of participating in one of these other relationships and occupying one of these other roles.

Qualifications

At this point, let me offer three qualifications that indicate where my Thomistic sketch departs from Thomas's views. First, Thomas assumes that the bodies of the blessed will be healed in every respect. He considers every disability a deficit that will be overcome.[53] I do not. On my account, citizenship in God's heavenly commonwealth requires a remedy for only the severest cognitive deficits. The blessed must be able to know and love God. Whether they will also have bodies healed and restored in every respect—about this I have doubts. At the very least, I want to acknowledge what Elizabeth Barnes and others have taught us about other, less severe disabilities.[54] There are many ways that one can enact a human persona. There are many kinds of human bodies. Some of these ways and bodies are considered lamentably disabled when in fact they exhibit human differences that require neither lament nor healing. In many cases, what they require is the recognition that a so-called impediment may in fact provide for a unique way of being human and loving God.[55]

Second, Thomas, I have said, assumes that sin's effects must be remedied before we can become citizens under the New Law. At the very least,

52. Thanks to Jeffrey Skaff for this insight and text.

53. *ST* Supplement, q. 80, a. 1; q. 84, a. 1; q. 85, a. 1.

54. Elizabeth Barnes, *The Minority Body: A Theory of Disability* (Oxford: Oxford University Press, 2016).

55. John Hare, *God's Command* (Oxford: Oxford University Press, 2015), 30.

he assumes that this healing makes this new role possible and so too its elevated dignity. But I am a Protestant and for reasons that motivated the Reformers, I'm inclined to reverse this order and say that by grace this citizenship comes first, only then the healing.

By Christ's sacrifice, our relationship with God is made right, and we are offered membership in a commonwealth of grace. We are made citizens under the New Law but without necessarily knowing and endorsing its demands or acting in accord with its precepts. These possibilities come later, fitfully and imperfectly through the sanctifying work of the Holy Spirit. In the terms I have been developing, this makes perfect sense. It is one thing to occupy the role of citizen, quite another to act in accord with that role. Christ's sacrifice creates citizens as it justifies sinners. The Holy Spirit sanctifies these citizens and makes it possible for them to act in accord with the New Law. Their elevated dignity comes by way of the role they occupy in God's gracious commonwealth, not from their holiness, not from their capacity to act in accord with that role.

Third, and related to this Reformed reversal, dignity comes with the role of citizen, I argue, with the fact that one occupies this role, not with the ability to act in accord with it, not by virtue of excellence with respect to action. Thomas disagrees. As he sees it, dignity comes by virtue of *playing* the role of citizen, not occupying it, and the better one plays it, the more dignity one has. His defense of capital punishment turns on precisely this distinction.[56] The argument goes like this. Human action is rational action. Rationality is its form. From this it follows that the more fully an action conforms to its form, to the order of reason (*ordine rationis*), the more rational it is, the more fully human it is, and, by virtue of that, the more human dignity it embodies. Thus the person who sins "departs from the order of reason, and consequently falls away from the dignity of his manhood." Still, so long as he sins voluntarily and thus knowingly, his actions remain rational, although imperfectly. His dignity remains, although diminished. Killing this sinner as punishment for crime would be unlawful, or so Thomas concludes. By contrast, someone who departs from the order of reason altogether, whose personhood is in doubt precisely because he is no longer subject to the natural law as a citizen who can know and endorse its demands—this "person" may be executed, not as perpetrator of a crime, but as someone who has slipped into the "slavish state of the beasts," someone whose very existence is "dangerous and infectious to the community."

56. *ST* II-II, q. 64, a. 2, ad 3.

Here we see two different ways to coordinate rationality, role, and dignity. Concentrate on the rationality, as Thomas does in this treatment of capital punishment, and you end up with his position. Personhood and dignity rise and fall as rationality does. Concentrate on the role made possible by the rationality, and you end up with mine. Personhood and dignity remain constant so long as the role is occupied. Indeed, they remain even in the case of persons whose ability to act rationally has departed altogether.

The Natural Law in Christianity's Civic Project

One last problem. Russell Hittinger has noted how "the Catholic understanding and presentation of natural law" received an upgrade "during the Wojtyła/Ratzinger era" and how this upgrade created a quandary. Both John Paul II and Benedict XVI shunned the "minimalist ethic of the manualists." They resisted the thought that the natural law could provide an alternative ethical theory, one different from the standard options on offer among the secular theorists. Instead, they tethered the natural law to "anthropology and theology," to scripture and revelation.[57] The problem is that these theologically rich terms make it difficult for the natural law to play one of its traditional roles, to function in Christianity's civic project. Presented in these terms, the natural law can no longer identify "common premises across religious and philosophical traditions," premises that can function in public debate about important matters, about the dignity of human persons and their immunity to domination.[58] Hittinger's recommendation is that Catholics retain the benefits of the theological upgrade while simultaneously seeking an alliance, theoretical and practical, with the "dignitarian humanism of the Enlightenment."[59]

My reinterpretation of the modern natural law tradition, of its account of human dignity and human rights, generates a version of this quandary. If you begin with the dignity that comes by way of our gracious recreation, by way of the role we have been given in the household of God, given by means of Christ's sacrifice, and if you regard the natural law and our natural human dignity on analogy with this gracious template, then your theological commitments may very well complicate your public engagements.

My suggestion, somewhat different from Hittinger's, is that we follow

57. Hittinger, "Natural Law and Public Discourse," 259.
58. Hittinger, "Natural Law and Public Discourse," 246.
59. Hittinger, "Natural Law and Public Discourse," 271.

Dr. King's example. If our own theological commitments make it difficult to express our care for justice and its common goods, for our shared human dignity and immunity from domination, without referring to the natural law, then Dr. King's practice is instructive, his implicit commitments compelling. Let me try to make them explicit. He assumes that his fellow citizens share a collection of proximate ends, above all the desire to set their various social and political relationships right. And he assumes they agree in broad outline about the character of a just relationship. At the very least, he doubts that anyone will call a relationship just that is marred by domination, where one party is at the mercy of another, left helpless before arbitrary power and made easy for exploitation. Domination and exploitation are species of injustice. Dr. King addresses his letter to white pastors who acknowledge these basic moral truths and express a vague commitment to opposing these forms of injustice while turning a blind eye to Jim Crow's concrete examples. They are insufficiently horrified by the injustice all around them, insufficiently ashamed by their desire to go slow, to oppose it incrementally.

So he engages in immanent criticism. Their lives, he tells them, do not embody their most basic moral convictions. Indeed, their refusal to oppose unjust positive laws and racist social mores casts doubt on their commitment to those convictions. When he speaks of the natural law, the point is to mark this distinction between conviction and convention and to locate it among his own theological commitments.[60] There are moral truths that transcend local, sinful convention. These belong to God's eternal law. The injustice of legally enforced domination and exploitation is one such example. Dr. King does not refer to the natural law in order to remind us that domination and exploitation are unjust. Rather, their injustice reminds us that there are moral truths that rule and measure positive law. Dr. King speaks of the natural law in order to bear witness to this fact.

Jim Crow America offered untold examples of social and political relationships distorted by domination and exploitation, that betray our recognition of their basic injustice, that violate the natural law's most basic prohibition.[61] Later in his life, Dr. King referred to others: economic exploitation at home and colonial domination in Vietnam. In our own day, we might

60. See Jeffrey Stout, *Democracy and Tradition* (Princeton, N.J.: Princeton University Press, 2004), 241, 244f.

61. "Nulli esse malum faciendum." The passage is normally translated "do no harm to another," but this misleads. Thomas's example is killing, which he plainly thinks is indifferent morally speaking until we describe the act, its ends, and its circumstances (*ST* I-II q, 1, a. 3 ad 3; q. 18, aa. 2–11). Only then will we be able to distinguish just from unjust killings, those that are evil deeds from those that are not. Given this, the phrase is best translated "do no injustice."

refer to sex trafficking, the mistreatment of immigrants, judicial torture, militarized policing, and mass incarceration of black and brown persons. We might also refer to the fact that vast differentials of power, wealth, and social position, combined with weak governmental institutions and strong market forces, have left far too many of our fellow citizens subject to the unaccountable power of others. Even when that power is not exercised, the threat of it leaves far too many feeling vulnerable, hopeless, and resentful. Some even fantasize about exercising arbitrary power of their own, about walling out, locking up, or expelling the scapegoats of their suffering. Others lay claim to that power in acts of organized violence and terror. These are obviously unjust responses, but they are not unintelligible.

It's against this backdrop, this contemporary unraveling, that Augustine's wisdom comes into focus. I'm not thinking of the image of Augustine that we find in contemporary political Augustinianism, the image first drawn by Robert Markus in his widely read and deeply influential work *Saeculum: History and Society in the Theology of St. Augustine*.[62] Markus gives us an Augustine attentive to the conflicts and divisions that afflict every social and political relationship disordered by sin. Since there is no overcoming these sources of sorrow without God's healing grace and (ultimately) before the eschaton, and since grace comes as grace will and the eschaton is long coming, our politics must be secular not sacred, its conflicts and divisions managed but never overcome. Markus recognizes the benefit this Augustinian image can bring to Christians who inhabit a liberal political order. It can be adapted and put to use in their civic projects and self-conceptions. It can provide theological warrants for resisting the temptation to sacralize the state or interfere in the religious lives of fellow citizens.

The trouble, however, the trouble as I see it, is that Augustine did not recommend anything like the liberal norm of non-interference. In part it's because he doubts that our social and political relationships can be truthfully described without acknowledging the many ways in which they are structured by laws that restrain action, customs that form habits, authorities that command obedience, and coercion that guarantees it. Persons and powers that interfere with human life and conduct: there's no escaping

62. Robert Markus, *Saeculum: History and Society in the Theology of St. Augustine* (Cambridge: Cambridge University Press, 1970). Recent work in political Augustinianism include Eric Gregory, *Politics and the Order of Love: An Augustinian Ethic of Democratic Citizenship* (Chicago: University of Chicago Press, 2008); Charles Mathewes, *The Republic of Grace: Augustinian Thoughts for Dark Times* (Grand Rapids, Mich.: Eerdmans, 2010); and John von Heyking, *Augustine and Politics as Longing in the World* (Columbia: University of Missouri Press, 2001).

them, or reason to think that we should. But more importantly it's because he has his attention fixed elsewhere, on the lust for domination that infects all human relationships this side of Adam's fall. It's this combination—the ordinary reality of interference in every human relationship and the lust for mastery disordering every human soul—that captures Augustine's imagination and that places a question mark over political society.

In his correspondence with North African magistrates, in his critique of Roman conquest, in his discussion of domestic and civil rule, and in his (somewhat surprising!) willingness to defend state action against his religious opponents, the Donatists—in each case we find Augustine asking whether the customs, commands, and laws at work in a relationship are external expressions of this internal disorder. Do they mask the arbitrary will of the powerful and their desire for mastery? Or are there reasons that warrant the constraints placed on human life and action, reasons that refer to the norms of justice and love, norms that can be used to hold power accountable?

Quite often it's Augustine himself in his role as bishop or pastor who does this work of accountability. These roles give him authority to press the powerful for reasons. And quite often we find him encouraging the occupant of some other paternal office—parent, priest, or magistrate—to act in accord with its norms. When he defends state action against the Donatists, his reasons refer to this same paternal logic. They are like children who have broken a promise and lost their way. He is like a father, who longs for their return and will do what he must in order to bring them home.[63]

Thankfully, our age is less willing to consider paternalistic relationships just. We distribute the authority to contest power more broadly, and we regard with suspicion those social and political relationships that resemble the relationship between parent and child. They are guilty until proven innocent.

These differences should not surprise us. Our age is not Augustine's. What matters, what we can learn from him nevertheless, is that domination is at work and dignity denied in far too many human relationships. As in *his* age, so in ours: power is too often distributed unequally and exercised arbitrarily, without reasons that can account for its merit or bear witness to the dignity of the persons involved. The lust to dominate, a deliverance of our deepest dislocation from God and neighbor, finds expression in precisely these circumstances.

63. For an excellent treatment of Augustine's relation to republicanism see Michael Lamb, "Augustine and Republican Liberty: Recontextualizing Coercion," *Augustinian Studies* 48, 1 (2017): 119–59.

The civic project of Christianity, however we regard it, should certainly include this aspect of Augustine's political thought. It should find a way to coordinate the concern for justice and its common good that we find in *Pacem in Terris* and *Gaudium et Spes*, the accent on law and citizenship, dignity and role that we find in Thomas, and the regard for domination and its lust that occupies Augustine. In this respect, as in so many others, Dr. King got it right.

Chapter 9

Gaudium et Spes and the Narrative Theology of George Lindbeck

Francesca Aran Murphy

The Lutheran theologian George Lindbeck was an official observer at Vatican II, "liv[ing] in Rome ... from 1962 to 1964" and attending all the conciliar sessions. Three decades later, Lindbeck recalled the primary, secondary, and tertiary causes that effected this: Pope Saint John XXIII asked for three observers apiece from each of the "world confessional organizations," and the Lutheran World Federation "decided they had to name an American as one of the three ... observers. The American would have to know Latin, German, and French, would have to have had some experience of Roman Catholic theology, and ... would have to get a leave of absence from his regular job. They scraped and scraped the barrel," Lindbeck explained, "and at the bottom there was an untenured Yale teacher whose dean and department were not bound by the draconian faculty employment rules now in effect."[1] As it was for other participant observers, Vatican II was for Lindbeck not only a block of documents but an event.

These three years in Rome were powerfully influential for Lindbeck. They launched the green "untenured Yale teacher" into his career as the godfather of narrative theology. At the same time, the young "teacher" interpreted the Council and *Gaudium et Spes* according to his own inner lights, the lights of a budding narrative theologian. What gripped Lindbeck

A version of this essay has appeared as "Telling the Story of *Gaudium et Spes*: George Lindbeck and the Catholic Recovery of Eschatology," in *Schools of Faith: Essays on Theology, Ethics and Education*, ed. David Fergusson and Bruce McCormack (London: Bloomsbury, 2019), 147–58.

1. Lindbeck, quoted in George Weigel, "Re-Viewing Vatican II: An Interview with George A. Lindbeck," *First Things* 48 (December 1994): 44–50.

about the "Pastoral Constitution on the Church in the Modern World" was its this-worldly eschatology.

Lindbeck thought the eschatological paradigm of *Gaudium et Spes* was new and fresh, differing from anything the Church had witnessed since the era of the Reformation. The difference which Lindbeck believed this new thing made is quite astonishing. In 1965, Lindbeck proposed that the eschatological framework that emerges through Schema 17 into Schema 13, that is, in the early drafts of *Gaudium et Spes*, constituted such an earthquake of a paradigm shift that it erased the chasm between Protestants and Catholics. Despite setbacks to the ecumenical movement, and the receding of the goal of full, sacramental reunion, Lindbeck never abandoned this intuition.

Lindbeck's interpretation of *Gaudium et Spes* is a creative misreading both of the event of the promulgation of this constitution and of the text itself. He misreads the event in the sense that he overstates the novelty of the Church's venture into eschatology. He thinks it is a radical departure from Tridentine tradition that the Catholics should be relating the movement of secular history to the construction of the City of God. But anti-liberal popes from Gregory XVI to Pius X and on to Leo XIII had already used the proximity of the City of God to the city of man to lash the Church to the Establishment. The nineteenth-century popes used the requirement of harmony of the two cities against those Catholic liberals who yearned for disestablishment. That goes together with an acknowledgment of the tension between the cities. Lindbeck seems never to have tasted the large dose of paradox in the constitution, its reiterated contention that history remains a struggle and a fight between the powers of darkness and the sons of light.

After much dining and cigar smoking amongst the French clerics, Lindbeck saw that the struggle and the fight between the old Scholastics and the New Theologians was profoundly rooted in diverse allegiances during the Occupation and the Second World War.[2] The Old Thomists were anti-

2. In his interview with Weigel, Lindbeck recalls: "You'd be sitting around drinking wine with the French, and just as you pierced the surface, they'd start talking about *Action Française* and all that. The French allies of the curial party, the French integralists, were more likely to have been in sympathy with *Action Française*, which the *nouvelle theologie* people never were. By and large, most of the integralists had not been sympathetic to the Resistance during the war, as de Lubac and others in his group had been. So there was this deep personal estrangement between the *nouvelle theologie* people and their critics, who believed that they had betrayed true French Catholicism, understood in monarchist terms. De Lubac illustrated the intensity of it when he quoted a critic of his to the effect that John XXIII had chosen Congar and de Lubac for the conciliar preparatory commissions because the Pope was wise enough to remember what had happened after Vatican I (1870), when the 'old Catholic' schism occurred, and wanted to make sure that dissidents didn't leave the Church this time around. . . . I always

liberals, like the nineteenth-century popes: they wanted the Church to speak for the common good and the common man. They saw liberalism as serving the elite. But they saddled their humanistic political theory with a pessimistic determination to attach the Church to the forces of political reaction and "realpolitik," for whom the deadly foe is utopianism. The agenda of the New Theologians was to toss out neo-scholastic anti-utopianism and instead root Catholic social anthropology in a natural desire for the supernatural God. In *Gaudium et Spes* both sides win: the Thomists get their common good and a thoroughgoing rejection of any kind of European-style "liberalism," and the New Theologians get to found this social anthropology in a Christ-haunted utopianism that is driven by the desire for God to build a new Jerusalem.

It goes without saying that it is cheating to sum up *Gaudium et Spes* in one or two paragraphs—the *real,* authentic, properly interpreted constitution—and then tell you how Lindbeck "misread it." Maybe I misread it too, and much less creatively than Lindbeck did! In this chapter I will lay out Lindbeck's interpretations of Schema 17 and 13, as they unfolded into *Gaudium et Spes*. Not everyone seized on "eschatology" as the driving force of the Pastoral Constitution, and Lindbeck was right to do so. He grasped it not only because it's there but also because "eschatology" gave Lindbeck the "new look" on Pauline Christianity which narrative theology requires. Let's get chopping with that before we come back to the question of readings and misreadings.

Lindbeck's Initial Reaction to *Gaudium et Spes*

Lindbeck's earliest reaction to *Gaudium et Spes* is in French, and to my knowledge it has never been translated in full. I kept looking for a missing *ne ... pas* when I read these paragraphs, which I shall quote in full, and with no ellipses that quietly remove some *plus maintenants* and *pas encores*. In 1965, when the Pastoral Constitution was still Schema 13, Lindbeck gave several ways in which the document changes Protestant-Catholic relations. Here are a couple: "When we employ eschatological categories," as the Schema does,

> particularly as combined with the personalist and existential vision of the historicity of human life, the ancient theological conflicts about *sola fide* and *sola gratia*, about free will and predestination, sin and concupiscence, purely and simply disappear.... For Catholics as well as Protestants, retrieve the biblical vision of salvation as a passage from the old age to the new age, a passage from slavery to demonic

found it desirable at any dinner party to find out where people stood on the Revolution before getting into any other discussion" (Lindbeck, quoted in Weigel, "Re-Viewing Vatican II").

powers to the freedom of the sons of God, deliverance from that fixation on the past which leads to attempts at self-justification to open the future to God. There is no way one could debate the old problems in the terms of that individualism which we have inherited from Augustine ... and which, by itself, gave a meaning to those disputes like the one about infused grace and extrinsic imputation. The surmounting of the individualism of the Western tradition draws our attention to a second domain, that of ecclesial reunion. Not only the Bible, but also history and sociology, have rendered us more conscious of the social nature of man than one could have been with Aristotle and his time.... Whoever concerns himself about an authentically personal life becomes a being who is profoundly preoccupied with the social context.... [I]t is only by means of that which can be transmitted in and through the Christian community, that a person can become consciously and actively a member of the body of Christ. The Church, not in the sense of an authoritarian institution, but as a communion, a community, is the mother to all of us—our mother country—and this is why her living continuity, her catholicity, and, in consequence, her unity are of an utmost importance.[3]

Lindbeck boldly announces that the "eschatological communion" theology of Schema 13 renders ecumenical divisions obsolete, and that as a result the benchmarks of the Lutheran Reformation, faith alone, grace alone, and predestination, cease to matter.

One can only imagine that Lindbeck sees the Pastoral Constitution's focus on historical-eschatology as re-setting the picture of the human person so that the old "introspective questions," the questions that arise from the examination of a person's own interiority and conscience, evaporate. A new, eschatological picture of man emerges, in which human beings are always already in active history and oriented toward the future *eschaton*, and are understood not as individuals who are preoccupied with the salvation of their own private souls, but rather as "collective humanity," preoccupied with the social construction of the earthly city.

A Reading and a Misreading

A Reading

Gaudium et Spes reiterates the social teaching of the Church of the past few centuries, especially its concern for the common good. It describes the natural law, which governs the morality of social and political endeavor, in terms of

3. George A. Lindbeck, "Le Cadre du Désaccord Catholique-Protestant," in *Théologie d'aujourd'hui et de demain*, ed. P. Burke, H. de Lubac, et al. (Paris: Cerf, 1967), 191–206 at 202–3.

the human "vocation"[4] or calling.[5] In keeping with many statements in earlier Catholic social teaching, *Gaudium et Spes* notes that as part of the human vocation to relate and bind the "city of man" to the city of God. The encyclical thus states that "while earthly progress must be carefully distinguished from the growth of Christ's kingdom, to the extent that the former [earthly progress] can contribute to the better ordering of society, it is of vital concern to the city of God."[6] The Pastoral Constitution schools us in presenting human effort to create a better world in eschatological terms: "the Church has a saving and eschatological purpose which can be fully attained only in the future world. But she is already present in this world, and is composed of men, that is, of members of the earthly city, who have a call to form the family of God's children." *Gaudium et Spes* speaks of a proleptic intermingling of the future synthesis of the earthly and the heavenly cities. It instructs us that the presence of the new Jerusalem within the city of man is visible only to the eyes of faith: "That the earthly and the heavenly city penetrate each other is a fact accessible to faith alone; it remains a mystery of human history."[7] The constitution disparages spiritual selfishness, or hiving off into one's own private hopes of heaven; the constitution would not have us think of ourselves merely as resident aliens:

> This council exhorts Christians, as citizens of two cities, to strive to discharge their earthly duties conscientiously and in response to the Gospel spirit. They are mistaken who, knowing that we have here no abiding city but seek one which is to come, think that they may therefore shirk their earthly responsibilities. For they are forgetting that by the faith itself they are more obliged than ever to measure up to these duties, each according to his proper vocation.[8]

Catholic theologians of the time recognized that *Gaudium et Spes*, so to speak, "eschatologizes" and to some extent "historicizes" the traditional Catholic thinking about nature and grace, turning human nature into an active, constructive future orientation, and grace as the historically future fulfillment of that orientation. Edward Schillebeeckx wrote, in 1967, that with the Pastoral Constitution, the old, overly abstract condundrums about nature and grace become, "a problem set out in terms of the relations that unite earthly expectation (or earthly activity) and the eschatological kingdom."[9] Or

4. *GS* §35.
5. *GS* §35.
6. *GS* §36.
7. *GS* §40.
8. *GS* §43.
9. Cited in Henri de Lubac, "The Total Meaning of Man and the World," *Communio* 35 (winter 2008): 613–41 at 629–30.

as Henri de Lubac put it, in a stylistically typical rhetorical inquiry: "Do not" *Gaudium et Spes*'s "expressions," such as "growth of the reign" or "sketch of the age to come," "seem ... to suggest a very close connection between man's final end and the things of the temporal order and of the earthly society?"[10]

Lindbeck's reading of *Gaudium et Spes* is squarely based on this central eschatological thread. Writing when the document was still Schema 13, Lindbeck was impressed by the Conciliar document's cosmic Christology, which "seems to suggest that ... the 'building up of the earthly city' is a participation in the cosmic redemptive activity of Christ." Lindbeck warmed to its "eschatological" dynamism. The document's teaching that "the redeemed must communicate ... their hope" of final, eschatological deliverance "by earthly agencies and conditions"[11] rocked Lindbeck's chimes. Like Schillebeeckx, Lindbeck perceives that the Schema to some extent reframes the old adage that grace fulfills nature within an historical-futuristic conception of "fulfillment." As Lindbeck reads the *Schema*, it exhorts "the Christian ... to throw himself wholeheartedly into the building up of the earthly city" just because the faithful citizen "thereby prepares the conditions for the final coming of the kingdom."[12] Lindbeck is taken with the non-chiliastic millennialism of the conciliar imagination; its plundering and re-baptizing of the old Joachimite image of the first fruits of the new Jerusalem sprouting in a renewed earth, here below; its recovery of Irenaeus's this worldly and optimistic eschatology. Lindbeck is clearly turned on to sit at the feet of the conciliar fathers and be told that "[h]uman advancement, even in scientific, technical and artistic domains ... is not irrelevant to the Christian's hope, but is in some sense a direct preparation for the final fulfillment, for the ultimate manifestation of the kingdom of God."[13]

Even between 1965 and 1967, Lindbeck had stated fair and square that "progress" delivers both cures for hitherto incurable diseases and the atomic bomb: he knew that progress is not linear and often circles back on itself. He knew, too, that *we do not necessarily* know what counts as progress, or what, in our earthly ascent, is actually contributing to laying the foundations of the new Jerusalem, and what is a wrecking ball, knocking the building back down. But Lindbeck does not think our lack of knowledge of what counts as "progress" matters, any more than the fact that the Greeks and

10. De Lubac, "The Total Meaning of Man and the World," 638.

11. George A. Lindbeck, *Dialogue on the Way: Protestant Report from Rome on the Vatican Council* (Minneapolis, Minn.: Augsburg, 1965), 240.

12. Lindbeck, *Dialogue on the Way*, 242.

13. Lindbeck, *Dialogue on the Way*, 244.

the Romans did not advertently recognize their cultural achievements as "preparatio evangeliae" matters. Lindbeck claims, "The world is not getting better in any unambiguous way any more than in the thousands of years before Christ. And yet, perhaps even our ambiguous secular achievements are being used by God to prepare the way for the consummation, just as he used the Greeks and the Romans to prepare for the coming of the kingdom in the person of Jesus."[14]

Lindbeck acknowledges, likewise, that what he sees as the Schema's focus on eschatology and the future good of humanity as a whole can "distract attention from the one thing necessary": how it stands right now between the believer and the Lord of history. Rather self-deprecatingly, Lindbeck assigns such a concern for the relation between the individual and Christ to the Reformation, and to a negative aspect of the Reformation: Lindbeck the Conciliar observer already has the "social" anthropology of his later, famous work on doctrine. He thus concedes the "individual" and his immortal soul to Catholic humanitarianism, inventing a rhetorical question of his own: "Catholics can justifiably ask us whether we have not so individualized, personalized, and existentialized the forgiveness of sins that we have forgotten its objective, ontological and cosmic dimensions. They can ask us whether we have not so much emphasized faith that we have neglected hope."[15]

Lindbeck has three levels of explanation of why Protestants and Catholics should give enthusiastic assent to the "eschatologism" of *Gaudium et Spes*. He has three reasons why the Conciliar "Joy and Hope" is a good thing. One is that the "Constitution on the Church in the Modern World" has assimilated the historicization of *modern* human consciousness. Modern people, as Lindbeck claims, seek transcendence in and through history: they envisage that which transcends them as being "before" them, not "above" them. Lindbeck seems to advocate what he calls the authentically "Biblical eschatology" not particularly on the grounds that it is biblical, but rather because this orientation to seek fulfillment in the future resonates with the way moderns experience their being in the world. Point one in favor of the eschatologism of the Pastoral Constitution is that it vibes with modernity. Lindbeck writes that "biblical eschatology . . . has not won the field because theologians believe themselves faithful to the witness of Scripture. Its success must be attributed to the fact that New Testament eschatology takes on, in the modern perspective, a meaning which it did not have in the classical perspective." And thus,

14. Lindbeck, *Dialogue on the Way*, 250.
15. Lindbeck, *Dialogue on the Way*, 251.

It can return anew to the center, in the way that hope, the foretaste and the opening to the future salvation that God prepares for the whole world can become once more a dimension and an essential source of Christian faith and love. It is in this renewal of biblical eschatology, bound to the modern sense of the historical character of existence which, I suggest, furnishes the new framework, the common framework, which will matter to both Catholic and Protestant theology in the times to come."[16]

Secondly, and more in tune with "classical Lindbeckian concerns," an eschatological perspective is susceptible of eschatological empirical verification.[17] Lindbeck notes that the only language that makes sense for the modern pragmatist is a language open to empirical verification. Eschatological language is proleptically verifiable. It's remarkable how many Protestant and Lutheran theologians of the 1960s bought into this raw, Hegelian model of truth.

Thirdly, and most importantly, Lindbeck proposed in 1970 that the "eschatological" orientation of the social teaching of *Gaudium et Spes* means that it presents the "good" to be achieved by humanity not propositionally but in terms of a story. Conciliar eschatology makes the social teaching of the constitution take a story form. It enables the document to conceive of "the world not in terms of endless sameness," not on a Greek or Cartesian or "two-story," propositional model, "[b]ut as the story of God's creative and redemptive action and man's ever new responses."[18]

Hence Lindbeck is able to claim that the eschatological perspective of *Gaudium et Spes*, itself a model of historical thinking, historically relativizes the traditional disputes between Protestants and Catholics, making those disputes "of their time," beaching them like old ships and sails in the sixteenth century. The historical perspective espoused by the Pastoral Constitution enables us to see, Lindbeck thinks, that the erstwhile antagonisms of Catholics and Protestants are "more complementary than contradictory."[19] Hence, Lindbeck's immediate response to Schema 13 was to propose that it renders the introspective minutiae of Catholic-Protestant conflict obsolete. Lindbeck offered as his "personal conclusion ... that, in the contemporary eschatological-historical framework of thought, it becomes more and more difficult to develop a complete and solid theological justification of Protestantism and of Catholicism as they now are"—meaning, as two opposed ver-

16. Lindbeck, "Le Cadre du Désaccord Catholique-Protestant," 197.

17. Lindbeck, "Le Cadre du Désaccord Catholique-Protestant," 199.

18. George A. Lindbeck, *The Future of Roman Catholic Theology: Vatican II—Catalytst for Change* (Philadelphia: Fortress Press, 1970), 13.

19. Lindbeck, "Le Cadre du Désaccord Catholique-Protestant," 205.

sions of Christianity. Lindbeck felt that "[e]ven at the heart of history, and without speaking of the reconciliation for which we hope at the end of time, we are constrained to aspire to *one* Church, to pray for *one* Church which would be simultaneously Catholic and reformed."[20] We can, as it were, live proleptically *now* in the reunited church, which has yet to materialize but which Christian hope lets us perceive as the ground of our enterprise: the future reunion of Christendom is at the root of our ecumenical project. It is fascinating to observe the extent to which the father of narrative theology is prepared to immolate all the traditional Protestant and Lutheran concerns on the altar of eschatology.

Lindbeck got colder feet as the years drew on, and by 1970 he was able to observe that a so-called "classical" or vertical perspective is there in *Gaudium et Spes*, alongside the historical-eschatological.[21] But as I shall say in more detail in a moment, I do not think Lindbeck ever drew back from the insights he formed at his first dizzying gaze upon Catholic eschatology.

A Mis-Reading

Lindbeck seizes upon the eschatological core of the document and accurately situates its eschatological orientation in the context of Catholic debates about the desirability of observing that human nature desires to behold its "alpha and omega" in the supernatural. And yet, at the same time, he misses and strikes out on seeing the resolution of the natural/supernatural controversies in the person of Jesus Christ. In keeping with his own Lutheran narrative theology, an "eschatological" story is taken to function like a futuristic version of "predestination," and to determine the uptick of human fortunes without the merely individualistic intervention of any particular persons, even and including the Second Person of the Trinity. Lindbeck misreads *Gaudium et Spes* to the extent that he fails to observe that its centerpiece, out of which its eschatological conjunction of nature and supernature flows, is Jesus Christ. And, frankly, he never observes it because his eye is on questions like whether salvation is being conceived merely individualistically—as by Protestant existentialism or Tridentine Catholicism—or communally. Like so many figures of his generation, both Catholic and Protestant, Lindbeck drops the theological ball because he is so preoccupied with theories that he loses sight of personalities, even that of Jesus Christ.

20. Lindbeck, "Le Cadre du Désaccord Catholique-Protestant," 206.
21. Lindbeck, *The Future of Roman Catholic Theology*, 23.

Many of the Protestant observers at Vatican II were perturbed by what they took to be the "optimism" of its social and political teachings. Along with Henry Bruston and Edmund Schlink, for example,[22] Lindbeck felt that *Gaudium et Spes* was "too optimistic" in what it expected from this-worldly history. The 1960s was an upbeat decade, and many pessimists have wondered, then and since, about the pastorial prudence of anchoring new magisterial developments in such a tuneful season as the 1960s. Like John Henry Newman with respect to the promulgation of papal infallibility at Vatican I, Lindbeck was an "inopportunist" with respect to the assumptions of *Gaudium et Spes* about social progress; he told George Weigel in 1994: "I had reservations about the document's opportuneness. I was already pessimistic about the state of the world.... [Y]ou could see 1968 coming in 1965."[23] On the one hand, it was a pleasant surprise to see the Catholics magisterially affirming modernity, but on the other, such a broad affirmation of modernity as an era of progress did not sit right with the young Lutheran professor.

What Lindbeck misses here is not simply the deft balance of pessimistic grays alongside the orange hues of eschatological hope in the "Pastoral Constitution on the Church in the Modern World." It's that the Pastoral Constitution uses "modernity" and "modern man" as tropes with which to illustrate and exemplify the human condition itself; its affirmation of "modernity" sets the scene for an analysis of the human person who strides upon this stage in history. To affirm modernity is to affirm the backdrop and scene within which modern people live, and one cannot ask people to interrogate themselves without acknowledging their context. But the point of this is to ask human beings what they are here for. It asks "what's up" with modern times in order to ask modern people "what is up" with them. It discusses the ups and downs of modernity in order to consider the ups and downs of historical human beings.

Gaudium et Spes describes "the modern world" as "at once powerful and weak": the absence of blanket affirming optimism leads into the inference that "the imbalances under which the modern world labors are linked with that core basic imbalance which is rooted in the heart of man."[24] In keeping with its inspiration in the Augustinian theme of the heart restless until it rests in God, and its constant Pascalian evocation of the grandeur and lowliness of man, the document notes that the internal conflicts which

22. Henry Bruston, "L'Église et la Vocation Humaine," in *Points de Vue de Théologiens Protestants: Études sur ls décrets du Concile Vatican II*, ed. J. Bosc et al. (Paris: Cerf, 1967), 173–203.

23. Lindbeck, quoted in Weigel, "Re-Viewing Vatican II."

24. *GS* §10.

each individual experiences are externalized in the division between those complacent moderns who "are convinced that the future rule of man over the earth will satisfy every desire of his heart" and the nihilistic moderns "who despair of any meaning to life and . . . think existence is devoid of . . . significance and strive to confer a total meaning on it by their own ingenuity alone."[25] The constitution teaches that the human being who sidesteps self-interrogation about his own "end and beginning," his purpose in life, either projects the desires of the restless heart outward and makes a sacrament of technology, or fixates on technological progress to make up for the intrinsic meaninglessness of it all. Trying to solve the human problem from "outside in" rather than from "inside out" leads us to turn our social reality into a projection of the human problem writ large. Modernity, with all its engineering masterworks, is a projection of the human problem across the face of the earth in ambivalent technical achievements.

The problem is that we have lost the key to the question: "What is man?" We do not grasp that as a result of a broken bond to the Creator, and therefore with all our fellow human beings, "man is split within himself." "As a result" of this "split," the document teaches:

> all of human life, whether individual or collective, shows itself to be a dramatic struggle between good and evil. . . . Indeed, man finds that by himself he is incapable of battling the assaults of evil successfully, so that everyone feels as though he is bound by chains. But the Lord Himself came to free and strengthen man, renewing him inwardly and casting out that "prince of this world" . . . who held him in the bondage of sin. For sin has diminished man, blocking his path to fulfillment.[26]

Lindbeck never mentions this introspective aspect of the document, although all of its eschatology is intended as a response to the real, historical situation of the human person, who is down in the hole and whose own efforts to escape simply enmire him further.

Gaudium et Spes was written by simple Catholic men who had been taught in their catechisms about the four last things. Across the spectrum of theologians who worked on the numerous schemas for the constitution—from Karol Wojtyła and Henri de Lubac to Msgr. Piolanti and Sebastian Tromp—for all of these men, eschatology is about death, judgment, heaven, hell. Thus paragraph 18 is about "the riddle of human existence grow[ing] most acute" in the face of "death." It is boldly Athanasian in its response: Man "rebels against death because he bears in himself an eternal seed

25. *GS* §10.
26. *GS* §12.

which cannot be reduced to sheer matter."[27] So the document leads back through the labyrinth of introspection, down into the "acute" questions raised by death, and through that door in the human soul to God:

> The Church holds that the recognition of God is in no way hostile to man's dignity, since this dignity is rooted and perfected in God. For man was made an intelligent and free member of society by God Who created him, but even more important, he is called as a son to commune with God and share in His happiness. She further teaches that a hope related to the end of time does not diminish the importance of intervening duties but rather undergirds the acquittal of them with fresh incentives.... [W]hen ... the hope of life eternal [is] wanting, man's dignity is most grievously lacerated, as current events often attest; riddles of life and death, of guilt and of grief go unsolved with the frequent result that men succumb to despair.[28]

The document contrasts the *despairing* attitude to modern technological society of secular agnosticism with the positive hopeful attitude to human progress that can be seriously entertained only by those who hope in eternity and eternal life. There's no question in the document about balancing optimism and pessimism about social progress: the contrast it makes is between Godless despair over the future and Christological hope in eternal life and, therefore, in this life here below.

So as John Paul II, who had labored over the various editions of this text, knew so well, the storm center of the eschatology of *Gaudium et Spes* is at paragraph 22: "only in the mystery of the incarnate Word does the mystery of man take on light.... Christ, by the revelation of the mystery of the Father ... fully reveals man to man himself and makes his supreme calling clear."[29] The content of the eschatological momentum of history is Christ, and to that extent, the issue of whether it is opportune or imprudent to be thinking of the presence of the new Jerusalem in the earthly city is off the mark. When we speak of the indwelling of the heavenly city in our earthly human exploits, we do not necessarily envisage the earthly city as a Camelot or as a city on a hill whose harmony with the new Jerusalem is all too clear. We simply mean that Christ, the Lord of history, is present in every stage of the communal biography of mankind. He was present in *samizdat* culture, amongst the querulous Russian Refusniks, and in the Polish Solidarity movement.

One of the central, significant contributions of the Protestant observers to the social documents of Vatican II, like *Gaudium et Spes* and *Dignitatae*

27. *GS* §18.
28. *GS* §21.
29. *GS* §22.

Humanae, was the notion of the Church as a "servant" presence in society. Originally proposed by the Lutheran Lukas Vischer, the idea of the "servant church" was an important inroad in the discussion of how the Church could be present *in public* without dominating that public space.[30] How could one steer between the unworkable integralism of the traditionalists and the liberal reduction of faith to passive private option? The Protestant observers suggested that the Church as "servant" operates in public but wields power only through service. George Lindbeck was very well aware of the importance and novelty of these manoeuvres. He spoke of

> glimmerings of the complete realistically eschatological answer as when the Constitution on the Church in the Modern World says that those who "dedicate themselves to the earthly service of men ... make ready the material of the celestial realm [and] devote themselves to that future when humanity itself will become an offering accepted by God" (art. 38). This suggests that the work of the earthly city is important, not necessarily because it contributes to the church, as the incarnationalist view holds, but because it supplies material for the kingdom at the end of history. Because God is guiding all the processes of nature and of history towards the consummation, his people are called upon to participate fully in his anonymous humanizing activity even when they do not thereby win members or Christianize the world in any overt way.[31]

This is a decent first attempt at understanding the document, but you cannot bypass the Incarnation without bypassing Christ.

Lindbeck does not perceive that, as the constitution would have it, Christ, and the kind of body Christ's is, is the means through which God's eschatological action is transforming the histories of individual men and women, and human history as a whole. The consequence of this inattention can be quite dire, as when the Yale theologian claims that, for the conciliar texts

> [t]he role of the church seems to be diminished in a realistically eschatological perspective because salvation is conceived not individualistically but rather in terms of the redemption of mankind as a whole and ... of the cosmos. In order to bring about such a stupendous result, God must be guiding all the processes of history towards the goal, not simply working redemptively in and through the church. The people of God is viewed much more than formerly as only one of the instruments of God's saving activity.[32]

30. Herbert Vorgrimler, ed., *Commentary on the Documents of Vatican II: Volume V: Pastoral Constitution on the Church in the Modern World*, trans. W. J. O'Hara (London: Burns and Oates, 1969), 20–25.

31. Lindbeck, *Future*, 49–50.

32. Lindbeck, *Future*, 35.

I do not understand what agents, instruments, or secondary causes could bring about this transformation if it is not the individual Christian persons who make up the body of Christ, and through whom the person of Christ acts in history. Lindbeck seems to have got mixed up and confused between "salvation" as a noun or end product and salvation as a verb or process. Salvation as an end will be social, and include our households and our animals, but this does not mean that the *savers*, the agents of salvation, are not individuals, and include the one, particular, Church as an individual person.

Lindbeck Walks It Back

Between 1965 and 1970, Lindbeck believed that the eschatological focus of documents like *Gaudium et Spes* rendered the Reformation disputes about faith and justification and Scripture obsolete. Lindbeck later came to appreciate that his immediate, spontaneous response to the Vatican II documents had been overly enthusiastic. He came to realize that changes in opinion about doctrines or dogmas would not, of themselves, overturn the entrenched divisions of the Churches. Lindbeck told George Weigel in 1994:

> [T]he circumstances that would make reunion possible had to do with much more than the discovery that these doctrines could be understood, without betraying one's own heritage, in ways that were not church-dividing. We learned a lot as time went on. And while we were never naive enough to think that that agreement was all that was needed, we did think that a meeting of minds on the sixteenth-century conflicts ... would make more difference ecumenically than in fact it has. We thought ... that specifically historical doctrinal issues were more decisive than they proved to be.[33]

But in another sense Lindbeck left the Council thinking the Reformation was over, and he never wholly went back on that insight. He told Weigel, "The agreements we reached are, of course, one of the conditions for reunion. And so, while I have no idea when this progress will contribute in substantial ways to the reunion of the churches, I find myself feeling a great sense of satisfaction that that job is in large part done."[34] Writing in 2003, at the time of the Lutheran-Roman Catholic statement on justification, Lindbeck observed that it looked like most people had given up on the original vision of ecumenism as aiming at the visible reunion of the Churches. But then he asked this seemingly rhetorical question:

33. Lindbeck, quoted in Weigel, "Re-Viewing Vatican II."
34. Lindbeck, quoted in Weigel, "Re-Viewing Vatican II."

What … if the influence of the Enlightenment on modern and postmodern religious developments is itself coming to an end? What if it is the currently regnant theologies with their indifference to unitive ecumenism that are the anomaly? Perhaps, in our post-Constantinian yet increasingly globalist age, the visible unity of the Christian Churches, no doubt in post-Constantinian forms, will come to seem more and more important.[35]

Let me put Lindbeck's thought like this, or at least offer a Catholic version of Lindbeck's thought process. Chiliasm arose early in Christian history and was not extinguished by Augustinian re-interpretations of the book of Revelation. The medieval church got itself up to its elbows in blood in the inquisitorial effort to stamp out chiliastic eschatology. The Lutheran Reformation was itself an offspring of a counter-ecclesial eschatological spirit. Trent and Tridentine Catholicism responded with rejection. But the Catholic Church found, over the next several hundred years, that its stamping out of the eschatological came at the cost of denying that human beings desire the eternal city at all. The Catholic Church then maintained her social and political order at the cost of denying that the eternal city has any deep relevance to human beings on this earth. Thus at Vatican II, in *Gaudium et Spes*, the Church Catholic re-baptized the eschatological impulse, and in so doing razed the bastions between herself and the Protestant churches of the Reformation. For Protestants like Lindbeck, the Reformation was over: "the job is in large part done."[36] Many other Protestants were stimulated by the Church's embrace of eschatology to retreat ever further from nature. It is this retreat and rejection of nature which now stands as a roadblock to ecumenical conversation.

35. George Lindbeck, "The University and Ecumenism," in *Justification and the Future of the Ecumenical Movement: The Joint Declaration on the Doctrine of Justification*, ed. William G. Rusch (Collegeville, Minn.: Liturgical Press, 2003), 1–13 at 10.

36. Lindbeck, quoted in Weigel, "Re-Viewing Vatican II."

Chapter 10

Meeting *par cum pari*

Unitatis Redintegratio and Ecumenical Progress

Hans Boersma

The spirit of mutual appreciation and friendship that permeated the conference on which this essay is based is reason for gratitude. Vatican II's Decree on Ecumenism, *Unitatis Redintegratio*, mentions how important it is for Catholics to "become familiar with the outlook of our separated brethren," and it goes on to call for "meetings of the two sides—especially for discussion of theological problems—where each can treat with the other on equal footing (*par cum pari*)."[1] The conference "*Ad Limina Apostolorum*: Vatican II and the Future of Catholic-Protestant Ecumenism" seems to me one such meeting intended by the Council in its decree, promulgated on November 21, 1964.[2] To be sure, the notion of meeting "on equal footing" (*par cum pari*) is

1. Decree on Ecumenism (*Unitatis Redintegratio* [*UR*]), in *The Conciliar and Postconciliar Documents*, vol. 1 of *Vatican Council II*, edited by Austin Flannery, rev. ed. (Northport, N.Y.: Costello; Dublin, Ireland: Dominican, 1975), no. 9 (p. 461); *Acta Apostolicae Sedis* (*AAS*) 57 (1965): 90–112, at 98. The notion of meeting *par cum pari* first occurred in the 1949 Instruction *Ecclesia Catholica* of the Holy Office, which for the first time and cautiously gave an opening to ecumenical dialogue with non-Catholics: "All the aforesaid conferences and meetings, public and non-public, large and small, which are called for the purpose of affording an opportunity for the Catholic and the non-Catholic party for the sake of discussion to treat of matters of faith and morals, each presenting on even terms (*par cum pari*) the doctrine of his own faith, are subject to the prescriptions of the Church which were recalled to mind in the *Monitum*, '*Cum compertum*,' of this Congregation under date of 5 June, 1948. Hence mixed congresses are not absolutely forbidden; but they are not to be held without the previous permission of the competent Ecclesiastical Authority" (https://www.ewtn.com/catholicism/library/on-the-ecumenical-movement-2070; *AAS* 42 [1950]: 142–47, at 145).

2. For a historical overview of the origin of the decree, see Werner Becker, "History of the Decree," in *Commentary on the Documents of Vatican II*, vol. 2, ed. Herbert Vorgrimler, trans. R. A. Wilson (New York: Herder and Herder, 1968), 1–62.

a delicate one. When Karl Barth used the expression *Ad Limina Apostolorum* for the title of the book in which he reported on his 1966 visit to Rome, which took place exactly fifty years prior to the conference with the same name, he playfully compared his visit to the quinquennial visits of Catholic bishops to the bishop of Rome, honoring with their visits not only the "thresholds of the apostles" (*limina apostolorum*) but also the universal jurisdiction of Rome.[3] His quasi-subservient attitude, however, did not prevent Barth from engaging in frank dialogue and asking probing questions. The elderly Swiss theologian evidently came away from Rome convinced that his meetings with Catholic leaders in Rome had conformed to the principle of meeting *par cum pari*.[4]

Unity and a New Spirit

In this chapter I intend to probe some of the difficulties surrounding the desire to meet "on equal footing." I will press the question of what unity means according to the Decree on Ecumenism, and the general drift of my considerations will be that the principle of meeting *par cum pari* is a difficult fit with the overall ecclesiology at work in *Unitatis Redintegratio* and, by extension, in Catholic doctrine. Before arriving at this more critical analysis, however, it is incumbent on me to observe that the decree presents a remarkable opening for ecumenical dialogue, one that would have been unthinkable in the context of earlier magisterial teaching on ecumenism. Although the language of the "spirit of Vatican II" may be controversial and can be misused, there is little doubt that the council documents breathe an unprecedented spirit of openness or *aggiornamento*. Johannes Feiner rightly observes that the attitude expressed in *Unitatis Redintegratio* toward ecumenism marks a new beginning:

> The content and tone of this evaluation [of the ecumenical movement] are in marked contrast to the encyclical *Mortalium Animos* of Pius XI (6 January 1928); but it is also more positive than the instruction *Ecclesia Catholica* of 20 December 1949, which

3. See Karl Barth, *Ad Limina Apostolorum: An Appraisal of Vatican* II, trans. Keith R. Crim (Richmond, Va.: John Knox, 1968) (hereafter, *ALA*). Barth's visit took place from September 22 to 29, 1966 (*ALA*, 11).

4. This is perhaps clearest from Barth's humorous description of his exchange with Pope Paul VI: "We did not pass over the difficult point of Mariology. The Pope had heard that I preferred Joseph, the foster father of Jesus, as the prototype of the nature and function of the church, to the 'handmaiden of the Lord' who was subsequently elevated to the position of Queen of Heaven. He assured me he would pray for me, that in my advanced age I would be given deeper insight into this problem" (*ALA*, 15). Barth reports the outcome of his visit with the comment: "I returned from Rome just as stubbornly evangelical—I would really rather say, evangelical-catholic—as before" (*ALA*, 18).

was the beginning of a change in the attitude of the Catholic Church. The decree begins by looking at the whole of Christianity, including Catholic and non-Catholic Christians, and affirms that the movement for unity in our own time has undergone a remarkable strengthening and extension.[5]

In good part as a result of this new ecumenical spirit of *Unitatis Redintegratio*, collegial friendships, shared academic endeavors, as well as numerous forms of ecumenical dialogue have flourished and created an atmosphere that is markedly different from that of the pre-Vatican II years. We may even gratefully acknowledge that doctrinally some progress has been made, perhaps most notably in the form of the much-applauded Lima statement of Faith and Order, *Baptism, Eucharist and Ministry* (1982) and the Catholic-Lutheran *Joint Declaration on the Doctrine of Justification* (1997).[6] The Evangelicals and Catholics Together statements too, though not all arriving at the kind of consensus one might hope for, have done a great deal to draw evangelicals and Catholics more closely together.[7]

Much of this ecumenical progress has become possible as a result of *Unitatis Redintegratio*. The decree evinces genuine openness to what it calls "separated churches and ecclesial communities," the members of which "the Catholic Church accepts ... with respect and affection as brothers," who are "in some, though imperfect (*etsi non perfecta*), communion with the Catholic Church."[8] What is more, *Unitatis Redintegratio* expresses joy "that our separated brethren look to Christ as the source and center of ecclesiastical communion."[9] "Very many" of the "most significant elements and endowments which together go to build up and give life to the Church itself, can exist outside of the boundaries of the Catholic Church," and here the decree makes mention particularly of "the written Word of God," of "the life of grace," of the theological virtues, and of various "visible elements."[10] Doctrinal divisions notwithstanding, the Second Vatican Council recognizes that a spiritual unity persists in the midst of serious disagreements.

5. Johannes Feiner, "Commentary on the Decree," in *Commentary on the Documents of Vatican II*, vol. 2, ed. Herbert Vorgrimler, trans. R. A. Wilson (New York: Herder and Herder, 1968), 57–164, at 60.

6. *Baptism, Eucharist, and Ministry*, Faith and Order Paper 111 (Geneva: World Council of Churches, 1983); The Lutheran World Federation and the Roman Catholic Church, *Joint Declaration on the Doctrine of Justification* (Grand Rapids, Mich.: Eerdmans, 2000).

7. For the ECT statements, see *Evangelicals and Catholics Together at Twenty: Vital Statements on Contested Topics*, ed. Timothy George and Thomas G. Guarino (Grand Rapids, Mich.: Brazos, 2015). For an (at this point somewhat outdated) discussion of developments surrounding ECT, see Mark Noll and Carolyn Nystrom, *Is the Reformation Over? An Evangelical Assessment of Roman Catholicism* (Grand Rapids, Mich.: Baker, 2005).

8. *UR* §3; *AAS* 57 (1965): 93.

9. *UR* §9; *AAS* 57 (1965): 105.

10. *UR* §3; *AAS* 57 (1965): 93.

Nor does this spiritual unity pertain only to individual relationships, as if it were abstracted from ecclesial life and practice. Repeatedly, the decree speaks of baptism as creating a common link. Some of those separated from the Church are "joined (*appositi*) to her by baptism."[11] With reference to Colossians 2:12—You were "buried with him in baptism, in which you were also raised with him through faith in the powerful working of God, who raised him from the dead"[12]—the decree insists that baptism "constitutes the sacramental bond of unity existing among all who through it are reborn."[13] This baptismal bond points to some kind of shared liturgical life, since the "brethren divided from us also carry out many liturgical actions (*actiones sacrae*) of the Christian religion."[14]

In what is perhaps the most remarkable acknowledgment of a shared ecclesial life, the decree insists that these liturgical actions "truly engender a life of grace, and, one must say, can aptly (*aptae dicendae sunt*) give access to the life of salvation."[15] Apparently, liturgical actions among the "separated brethren" can function as means of divine grace.[16] As such, the practice of baptism is part and parcel of a rich devotional and liturgical life among the "separated brethren":

> The Christian way of life of these brethren is nourished by faith in Christ. It is strengthened by the grace of baptism and the hearing of the Word of God. This way of life expresses itself in private prayer, in meditation on the scriptures, in the life of a Christian family, and in the worship of the community gathered together to praise God. Furthermore, their worship sometimes displays notable features of a liturgy once shared in common.[17]

The recognition of fraternity on the part of Vatican II goes well beyond a meager acknowledgment that God is at work within individuals separated from the church. To my mind, this recognition must be applauded without reserve as it bequeathed a different spirit both to the Council and to ecumenical discussion ever since.

11. *UR* §4; *AAS* 57 (1965): 96.
12. Throughout I quote from the *English Standard Version*.
13. *UR* §22; *AAS* 57 (1965): 105.
14. *UR* §3; *AAS* 57 (1965): 93.
15. *UR* §3; *AAS* 57 (1965): 93.
16. Cf. Johannes Feiner's comment that it is not the case "that non-Catholics can attain salvation, *although* they live outside the Catholic Church. Rather, one must say that Christ gives them salvation through the reality of non-Catholic communities ... in so far as within them the effect is present of the elements of the Church through which Christ effects the salvation of the faithful in the Catholic Church also" ("Commentary on the Decree," 76).
17. *UR* §23; *AAS* 57 (1965): 106.

In this light, it may not go unmentioned that the council fathers speak both generously and truthfully when they maintain that for the separation of the church often "both sides were to blame,"[18] so that the council fathers "beg pardon of God and of our separated brethren."[19] Both sides of the Reformation divide have guilt to admit, and although this acknowledgment lacks specificity, the plea for forgiveness does express a welcome desire to heal the horrible rift to which both parties of the sixteenth-century schism were guilty.[20] Both the Catholic Church and the Reformation churches need to address past wrongs and hurts in charting a common path forward toward a full and complete restoration of unity.[21]

Unity and Other Churches

Also important, from an ecumenical perspective, is the decree's language of the church's unity subsisting (*subsistere*) in the Catholic Church. To Protestants this may seem like a massive claim, but it nonetheless carefully delineates the manner in which the Catholic Church is identified with the one, holy, catholic, and apostolic church of the creed. The verb *subsistere* occurs most famously in paragraph 8 of *Lumen Gentium*:

> This Church, constituted and organized as a society in the present world, subsists in (*subsistit in*) the Catholic Church, which is governed by the successor of Peter and by the bishops in communion with him. Nevertheless, many elements of sanctification and of truth are found outside its visible confines. Since these are gifts belonging to the Church of Christ, they are forces impelling towards Catholic unity.[22]

18. *UR* §3; *AAS* 57 (1965): 93.

19. *UR* §7; *AAS* 57 (1965): 97. Cf. Timothy George, "*Unitatis Redintegratio* after Fifty Years: A Protestant Reading," *Pro Ecclesia* 25 (2016): 53–70, at 58–60.

20. The plea for forgiveness was not included in the initial 1963 schema *De Oecumenismo* and was added because many of the written submissions of the council fathers "demanded a humble confession of the guilt which also lies upon Catholics for the separation of Christians" (Becker, "History of the Decree," 26–27).

21. The overall tone of openness toward non-Catholics in *Unitatis Redintegratio* was a deliberate corrective move on the part of the council after the early schema *De Ecclesiae Unitate* (*Ut omnes unum sint*), dealing with the Eastern Churches, had largely been received negatively by the council fathers in their debate from November 26 to November 30, 1962 (Becker, "History of the Decree," 7–19). The schema that directly lies at the basis of *Unitatis Redintegratio*, *De Oecumenismo*, was initially drawn up in the spring of 1963 by the Secretariat for Promoting Christian Unity, headed by Cardinal Augustin Bea (along with Mgr. J. G. M. Willebrands). The SPCU had been established in November 1960, and on October 22, 1962 Pope John XXIII had given it the same rank as the other commissions within the Vatican Council (Becker, "History of the Decree," 6).

22. "Dogmatic Constitution of the Church" (*Lumen Gentium* [*LG*]), in *The Conciliar and Postconciliar Documents*, vol. 1 of *Vatican Council II*, edited by Austin Flannery, rev. ed. (Northport, N.Y.: Costello; Dublin, Ireland: Dominican, 1975), §8 (p. 357); *AAS* 57 (1965): 5–67, at 12.

Whereas in 1950 *Humani Generis* had stated that "the Mystical Body of Christ and the Roman Catholic Church are one and the same thing,"[23] *Lumen Gentium* modifies this language by replacing *est* with *subsistit in.*

To be sure, many Catholics will be quick to clarify that the change in wording is not a change in teaching. Avery Cardinal Dulles has gone so far as to suggest that "the council agreed with *Mystici Corporis* that the mystical Body had full or substantive existence in the Catholic Church *and nowhere else.*"[24] This analysis is borne out by a 2007 statement of the Congregation for the Doctrine of the Faith, which explains that the language of "subsistence" refers to the "perduring, historical continuity and the permanence of all the elements instituted by Christ in the Catholic Church, in which the Church of Christ is concretely found on this earth."[25] In terms of the difference between "subsists in" and "is," the Congregation explains that

> this expression [i.e., "subsists in"], which indicates the full identity (*plenam identitatem*) of the Church of Christ with the Catholic Church, does not change the doctrine on the Church. Rather, it comes from and brings out more clearly the fact that there are "numerous elements of sanctification and of truth" which are found outside her structure, but which "as gifts properly belonging to the Church of Christ, impel towards Catholic Unity."[26]

Thus does the Congregation for the Doctrine of the Faith reassert the earlier insistence on the proper identity between the church of Christ and the Catholic Church, while at the same time making clear by the language of *subsistere* that the separated brethren also have a link with the Catholic Church.

As an aside, I must confess that I find the Congregation's clarification less than compelling. If it is true that "subsists in" intimates full identity between the church of Christ and the Catholic Church, then how can that same verb bring out more clearly the presence of truth elements among the

23. *Humani Generis* (*HG*), §27; http://w2.vatican.va/content/pius-xii/en/encyclicals/documents/hf_p-xii_enc_12081950_humani-generis.html; *AAS* 42 (1950): 561–78, at 571.

24. Avery Cardinal Dulles, "Nature, Mission, and Structure of the Church," in *Vatican II: Renewal within Tradition*, ed. Matthew L. Lamb and Matthew Levering (New York: Oxford University Press, 2008), 25–36, at 28; emphasis added. Dulles points out that in response to complaints about the word "is" (*est*) in an early draft, a subcommittee replaced it with "is present in" (*adest in*). He goes on to write: "However, the council fathers were not content to assert that the Church of Christ is present in Roman Catholicism, which had always claimed to possess in itself the fullness of the Church. Thus the Theological Commission on November 25, 1963, dropped the term 'adest' and replaced it with 'subsistit.' The new term was proposed by Sebastian Tromp, SJ, who had previously favored 'est' and was a stout defender of the positions of *Mystici Corporis*" (ibid.).

25. Congregation for the Doctrine of the Faith, "Responses to Some Questions regarding Certain Aspects of the Doctrine on the Church"; http://www.vatican.va/roman_curia/congregations/cfaith/documents/rc_con_cfaith_doc_20070629_responsa-quaestiones_en.html; *AAS* 99 (2007): 604–8, at 606.

26. "Responses to Some Questions"; *AAS* 99 (2007): 607.

"separated brethren"? It seems to me that only if it weakens the identity between the church of Christ and the Catholic Church, can the language of *subsistere* be of help in bringing to the fore "elements of sanctification and of truth" outside the Roman Catholic structure. Only if *subsistere* is less intensive than *est* does it facilitate recognition of ecclesial elements outside the Roman Catholic Church.

The overall point nonetheless remains: in several key places the documents of Vatican II use the verb *subsistere* rather than *esse* to identify the relationship between the church of Christ and the Roman Catholic Church, and the purpose, according to the Congregation for the Doctrine of the Faith, is to draw attention to the numerous elements of sanctification and truth found outside the institution of the Catholic Church. As such, there is an acknowledgment that the separation of fellow Christians from the unity of the church of Christ wounds also the unity of the Roman Catholic Church.[27]

All this is in line, I think, with *Lumen Gentium*'s insistence that there are multiple ways of being related to the catholic unity of the church: "The Catholic faithful, others who believe in Christ, and finally all mankind" belong to or are related to (*pertinent vel ordinantur*) the church's unity in different ways.[28] After mentioning those who belong to the visible Catholic Church—adding the salutary warning that "even though incorporated into the Church, one who does not ... persevere in charity is not saved"[29]—*Lumen Gentium* goes on to speak of other baptized Christians "who do not ... profess the Catholic faith in its entirety or have not preserved unity or communion under the successor of Peter."[30] Here the Dogmatic Constitution on the Church deals with believers in various "Churches or ecclesial communities" that display varying degrees of adherence to the truth of the gospel. In a manner consonant with *Unitatis Redintegratio*, the Dogmatic Constitution speaks of Christians being "in some real way joined to us in the Holy Spirit," who "stirs up desires and actions in all of Christ's disciples in order that all may be peaceably united."[31] Finally, *Lumen Gentium* turns to "those who have not yet received the Gospel," dealing in turn with Jewish believers, Muslims, as well as others "who, through no fault of their own,

27. Cf. the *Catechism of the Catholic Church*: "The ruptures that wound the unity of Christ's Body—here we must distinguish heresy, apostasy, and schism—do not occur without human sin" (2nd ed. [Vatican City: Libreria Editrice Vaticana, 2000], §817 [p. 216]).

28. *LG* §13; *AAS* 57 (1965): 18.

29. *LG* §14; *AAS* 57 (1965): 19.

30. *LG* §15; *AAS* 57 (1965): 19.

31. *LG* §15; *AAS* 57 (1965): 19.

do not know the Gospel of Christ or his Church."[32] Even concerning this last category the council fathers acknowledge (though with some important qualifications) that "whatever good or truth is found amongst them is considered by the Church to be a preparation for the Gospel."[33]

In short, the various ways in which people belong to or are related to the people of God may be depicted by way of a widening set of concentric circles, with Catholic believers in the center, and moving outward via other Christians to Jews, Muslims, and non-believers.[34] Also here, though the constitution in no way negates that the church's unity fully and only subsists within the Catholic Church (and other Christians are not explicitly said to "belong" [*pertinere*] to the church of Christ),[35] *Lumen Gentium* does attempt to do justice to the complexity of the various ways there are of relating to the gospel and to the church: Eastern Orthodox believers, and to some degree also Protestants, are more closely related to the church than are others.

Unity and Hierarchy of Truths

We should also duly note that *Unitatis Redintegratio* does not treat every aspect of Catholic teaching as equally central to the church's unity. By insisting on a "hierarchy of truths" in paragraph 11, the Vatican Council intended to give a new impetus to ecumenical dialogue:

> Furthermore, in ecumenical dialogue, Catholic theologians, standing fast by the teaching of the Church yet searching together with separated brethren into the di-

32. *LG* §16; *AAS* 57 (1965): 20.

33. *LG* §16; *AAS* 57 (1965): 20.

34. Cf. the critical description in Gregg R. Allison, *Roman Catholic Theology and Practice: An Evangelical Assessment* (Wheaton, Ill.: Crossway, 2014), 175–77.

35. In part because the bull *Exultate Deo* (1439) insists that through baptism "we are made members of Christ and of the body of the Church," the Council was unwilling to deny that also Protestants in some way belong to the church. See Henry Denzinger, *The Sources of Catholic Dogma*, trans. Roy J. Deferrari (Saint Louis, Mo.: Herder, 1955), no. 696 (p. 221). The notion of "imperfect" (*non perfecta*) communion (*UR* §3; *AAS* 57 [1965]: 93) with the church, conjoined with the statement that all baptized people are "incorporated into Christ" (*Christo incorporantur*) (*UR* §3; *AAS* 57 [1965]: 93), suggests that all baptized Christians can in some way be considered to belong to the church. Charles Morerod comments: "All baptized people are 'members of Christ's body,' which means of the Church (or of the communion of the Church, at least imperfectly)" ("The Decree on Ecumenism, *Unitatis Redintegratio*," in *Vatican* II, ed. Lamb and Levering, 311–41, at 316). Cf. also Johannes Feiner's comment that this phrasing of the decree "is based upon a vision which on the one hand does not regard the body of Christ and the Catholic Church as two separate entities, but on the other hand does not regard them as simply identical. Those who are outside the communion of the Catholic Church are brought to faith in Christ and are baptized, are incorporated into the mystical body of Christ; thus while they do not belong to the Catholic Church as this clearly defined community of faith with the ordered structure of a society, nevertheless they are fundamentally in communion with it through faith and baptism" ("Commentary on the Decree," 73).

vine mysteries, should do so with love for the truth, with charity, and with humility. When comparing doctrines with one another, they should remember that in Catholic doctrine there exists an order or "hierarchy" of truths (*'hierarchiam' veritatum*), since they vary in their relation to the foundation (*fundamento*) of the Christian faith. Thus the way will be opened whereby this kind of "fraternal rivalry" will incite all to a deeper realization and a clearer expression of the unfathomable riches of Christ.[36]

Many have commented on the ecumenical import of this statement, the wording of which appears to have been influenced by the Lutheran ecumenical theologian Oscar Cullmann.[37] Undoubtedly inspired in good part by this paragraph, Cullmann himself commented: "This is more than the opening of a door; new ground has been broken. No Catholic document has ever spoken of non-Catholic Christians in this way."[38] The Dutch Reformed theologian Gerrit C. Berkouwer went even further in commenting on the notion of a hierarchy of truths: "It is not enough to merely gauge the meaning and scope of this expression. It is undoubtedly flabbergasting that this 'concentration' (on the fundamentals) that pretty much occupies all churches today is unexpectedly set forth in a conciliar decree and that this did not elicit more opposition despite its 'strangeness'."[39]

It is important, however, carefully to note what paragraph 11 does and does not affirm by speaking of a "hierarchy of truths." The quotation given above begins by stating that Catholic theologians engage in ecumenical dialogue while "standing fast by the teaching of the Church," and it is preceded by the important caveats that it is "essential that the doctrine be clearly presented in its entirety" and that "nothing is so foreign to the spirit of ecumenism as a false irenicism (*ille falsus irenismus*) which harms the purity of Catholic doctrine and obscures its genuine and certain meaning."[40] These preliminary comments make clear that a hierarchy of truths should not be construed as an excuse to render irrelevant those doctrinal issues on which Catholics and Protestants may disagree.

Eduardo Echeverria, in his treatment of Berkouwer, cautions against an understanding of a hierarchy of truths that "breeds theological indiffer-

36. *UR* §11; *AAS* 57 (1965): 99.

37. Edward Iris Cassidy, *Ecumenism and Interreligious Dialogue: Unitatis Redintegratio, Nostra Aetate* (New York: Paulist Press, 2005), 10–11, drawing on Thomas Stransky, "The Observers at Vatican II: A Unique Experience of Dialogue," *Centro pro Unione Bulletin*, no. 63 (Spring 2003): 8–14.

38. As quoted in Cassidy, *Ecumenism and Interreligious Dialogue*, 11.

39. G. C. Berkouwer, *Nabetrachting op het Concilie* (Kampen: Kok, 1968), 103; as quoted in Eduardo Echeverria, *Berkouwer and Catholicism: Disputed Questions*, Studies in Reformed Theology 24 (Leiden: Brill, 2013), 103.

40. *UR* §11; *AAS* 57 (1965): 99.

ence," as if, for example, the Assumption of Mary can "no longer remain a church-dividing issue because of its low rank—nonfundamental truths—in regard to the foundation of faith and hence the fundamental revealed truths at its base."[41] Berkouwer, explains Echeverria, recognized that this would be a wrong understanding of a hierarchy of truths. Instead, as Berkouwer put it, "Embedded in this expression in the decree is the question of the connection that binds together the 'elements' of doctrine, and above all the 'nexus' with Christ as the foundation, and of the variation in the connection with this foundation."[42]

Archbishop Andrea Pangrazio of Gorizia, Italy, made this exact same point in presenting the expression "hierarchy of truths" to the council, commenting:

> There should be a centre to which these [individual ecclesial] elements are to be related and without which they cannot be explained. This binding factor and this centre is Christ himself, whom all Christians confess as the Lord of the Church, whom undoubtedly Christians of all communities strive to serve faithfully and who condescends to work wonderful things even in the communities separated from us through his active presence in the Holy Spirit. . . . Even though all revealed truths must be believed with the same divine faith and all constitutive elements of the Church have to be faithfully retained, yet they are not all of the same importance.[43]

Archbishop Pangrazio's point appears to be that we may rejoice in our common agreement on the fundamental truths that belong to the *end* of the Christian faith (Trinity, Incarnation, redemption, God's love for sinful humanity, eternal life in God's kingdom, and so on); and that we also may rejoice that the areas of disagreement do not concern the end itself but only the *means* (doctrinal claims concerning the seven sacraments, the hierarchical structure of the church, apostolic succession).[44] The notion of a "hierarchy of truths" is thus, first and foremost, meant to elucidate the character of our disagreements, that is to say, to make clear that they concern not matters belonging to the centre or the end, but matters only of means. Not all doctrines have equal weight.[45]

41. Echeverria, *Berkouwer and Catholicism*, 104.

42. Berkouwer, *Nabetrachting*, 103; as quoted in Echeverria, *Berkouwer and Catholicism*, 104.

43. Speech of Archbishop Pangrazio, November 25, 1964, as translated in Lorenz Jaeger, *A Stand on Ecumenism: The Council's Decree*, trans. Hilda Graef (New York: Kenedy, 1965), 114–15. Cf. Morerod, "The Decree on Ecumenism," 322.

44. Both the language of "end" and "means" and the examples are Pangrazio's (in Jaeger, *Stand on Ecumenism*, 115).

45. See Thomas G. Guarino, *Revelation and Truth: Unity and Plurality in Contemporary Theology* (Scranton, Pa.: University of Scranton Press, 1993), 142–43.

None of this resolves the ecumenical dilemma. After all, as we just saw, Pangrazio also makes the comment that "all revealed truths must be believed with the same divine faith and all constitutive elements of the Church have to be faithfully retained." Echeverria helpfully clarifies by drawing from Yves Congar the distinction between the *quod* and the *quo* of the faith. The *quod* is the material contents of the faith. Here not everything is equally close to the heart of the gospel. Some doctrines are more important than others. The *quo* is the formal authority that doctrines carry by virtue of their being proclaimed infallibly. In that sense all doctrines are equal and must be accepted in faith.[46] The Swiss Dominican, Charles Morerod, OP, captures this same distinction when he comments that the council fathers had in mind

> two elements: (1) a hierarchy among truths as a result of their different relation to the center of revelation (that is, Christ and his mystery) and (2) a proposition that all revealed truths must be held because they are revealed, although some are more important than others. The text of the decree does not explicitly mention the second element, but the context of article 11 ('doctrine should be clearly presented in its entirety') implies it.[47]

Thus, although Morerod acknowledges that *Unitatis Redintegratio* does not explicitly make the point that all doctrines, regardless of their ranking within the overall hierarchy, must be accepted in faith, he is right—along with Echeverria and others—that this is how we should read the decree. And, if this is true, then the "hierarchy of truths" isn't as ecumenically promising as Cullmann and Berkouwer seem to have thought. Certainly the notion does not function as some kind of *deus ex machina* with regard to the unity of the church.

Still, the decree does spell out *how* the hierarchy of truths can assist ecumenical dialogue. It states that when we compare doctrines in ecumenical dialogue we should keep in mind that they are not all equally important. This, the decree continues, may trigger a kind of "fraternal rivalry," which "will incite all to a deeper realization and a clearer expression of the unfathomable riches of Christ."[48] Without in any way suggesting that Catholic doctrines can be surrendered in dialogue, this wording nonetheless seems

46. Echeverria, *Berkouwer and Catholicism*, 106–7, drawing on Yves M.-J. Congar, *Diversity and Communion*, trans. John Bowden (London: SMC, 1984), 119. Cf. Johannes Feiner's comment: "The statement in the decree concerning the hierarchy of truths is in any case a demand (addressed in the first instance to partners in dialogue, but ultimately to all Catholics), not to think, with regard to the truths taught by the Church, only of the formal element common to them all, that they are revealed, but also to bear in mind the significance of their content" (Feiner, "Commentary on the Decree," 119).

47. Morerod, "The Decree on Ecumenism," 323.

48. *UR* §11; *AAS* 57 (1965): 99.

to suggest that we must deal differently with doctrines that are at the heart of the faith than with those of lesser significance. Even though it is not immediately clear how the "fraternal rivalry" may allow us to make progress in discussing less fundamental doctrines (since every doctrine has the same formal authority), the decree does appear to envisage some ecumenical leeway at this point.

It also can hardly have escaped the council fathers' attention that by introducing a hierarchy of truths they were at odds, if not with the letter, then at least with the spirit of Pius XI's 1928 encyclical, *Mortalium Animos*. It had sharply rejected the distinction between fundamental and non-fundamental articles of faith:

> In connection with things which must be believed, it is nowise licit to use that distinction which some have seen fit to introduce between those articles of faith which are *fundamental* and those which are not fundamental (*capita fidei fundamentalia et non fundamentalia*), as they say, as if the former are to be accepted by all, while the latter may be left to the free assent of the faithful: for the supernatural virtue of faith has a formal cause, namely the authority of God revealing, and this is patient of no such distinction. For this reason it is that all who are truly Christ's believe, for example, the Conception of the Mother of God without stain of original sin with the same faith as they believe the mystery of the August Trinity, and the Incarnation of our Lord just as they do the infallible teaching authority of the Roman Pontiff, according to the sense in which it was defined by the Ecumenical Council of the Vatican. Are these truths not equally certain, or not equally to be believed, because the Church has solemnly sanctioned and defined them, some in one age and some in another, even in those times immediately before our own? Has not God revealed them all?[49]

Pius XI, by appealing to the teaching role of the church (the *quo* of formal authority), seemed to reject the very distinction between fundamental and non-fundamental articles.[50] Although *Unitatis Redintegratio* does not use this distinction, and although it does not in any way question the authority of less important doctrines, nonetheless, its notion of a "hierarchy of truths" comports rather well with the distinction between fundamental and non-fundamental articles, and the decree explicitly states that doctrines "vary in their relation to the foundation (*fundamento*) of the Christian faith."[51] It is hard to avoid the conclusion that the council fathers delib-

49. *Mortalium Animos*, §9; http://w2.vatican.va/content/pius-xi/en/encyclicals/documents/hf_p-xi_enc_19280106_mortalium-animos.html; *AAS* 20 (1928): 5–16, at 13.

50. To be sure, one may read the statement in such a way that the pope merely condemns a wrong use of the distinction between fundamental and non-fundamental articles. Still, the overall drift of *Mortalium Animos* is almost diametrically opposed to that of *Unitatis Redintegratio*.

51. *UR* §11; *AAS* 57 (1965): 99.

erately moved beyond Pius XI's 1928 encyclical. The Council's purpose in doing this was to create room for ecumenical dialogue and so to heal the wound that history has inflicted on the unity of the church.

The question does remain: how does the Council's desire to promote dialogue by inciting "fraternal rivalry" actually help us in practice? After all, regardless of the council fathers' intentions, on one point the Decree on Ecumenism does not contradict *Mortalium Animos*: Morerod and Echeverria are right to suggest that also the Decree on Ecumenism holds that no Catholic doctrine can be reformed, regardless of its place within the hierarchical ordering of truths. Therefore, whereas the council fathers spoke of a hierarchy of truths with the intent of enabling meaningful dialogue, they nonetheless leave us with a quandary: how are we to make progress in dialogue if we know beforehand that the only acceptable progress will be for Protestant dialogue partners to accept the entirety of the doctrinal deposit as it is perceived by and articulated in the Catholic Church?

At this point, Catholic ecumenical theologians often point to the distinction between affirmations and representations, a notion that Henri Bouillard brought to the fore in his controversial 1944 publication, *Conversion et grâce*:

> History does not, however, lead to relativism. It allows us to know, in the midst of theological evolution, an absolute—not an absolute of representation, but an absolute of affirmation. Whereas notions, methods, and systems change over time, the affirmations that they contain remain, even though they are expressed by means of other categories. Moreover, it is the affirmations themselves that, in order to keep their meaning in a new intellectual universe, determine new notions, methods, and systems in correspondence with that universe.... History thus manifests at the same time the relativity of notions, of schemes in which theology takes shape, and the permanent affirmation that governs them. It is necessary to know the temporal condition of theology and, at the same time, to offer with regard to the faith the absolute affirmation, the divine Word that has become incarnate.[52]

Bouillard, Henri de Lubac's younger colleague at the Fourvière scholasticate, distinguishes here between affirmations, which remain absolute, and representations, which may change.[53] Theological notions and schemes come and go within the context of the permanent, absolute affirmation of

52. Henri Bouillard, *Conversion et grâce chez S. Thomas d'Aquin: Étude historique*, Théologie 1 (Paris: Aubier, 1944), 120–21.

53. For the controversy surrounding Bouillard's book, see Cf. Thomas G. Guarino, "Henri Bouillard and the Truth-Status of Dogmatic Statements," *Science et Esprit* 39 (1987): 331–43; Hans Boersma, *Nouvelle Théologie and Sacramental Ontology: A Return to Mystery* (Oxford: Oxford University Press, 2009), 99–104.

the divine Word. Bouillard's approach drew sharp criticism at the time, particularly from Réginald Garrigou-Lagrange, who insisted, "It is very dangerous to say, 'Notions change, affirmations remain.' If the notion of truth itself is going to change, the affirmations no longer remain true in the same manner, nor with the same meaning."[54] Pius XII appeared to adjudicate the disagreement in 1950, when in *Humani Generis* he took aim at some who

> hold that the mysteries of faith are never expressed by truly adequate concepts but only by approximate and ever changeable notions, in which the truth is to some extent expressed, but is necessarily distorted. Wherefore they do not consider it absurd, but altogether necessary, that theology should substitute new concepts in place of the old ones in keeping with the various philosophies which in the course of time it uses as its instruments, so that it should give human expression to divine truths in various ways which are even somewhat opposed, but still equivalent, as they say. They add that the history of dogmas consists in the reporting of the various forms in which revealed truth has been clothed, forms that have succeeded one another in accordance with the different teachings and opinions that have arisen over the course of the centuries.[55]

Pope Pius XII sharply rejected that notions and concepts are easily malleable and changeable while the truth itself remains the same, and he criticized this as "dogmatic relativism."[56] Interestingly, *Humani Generis* also drew attention to the ecumenical agenda behind the distinction: "They cherish the hope that when dogma is stripped of the elements which they hold to be extrinsic to divine revelation, it will compare advantageously with the dogmatic opinions of those who are separated from the unity of the Church and that in this way they will gradually arrive at a mutual assimilation of Catholic dogma with the tenets of the dissidents."[57] It is not difficult to see that the distinction between affirmation and representation can be fruitful ecumenically. It allows one to place particular representations, presumably less directly related to the absolute truth of God's self-revelation in Christ, lower on the scale of the "hierarchy of truths." Thus, a degree of relativity with regard to doctrinal apprehensions would allow believers to live together despite (relatively minor) differences in doctrine.

The apprehension regarding Bouillard's distinction—even the charge of "dogmatic relativism"—is understandable, however, for at least two reasons. First, Bouillard contrasted the permanent affirmation as "the divine

54. Garrigou-Lagrange, "La Nouvelle théologie, où va-t-elle?" *Angelicum* 23 (1946): 126–45, at 130.
55. *HG* §15; *AAS* 42 (1950): 566.
56. *HG* §16; *AAS* 42 (1950): 566.
57. *HG* §14; *AAS* 42 (1950): 565.

Word that has become incarnate" with changing representations subject to the "relativity of notions, of schemes in which theology takes shape." At the very least Bouillard could have made clearer precisely how changing notions relate to the permanence of the doctrine that is firmly anchored in Christ. Presumably not every notion or theological system relates equally well to the Christological deposit of faith, and so the theological task remains to articulate precisely how, in individual cases, a certain belief or articulation relates to the incarnate Word.

Second, *Humani Generis* rightly points out that it is not indifferent which theological notions (or representations) we use. Not all changes in theological notions leave the Christological foundation untouched. Indeed, though he may well have exaggerated, Pope Pius wasn't devoid of insight when he claimed: "The contempt for terms and notions habitually used by scholastic theologians leads of itself to the weakening of what they call speculative theology, a discipline which these men consider devoid of true certitude because it is based on theological reasoning."[58]

It is against the backdrop of these controversies over the *nouvelle théologie* of Bouillard and others, and of the fairly unequivocal denunciations of the same in *Humani Generis*, that on October 11, 1962, Pope John XXIII opened the Second Vatican Council with the oft-repeated comment: "The substance of the ancient doctrine of the deposit of faith is one thing, and the way in which it is presented is another. And it is the latter that must be taken into great consideration with patience if necessary, everything being measured in the forms and proportions of a magisterium which is predominantly pastoral in character."[59] The pope did not explicitly choose sides in the disagreements surrounding *nouvelle théologie*, but by making a distinction between the substance and the mode of presentation he made clear where his sympathies lay and likely intended to create room for ecumenical discussion.[60] By reintroducing a much-controverted distinction, the pope placed on the Council's agenda the question of how to deal with less significant doctrines in dialogue with non-Catholic believers.[61] Whereas the

58. *HG* §17; *AAS* 42 (1950): 567.

59. *Gaudet Mater Ecclesia*; http://vatican2voice.org/91docs/opening_speech.htm; *AAS* 54 (1962): 786–95, at 792.

60. See Thomas G. Guarino, *Foundations of Systematic Theology* (New York: T&T Clark, 2005), 148–49.

61. In line with this, *Unitatis Redintegratio* specifically accepts variations "even in the theological elaborations of revealed truth" (*UR* §4; *AAS* 57 [1965]: 95). With regard to Eastern Orthodoxy, the decree comments, "What has already been said about legitimate variety we are pleased to apply to differences in theological expressions of doctrine" (*UR* §17; *AAS* 57 [1965]: 103). Cf. Eduardo J. Echeverria,

pope in no way conveyed a desire to upend Catholic doctrine, his opening words did convey sympathy for the direction charted by *nouvelle théologie* and certainly breathed a different spirit than did *Mortalium Animos* in 1928.

Unity and Fullness

So far, the Decree on Ecumenism may seem relatively promising. Not only does it acknowledge that we all share in the guilt of disunity, that we do have a shared baptismal bond of unity, and that we are already united in Christ, but *Unitatis Redintegratio* deliberately uses language that stops short of simply identifying the Roman Catholic Church with the Church of Christ (by using the verb *subsistere*), and it at least genuinely attempts to employ the notion of a "hierarchy of truths" in an effort to create fruitful dialogue with non-Catholics. Even though the hierarchy of truths still leaves us with the difficulty of how to solve the serious ecumenical issue of the formal authority of doctrine (its *quo*), it may not be a priori impossible to make headway also on this score, by distinguishing between affirmations and representations, between substance and manner of presentation.

Still, despite all these gains, and despite the rather momentous change in ecumenical atmosphere since Barth's visit *ad limina* fifty years ago, I am less than confident that an ecumenical breakthrough is just around the corner. The reason for my lack of optimism lies in the perceptive critical question that Barth raised, reflecting on his visit *ad limina*: "What is the significance for the definition 'separated brethren' (lack of 'fullness') of the statement (4, 10) that it is difficult for the Catholic Church herself 'to express in actual life her full catholicity in all its aspects'?"[62] In other words, if the Catholic Church is truly convinced that it is difficult for her to express "full catholicity" (*plenitudo catholicitatis*), then how is the lack of fullness among the "separated brethren" different from that of Catholics? This question, it seems to me, uncovers what remains *Unitatis Redintegratio*'s greatest obstacle to progress: although the Catholic Church may find it difficult to *express* "full catholicity," this does not mean an acknowledgment that it is not present.

A careful reading of *Unitatis Redintegratio* makes clear that the council

---

Dialogue of Love: Confessions of an Evangelical Catholic Ecumenist (Eugene, Ore.: Wipf and Stock, 2010), 15–18.

62. Barth, *Ad Limina Apostolorum*, 30. *UR* §4 states that because of divisions "the Church herself finds it more difficult to express (*exprimere*) in actual life her full catholicity (*plenitudinem catholicitatis*) in all its aspects" (*AAS* 57 [1965]: 96).

fathers treated the lack of unity (and catholicity) among Catholics rather differently from the lack of unity (and catholicity) of the "separated brethren." Throughout, *Unitatis Redintegratio* maintains that the fullness of unity is already present in the Roman Catholic Church, so that the problem of separation is much more one of the "separated brethren" than of the Roman Catholic Church. As a result, meeting on "equal footing" (*par cum pari*) in ecumenical dialogue becomes more difficult, and ecumenical progress remains elusive.

Paragraph 3, arguably the most ecumenical in the decree, is at the same time one of most problematic ones. Though both sides are said to share blame for the Reformation, this acknowledgment is preceded by the comment that "large communities became separated from full communion (*a plena communione*) with the Catholic Church."[63] It is only the "separated brethren" who "are not blessed with that unity which Jesus Christ wished to bestow on all those to whom he has given new birth into one body."[64] In line with this, despite its genuine outreach to "separated brethren"—and the Council's proceedings make clear that we should in no way minimize the efforts the council fathers made in this regard—the Council nonetheless maintains that it is "through Christ's Catholic Church alone ... that the fullness (*plenitudo*) of the means of salvation can be obtained," and "into which all those should be fully (*plene*) incorporated who belong in any way to the people of God."[65] Furthermore, *Unitatis Redintegratio* connects this statement explicitly with the "apostolic college" of which "Peter is the head,"[66] thereby making clear that restoration of unity can come about only through unity with Rome, since it alone has the *plenitudo* of the means of salvation.

Accordingly, in paragraph 4 the decree goes on to articulate the hope that through ecumenical dialogue "all Christians will be gathered, in a common celebration of the Eucharist, into the unity of the one and only Church, which Christ bestowed on his Church from the beginning. This unity, we believe, subsists in the Catholic Church as something she can never lose (*inamissibilem*), and we hope that it will continue to increase until the end of time."[67] Despite the shared guilt of the Catholic Church, it is not Rome

63. *UR* §3; *AAS* 57 (1965): 92–93.
64. *UR* §3; *AAS* 57 (1965): 93–94.
65. *UR* §3; *AAS* 57 (1965): 94.
66. *UR* §4; *AAS* 57 (1965): 95.
67. *UR* §4; *AAS* 57 (1965): 95: "Omnes Christiani, in una Eucharistiae celebratione, in unius unicaeque Ecclesiae unitatem congregentur quam Christus ab initio Ecclesiae suae largitus est, quamque inamissibilem in Ecclesia catholica subsistere credimus et usque ad consummationem saeculi in dies crescere speramus."

but Protestants who are separated. The very phrase, "separated brethren" (*fratres seiuncti*), indicates as much.[68] The decree says that "we believe" (*credimus*) that the unity of the Catholic Church is something she "can never lose" (*inamissibilem*); and although the text goes on to express the hope (*speramus*) that the unity of the Catholic Church may "increase until the end of time," it is not clear how this hope can possibly be thwarted in light of the belief that the unity of the church already subsists in the Catholic Church and can never be lost.

Thus, though an increase in unity is possible, even for believers in the Catholic Church, the decree nonetheless qualifies this in two ways. First, as we have already seen, the unity of the church already securely "subsists" in the Roman Catholic Church. Second, it is only in those who are separated that this unity of the Catholic Church is not fully realized. Paragraph 4 maintains that divisions "prevent the Church from realizing the fullness of catholicity (*plenitudinem catholicitatis*) proper to her *in those of her sons who … are … separated from full* (plena) *communion with her*."[69] This carefully worded sentence seems to me remarkably one-sided. Only the separated brethren are lacking in terms of the fullness of the catholicity of the church. The problem experienced by the Catholic Church, then, is not a lack of unity—this cannot possibly be lost; it is proper to her—but merely the *expression* of this unity through full fellowship with Christians beyond the visible bounds of the Roman Catholic Church: the church merely finds it "more difficult to express (*exprimere*) in actual life her full catholicity (*plenitudinem catholicitatis*) in all its aspects."[70] The unity of the church, so it seems, is not really endangered by the Reformation—with two exceptions: (1) separated brethren are lacking in unity since they do not yet share the Eucharist of the Catholic Church and as such do not yet fully share in the full unity that

68. Pope Leo XIII is sometimes credited with first using the expression "separated brethren." Thomas Cahill, for instance, comments: "He was the first pope to speak of Protestant and Orthodox Christians as 'separated brethren,' rather than as heretics and schismatics" (*Pope John XXIII: A Life* [London: Penguin, 2002], 78). It is not clear to me, however, that Pope Leo XIII actually used this term. I have not been able to locate instances of Pope Leo XIII referring to Orthodox or Protestant believers as "separated brethren." English translations of Pope John XXIII's encyclicals do use the phrase "separated brethren." But even in the case of John XXIII's encyclicals, the term "separated brethren" usually translates the term *dissidentes*. I am grateful for conversation with Michael Root on this point.

I should add that although the expression *fratres seiuncti* is usually translated as "separated brethren," the phrase replaced the earlier *fratres separati*, which had been used in the schema *De Oecumenismo*. This change allows for the interpretation that it is not only the non-Catholics who have separated (Becker, "History of the Decree," 35, 39). Feiner observes that the verb "*seiungere* expresses a less profound separation than *separare*. In English (as in German), however, the nuance is difficult to reproduce" ("Commentary on the Decree," 70).

69. *UR* §4 (emphasis added); *AAS* 57 (1965): 96.

70. *UR* §4; *AAS* 57 (1965): 96.

subsists in her; and (2) the Catholic Church herself has difficulty expressing the unity that is indefectibly and properly hers.[71]

If this is a fair reading of the Decree on Ecumenism, I cannot but wonder what the next paragraph means when it opens with the comment that "the concern for restoring (*instaurandae*) unity concerns the whole church, faithful and clergy alike."[72] If unity was never lost—except from the side of those who are separated from the Catholic Church and except for certain expressions of the unity of the Catholic Church—what is there to restore? To be sure, *Unitatis Redintegratio* gives somewhat of an answer to this question when it speaks of the need for a "continual reformation" (*perennem reformationem*) in terms of moral conduct, church discipline, and even the way doctrine is formulated. Any deficiencies in this regard must be "set right" (*instaurentur*).[73] Accordingly, the decree applauds the "cooperation in social matters," which today "is widespread" (*latissime instauretur*).[74] Cooperation among Christians "has already begun (*iam instaurata*) in many countries" and "should be developed more and more."[75] Restoration of full communion in the unity of the church is a worthy goal.[76] But the process of restoring (*instaurare*) this unity cannot hide that unity already subsists in the Catholic Church and that, according to the Decree on Ecumenism, it is lacking among the "separated brethren."

Unity and the Eschaton

It is hardly a secret that the ecumenical movement has lost much of its initial vitality. A number of factors contribute to this ecumenical malaise, several of which are internal to Protestantism, such as the decline of mainline Protestantism and the common practice of open communion among Protestant churches, which removes much of the urgency of ecumenical dialogue.[77]

71. It is interesting to observe, therefore, that one of the written submissions in response to the scheme *De Oecumenismo* in the summer of 1963 suggested "that the schema should provide an answer to the question whether by a schism 'merely a large number of former members of the Catholic Church became separated, while the Church remained perfect and undivided', or whether in this division, which has taken place against the will of God, the Church itself was divided in some sense'" (Becker, "History of the Decree," 27).

72. *UR* §5; *AAS* 57 (1965): 96.

73. *UR* §6; *AAS* 57 (1965): 97.

74. *UR* §12; *AAS* 57 (1965): 99.

75. *UR* §12; *AAS* 57 (1965): 100.

76. The decree also speaks of working toward "restoration (*instaurationem*) of the full communion that is desired between the Eastern Churches and the Catholic Church" (*UR* §14; *AAS* 57 [1965]: 101).

77. John Paul II's encyclical, *Ecclesia de Eucharistia* (2003) makes a worthwhile observation in this regard: "Precisely because the Church's unity, which the Eucharist brings about through the Lord's

Among Protestants, evangelicals are probably closest to Catholicism—witness, for instance, the growth of the contingent of evangelical Catholics as a result of the past several papacies, of which George Weigel has given an account in his book, *Evangelical Catholicism*.[78] At the same time, the kinship between Catholics and evangelicals has primarily been due to shared moral values, of which *Unitatis Redintegratio* speaks in commenting that "ecumenical dialogue could start with the moral application of the Gospel."[79] This "ecumenism of the trenches," as Timothy George has called it, does lead to genuine co-belligerency, and it also lays the groundwork for discussions about ecclesial unity. But the lack of historical and liturgical awareness among evangelicals should remind us of the tremendous difficulties that we face in terms of ecumenical prospects. All this is simply to say that issues internal to Protestantism are in part responsible for the lack of progress in implementing the agenda, if we may call it that, of *Unitatis Redintegratio*.

Since, however, I have been analyzing the Decree on Ecumenism, I want to focus on what I believe to be a serious obstacle to unity within *Unitatis Redintegratio* itself. Perhaps I can best illustrate my concern by means of a question that Charles Morerod raises in his discussion of the document. He asks: "Since all Christian communities are divided, should we not say that the Catholic Church is also not blessed with 'that unity which Jesus Christ wished to bestow'?"[80] Though Morerod recognizes the strength of this argument, he counters it with two comments, from Pope Paul VI and Pope John Paul II respectively, in which they affirm the fullness of the unity of the

---

sacrifice and by communion in his body and blood, absolutely requires full communion in the bonds of the profession of faith, the sacraments and ecclesiastical governance, it is not possible to celebrate together the same Eucharistic liturgy until those bonds are fully re-established. Any such concelebration would not be a valid means, and might well prove instead to be *an obstacle, to the attainment of full communion*, by weakening the sense of how far we remain from this goal and by introducing or exacerbating ambiguities with regard to one or another truth of the faith. The path towards full unity can only be undertaken in truth" (§44; emphasis in original); http://www.vatican.va/holy_father/special_features/encyclicals/documents/hf_jp-ii_enc_20030417_ecclesia_eucharistia_en.html; *AAS* 95 (2003): 433–75, at 462. In an earlier publication, I was more positive about the practice of "Eucharistic hospitality" (*Violence, Hospitality, and the Cross: Reappropriating the Atonement Tradition* [Grand Rapids, Mich.: Baker Academic, 2004], 215–22). I have come to see more clearly the problems that such a practice entails. It not only imperils ecumenism—since the Eucharist marks the high point of ecclesial unity—but it also sacrifices the visibility of the church's structures, reduces the church to a private as opposed to a public entity, and makes church discipline and supervision all but impossible. In short, I worry that the practice of intercommunion renders the individual rather than the corporate church responsible for judging matters of faith and morals.

78. George Weigel, *Evangelical Catholicism: Deep Reform in the 21st-Century Church* (New York: Basic—Perseus, 2014).

79. *UR* §23; *AAS* 57 (1965): 106.

80. Morerod, "The Decree on Ecumenism," 317.

Catholic Church, and Morerod concludes from this: "Catholic theologians must deal with a paradox: All Christians are divided, and Catholics are in this situation of division, but the Catholic Church alone has never lost full unity."[81] While I appreciate the appeal to the two pontiffs, it is not enough to appeal to the Catholic magisterium in support for the full and perduring unity of the Catholic Church. The paradox on which Morerod insists needs not just a formal but also a material theological argument.

Catholicism suffers a much deeper wound than Morerod (and, I think, the Decree on Ecumenism itself) appears ready to acknowledge. The inability of admitting this comes to the fore perhaps most clearly in the way the council fathers deal with the Catholic theological heritage. My earlier discussion regarding the notion of a hierarchy of truths is indicative of this inability. The formal authority of Catholic doctrines, including those that some may call "non-fundamental" or that at least are less important (such as transubstantiation, the immaculate conception of Mary, and so on), cannot ever be called into question. Although the Council goes as far as it possibly can by linking the hierarchy of truths to the prospects for ecumenical dialogue, I already indicated that it is not at all clear that the hierarchy of truths can assist such dialogue *in actual fact*. For that to happen, the Catholic Church would at the very least have to acknowledge that some doctrines are not essential to the unity of the church and that in those cases we can accept different points of view. It seems to me that the strictly irreformable character of Catholic teaching prevents the hierarchy of truths from serving a truly ecumenical role. Ecumenical progress hinges, therefore, on a more robust functioning of the distinction between affirmations and representations. By no means do I mean to promote a relativist attitude toward Christian doctrine. But it strains credulity that brothers and sisters in Christ, who love and care for one another, must either continue in their divided paths or accept that the uniquely Roman Catholic representations of certain doctrines are essential to Christian unity.

From all I can see, the approach to unity in *Unitatis Redintegratio* does not sufficiently take into account that the church's unity is an eschatological reality, which, although it breaks into this world and allows us provisionally to share in it through the preaching of the gospel and the celebration of the Eucharist, does not visibly take shape today as fully as it will in the hereafter. The ultimate reason, therefore, why the language of *subsistere*, the use of a set of concentric circles, and the notion of a hierarchy of truths all fail

81. Morerod, "The Decree on Ecumenism," 317.

to bring us to the point of unity is that they obscure the underlying problem, namely, that *Unitatis Redintegratio* still does not do sufficient justice to the eschatological character of the church's unity.[82]

To be sure, paragraph 4 does quote Ephesians 5:27, where Saint Paul mentions the church as Christ's bride "without spot or wrinkle," and the council fathers envision this as an eschatological reality to which we may look forward: "Every Catholic must therefore aim at Christian perfection and, each according to his station, play his part, that the Church, which bears in her own body the humility and dying of Jesus, may daily be more purified and renewed, against the day when Christ will present her to himself in all her glory without spot or wrinkle."[83] This eschatological reading of Ephesians 5:27 is an important recognition that it is at the end time that the church will be without spot or wrinkle.

But the decree precedes this statement with the comment: "Although the Catholic Church has been endowed with all divinely revealed truth and with all means of grace, yet its members fail to live by them with all the fervor that they should."[84] This statement distinguishes between the church and its members, or, we could also say, between unity *of* the church and unity *in* the church. Unity *of* the church (the church itself) is rooted in the apostolic tradition that ultimately goes back to the eternal missions of the Son and of the Spirit; unity *in* the church (that of the members) is the way in which people give expression to this unity in their everyday lives.[85] The distinction is a legitimate one, I think, as long as we keep in mind that the unity *of* the church first of all concerns the church of the *eschaton*, which does not fully manifest itself in structural unity here on earth. Perhaps, therefore, we should entertain the possibility that full unity comes to us from the end,

82. Cf. Geoffrey Wainwright's comment: "I wish to suggest that a genuinely eschatological tension allows all the notes of the church to be confessed in a dynamic sense that fosters their perfect and tangible attainment, albeit within the limits of a pilgrim existence. In that way, other authentically Trinitarian churches and ecclesial communities—marked by the Gospel, the Scriptures, baptism, the Lord's Supper, and active faith (cf. *Unitatis Redintegratio*, 20–23)—could be regarded as *part of* the 'one holy catholic Church' while praying and working toward the fullness that would come to them—and to the Roman Church—on the establishment of communion with the apostolic Petrine see in structures that still demand elaboration" ("*Unitatis Redintegratio* in a Protestant Perspective," *Pro Ecclesia* 15, no. [2006], 172–85, at 185).

83. *UR* §4; *AAS* 57 (1965): 95.

84. *UR* §4; *AAS* 57 (1965): 95.

85. Though the distinction between unity *of* the church and unity *in* the church is mine, it does justice to paragraph 4, as it is patterned on the International Theological Commission's 1999 statement, *Memory and Reconciliation: The Church and the Faults of the Past*, which distinguishes between holiness *of* the church and holiness *in* the church, with the former remaining inviolable despite problems with the latter (*MR* 3.2; http://www.vatican.va/roman_curia/congregations/cfaith/cti_documents/rc_con_cfaith_doc_20000307_memory-reconc-itc_en.html).

the eschatological unity to which the apostle Paul refers. To my mind, paragraph 4 is too quick in appropriating to the Catholic Church "all divinely revealed truth" and relegates any problems in this regard too easily to its members who fail to live up to it.

I applaud the Decree on Ecumenism's encouragement that Catholics meet with non-Catholics "on equal footing" (*par cum pari*), and I am grateful for this volume of essays (and the conference on which it is based) as an example of this. Nonetheless, one of the greatest obstacles toward full unity remains the conviction that this principle of meeting *par cum pari* does not apply to the Roman Catholic Church as an institution. Individual Catholics are encouraged to meet *par cum pari*; but the discourse of *Unitatis Redintegratio* does not suggest that the Catholic Church is on equal footing with "separated brethren." I suspect that if the principle of meeting *par cum pari* is allowed materially to affect Catholic ecclesiology more robustly than it does in the Decree on Ecumenism, ecumenical progress will become a genuine possibility.

Chapter 11

Catholic Ecumenical Doctrine and Commitment—Irrevocable and Persistent

Unitatis Redintegratio as a Case of an Authentic Development of Doctrine

Reinhard Hütter

> Half the controversies in the world are verbal ones; and could they be brought to a plain issue, they would be brought to a prompt termination. Parties engaged in them would then perceive, either that in their substance they agreed together, or that their difference was one of first principles.... When men understand what each other mean, they see, for the most part, that controversy is either superfluous or hopeless.
>
> —John Henry Newman

> Modern Catholicism is nothing else but simply the legitimate growth and complement, that is, the natural and necessary development, of the doctrine of the early church, and ... its divine authority is included in the divinity of Christianity.
>
> —John Henry Newman

I am indebted to David L. Augustine, Josef Freitag, Nancy Heitzenrater Hütter, Michael Root, and Richard Schenk, OP, for helpful suggestions, corrections, and criticisms to this chapter. The epigraphs are, respectively, from John Henry Newman, *Fifteen Sermons Preached before the University of Oxford Between A.D. 1826 and 1843*, introd. Mary Katherine Tillman (Notre Dame, Ind.: University of Notre Dame Press, 1997), 200–201; and John Henry Cardinal Newman, *An Essay on the Development of Doctrine*, foreword by Ian Ker (Notre Dame, Ind.: University of Notre Dame Press, 1989), 169. (Hereafter, Newman, *Dev.*)

Karl Barth and ecumenism? As one might expect from a theologian of his surpassing stature and significance, the two sets of questions, interpretive and critical, that Karl Barth formulated in the pertinent section of his *opusculum, Ad Limina Apostolorum*, in relationship to the Second Vatican Council's Decree on Ecumenism, *Unitatis Redintegratio*, are perceptive, astute, and—at the time they were raised—relevant.[1] But these questions also make every ecumenically attuned reader immediately aware of the nothing less than astonishing fecundity of ecumenical events, accomplishments, and simple givens that stand between us and Karl Barth's visit to the Vatican more than fifty years ago. To name just a few of them:

First, and in many ways most importantly, the last century and the beginning years of the new millennium were rich in an unprecedented ecumenism of martyrdom, especially in Africa, Asia, and the Middle East. In his 1995 encyclical letter "On Commitment to Ecumenism," *Ut Unum Sint*, Pope John Paul II refers to a common martyrology and states:

> This also includes the martyrs of our own century, more numerous than one might think, and it shows how, at a profound level, God preserves communion among the baptized in the supreme demand of faith, manifested in the sacrifice of life itself.... These *Saints* come from all the Churches and Ecclesial Communities which gave them entrance into the communion of salvation.[2]

Second, mention needs to be made of an ecumenically crucial document, adopted by Faith and Order at its plenary commission meeting in Lima, Peru,

1. I am perusing the edition printed in Communist East Germany, Karl Barth, *Ad Limina Apostolorum* (Berlin: Evangelische Verlagsanstalt, 1967) and the English translation, Karl Barth, *Ad Limina Apostolorum: An Appraisal of Vatican II*, trans. Keith R. Crim (Westminster, Md.: John Knox Press, 1968; reprinted: Eugene, Ore.: Wipf and Stock, 2016). (Hereafter, *ALA*.) For a recent introduction and interpretation of *Unitatis Redintegratio*, see Charles Morerod, OP, "The Decree on Ecumenism, *Unitatis Redintegratio*," in *Vatican II: Renewal within Tradition*, ed. Matthew Lamb and Matthew Levering (Oxford: Oxford University Press, 2008), 311–41. For one of the first substantive and extensive introductions to and commentaries of the Decree on Ecumenism, see *Dekret über den Ökumenismus* (Decretum de Oecumenismo "Unitatis Redintegratio"), in *Das Zweite Vatikanische Konzil: Dokumente und Kommentare. Teil II* (Ergänzungsbände zu *Lexikon für Theologie und Kirche*) (Freiburg: Herder, 1967); introduction by Werner Becker, 11–39; commentary by Johannes Feiner, 40–126.

2. *Ut Unum Sint* (*UUS*) §84. For a crucial study on this topic, actually commissioned by the Catholic Church, see the important work by the noted Italian historian and founder of the St. Egidio Community, Andrea Riccardi, *Il secolo del martirio. I cristiani nel Novecento* (Milan: Mondolibri, 2000) (French translation: *Ils sont morts pour leur foi. La persécution des chrétiens au XXe siècle* [Paris: Omnibus, 2002]; German translation: *Salz der Erde, Licht der Welt: Glaubenszeugnis und Christenverfolgung im 20. Jahrhundert* [Freiburg: Herder, 2002]. Surprisingly and disconcertingly, there does not seem to exist an English translation of this work.)

in 1982, the "Lima Text" *Baptism, Eucharist, and Ministry* (*BEM*).[3] This indeed famous text explores the growing agreement and remaining differences in fundamental areas of the faith and life of Christian churches. This probably most widely distributed and studied ecumenical document not only achieved a breakthrough regarding an emerging common understanding and mutual recognition of baptism but also has been the basis for many "mutual recognition" agreements among churches and remains an ongoing crucial reference point for ecumenical dialogue.

Third, in 1999, as the result of an extensive ecumenical dialogue and with *BEM* as its indispensable forerunner and station on the way, the *Joint Declaration on the Doctrine of Justification* was drafted by the Pontifical Council for Promoting Christian Unity and the Lutheran World Federation and affirmed in its entirety by the Catholic Church and the leading representatives of the Lutheran World Federation.[4] The document states famously: "Together we confess: By grace alone, in faith in Christ's saving work and not because of any merit on our part, we are accepted by God and receive the Holy Spirit, who renews our hearts while equipping and calling us to

3. The Commission on Faith and Order is what one might best characterize as a think tank of the World Council of Churches constituted by official representatives of all major historical Christian communions. The studies produced by the Faith and Order Commission pertain primarily to questions of faith (doctrine) and order (the ministerial structure of the church). This document is available at http://www.oikoumene.org/en/resources/documents/commissions/faith-and-order/i-unity-the-church-and-its-mission/baptism-eucharist-and-ministry-faith-and-order-paper-no-111-the-lima-text. For "An Agreed Statement on the Lima Document: Baptism, Eucharist, Ministry" by the Eastern Orthodox/Roman Catholic Consultation in the United States, during its 28th and 29th meetings (1983–84), see http://www.usccb.org/beliefs-and-teachings/ecumenical-and-interreligious/ecumenical/orthodox/statement-lima-baptism-eucharist-and-ministry.cfm.

4. Cardinal Cassidy, in his function as secretary of the Pontifical Council for the Promotion of Christian Unity signed the document as the Pope's representative in ecumenical matters at the instruction of Pope John Paul II. The *Official Common Statement* ends with the following phrase: "By this act of signing The Catholic Church and The Lutheran World Federation confirm the Joint Declaration on the Doctrine of Justification in its entirety." For the full text, see the Lutheran World Federation and the Roman Catholic Church, *Joint Declaration on the Doctrine of Justification* (Grand Rapids, Mich.: Eerdmans, 2000) and http://www.vatican.va/roman_curia/pontifical_councils/chrstuni/documents/rc_pc_chrstuni_doc_31101999_cath-luth-joint-declaration_en.html. For an informative recent study of the complexities of the document, see Pieter de Witte, *Doctrine, Dynamic, and Difference: To the Heart of the Lutheran-Roman Catholic Differentiated Consensus on Justification* (London: T&T Clark International, 2012); for a critical analysis by a Catholic theologian, see Christopher J. Malloy, *Engrafted into Christ: A Critique of the Joint Declaration* (New York: Peter Lang, 2005) and for the most strident critique of the antecedent theological study and of the *JDDJ* itself from a Lutheran theologian, see Jörg Baur, *Einig in Sachen Rechtfertigung? Zur Prüfung des Rechtfertigungskapitels der Studie des Ökumenischen Arbeitskreises Evangelischer und Katholischer Theologen, "Lehrverurteilungen, kirchentrennend?"* (Tübingen: Mohr Siebeck, 1989), and idem, *Frei durch Rechtfertigung: Vorträge anläßlich der römisch-katholisch lutherischen "Gemeinsamen Erklärung"* (Tübingen: Mohr Siebeck, 1999). For an astute rejoinder to Baur's first book, see Ulrich Kühn and Otto H. Pesch, *Rechtfertigung im Disput: Eine freundliche Antwort an Jörg Baur auf seine Prüfung des Rechtfertigungskapitels in der Studie des Ökumenischen Arbeitskreises evangelischer und katholischer Theologen: "Lehrverurteilungen—kirchentrennend?"* (Tübingen: Mohr Siebeck, 1991).

good works."[5] On July 23, 2006, in Seoul, Korea, the World Methodist Council voted unanimously to adopt the *Joint Declaration on the Doctrine of Justification*, presented its own declaration, the *World Methodist Council Statement of Association with the Joint Declaration on the Doctrine of Justification*, which was accompanied by the "Official Common Affirmation" signed by representatives of the Catholic Church, the Lutheran World Federation and the World Methodist Council.[6]

Fourth, there exist now bilateral ecumenical dialogues between the Catholic Church and all of the major Protestant denominations. Not only does the Catholic Church have bilateral dialogues with all of the old mainline denominations but also with newer Christian movements.[7] One of the oldest bilateral dialogues is the international Catholic-Pentecostal dialogue, which began in 1972. But now, there also seem to be bilateral dialogues emerging on the horizon with denominations that are doctrinally separated from or not in Eucharistic communion with similar sister-denominations. So, for example, quite recently an unofficial academic conversation began between Catholic theologians and theologians of the International Lutheran Council (ILC), of which the Lutheran Church Missouri Synod is the largest and most important member, with the task of clarifying whether an official bilateral dialogue should be launched.

Fifth, there is the phenomenon of the ecumenical monastic community of Taizé in France, to which Pope John XXIII once referred as "that little spring time." Under the visionary leadership of Frère Roger Schutz (1915–2005) the Taizé community, by way of its annual Youth Council, has wielded an incalculable ecumenical influence on more than two generations of European and North American Catholics and Protestants.

Sixth, consider a recent ecumenical gesture of significance—inconceivable to Catholics and Protestants fifty years ago: At the Solemnity of Saints Peter and Paul in St. Peter's Basilica, during the Solemn Mass when the Holy Father bestows the pallium on metropolitan archbishops and primates as a symbol of their unity with the Holy See, in recent years the choral mu-

5. *JDDJ* §15.

6. For the complete text, see http://www.vatican.va/roman_curia/pontifical_councils/chrstuni/meth-council-docs/rc_pc_chrstuni_doc_20060723_text-association_en.html. The singular facilitator of the "Official Common Affirmation" and a key drafter of the "Statement of Association" was Geoffrey Wainwright. The leading Methodist ecumenist of his generation, a British Methodist, and personal friend of Pope Benedict XVI, he was first my teacher and later my colleague and friend at Duke University Divinity School.

7. For a list of all bilateral dialogues, see the website of the Pontifical Council of Promoting Christian Unity, http://www.vatican.va/roman_curia/pontifical_councils/chrstuni/index.htm.

sic during the solemn liturgy has been provided not only by the Vatican boys' choir but also by an invited Lutheran boys' choir. One year it was the Windsbacher Knabenchor, another year the Leipziger Thomanerchor, and I am quite sure that Anglican boys' choirs will follow.

Last but not least, one can make a reasonably strong case that—if not all of the concerns Karl Barth raised in the section "Critical Questions"[8] of his *Ad Limina Apostolorum* about the Decree on Ecumenism—at least all of his concerns raised in the section "Questions for Clarification" regarding the Decree on Ecumenism have been addressed in subsequent documents of the Catholic magisterium, first and foremost in the above-mentioned encyclical letter, On Commitment to Ecumenism, *Ut Unum Sint,* by Pope John Paul II.[9] What are Barth's questions for clarification? Consider the first two questions:

1. Are all (including Catholics) called on in this ecumenical dialogue:
   (a) "to examine their own faithfulness to Christ's will for the Church and wherever necessary, undertake with vigor the task of renewal and reform" (4, 2)?
   (b) to make the first approaches to the separated brethren (4, 5)?
   (c) but above all "to make an honest and careful appraisal of whatever needs to be renewed and achieved in the Catholic household itself" (4, 5)?

2. Is it permissible (or perhaps necessary) in the future to regard the Catholic Church as involved in "that continual reformation of which she always has need" (6, 2)?[10]

Ut Unum Sint, in its introduction and in paragraph 16 offers a positive response to Barth's first question of clarification. Also the second question receives a positive answer, but here the difficult matter of first principles emerges. "[T]hat continual reformation of which she always has need," its scope, and its entailments might turn out to be completely different when approached from the principle operative in the ecclesiology of the Reformed communions to which Barth is committed or when approached from the principle of Catholic ecclesiology as laid out in Vatican II's Dogmatic Constitution on the Church, *Lumen Gentium*. From a Catholic point of view, it is quite obvious that

8. I shall address Barth's "Critical Questions" at a later point.

9. See among others also the 2000 Declaration *"Dominus Iesus:" On the Unicity and Salvific Universality of Jesus Christ and the Church* from the Congregation of the Doctrine of the Faith and the 2001 study *The Jewish People and Their Sacred Scriptures in the Christian Bible* from the Pontifical Biblical Commission. (Of course, these documents are of considerably different magisterial weight.)

10. Barth, *ALA*, 29. The in-text references are to *UR*.

Unitatis Redintegratio appeals to a principle in operation since the days of the apostles, a principle made concrete in *Ut Unum Sint* in the specification that the ecumenical commitment of the Catholic Church is irrevocable. By way of this specification *Ut Unum Sint* gives a genuinely Catholic answer to Barth's question, an answer that makes clear that the principle of the "continual reformation of which she always has need" cannot be conceived in an abstract *a priori* fashion and then applied across the board in a programmatic and deductive way, but that the continual reform rather unfolds concretely under the guidance of the magisterium and in the framework of a developing tradition.[11]

Consider Barth's third question for clarification: "3. What is the meaning of 'an order or "hierarchy" of truths' in Catholic teaching, which 'vary in their relationship to the foundation of the Christian faith' (11, 3)? What are the 'essentials [the *necessaria*]' (4, 7)?"[12] Familiar Protestant ways—mutually incompatible, I should note—of identifying these *necessaria* are (a) the *consensus quinquesaecularis*, that is, the doctrinal consensus of the first five centuries,[13] (b) the *doctrina* that "Scripture alone" yields,[14] and (c) the Gospel as the pure *norma normans* within Scripture, as the one and only thing truly necessary; that is, the doctrine of justification by faith alone as the sole criterion that norms, judges, and conditions not only the reading of the canon of Scripture but also all other doctrinal formulations.[15] An initial understanding of what the Council Fathers meant by the *necessaria* in paragraph 4 of *Unitatis Redintegratio* might be gathered from the speech of Archbishop Andrea Pangrazio of Gorizia, Italy, who proposed the expression "hierarchy of truths" to the Council:

> There are truths that belong to the order of the end, such as the mystery of the most holy Trinity, of the incarnation of the Word and the redemption.... But there are other truths, which belong to the order of the means of salvation, as for example

11. For an excellent theological study that clarifies this complex and central matter with great lucidity, see Yves Congar's important work, *True and False Reform in the Church*, trans. Paul Philibert, OP (Collegeville, Minn.: Liturgical Press, 2011).

12. Barth, *ALA*, 29.

13. One might think here of the German Lutheran theologian Georg Calixt (1586–1656) who aimed at reconciling Christendom based on this consensus. An analogous concept is involved in the Anglican branch theory advanced by the Anglican John Henry Newman in one of his most important theoretical contributions to the Oxford Movement, his 1837 *Lectures on the Prophetical Office of the Church*.

14. A useful recent example of this approach can be found in *Scripture's Doctrine and Theology's Bible: How the New Testament Shapes Christian Dogmatics*, ed. Markus Bockmuehl and Alan J. Torrance (Grand Rapids, Mich.: Eerdmans, 2008).

15. For paradigmatic examples, see Eberhard Jüngel, *Justification: The Heart of the Christian Faith*, trans. Jeffrey F. Cayzer, introd. John Webster (London: Bloomsbury T&T Clark, 2006) and Mark C. Mattes, *The Role of Justification in Contemporary Theology*, Foreword by Klaus Schwarzwäller (Grand Rapids, Mich.: Eerdmans, 2004).

the truth of the seven sacraments, of the hierarchical structure of the Church, of the apostolic succession and others.... In fact, the doctrinal differences among Christians are less concerned with the truths that belong to the order of the end, and more with those concerning the order of the means, which are undoubtedly subordinate to the former.[16]

The distinction between the "order of the end" and the "order of the means" affords an understanding of the *necessaria*. The *necessaria* pertain clearly first and foremost to the "order of the end." But do they strictly only comprise the "order of the end" and relegate the "order of the means" to the status of *adiaphora*? Hardly so, for in *modus 49*, which is attributed to Cardinal König of Vienna, the secretariat explained the term "hierarchy of truths" to the Council the following way:

It seems most important for ecumenical dialogue, that the truths about which all Christians agree as well as those about which they differ, be rather evaluated than enumerated. Without any doubt all revealed truths must be held with the same divine faith, but their importance and "weight" differ in reason of their link with the history of salvation and the mystery of Christ.[17]

Modus 49 suggests implicitly that the *necessaria* do indeed comprise the "order of the end" as well as the "order of the means," yet in a hierarchy of truths of differing importance.

But how precisely is one to understand the "hierarchy of truths"? *Modus 49* already makes plain that the use of this term emphatically does not suggest that some revealed truths are less true than others or that some revealed truths are to be held by divine faith and others not. This interpretation (found in *Modus 49*) is affirmed in a noteworthy document drafted in 1990 by a joint working group of the Roman Catholic Church and the World Council of Churches:

First of all, the council's sentence does not mean that there is only a more or less incidental relationship between these truths and the foundation, so that a merely relative character stamps them, and one can consider them optional in the life of faith. Still less does the decree's sentence consider truths of faith as more or less necessary for salvation, or suggest degrees in our obligation to believe in all that God has revealed. When one fully responds to God's self-revelation in faith, one accepts that Revelation as a whole. There is no picking and choosing of what God has revealed, because there is no picking or choosing of what Revelation is—our salvation. Hence, there are no degrees in the obligation to believe all that God has revealed.[18]

16. Morerod, "The Decree on Ecumenism, *Unitatis Redintegratio*," 322–23.
17. Morerod, "The Decree on Ecumenism, *Unitatis Redintegratio*," 323.
18. Joint working group of the Roman Catholic Church and the World Council of Churches, "The

Five years later, in 1995, Pope John Paul II seems to follow the thrust of this explanation when he states in paragraph 37 of *Ut Unum Sint* that the "order or 'hierarchy' of truths" "indicates a criterion to be followed when Catholics are presenting or comparing doctrines"[19] and in paragraph 39 that "[t]he examination of such disagreements has two essential points of reference: Sacred Scripture and the great Tradition of the Church. Catholics have the help of the Church's living Magisterium."[20] In light of these guidelines, the "hierarchy of truths" can only be understood to denote the comprehensive network of all revealed truths of the deposit of faith, communicated in the sacred scriptures and apostolic tradition, unfolded and specified in the post-apostolic tradition of the Church, and definitively promulgated by the Church's magisterium. This whole network relates, in varying ways, to the one sole foundational "Dogma," the person, teaching, and salvific work of the Incarnate Lord, Jesus Christ. The term "hierarchy" in "hierarchy of truth" connotes a web of irreversible, non-symmetrical relationships of doctrinal dependence. What is lower in the hierarchy of truths is therefore by no means less true. Rather, these truths vary in their relationship of dependence upon the foundation of the Christian faith from which they arise, the *Prima Veritas*, the Triune God, and the Incarnate Lord, who said of himself, "I am the way, the truth, and the life." As Bishop Morerod helpfully states:

> The hierarchy of truths simply means that any truth received from divine revelation must be connected to the central mysteries. For instance, the dogma of the Assumption depends on the dogma of Mary's divine motherhood, which implies the more central truth that Jesus is God and man. Theology should begin with the more central truths and then explain the others progressively.[21]

Hence, invoking the "hierarchy of truths" in an ecumenical context amounts to nothing less than extending the invitation of *Unitatis Redintegratio,*[22] *which was* renewed by *Ut Unum Sint,* "for this kind of fraternal rivalry to incite all to a deeper realization and a clearer expression of the unfathomable riches of Christ."[23]

Consider finally the last double question for clarification:

Notion of 'Hierarchy of Truths': An Ecumenical Interpretation," *Faith and Order Paper n. 150* (Geneva: WCC Publications, 1990), no. 25, p. 20.

19. *UUS* §37.

20. *UUS* §39.

21. Morerod, OP, "The Decree on Ecumenism, *Unitatis Redintegratio,*" 324.

22. See *UR* §11.

23. *UUS* §37.

4. Are the following statements (17, 1) applicable only to the Eastern "separated brethren":

(a) the statement that "sometimes one tradition has come nearer than the other to an apt appreciation of certain aspects of a revealed mystery";

the statement that "these various theological formulations are often to be considered as complementary rather than conflicting"?[24]

The first part of this question (a) finds a pertinent response in *Ut Unum Sint*: "It is not that beyond the boundaries of the Catholic community there is an ecclesial vacuum. Many elements of great value (*eximia*), which in the Catholic Church are part of the fullness of the means of salvation and of the gifts of grace which make up the Church, also are found in the other Christian Communities,"[25] "where certain features of the Christian mystery have at times been more effectively emphasized."[26] Quite obviously, *Ut Unum Sint* acknowledges this important pneumatological phenomenon across the spectrum of Christian communions, including especially also the various and multiform Protestant communities.

This important passage from *Ut Unum Sint* also offers a pertinent answer to the fourth critical question, which we shall therefore address at this point. Barth asks:

> What is the significance for the definition of the concept "separated brethren" (lack of "fullness") of the statement (4, 10) that it is difficult for the Catholic Church herself "to express in actual life her full catholicity in all its aspects"?[27]

The last sentence in paragraph 14 of *Ut Unum Sint* states, "Ecumenism is directed precisely to making the partial communion existing between Christians grow towards full communion in truth and charity." Hence, the "separated brethren" are brethren inasmuch as they are objectively ordered to full communion with the Catholic Church, and their objective separation from this full communion weakens the actual life of the Catholic Church, that is, the visible actualization of the fullness of her catholicity. In "separated brethren," while "separated" is a qualifier naming the absence of the fullness of communion, "brethren" refers to the substance of the extant communion. In paragraph 3, *Unitatis Redintegratio* states the matter with all desirable clarity, and *Ut Unum Sint* quotes this crucial passage in paragraph 13: "All those justified by faith

24. Barth, *ALA*, 29.
25. *UUS* §13.
26. *UUS* §14.
27. Barth, *ALA*, 30.

through Baptism are incorporated into Christ. They therefore have a right to be honored by the title of Christian, and are properly regarded as brothers and sisters in the Lord by the sons and daughters of the Church."[28] Since the catholicity of the Catholic Church is not achieved simply additively but is in a certain way extant from the beginning since the Church of Christ subsists in the Catholic Church and since the event of Pentecost reached out to all peoples of the then known *oikoumene*,[29] the inclusion of the separated brethren does not bring about a hitherto absent catholicity. But the existence of separated brethren is an objective obstacle to the full visible realization of the Church's catholicity. For those "certain features of the Christian mystery" which "have at times been more effectively emphasized"[30] among the "separated brethren," to use the terminology of *Unitatis Redintegratio*, would indeed greatly contribute to the full visible realization of the Church's catholicity.

It is quite apposite now to turn to the second part of Barth's fourth question for clarification, where he wonders whether the possible complementarity of theological formulations might not only pertain to "Eastern 'separated brethren'" but also to Protestants. This pertinent question finds a relevant answer in paragraph 38 of *Ut Unum Sint*, where Pope John Paul II describes a crucial ecumenical hermeneutics allowing for such complementarity of theological formulations:

> In dialogue, one inevitably comes up against the problem of the different formulations whereby doctrine is expressed in the various Churches and Ecclesial Communities. This has more than one consequence for the work of ecumenism. In the first place, with regard to doctrinal formulations which differ from those normally in use in the community to which one belongs, it is certainly right to determine whether the words involved say the same thing. This has been ascertained in the case for example of the recent common declarations signed by my Predecessors or by myself with the Patriarchs of Churches with which for centuries there have been disputes about Christology. As far as the formulation of revealed truths is concerned, the Declaration *Mysterium Ecclesiae* states: "Even though the truths which the Church intends to teach through her dogmatic formulas are distinct from the changeable conceptions of a given epoch and can be expressed without them, nevertheless it can sometimes happen that these truths may be enunciated by the Sacred Magisterium

28. *UUS* §13, citing *UR* §3.

29. Henri de Lubac, in his *The Splendor of the Church*, trans. Michael Mason (New York: Sheed & Ward, 1956; San Francisco: Ignatius Press, 1999) puts the matter succinctly: "Even when, at her beginning, she was containable in the upper room at Jerusalem, she had already reached out to all the people of the world in virtue of the miracle of the many tongues, and she knew that she had received these peoples as her inheritance. She was, in fact, to appropriate to her own use the idea of the *oikoumene* as soon as she came into contact with it" (52).

30. *UUS* §14.

in terms that bear traces of such conceptions. In view of this, it must be stated that the dogmatic *formulas* of the Church's Magisterium were from the very beginning suitable for communicating revealed truth, and that as they are they remain for ever suitable for communicating this truth to those who interpret them correctly" [Congregation for the Doctrine of the Faith, Declaration in Defence of Catholic Doctrine on the Church *Mysterium Ecclesiae*, 5: *AAS* 65 (1973), 403]. In this regard, ecumenical dialogue, which prompts the parties involved to question each other, to understand each other and to explain their positions to each other, makes surprising discoveries possible. Intolerant polemics and controversies have made incompatible assertions out of what was really the result of two different ways of looking at the same reality. Nowadays we need to find the formula which, by capturing the reality in its entirety, will enable us to move beyond partial readings and eliminate false interpretations.[31]

The *Joint Declaration on the Doctrine of Justification* must be understood as the most relevant example of an acknowledgment of this complementarity of theological formulations to obtain now between Lutherans and Catholics regarding their now shared understanding of the core of the doctrine of justification. And so, since the signing of the *Joint Declaration on the Doctrine of Justification*, Barth's question can be answered factually, namely, that indeed the possible complementarity of theological formulations might pertain not only to "Eastern 'separated brethren'" but also now to Protestants in reference to the very heart of that article of faith by which, according to traditional Protestant theology, the church stands and falls.

In sum, while Barth's "Questions for Clarification" still are of some moderate historical interest, they have lost virtually all of their heuristic force and function. In retrospect it has become plain that in the course of the magisterial explication of *Unitatis Redintegratio*, especially in Pope John Paul II's encyclical letter *Ut Unum Sint*, they have all found an answer in one way or another. With respect to the specific topic at hand, this is probably the most noteworthy of the positive ecumenical facts, accomplishments, and simple givens that stand between us and Karl Barth's journey *ad Limina Apostolorum* more than fifty years ago.

But there are also other, negative ecumenical experiences that stand between us and Barth's questions. Ecumenical agreements ironically have caused new tensions, estrangements, and even splits; one might think, among numerous other examples, of the Episcopal-Lutheran "Concord of Agreement" that set into motion the "Word Alone Movement," a splintering of a network of congregations from the Evangelical Lutheran Church of

31. *UUS* §38.

America. Moreover, consider the deep disagreements in and between Christian communions about matters of sexual morality and about the levels of accommodation in sexual and other matters to an increasingly aggressive ideology of subjective sovereignty fostered by a global consumer capitalism. These disagreements have led to grave tensions within the Catholic Church and to serious estrangements and new splits in the Anglican communion and in various other Protestant denominations. The recent formation of the North American Lutheran Church comes to mind. Last but not least, mainline Protestant ecumenism in a liberal theological key has quite successfully coined an ecumenical success term—"reconciled diversity," a term that describes a reality that one might more precisely characterize as a complacent state of "reconciled indifference"—the reality of a broad, amorphous, undifferentiated mutual acceptance in an overall post-doctrinal ambience, an ambience in which the original goal of full visible, organic, and institutional unity is not even remembered anymore.

In addition to this mainline Protestant ecumenism in a liberal key, which one might most precisely call "premature victory ecumenism," there are ecumenisms that have not lost sight of the goal of visible unity but have lost the hope that is perfected in patience. They represent the strand of "ecumenical enthusiasm," which is a subcategory of a much broader phenomenon best characterized as "ecclesial presentism."[32] For ecclesial presentism, all that counts are the collective convictions we hold right now in the present as we move into the future. Ecclesial presentism holds the Church to be a self-actuating and self-norming body empowered by the Spirit. Rupture is an inbuilt moment of this dynamic. It is the Spirit-granted liberation from a past that once was the self-actuation of what is now the Church of the past. The dynamic, rupture-filled, and spontaneous fluidity of ongoing ecclesial self-actuation is the ideal of ecclesial presentism—the interminable process of shaking off the shackles of past ecclesial self-actuations and bringing about the self-actuation of the new Church of the present. The notion that differentiates between the outgoing and the incoming Church of the present is "future." The very shape the future is supposed or desired to take based on the purportedly collective convictions of the present becomes the blueprint for the self-actuation of the new incoming Church of the present and the criterion by which the outgoing Church of the present, now the Church

32. In the following, I understand "ecumenical enthusiasm" and "ecclesial presentism" as ideal types, heuristic devices for identifying theologically problematic and ecumenically detrimental attitudes, tendencies, and programs. In concrete lived reality, they occur in mixed forms, are qualified by other factors, and appear in varying degrees of intensity.

of the past, is purged, corrected, and remodeled. For ecclesial presentism the necessity of *ecclesia semper reformanda* does not arise from the fact that the visible Church is a *corpus permixtum*, and that its personnel—to use Jacques Maritain's apposite phrase—is fragile, sinful, and at times corrupt.[33] On the contrary, for ecclesial presentism, *ecclesia semper reformanda* simply captures the very dynamic of the Church's ongoing self-actuation.

Unsurprisingly, ecclesial presentism's large subgroup of ecumenical enthusiasm demands "unity now," ideally in the symbolic form of instant intercommunion. Ecumenical enthusiasts can dispense with visible organic and institutional unity reflecting the unity of faith. They simply regard this ecumenical goal as a tenet characteristic of the Church of the recent past. For the new Church of the present—sensitive to the dominant self-image of subjective sovereignty and the consequent dynamic fluidity and irreducible diversity among all Christians in their respective communions and among all Christian communions—visible, organic, and institutional unity is seen, at best, as a benign *adiaphoron*—a sentimental concession to the ecumenical goals of the Church of the recent past, or worse, as an unrealistic goal and indeed a paralyzing ideal that obstructs the tangible ecumenical progress to a universal state of reconciled diversity, that is, indifference.

And unsurprisingly again, for ecumenical enthusiasts, whether Protestant or Catholic, the Catholic Church has been and continues to be a considerable stumbling block. First and foremost, the Catholic Church does not accommodate at all well, to say the least, to the ideal of ecclesial presentism. The Catholic Church joined the ecumenical movement late but now seems to dominate it by her sheer size, the global omnipresence of her organizational structure, and her innumerable bilateral dialogues. What must for ecclesial presentists look like doctrinal intransigence slows down ecumenical progress to a glacial pace and seems to submit it constantly to unintelligible theological complications of all sorts.

Even in a theologian of such surpassing stature and significance as Karl Barth, one can discern a faint echo of such an irritation. In the first two of his critical questions posed in regard to *Unitatis Redintegratio*, he observes that "the ecumenical movement arose outside the Catholic Church" and only with the Decree on Ecumenism, "Catholics are now at last called to participate in it," and then asks "Why is this initiative of the non-Catholic churches not explicitly recognized?"[34]

33. See Jacques Maritain, *On the Church of Christ: The Person of the Church and Her Personnel*, trans. Joseph W. Evans (Notre Dame, Ind.: University of Notre Dame Press, 1973).

34. Karl Barth, *ALA*, 30. As one might expect, the critical questions that Barth formulates in rela-

At first blush the conciliar text seems to support the observation entailed in Barth's critical question: the crucial initiative of the Christian communions that brought about and for a considerable time sustained the ecumenical movement is not explicitly recognized in *Unitatis Redintegratio*. However, a closer and more exacting reading of the decree's Introduction yields a somewhat different picture. Consider the following passage:

> But the Lord of Ages wisely and patiently follows out the plan of grace on our behalf, sinners that we are. In recent times more than ever before, He has been rousing divided Christians to remorse over their divisions and to a longing for unity. Everywhere large numbers have felt the impulse of this grace, and among our separated brethren also there increases from day to day the movement, fostered by the grace of the Holy Spirit, for the restoration of unity among all Christians. This movement toward unity is called "ecumenical." Those belong to it who invoke the Triune God and confess Jesus as Lord and Savior, doing this not merely as individuals but also as corporate bodies. For almost everyone regards the body in which he has heard the Gospel as his Church and indeed, God's Church. All however, though in different ways, long for the one visible Church of God, a Church truly universal and set forth into the world that the world may be converted to the Gospel and so be saved, to the glory of God.[35]

The phrase "who invoke the Triune God and confess Jesus as Lord and Savior" alludes to the Trinitarian and Christological formula to be found at the beginning of the *Constitution of the World Council of Churches* (WCC). There the Constitution states: "The World Council of Churches is a fellowship of churches which confess the Lord Jesus Christ as God and Saviour according to the scriptures and therefore seek to fulfil together their common calling to the glory of the one God, Father, Son and Holy Spirit."[36] For those familiar with this constitution and the work of the WCC, this phrase is a rather

---

tionship to all the documents of Vatican II are significantly shaped by the normative commitments of his theology, and the critical questions posed to *Lumen Gentium* and *Unitatis Redintegratio* are deeply informed by his unique adaptation of Reformed ecclesiology. I had occasion to analyze the latter critically quite a while ago and have seen since then no reason to change my analysis and critique. See the relevant chapters in my book *Suffering Divine Things: Theology as Church Practice* (Grand Rapids, Mich.: Eerdmans, 2000) and also the chapter "Karl Barth's 'Dialectical Catholicity': Sic et Non," in my book *Bound to Be Free: Evangelical Catholic Engagements in Ecclesiology, Ethics, and Ecumenism* (Grand Rapids, Mich.: Eerdmans, 2004), 78–94, 242–49. For an instructive study of the critical engagement and constructive reception of Karl Barth's theology by German and Swiss Catholic theologians after WWI and before Vatican II, see Benjamin Dahlke, *Karl Barth, Catholic Renewal, and Vatican II* (London: Bloomsbury, 2012).

35. http://www.vatican.va/archive/hist_councils/ii_vatican_council/documents/vat-ii_decree_19641121_unitatis-redintegratio_en.html.

36. http://www.oikoumene.org/en/resources/documents/assembly/2013-busan/adopted-documents-statements/wcc-constitution-and-rules. For a helpful discussion of this matter, see the commentary by Johannes Feiner, *Das Zweite Vatikanische Konzil: Dokumente und Kommentare. Teil II*, 42–43.

obvious reference to and acknowledgment of the antecedent initiative of the Christian communions that have brought about the WCC. This whole initiative is seen in the Introduction through the eyes of faith as the work of "the Lord of Ages" (*Dominus saeculorum*), a work of his providence effected by his grace. The Decree on Ecumenism states explicitly that this divine initiative does not only encompass individual Christians separated from the Catholic Church but that this work, integral to the economy of salvation, also encompasses their "corporate bodies." Thus, arguably, *Unitatis Redintegratio* does recognize the initiative of the non-Catholic Christian communions, albeit admittedly somewhat obliquely. Only in Pope John Paul II's 1995 encyclical letter *Ut Unum Sint* do we find the explicit magisterial recognition Karl Barth was searching for in the Decree on Ecumenism: "The ecumenical movement really began within the Churches and Ecclesial Communities of the Reform. At about the same time, in January 1920, the Ecumenical Patriarchate expressed the hope that some kind of cooperation among the Christian Communions could be organized."[37]

Fifty years after Barth expressed this mild and in his case arguably quite legitimate irritation and surprise, we are facing quite a different situation. Many Protestant communions have exhausted themselves ecumenically, have settled for reconciled indifference, and have given up on the goal of full visible unity; some have even split up into new entities. At the same time, the Catholic Church holds onto the full ecumenical vision, yet proceeds at a pace and in a *modus operandi* unintelligible to most Protestants and many a Catholic. What might account for this fact? And why are the Catholic Church's ecumenical pace and *modus operandi* at the same time so unintelligible to most Protestants and to many a Catholic—rather than to be expected and possibly even appreciated for what they actually are?

"To Be Deep in History Is to Cease to Be a Protestant"

In order to answer these questions I shall advance a modest proposal. This proposal takes its departure from a not altogether uncontroversial adage of John Henry Newman. He famously stated in the opening pages of his seminal *Essay on the Development of Doctrine*: "To be deep in history is to cease

37. *UUS* §65. http://w2.vatican.va/content/john-paul-ii/en/encyclicals/documents/hf_jp-ii_enc_25051995_ut-unum-sint.html.

to be a Protestant."[38] The history Newman refers to in this aphorism is, of course, not the history presented by *The History Channel* on TV; nor is it the total sum of historical facts one might learn by heart in order to shine at Trivial Pursuit; nor is it the suggested "history" craftily insinuated to the reader's unguarded imagination in the wave of recent anti-Catholic novels, from Dan Brown's *The DaVinci Code* to Colm Tóibín's *The Testament of Mary*; nor is it even the substantive history taught before its recent replacement by social studies at American colleges, in the days when they still maintained an authentic liberal arts curriculum. Rather, the history Newman refers to with his evocative expression "to be deep in history" is the Spirit-guided and Spirit-filled history of salvation that the living Church holds in her memory. It is the Church's memory of the living Christ, the Bridegroom, who guides his bride, the Church by way of the Comforter he promised to send. The Church's memory is deeply informed by Christ's words as communicated by St. John: "I have yet many things to say to you, but you cannot bear them now. When the Spirit of truth comes, he will guide you into all the truth" (Jn 16:13; RSV). It is the history of the unfolding truth into which the Spirit guides. It is for this reason that a Catholic is "deep in history." And it is for the self-same reason that a Catholic is deep in the Christ-centered and Spirit-filled present. These are two sides of one single reality, the reality of the living, Christ-rooted and Spirit-filled Church. This single reality of the ever unfolding truth of revelation, the Christ-rooted and Spirit-filled Church, has a *sacramental* expression, first and foremost in the sacrifice of the Mass, in Holy Communion, and in the priestly vocation; an *institutional* expression, the episcopal hierarchy in apostolic succession in union with the See of Peter; a *charismatic* expression, the monastic orders, the religious communities, the ecclesial movements, and the daily Spirit-guided witness of all the faithful; a *prophetic* expression, the theologians; a *doctrinal* expression, revelation by way of the Holy Scriptures and holy tradition, being continuously made explicit and thus being ever alive in the ongoing development of doctrine; and related to the doctrinal expression, finally, the *magisterial* expression, the college of bishops in union with the pope.

All of these expressions of the unfolding truth—sacramental, institutional, charismatic, prophetic, doctrinal, and magisterial—are integral parts of the extension of the Incarnate Lord, Christ's body, the living Church. To see this ecclesial reality through the eyes of faith is to understand the

38. Newman, *Dev.*, 8.

peculiar way of the Catholic Church's ecumenical engagement and procedure. Most characteristic and important for the topic at hand is the development of doctrine. Granted, immediate ecumenical progress occurs first and foremost by way of constant prayer, conversion to reconciliation and unity, honest critical self-examination, and ongoing ecumenical sign-acts of a prophetic and reconciliatory nature. But all of this bears lasting and irrevocable fruit ultimately only when unity in the truth is achieved and doctrinal agreement comes about. And any doctrinal agreement will, for the Catholic Church at least, have to fall within the parameters of the complex and slow-moving reality called development of doctrine. At the same time, the Catholic Church's ecumenical doctrine and practice must itself be understood and appreciated in light of the development of doctrine. That is, one must come to understand *Unitatis Redintegratio* as a milestone of the development of doctrine in order to appreciate the decree for what it is, and not mistake it for a well-camouflaged Tridentine "return to Rome" strategy, as some Protestant theologians have feared and still fear, nor mistake it for a well-camouflaged rupture with the tradition, as some ecclesial presentists have argued all along, taking the Decree on Ecumenism for a rupture that justifies other ruptures and finally shows what the Church purportedly was all along—a self-actuating reality moving from rupture to rupture. In light of the development of doctrine it would also be wrong, for that matter, to take *Unitatis Redintegratio* together with *Dignitatis Humanae* as the sole fatal rupture with the authentic Catholic tradition, as Lefebvrists would have it, a rupture that purportedly has sent post-Vatican II Catholicism on the path of errancy.

Also, it is worth recalling that in the close to one hundred years between the First and the Second Vatican Councils fell an extremely rich harvest of Catholic theological reflection on the development of doctrine. John Henry Newman, Maurice Blondel, Francisco Marin-Sola, Ambrose Gardeil, Léonce de Grandmaison, Henri de Lubac, Charles Journet, Yves Congar, Karl Rahner, and other theologians composed significant works on the development of doctrine. It might have been due to the abundance of theoretical proposals on the development of doctrine and the simultaneous paucity of a comprehensive consensus among theologians that the Council Fathers' teaching on this topic was relatively sparse. Nevertheless, they teach the central matter with sufficient clarity in the Dogmatic Constitution on Divine Revelation, *Dei Verbum*:

> This tradition which comes from the Apostles develops in the Church with the help of the Holy Spirit. For there is a growth in the understanding of the realities and the words which have been handed down. This happens through the contemplation and study made by believers, who treasure these things in their hearts (see Luke, 2:19, 51) through a penetrating understanding of the spiritual realities which they experience, and through the preaching of those who have received through Episcopal succession the sure gift of truth. For as the centuries succeed one another, the Church constantly moves forward toward the fullness of divine truth until the words of God reach their complete fulfillment in her.[39]

Given this teaching of *Dei Verbum*, how does one distinguish between authentic developments of doctrine and "developments" that are actually corruptions of doctrine? Quite obviously, not every "development" is necessarily an authentic development.

John Henry Newman's Seven Notes of an Authentic Development of Doctrine

The still unsurpassed resource for gaining clarity on this matter, I would like to suggest, is the great classic that initiated the modern theological reflection on the development of doctrine, John Henry Newman's *Essay on the Development of Christian Doctrine*. Newman originally published this work in 1845 while he "was in the throes of reception into the Catholic Church."[40] In 1878, after Newman had been made a cardinal by Pope Leo XIII, he published a second, better organized and explicitly Catholic version.

In an instructive book on Newman's thought, the late Cardinal Avery Dulles calls "Newman's *Essay on the Development of Christian Doctrine* … one of the most seminal works of nineteenth-century theology."[41] He observes that "Newman gave no quarter to dogmatic relativism. He argued vigorously for the irreversibility of dogmas, not necessarily in their wording, but in their meaning. His balanced position represents a middle course between a fluid historicism and a rigid dogmatism."[42] Dulles continues:

> From the very outset Newman opposes the "transformist" view that Christianity is ever in flux and accommodates itself to the times. For him it is axiomatic that the

39. *DV* §8. http://www.vatican.va/archive/hist_councils/ii_vatican_council/documents/vat-ii_const_19651118_dei-verbum_en.html.

40. Aidan Nichols, OP, *From Newman to Congar: The Idea of Doctrinal Development from the Victorians to the Second Vatican Council* (Edinburgh: T&T Clark, 1990), 45.

41. Avery Cardinal Dulles, SJ, *John Henry Newman* (London: Continuum, 2002), 79.

42. Dulles, *John Henry Newman*, 79.

faith of the apostles must perdure. But in order to retain its vitality and ward off new errors, the living Church will sometimes have to articulate its faith in new ways. Granted that development must occur, it must still be asked whether the new formulations are in accord with the ancient faith. To respond to this difficult question he proposed seven tests for authentic development.[43]

These seven tests or, as Newman calls them in the 1878 edition, notes of an authentic development of doctrine are: preservation of type, continuity of principles, power of assimilation, logical sequence, anticipation of its own future, conservative action on its own past, and finally, chronic vigor. It will be helpful to take a brief look at each one of these notes.

The first note is *preservation of type*. Newman illustrates this note with the help of an analogy from biological life:

> [Preservation of type] is readily suggested by the analogy of physical growth, which is such that the parts and proportions of the developed form, however altered, correspond to those which belong to its rudiments. The adult animal has the same make, as it had on its birth; young birds do not grow into fishes, nor does the child degenerate into the brute, wild or domestic, of which he is by inheritance lord. Vincentius of Lerins adopts this illustration in distinct reference to Christian doctrine: "Let the soul's religion," he says, "imitate the law of the body, which, as years go on, developes indeed and opens out its due proportions, and yet remains identically what it was. Small are a baby's limbs, a youth's are larger, yet they are the same."[44]

Thus, for example, monasticism emerged as the first charismatic and ascetic movement in the early Church East and West and has grown into many diverse branches. And while it still exists and flourishes in the Catholic Church, it is not found among Methodist, Presbyterian, or Baptist ecclesial communities. The Catholic Church displays the note of preservation of type, while most Protestant ecclesial communions do not.[45]

The second note is *continuity of principles*. It is intimately connected to the first note. For in order to preserve its type, the Church must be faithful to its foundational principles. Newman proposes nine such principles: the principle of dogma, the principle of faith, the principle of theology, the sacramental principle, the principle of the spiritual sense of Scripture, the principle of grace, the principle of asceticism, the principle of the malignity of sin, the principle that matter and the mind are capable of sanctification.

43. Dulles, *John Henry Newman*, 79.

44. Newman, *Dev.*, 171f.

45. Among Lutherans in Germany—thanks to the *Hochkirchliche Bewegung*—and among Anglicans in England—thanks to the Oxford Movement—some forms of religious and monastic life were recovered in the latter part of the nineteenth and the early twentieth century.

At the end of the list he adds a tenth principle, the principle of the development of doctrine.[46] Abandon any one of these principles and Christianity will be diminished and even distorted in one or the other respect. Standing by all of these principles and assuring their continuity is tantamount with the life and vigor of the Church.

The third note is *power of assimilation,* which Newman explains pithily thus: "Development is a process of incorporation."[47] Dulles renders this note in an evocative image: "As a healthy organism builds itself up by ingesting food, so the Church takes in what is assimilable in the cultures it meets, and transforms what it appropriates. The Church and its faith have matured by interaction with the great civilizations of Greece and Rome."[48]

The fourth note is *logical sequence*. Here Newman has in mind the fact that in retrospect "the process of development" is "capable of a logical expression."[49] He states: "A doctrine ... professed in its mature years by a philosophy or religion, is likely to be a true development, not a corruption, in proportion as it seems to be the *logical issue* of its original teaching."[50] *Nota bene*, Dulles observes correctly that "Newman's term 'logical sequence' is much broader in scope than formal inference of conclusions from premises, although Newman does not exclude deductive argument."[51] Hence, according to Newman's capacious understanding of logical sequence, there arguably obtains a logical sequence between the dogma of the Blessed Virgin Mary as *Theotokos*, as God-bearer, promulgated at the Council of Ephesus, and the Dogmas of the Immaculate Conception of the Mother of God and of her Assumption, body and soul, into Heaven.

The fifth note is *anticipation of its own future*. An ultimate development may be authentic when there is a "*definite anticipation* at an early period in the history of the idea to which it belongs."[52] One might think of the veneration of relics of the martyrs as a certain anticipation of and preparation for the invocation of the saints. Newman observes that "the fact, then, of such early or recurring intimations of tendencies which afterwards are fully realized, is a sort of evidence that those later and more systematic fulfilments are only in accordance with the original idea."[53]

46. For the complete list, see Newman, *Dev.*, 325.
47. Newman, *Dev.*, 186f.
48. Dulles, *John Henry Newman*, 75.
49. Newman, *Dev.*, 191.
50. Newman, *Dev.*, 195.
51. Dulles, *John Henry Newman*, 75.
52. Newman, *Dev.*, 199.
53. Newman, *Dev.*, 196.

The sixth note is *conservative action on its own past*. "A true development ... may be described as one which is conservative of the course of antecedent developments being really those antecedents and something besides them: it is an addition which illustrates, not obscures, corroborates, not corrects, the body of thought from which it proceeds; and this is its characteristic as contrasted with a corruption."[54] Newman, for example, argues that, when rightly understood, the doctrine of the Holy Trinity does not attenuate or even erode, but does rather assert and even guarantee the prior and more fundamental doctrine of monotheism. Equally, the Marian dogmas of the Immaculate Conception and the Assumption do not undermine the absolute and surpassing centrality of the Incarnate Logos and his exclusive and universal role as Savior, but rather affirm it.

The seventh note is *chronic vigor*. By retaining its youthful vigor regardless of its antiquity, the Church with its development of doctrine may be presumed to be authentic. By contrast, "a corruption, if vigorous, is of brief duration, runs itself out quickly, and ends in death; on the other hand, if it lasts, it fails in vigour and passes into a decay."[55] Ongoing reform, ongoing charismatic renewal, and ongoing development of doctrine are signs of the Church's chronic vigor.

The seven notes of authentic development indicate quite clearly that Newman understands development as the sign and characteristic of ongoing, but deepening and more explicit identity. He states:

> It is indeed sometimes said that the stream is clearest near the spring. Whatever use may fairly be made of this image, it does not apply to the history of a philosophy or belief, which on the contrary is more equable, and purer, and stronger, when its bed has become deep, and broad, and full.... In a higher world it is otherwise, but here below to live is to change, and to be perfect is to have changed often.[56]

Authentic change is a function of the ongoing identity of meaning, of faithfulness to the principles given in the one single and self-same deposit of faith. Significantly, Newman saw his notes as applicable to the "actual decisions of authority,"[57] that is, to a promulgated teaching; they are not at all meant to help project, predict, or even somehow encourage and bring about future developments. Development of doctrine, as Newman understands it, is not the tool of ongoing change managed by self-appointed developers of doctrine in

54. Newman, *Dev.*, 200.
55. Newman, *Dev.*, 437.
56. Newman, *Dev.*, 40.
57. Newman, *Dev.*, 78.

view of a desired future Church whose teaching is to be designed in advance by the self-actuating Church of the present.[58] Such a grave misunderstanding of the development of doctrine could, according to Newman, lead only to doctrinal corruptions, not to an authentic development of doctrine.

The apposite point has been reached to ask whether *Unitatis Redintegratio* displays Newman's seven notes of an authentic development of doctrine. *Nota bene*, though: The way Newman characterizes the seven notes of an authentic development of doctrine and the kinds of examples he adduces suggest that he operates with a rather capacious concept of doctrine, a notion that does not only encompass doctrines in the narrow and precise sense but also practices, offices, and pious customs. Hence, despite the fact that *Unitatis Redintegratio* did not promulgate a definitive teaching, a doctrine in the narrow sense, the Decree on Ecumenism nevertheless falls in the purview of the criteriology of Newman's seven notes.

A Newmanian Reading of *Unitatis Redintegratio* as Authentic Development of Doctrine

Regarding the first note, *preservation of type*, Newman emphasizes that "this unity of type, characteristic as it is of faithful developments, must not be pressed to the extent of denying all variation, nay, considerable alteration of proportion and relation, as time goes on, in the parts or aspects of an idea."[59] It belongs to the very nature of an ecumenical council of the Catholic Church to restore unity and to overcome schism or at least to work toward the restoration of unity and the overcoming of schism. Throughout the centuries, councils took many shapes and forms, but the type is preserved, the type that is indicative of the very nature of an ecumenical council of the Catholic Church. Even a primarily pastoral council, as Pope John XXIII intended the Second Vatican Council to be, preserves the type. This preservation of type finds its precise expression in the opening lines of *Unitatis Redintegratio*:

> The restoration of unity among all Christians is one of the principal concerns of the Second Vatican Council. Christ the Lord founded one Church and one Church only. However, many Christian communions present themselves to men as the true inher-

58. See Jon D. Levenson, *The Hebrew Bible, the Old Testament, and Historical Criticism: Jews and Christians in Biblical Studies* (Louisville, Ky.: Westminster John Knox Press, 1993), 7: "Historical criticism is invaluable to the venerable liberal (and, in my view, illogical) argument that the inevitability of unwilled change legitimates willed change, that the historical reality that the tradition was, de facto, always changing validates, de jure, contemporary efforts to alter it."

59. Newman, *Dev.*, 173.

itors of Jesus Christ; all indeed profess to be followers of the Lord but differ in mind and go their different ways, as if Christ Himself were divided. Such division openly contradicts the will of Christ, scandalizes the world, and damages the holy cause of preaching the Gospel to every creature.[60]

Unitatis Redintegratio articulates and develops some of the most central ecumenical implications of the ecclesiology of *Lumen Gentium*. Had the Council Fathers failed in this task by refraining from drawing the right conclusions from *Lumen Gentium*, there would have been a very real danger of a corruption arising in Catholic theology, since, as Newman points out, "one cause of corruption in religion is the refusal to follow the course of doctrine as it moves on, and an obstinacy in the notions of the past."[61]

Recall Newman's second note, *continuity of principles*. Newman recognizes that the difference between doctrines and principles sometimes depends on how one looks at them; he states that the "life of doctrines may be said to consist in the law or principle which they embody."[62] One should rightly expect a decree on ecumenism not to advance a specific doctrine, let alone promulgate a dogma, but rather articulate the fundamental laws or sets of principle that inform and structure all of the Church's teaching. And precisely this *Unitatis Redintegratio* articulates with all desirable clarity:

In order to establish this His Holy Church everywhere in the world till the end of time, Christ entrusted to the College of the Twelve the task of teaching, ruling and sanctifying. Among their number He selected Peter, and after his confession of faith determined that on him He would build His Church. Also to Peter He promised the keys of the kingdom of heaven, and after His profession of love, entrusted all His sheep to him to be confirmed in faith and shepherded in perfect unity. Christ Jesus Himself was forever to remain the chief cornerstone and shepherd of our souls.

Jesus Christ, then, willed that the apostles and their successors—the bishops with Peter's successor at their head—should preach the Gospel faithfully, administer the sacraments, and rule the Church in love. It is thus, under the action of the Holy Spirit, that Christ wills His people to increase, and He perfects His people's fellowship in unity: in their confessing the one faith, celebrating divine worship in common, and keeping the fraternal harmony of the family of God.

The Church, then, is God's only flock; it is like a standard lifted high for the nations to see it: for it serves all mankind through the Gospel of peace as it makes its pilgrim way in hope toward the goal of the fatherland above.

This is the sacred mystery of the unity of the Church, in Christ and through Christ, the Holy Spirit energizing its various functions. It is a mystery that finds its

60. *UR* §1.
61. Newman, *Dev.*, 177.
62. Newman, *Dev.*, 178.

highest exemplar and source in the unity of the Persons of the Trinity: the Father and the Son in the Holy Spirit, one God.[63]

It is the continuity of these sets of principles that allow the Council Fathers to evoke the hierarchy of revealed truths, an ordered whole where some truths are constitutive of others and where all of them are rooted in the mystery of the Trinity.

Newman's third note is the *power of assimilation*, or, *unitive power*. He observes that "doctrines and views which relate to man are not placed in a void, but in the crowded world, and make way for themselves by interpenetration, and develope by absorption"[64] and concludes that the Catholic Church "can consult expedience more freely than other bodies, as trusting to her living tradition, and is sometimes thought to disregard principle and scruple, when she is but dispensing with forms."[65] The Second Vatican Council's Declaration on Religious Freedom, *Dignitatis Humanae*, in its opening paragraph explicitly recognizes

> ... that the Council is responding to external influences when it refers to the growing sense of the dignity of the human person and the importance of responsible freedom as opposed to state coercion. In other words, the Church is willing to absorb ideas emanating from secular thought without fear of compromising her own essential doctrines.[66]

Also, *Unitatis Redintegratio* states clearly that the Church's development of an explicit commitment to ecumenism came about in the middle of manifold concrete encounters and by way of assimilating important insights and impulses from other Christian communions. Consider this passage from *Unitatis Redintegratio*:

> Catholics must gladly acknowledge and esteem the truly Christian endowments from our common heritage which are to be found among our separated brethren. It is right and salutary to recognize the riches of Christ and virtuous works in the lives of others who are bearing witness to Christ, sometimes even to the shedding of their blood. For God is always wonderful in His works and worthy of all praise. Nor should we forget that anything wrought by the grace of the Holy Spirit in the hearts of our separated brethren can be a help to our own edification. Whatever is truly Christian is never contrary to what genuinely belongs to the faith; indeed, it can always bring a deeper realization of the mystery of Christ and the Church.[67]

63. *UR* §2.
64. Newman, *Dev.*, 186.
65. Newman, *Dev.*, 189.
66. Ian Ker, *Newman on Vatican II* (Oxford: Oxford University Press, 2014), 68.
67. *UR* §4. Pope John Paul II, in an important passage in *Ut Unum Sint*, articulates not only the

In light of this statement the nothing-less-than-astounding reception of the rich Protestant hymnody into the post–Vatican II Catholic hymnals is not all that surprising.

Newman's fourth note is *logical sequence*. We should observe that this note does not necessarily mean "a conscious reasoning from premisses to conclusion."[68] All that is required is that a doctrine should seem to be "the *logical issue* of its original teaching."[69] This note requires an exposition and argumentation that exceeds the scope of this chapter. But it is clear that Pope John Paul II in *Ut Unum Sint* receives *Unitatis Redintegratio* in precisely this sense, "as the logical issue of its original teaching." He states:

> In indicating the Catholic principles of ecumenism, the Decree *Unitatis Redintegratio* recalls above all the teaching on the Church set forth in the Dogmatic Constitution *Lumen Gentium* in its chapter on the People of God. At the same time, it takes into account everything affirmed in the Council's Declaration on Religious Freedom *Dignitatis Humanae*.[70]

According to *Ut Unum Sint*, *Unitatis Redintegratio* is to be read in the context of the complete teaching of Vatican II. And Vatican II, as Pope Benedict XVI has consistently taught, and as Pope Francis has affirmed, can be properly understood and received only by way of what I would call a genuinely Newmanian hermeneutic. For good reasons Pope Benedict did not call it thus, but rather, in his memorable 2005 Christmas greetings to the Roman curia called it a "'hermeneutic of reform,' of renewal in the continuity of the one subject-Church which the Lord has given to us." He continues: "She is a subject which increases in time and develops, yet always remaining the same, the

---

note of *continuity of principles* but also that of *the power of assimilation*. He makes his case by building upon the already above-cited introduction of *Unitatis Redintegratio*: "'The Lord of the Ages wisely and patiently follows out the plan of his grace on behalf of us sinners. In recent times he has begun to bestow more generously upon divided Christians remorse over their divisions and a longing for unity. Everywhere, large numbers have felt the impulse of this grace, and among our separated brethren also *there increases from day to day a movement*, fostered by the grace of the Holy Spirit, *for the restoration of unity among all Christians*. Taking part in this movement, which is called ecumenical, are those who invoke the Triune God and confess Jesus as Lord and Saviour. They join in not merely as individuals but also as members of the corporate groups in which they have heard the Gospel, and which each regards as his Church and, indeed, God's. And yet almost everyone, though in different ways, *longs that there may be one visible Church of God*, a Church truly universal and sent forth to the whole world that the world may be converted to the Gospel and so be saved, to the glory of God.' This statement of the Decree *Unitatis Redintegratio* is to be read in the context of the complete teaching of the Second Vatican Council. The Council expresses the Church's decision to take up the ecumenical task of working for Christian unity and to propose it with conviction and vigour: 'This sacred Synod exhorts all the Catholic faithful to recognize the signs of the times and to participate actively in the work of ecumenism'" (*UUS* §7 & §8).

68. Newman, *Dev.*, 189.

69. Newman, *Dev.* 195.

70. *UUS* §8.

one subject of the journeying People of God."[71] This identity of the one subject, the Church, is simply inconceivable without the notes of *preservation of type*, *continuity of principles*, *power of assimilation*, and *logical sequence*.

What about Newman's fifth note, *anticipation of the future*, whereby "here and there definite specimens of advanced teaching ... very clearly occur, which in the historical course are not found till a late day"?[72] Here would be the place to recount not only all the early efforts at reunion after the acceleration of the 1517 events and their European aftermaths and then again after the devastating religious wars of the seventeenth century, but also the efforts markedly increased by each cataclysmic European political earthquake, first the French Revolution and the subsequent Napoleonic Wars, then the First World War, and finally, the Second World War. Early initiatives in France and Belgium were followed by the *Una Sancta* Movement, by unofficial ecumenical encounters in the German cities Berlin, Kassel, and Leipzig, and later, also in Germany, by the famous Jaeger-Stählin working circle and, in France, by the Groupe des Dombes, a gathering of twenty Roman Catholic and twenty Protestant, mainly Reformed, theologians that has met regularly since 1937, and from 1968 until 1997 in the former Trappist Abbey of Notre-Dame des Dombes near Lyon in France, to mention just a few of the many unofficial ecumenical initiatives.[73] They support quite well Newman's note, indeed, they amount to "a sort of evidence."[74]

71. http://w2.vatican.va/content/benedict-xvi/en/speeches/2005/december/documents/hf_ben_xvi_spe_20051222_roman-curia.html

72. Newman, *Dev.*, 196.

73. For those early meetings before World War II, see Reinhard Slenczka, "Das evangelisch-katholische Gespräch in Deutschland," *Zeitwende* 33 (1962): 815–25; and for the Jaeger-Stählin-Kreis (named after its founding figures, the archbishop of Paderborn, Lorenz Kardinal Jaeger, and the bishop of the Evangelical-Lutheran Church of Oldenburg, Wilhelm Stählin), later called "Ökumenischer Arbeitskreis," see Ulrich Ruh, "50 Jahre Ökumenischer Arbeitskreis," *Herder Korrespondenz* 5 (1996): 230–32; and Barbara Schwahn, *Der Ökumenische Arbeitskreis evangelischer und katholischer Theologen von 1946 bis 1975* (Göttingen: Vandenhoeck & Ruprecht, 1996). For a brief account of the history of the Groupe des Dombes, see Frère Étienne Goutagny, "Histoire du Groupe des Dombes," http://www.arccis.org/downloads/groupedesdombesi.pdf. For informative accounts of the ecumenical movement, see from a Lutheran theological perspective Reinhard Slenczka's monographic entry "Dogma und Kircheneinheit" in *Handbuch der Dogmen- und Theologiegeschichte*, vol. 3, ed. Carl Andresen, Adolf M. Ritter, and Gustav A. Benrath (Göttingen: Vandenhoeck & Ruprecht, 1984), 426–603, and from a Catholic perspective the remarkable project sponsored by the Johann-Adam-Möhler-Institut für Ökumenik in Paderborn, Germany, see the *Handbuch der Ökumenik*, 3 Parts in 4 vols., ed. Hans Jörg Urban and Harald Wagner (Paderborn: Bonifatius, 1985–87). For a fuller and more recent discussion of the ecumenical developments on the European continent and the Catholic Church's increasing participation in it, see *Die Entdeckung der Ökumene: Zur Beteiligung der katholischen Kirche an der ökumenischen Bewegung*, ed. Jörg Ernesti and Wolfgang Thönissen (Paderborn/Frankfurt: Bonifatius/M: O. Lembeck, 2008), and *Toward a History of the Desire for Christian Unity: Preliminary Research Papers*, Proceedings of the International Conference at the Monastery of Bose, ed. Luca Ferracci (November 2014) (Vienna: LIT, 2015).

74. Newman, *Dev.*, 196.

Newman's sixth note, *conservative action upon its past*, identifies a development "which is conservative of the course of antecedent developments being really those antecedents and something besides them: it is an addition which illustrates, not obscures, corroborates, not corrects, the body of thought from which it proceeds," "a *tendency conservative* of what has gone before it."[75] While this is an indispensable note, in ecumenical circles any expressions of it have been usually received with irritation and impatience, by Protestants as well as Catholics. Not only does the so-called "conservative" interpretation of the famous "subsistit in"[76]—designating the full identity of the Church of Christ with the Catholic Church—belong to this note, but also the declaration *Dominus Iesus* from the year 2000, approved by Pope John Paul II, that reserves the term "Church" for bodies that have preserved a "valid episcopate and the genuine and integral substance of the Eucharistic mystery" in distinction from "ecclesial communions" that lack these traits. But *Unitatis Redintegratio* already very clearly articulates this note. Consider the following passage:

> Nevertheless, our separated brethren, whether considered as individuals or as Communities and Churches, are not blessed with that unity which Jesus Christ wished to bestow on all those who through Him were born again into one body, and with Him quickened to newness of life—that unity which the Holy Scriptures and the ancient Tradition of the Church proclaim. For it is only through Christ's Catholic Church, which is "the all-embracing means of salvation," that they can benefit fully from the means of salvation. We believe that Our Lord entrusted all the blessings of the New Covenant to the apostolic college alone, of which Peter is the head, in order to establish the one Body of Christ on earth to which all should be fully incorporated who belong in any way to the people of God. This people of God, though still in its members liable to sin, is ever growing in Christ during its pilgrimage on earth, and is guided by God's gentle wisdom, according to His hidden designs, until it shall happily arrive at the fullness of eternal glory in the heavenly Jerusalem.[77]

If there is one stumbling block for ecumenical enthusiasts among all of Newman's seven notes of an authentic development of doctrine, it is this one, *conservative action upon its past*, which means in ecumenical matters an ongoing affirmation of the identity of "Christ's Catholic Church."

75. Newman, *Dev.*, 200, 203.

76. For important studies about the controverted meaning of "subsistit in" in *Lumen Gentium* 8, see Alexandra von Teuffenbach, *Die Bedeutung des subsistit in (LG 8): Zum Selbstverständnis der katholischen Kirche* (Munich: Herbert Utz Verlag, 2002), and more accessibly, Christopher Malloy, "*Subsistit In*: Nonexclusive Identity or Full Identity?" *The Thomist* 72, no. 1 (2008): 1–44, and Stephen A. Hipp, *The One Church of Christ: Understanding Vatican II* (Steubenville, Ohio: Emmaus Academic, 2018).

77. *UR* §3. See also *UR* §§10; 14; 38; 64.

Last but not least there is *chronic vigor*, the seventh note of an authentic development of doctrine. In order to establish what Newman calls the chronic vigor of the development of doctrine—a development that the Decree on Ecumenism exemplifies, articulates, focuses, and strengthens—it shall suffice to point to Pope John Paul II's declaration in *Ut Unum Sint* that the Catholic ecumenical commitment is irrevocable,[78] and the concrete exemplifications of this commitment in the plethora of ongoing bilateral ecumenical dialogues; the ongoing work of Catholic ecumenical grass-root movements as, for example, the Focolare Movement or the Chemin Neuf Community; Pope Francis's recent efforts (continuing the efforts of popes Paul VI, John Paul II, and Benedict XVI) to begin mending the schism with the Orthodox Churches, not to mention Pope Francis's numerous ecumenical sign-acts; and, last but not least, the ecumenical commemorations of the 500th anniversary of the 1517 Wittenberg event.[79]

In sum, a reading of *Unitatis Redintegratio* in light of Newman's notes yields a veritable line of converging probabilities. In accumulation they constitute a robust, indeed "irrefragable"[80] argument demonstrating that the teaching advanced by *Unitatis Redintegratio* does indeed represent an authentic development of doctrine. As already mentioned above, Newman's capacious concept of doctrine make it possible to apply the criteriology of the seven notes to *Unitatis Redintegratio*—without the Decree on Ecumenism having to promulgate a distinct doctrine. Still, the Decree's first chapter,

78. *UUS* §3.

79. One might think especially of the joint ecumenical commemoration of the Reformation on October 31, 2016, in Lund, Sweden, by the Lutheran World Federation (LWF) and the Roman Catholic Church, the latter represented by Pope Francis himself. For an anticipatory set of ecumenical theological reflections from the *Ökumenische Arbeitskreis*, see *Reformation 1517–2017: Ökumenische Perspektiven*, ed. Volker Leppin and Dorothea Sattler (Freiburg/Br.: Herder, 2015), and for an ecumenical preparatory document *secundum quid*, see *Declaration on the Way: Church, Ministry and Eucharist*, a document that was developed as a resource by the Committee on Ecumenical and Interreligious Affairs of the United States Conference of Catholic Bishops (USCCB) and Ecumenical and Inter-Religious Relations in the Office of the Presiding Bishop of the Evangelical Lutheran Church in America (ELCA). The text of the document may be found on the website of the USCCB. For an instructive and informative brief account of the background to the Lund commemoration, see Michael Root, "Remembering the Reformation—with the pope," *The Christian Century*, September 6, 2016; online at http://www.christiancentury.org/article/2016-08/catholics-gathering. Noteworthy also is the joint statement of the Evangelische Kirche in Deutschland and the Deutsche Katholische Bischofskonferenz, *Erinnerung heilen—Jesus Christus bezeugen: Ein gemeinsames Wort zum Jahr 2017*.

80. Newman gave one of the best explanations for his method in a letter to Canon Walker from July 6, 1864: "The best illustration of what I hold is that of a cable, which is made up of a number of separate threads, each feeble, yet together as sufficient as an iron rod. An iron rod represents mathematical or strict demonstration; a cable represents moral demonstration, which is an assemblage of probabilities, separately insufficient for certainty, but, when put together, irrefragable" (Wilfrid Ward, *The Life of John Henry Cardinal Newman*, vol. II [London: Longmans, Green and Co., 1912], 43).

"Catholic Principles of Ecumenism," constitutes the heart of what pertains to an authentic development of doctrine. Essentially, the core of this development of doctrine, capaciously understood, comprises (1) a central theological insight, (2) a practical consequence formulated as a guideline for Catholic ecumenical practice, and (3) an exhortation that echoes the Second Vatican's comprehensive call to holiness:

> 1. Some and even very many of the significant elements and endowments which together go to build up and give life to the Church itself, can exist outside the visible boundaries of the Catholic Church: the written word of God; the life of grace; faith, hope and charity, with the other interior gifts of the Holy Spirit, and visible elements too. All of these, which come from Christ and lead back to Christ, belong by right to the one Church of Christ. The brethren divided from us also use many liturgical actions of the Christian religion. These most certainly can truly engender a life of grace in ways that vary according to the condition of each Church or Community. These liturgical actions must be regarded as capable of giving access to the community of salvation. It follows that the separated Churches and Communities as such, though we believe them to be deficient in some respects, have been by no means deprived of significance and importance in the mystery of salvation. For the Spirit of Christ has not refrained from using them as means of salvation which derive their efficacy from the very fullness of grace and truth entrusted to the Church.[81]
>
> 2. Today, in many parts of the world, under the inspiring grace of the Holy Spirit, many efforts are being made in prayer, word and action to attain that fullness of unity which Jesus Christ desires. The Sacred Council exhorts all the Catholic faithful to recognize the signs of the times and to take an active and intelligent part in the work of ecumenism.[82]
>
> 3. Catholics, in their ecumenical work, must assuredly be concerned for their separated brethren, praying for them, keeping them informed about the Church, making the first approaches toward them. But their primary duty is to make a careful and honest appraisal of whatever needs to be done or renewed in the Catholic household itself, in order that its life may bear witness more clearly and faithfully to the teachings and institutions which have come to it from Christ through the Apostles. For although the Catholic Church has been endowed with all divinely revealed truth and with all means of grace, yet its members fail to live by them with all the fervor that they should, so that the radiance of the Church's image is less clear in the eyes of our separated brethren and of the world at large, and the growth of God's kingdom is delayed. All Catholics must therefore aim at Christian perfection and, each according to his station, play his part that the Church may daily be more purified and renewed. For the Church must bear in her own body the humility and dying

81. *UR* §3.
82. *UR* §4.

of Jesus, against the day when Christ will present her to Himself in all her glory without spot or wrinkle.[83]

The ultimate warrant for such a theologically advanced argument is of course provided by the Church's ordinary magisterium itself and rests, as Newman stressed, in the "infallibility of the Church."[84] Consider the following passage from Pope John Paul II's encyclical letter *Ut Unum Sint*:

> Taking up an idea expressed by Pope John XXIII at the opening of the Council, the Decree on Ecumenism mentions the way of formulating doctrine as one of the elements of a continuing reform. Here it is not a question of altering the deposit of faith, changing the meaning of dogmas, eliminating essential words from them, accommodating truth to the preferences of a particular age, or suppressing certain articles of the *Creed* under the false pretext that they are no longer understood today. The unity willed by God can be attained only by the adherence of all to the content of revealed faith in its entirety. In matters of faith, compromise is in contradiction with God who is Truth. In the Body of Christ, "the way, and the truth, and the life" (*Jn* 14:6), who could consider legitimate a reconciliation brought about at the expense of the truth?[85]

Ecclesial presentists who welcome *Unitatis Redintegratio* as a rupture with the tradition and who reject Newman's notes as "general criteria for distinguishing sound from unsound developments,"[86] are faced with the fact that the ordinary papal magisterium in retrospect reads *Unitatis Redintegratio* very much in light of Newman's famous adage that Christianity "changes . . . in order to remain the same."[87] What Pope John Paul II affirms in *Ut Unum Sint* specifically regarding *Unitatis Redintegratio*, Pope Benedict XVI did for the Second Vatican Council as a whole in his homily at the opening of the Year of Faith, October 11, 2012: "The Council did not formulate anything new in matters of faith, nor did it wish to replace what was ancient. Rather, it concerned itself with seeing that the same faith might continue to be lived in the present day, that it might remain a living faith in a world of change."[88]

To conclude, Newman's notes of an authentic development of doctrine not only give us good reasons to appreciate *Unitatis Redintegratio* as an au-

83. *UR* §4.

84. Newman, *Dev.*, 78.

85. *UUS* §18.

86. Nicholas Lash, *Change in Focus: A Study of Doctrinal Change and Continuity* (London: Sheed and Ward, 1973), 97.

87. Newman, *Dev.*, 40.

88. http://w2.vatican.va/content/benedict-xvi/en/homilies/2012/documents/hf_ben-xvi_hom_20121011_anno-fede.html.

thentic development of doctrine. But *Newman's notes also make it possible to understand why the Catholic Church came late to the ecumenical movement and why she now continues the ecumenical commitment "in season and out of season" consistently, irrevocably, and therefore persistently and patiently.*

Furthermore, Newman's account of an authentic development of doctrine opens a way to respond to Barth's first two critical questions:

1. What is the meaning of "among separated brethren also" (1, 3), since the ecumenical movement arose outside the Catholic Church, and since Catholics are now at last called on to participate in it (4, 1; 4, 11; 24, 2)?

2. Why is this initiative of the non-Catholic churches not explicitly recognized (3, 1–4; 7ff.)?[89]

Probably the most effective way to draw on Newman's insight is to have recourse to one of the most famous images he uses in order to elucidate the development of a great idea that impresses itself upon human minds. Let us assume ecumenism to be one such great idea:

> [A great idea] is elicited and expanded by trial, and battles into perfection and supremacy.... It is indeed sometimes said that the stream is clearest near the spring. Whatever use may fairly be made of this image, it does not apply to the history of a philosophy or belief, which on the contrary is more equable, and purer, and stronger, when its bed has become deep and broad, and full. It necessarily rises out of an existing state of things, and for a time savours of the soil. Its vital element needs disengaging from what is foreign and temporary, and is employed in efforts after freedom which become more vigorous and hopeful as its years increase. Its beginnings are no measure of its capabilities, nor of its scope.[90]

On the presupposition that the Fathers of the Second Vatican Council shared at least in its broadest outlines Newman's understanding of the development of doctrine, they would have regarded an initiative taken at the beginning of the twentieth century, by the Church's understanding of time, as quite an inchoate phenomenon in need of clarification, purification, and development. Hence, in these matters simply to take the initiative and be off first does not at all amount to some kind of advanced position (*Vorsprung*) like in a car race. Granted, to begin is indispensable, but to bring to completion and do so rightly is of surpassing significance. Hence, only in light of the discernment by the Council Fathers that this initiative was indeed the

89. Barth, *ALA*, 30.
90. Newman, *Dev.*, 40.

work of the Holy Spirit did they deem it important. Indeed, they deemed it imperative that the Catholic Church take part in this initiative in order to contribute its own part to its course—and in the process they engaged in an authentic development of doctrine, as part of the journey toward the fullest possible expression and realization of the Church's catholicity in unity, but not uniformity.

Also Barth's third critical question might find an answer in light of Newman's understanding of the development of doctrine: "Is 3, 5 intended to imply that the party of Cephas mentioned in 1 Corinthians 1:12, in distinction from the other three, was the one complete Catholic Church?"[91] Barth's question pertains to the following passage from *Unitatis Redintegratio*:

> Even at the beginnings of this one and only Church of God [*in hac una et unica Dei ecclesia*] there arose certain rifts [*scissurae quaedam*], [Cf. 1 Cor. 11:18–19; Gal. 1:6–9; 1 Jn 2:18–19] which the Apostle strongly condemned. [Cf. 1 Cor. 1:11ff; 11:22] But in subsequent centuries much more serious dissensions made their appearance and quite large communities came to be separated from full communion with the Catholic Church—for which, often enough, men of both sides were to blame. (*UR* §3)

While in one sense, the complete Catholic Church (the *una et unica Dei ecclesia*) was already present *in nuce* when the Apostles and the Blessed Virgin were gathered in order to receive the Holy Spirit both individually (Jn 20:19–23) and collectively and publicly (Acts 2:1–4), the unique and surpassing role of Cephas/Peter for the whole Church, and indeed for the unity of the Church (while intimated in John 21:15–19), unfolds only over time; congruently, the doctrine of the Petrine office develops. Hence it is antecedently highly unlikely that—being deep in history—the Council Fathers, in *Unitatis Redintegratio* §3, could meaningfully intend to imply that "the party of Cephas" referred to by the Apostle Paul in 1 Corinthians 1:12 represented what Barth in his question called "the one complete Catholic Church." That would border on the absurd. The party of Cephas cannot refer meaningfully to the completeness of the Catholic Church *in nuce* that antecedes all parties mentioned in 1 Corinthians 1:12 and is presupposed by them, nor can it refer meaningfully to the unfolded and clarified understanding of the fullness of the Catholic Church and the unique role of the Petrine office as it develops in the subsequent centuries with the Council of Chalcedon in 451 and Pope Leo I's famous intervention by way of the so-called *Tome to Flavian* as one

91. Barth, *ALA*, 30.

important high point of this process of clarification. It has been preserved in the Acts of the Council that after the public reading of Pope Leo's letter the Council Fathers announced in unison: "Peter has spoken through the mouth of Leo."[92] It seems quite obvious that the Council Fathers of the Second Vatican Council, in *Unitatis Redintegratio* §3, wish 1 Corinthians 1:12 to be read and understood in the context of 1 Corinthians 11:18–19; Galatians 1:6–9; and 1 John 2:18–19. And such a canonical reading entails that the "party of Cephas," of which the Apostle Paul seems to know only by hearsay, refers to a particular grouping, a party analogous to those quite different problematics referred to in 1 Corinthians 11:17–22 and in Galatians 1:6–9. Since in *Lumen Gentium* the Council Fathers quite obviously do not assume a primordial diversity and plurality of original congregations, but rather from the beginning the *una et unica Dei ecclesia*, all these very early conflicts and tensions, *scissurae quaedam*, are understood to arise from within the one Church and are forerunners of the later *ampliores dissensiones*. The later dissensions that lead up to the ecumenical councils of Nicea and Chalcedon are indeed of much greater gravity and consequence than the early rifts of the apostolic Church precisely because, with the unfolding of a deeper understanding of the received truth of revelation, persistent error and intentional departures from the deposit of the faith and from the unity of the Church become ever graver in their ecclesial implications, indeed eventually detrimental to the fullness of communion for those who insist on them.

One might wonder, had Karl Barth ever taken the time and immersed himself deeply and in a sustained way—and guided by a hermeneutics of trust, or should I say, a genuinely ecumenical hermeneutics—in Newman's works, especially in the 1878 version of the *Essay on the Development of Doctrine*, what difference such a study might have made in the formulation of his questions "ad limina Apostolorum"?[93] He might possibly have discovered

92. For a brief and lucid account of St. Leo the Great, see Pope Benedict XVI's General Audience from March 5, 2008. The most relevant passage for our present purpose is the following: "From this intervention in particular, but also from others made during the Christological controversy in those years, it is clear that the Pope felt with special urgency his responsibilities as Successor of Peter, whose role in the Church is unique since 'to one Apostle alone was entrusted what was communicated to all the Apostles,' as Leo said in one of his sermons for the Feast of Sts Peter and Paul (83, 2). And the Pontiff was able to exercise these responsibilities, in the West as in the East, intervening in various circumstances with caution, firmness and lucidity through his writings and legates. In this manner he showed how exercising the Roman Primacy was as necessary then as it is today to effectively serve communion, a characteristic of Christ's one Church." http://w2.vatican.va/content/benedict-xvi/en/audiences/2008/documents/hf_ben-xvi_aud_20080305.html

93. In the 1920s, the politically and intellectually turbulent period immediately after the end of the First World War, the end of the Wilhelmine empire, and the beginning years of the Weimar Republic,

long before Ian Ker made it the theme of a noteworthy book that the Second Vatican Council was Newman's council and that it was for deeply Catholic reasons that the Catholic Church came late to the ecumenical venture.[94] He might also have realized to his own, undoubtedly welcome, surprise that he found in Newman's works pertinent answers, or at least their forerunners, to most of the critical questions he posed *ad limina Apostolorum* to the Decree on Ecumenism. And he might finally have realized that in doing theology it is impossible to leap over history in order to pretend a synchronicity between oneself as a theologian and all other theological interlocutors—Augustine, Aquinas, Calvin, Protestant orthodoxy, Schleiermacher, or for that matter, the ecumenical councils of the Catholic Church—under the Word of God as witnessed to in Holy Scripture. While Barth's synchronic approach, characteristic of his *Church Dogmatics*, surely avoids the dangers of liberal Protestant historicism, it fails to do justice to the fullness of Revelation as the ongoing unfolding of a living truth.

One of the few places in Barth's vast *magnum opus*, the *Church Dogmatics*, where his theological discourse approximates most closely Newman's central concerns and where the glaring absence of any awareness of Newman, let alone any discussion of his *Essay on the Development of Doctrine*, is most keenly felt, is the long excursus in *Church Dogmatics* I/2, which is part of §20, "Authority in the Church," 1. "The Authority of the Word."[95] In

there occurs a remarkable reception of Newman's thought in Germany. In 1921 Theodor Haecker translated into German Newman's *Essay in Aid of a Grammar of Assent* (published in 1921 as *Philosophie des Glaubens*) and subsequently the *Essay on the Development of Doctrine* (published in 1922 as *Die Entwicklung der christlichen Lehre und der Begriff der Entwicklung*). Erich Przywara, SJ, encouraged Edith Stein to translate a selection of Newman's Anglican letters and diary entries (*Briefe und Tagebücher bis zum Übertritt zur Kirche 1801–1845*, introd. Francis Bacchus and Henry Tristram, trans. Edith Stein, ed. Erich Przywara SJ [Munich: Theatiner, 1928]) and also *The Idea of a University*. (Although she completed the translation of *The Idea of a University*, this translation was only published in 2002 in the context of a new German edition of Edith Stein's complete works.) In order to introduce Newman to a German readership, Erich Przywara, SJ, wrote two monographs: *Einführung in Newmans Wesen und Werk* (1922) and *Religionsbegründung: Max Scheler—J. H. Newman* (1923). Barth seemed not to have taken intellectual and theological note of any of this. Immediately after the Second World War, beginning in the late 1940s, there occurred the second wave of a deeper, more nuanced, and more comprehensive reception of Newman's thought in Germany, resulting in a multi-volume edition of his works. This second reception of Newman had a deep impact on, among numerous other German theologians, Joseph Ratzinger, but it also seemed to have been missed by Karl Barth, who by now was of rather advanced age.

94. It would be quite worthwhile considering the astutely argued study by Ian Ker, *Newman on Vatican II*, under this aspect. What other aspects about the Second Vatican Council might Karl Barth have understood to a greater extent and appreciated more deeply, if in the course of his long theological life he had made the study of Newman's thought a priority in his dialogue with theologians of the past?

95. Karl Barth, *Church Dogmatics I: The Doctrine of the Word of God. Part 2* [*CD* I/2], trans. G. T. Thomason and Harold Knight (Edinburgh: T&T Clark, 1956), 544–72.

his detailed discussion of the Apostolic tradition as well as the post-Apostolic tradition and then again in informed and sympathetic discussion of Johann Adam Möhler (not taking into account though the interspersed, all too brief and rather uninformed sketch of Matthias Joseph Scheeben), Barth comes as close as ever to understanding the issues that preoccupied Newman in his *Essay on the Development of Doctrine* (and much later Yves Congar in his *Tradition and Traditions*).[96] Yet Barth creates an obstacle that bars him from a genuine encounter with the phenomenon of the development of doctrine—his rather transparent dialectical strategy, or quite obvious *Systemlogik*. Central to Barth's attempt in the extensive Prolegomena to the *Church Dogmatics* I/1 and I/2 of recovering a genuine Reformation theology under modern conditions is his construal of a twofold modern usurpation of the divine prerogative of sovereignty.[97] According to Barth's construal, neo-Protestantism achieves this usurpation for the sake of the individual subject, Roman Catholicism for the sake of the collective subject of the Church. God's free and sovereign self-revelation is domesticated on the one side by the controlling forces of humanly created "religion" and subjective sovereignty and on the other side by the controlling forces of an ecclesiastically constructed tradition and an infallible magisterium. The dialectical opposition of these two, according to Barth deeply erroneous, positions opens up the place for what he considers to be a genuine renewal of Reformation theology. Barth lays out this strategy in a rather transparent way in the opening pages of his long excursus.[98] Yet what in other places I have called Barth's "dialectical evangelical catholicity"[99] gives with one hand what it takes away again with the other. The deceptively rich and detailed presentation of historical matters in the excursus stands in service of a single principle: the event-character of "church" as a community that gives obedient witness to the word of revelation occurring again and again, a word of revelation that is "not the Church's own word, but the outside word which is spoken to it, so that it cannot seize or possess or control

96. See *CD* I/2, 458f. and 561–66. For an excellent study of Congar's comprehensive reception of Newman's understanding of the development of doctrine into his own theology of tradition, see Andrew Meszaros, *The Prophetic Church: History and Doctrinal Development in John Henry Newman and Yves Congar* (Oxford: Oxford University Press, 2016).

97. For the most exacting and astute analysis and description in English of what Barth took to be the unavoidable epistemic strictures caused by Kant's *Critique of Pure Reason* for any modern theology, see Bruce McCormack, *Karl Barth's Critically Realistic Dialectical Theology: Its Genesis and Development 1909–1936* (Oxford: Oxford University Press, 1995), and idem, *Orthodox and Modern: Studies in the Theology of Karl Barth* (Grand Rapids, Mich.: Baker, 2008).

98. See *CD* I/2, 544f.

99. See footnote 34.

that revelation."[100] Barth's dialectical strategy constrains him to construe the Roman Catholic Church in such a way that it is in no way able to consent to this statement without giving up its purported Catholic identity. This is one tangible instance of Barth becoming a prisoner of his own dialectical strategy. A serious study of Newman's *Essay on the Development of Doctrine* might have had the most salutary effect of inviting him deep into history. It is precisely the artificial and, to say the least, utterly far-fetched construal of Roman Catholicism as the mirror-image of neo-Protestantism that prevents Barth from being deep in history. Newman might have liberated Barth from the cage of his abstract *Systemlogik* and helped him to learn as a theologian how to be deep in history. And the rest, as they say, might have been history.

Facing the Outermost Ecumenical Horizon—The Fundamental Schism between Church and Synagogue

The attentive reader who might have followed these considerations with his or her own copy of Karl Barth's *Ad Limina Apostolorum* will have realized that one of Barth's critical questions has not yet been addressed. This last of Barth's critical questions turns out to be the most difficult one:

> 5. Why is the most grievous, the fundamental schism—the opposition of Church and synagogue (Rom. 9–11; Eph. 2)—not dealt with here, but only spoken of as the relation of the Church to "Abraham's stock" in the Declaration on the Relationship to Non-Christian Religions?[101]

It is the most difficult of the critical questions because it gestures to the outermost ecumenical horizon, so to speak, short of the *eschaton* and the end of history itself, as we know it. This at least is the case if we suppose the Apostle Paul to be right: "Lest you be wise in your own conceits, I want you to understand this mystery, brethren: a hardening has come upon part of Israel, until the full number of the Gentiles come in, and so all Israel will be saved" (Rm 11:25). In this last of the critical questions, Barth names the eschatological horizon that encompasses the totality of all possible ecumenical efforts. Yet what he calls "the most grievous, the fundamental schism" lies hidden in the mystery of divine providence on the other side

100. *CD* I/2, 545.
101. Barth, *ALA*, 30.

of the outermost horizon of the Church's unity, holiness, catholicity, and apostolicity. If this is true, then attempting to integrate this mystery into *Unitatis Redintegratio either* would have domesticated it by "normalizing" it as just one more item on the ecumenical agenda, *or* would have expanded the very scope of the ecumenical horizon to such a degree as to rob the Decree on Ecumenism of any theological coherence and ecclesial focus. At the very heart of the mystery of this fundamental schism rests the identity and mission of the Incarnate Lord, Jesus Christ. He is the sole occasion for this fundamental schism, the stumbling block, the stone that was rejected that became the corner stone, and he is the sole final cause of the eventual overcoming of this fundamental schism. It cannot be prematurely resolved by way of an enthusiasm characteristic of some Christian attempts to resolve this mystery here and now. This enthusiasm may take a neo-Marcionite form represented by theologians like Adolf von Harnack and more recently Notger Slenczka, who resolve the mystery by declaring that there does not obtain any fundamental schism whatsoever. For these theologians, because Judaism is a religion genuinely and categorically different from Christianity, the Hebrew canon therefore neither has intrinsic revelatory validity for Christianity nor is in any shape or form binding for the Christian faith.[102] Or this enthusiasm may take a neo-Ebionite form represented most recently by not a few post-Holocaust theologians eager to avoid the slightest intimations of Christian supersessionism by endorsing a two-covenant theology, which again resolves the matter by declaring that there does not obtain any fundamental schism whatsoever, but rather two strictly parallel and non-interfering covenants.[103]

102. Notger Slenczka, following Harnack, proposes to regard the whole Old Testament in a way analogous to the way in which Protestant theology has regarded the so-called "Apocrypha," namely, as useful and instructive to read, but as devoid of any revelatory validity and normative import for the Christian faith. Regarding Adolf von Harnack's position I indulge in citing his famous passage from his monograph on Marcion: "The thesis that is to be argued in the following may be stated thus: *the rejection of the Old Testament in the second century was a mistake which the great church rightly avoided; to maintain it in the sixteenth century was a fate from which the Reformation was not yet able to escape; but still to preserve it in Protestantism as a canonical document since the nineteenth century is the consequence of a religious and ecclesiastical crippling*" (Adolf von Harnack, *Marcion: The Gospel of the Alien God*, trans. John E. Steely and Lyle D. Bierma [Durham, N.C.: Labyrinth Press, 1990], 134). For Notger Slenczka, see his programmatic and learned essay "Die Kirche und das Alte Testament," in *Das Alte Testament in der Theologie* (Marburger Jahrbuch Theologie XXV), ed. Elisabeth Gräb-Schmidt and Reiner Preul (Leipzig: Evangelische Verlagsanstalt, 2013), 83–119. Adolf von Harnack and Notger Slenczka renew positions held in the sixteenth century by the German Lutheran theologian Johann Agricola (notorious for his antinomianism) and in the nineteenth century by the paragon of liberal Protestantism, Friedrich Schleiermacher (see paradigmatically his *magnum opus*, *The Christian Faith*, ed. H. R. Mackintosh and J. S. Stewart [Edinburgh: T&T Clark, 1968], vol. II, 608–11, §132).

103. For one paradigmatic instantiation of this program, see Paul M. Van Buren, *A Theology of*

In short, because this schism has its very root and origin in the identity of the Incarnate Lord, it cannot be addressed in the horizon that makes possible all other ecumenical dialogues, namely, the very identity of the Incarnate Lord himself and of the incorporation into him by way of baptism. Ignoring this fundamental fact would only lead to the temptation to resolve the mystery prematurely and forcefully in one of the two above ways, a supersessionist or a two-covenant theology. Though individual Catholic theologians may have tended in one or the other of these two directions, neither is really a doctrinal possibility for the Catholic Church. This fundamental schism does not fall under the ecumenical competency of the Catholic Church because it is *sui generis* in its eschatological qualification.[104]

The Future of Catholic-Protestant Ecumenism in a Properly Eschatological Perspective

Last but not least, it is apposite to ask what the future of Catholic-Protestant ecumenism might be. I am not a prophet, nor the son of a prophet, but if there is any future to such ecumenism—and precisely by praying and working for it Catholics faithful to *Unitatis Redintegratio* and *Ut Unum Sint* express their expectation of such a future—it seems clear that Catholics and Protestants would profit greatly from paying a renewed and more sustained attention to the thought of John Henry Newman. He is not behind us but still ahead of us, I think. His understanding of the development of doctrine points out the profound error of ecclesial presentism. Not to become presumptuously and impatiently enthusiastic and imprudently zealous about ecumenical progress, nor to become slothful, cynical, and even despairing

the Jewish-Christian Reality. Part 1: Discerning the Way (San Francisco: Harper and Row, 1980); *Part 2: A Christian Theology of the People of Israel* (San Francisco: Harper and Row, 1984); *Part 3: Christ in Context* (San Francisco: Harper and Row, 1988). *Nota bene*: The complexities, challenges, and opportunities that Messianic Judaism raises after and in light of *Nostra Aetate* does not fall under this category. For what is entailed in occupying faithfully and thoughtfully the theological space opened up by the tension between *Nostra Aetate* and *Ad Gentes*, see the lucidly argued and greatly instructive chapter by Bruce Marshall on *Nostra Aetate* in this volume.

104. This is an argument of fittingness that, as far as I can see, actually very few Council Fathers advanced. For there was indeed an exceedingly complex debate over whether or not the second declaration, that is, the third draft of what was then called *Decretum de Iudaeis*—a document solely on the Jewish people, which was later to become part of *Nostra Aetate*—was to form chapter IV of the Decree on Ecumenism (and whether *Dignitatis Humanae* was to form possibly chapter V of the Decree on Ecumenism). For a detailed and exacting account of the prehistory of *Nostra Aetate*, see the monographic "Kommentierende Einleitung" by Johannes Oesterreicher, in *Das Zweite Vatikanische Konzil: Dokumente und Kommentare. Teil II* (Ergänzungsbände zu *Lexikon für Theologie und Kirche*) (Freiburg: Herder, 1967), 406–78.

about it, requires nothing less than to be deep in history. The irony is this: the deeper we are in history—seeing matters through the eyes of faith—the more do we become aware of the eschatological horizon in which all history unfolds; and the more eschatological and the less managerial and operational our hope for ecumenical progress becomes, the more patient and the more intense it becomes. Not only do the life and work of John Henry Newman give witness to this reality, but it is also a reality of which the Council Fathers were deeply aware. And for this very reason we must always heed their exhortation to a hope that bears fruit in patience:

> This Sacred Council exhorts the faithful to refrain from superficiality and imprudent zeal, which can hinder real progress toward unity. Their ecumenical action must be fully and sincerely Catholic, that is to say, faithful to the truth which we have received from the apostles and Fathers of the Church, in harmony with the faith which the Catholic Church has always professed, and at the same time directed toward that fullness to which Our Lord wills His Body to grow in the course of time. (*UR* §24)

This exhortation helps us remember that the question of the ecumenical future falls, of course, fully under the scope of divine providence. This exhortation thereby also helps us resist the temptation to regard ecumenical progress as an ever-proceeding, quasi-asymptotic advance of human good will and effort that will eventually coincide with the realization of the Kingdom of God in this world, an imagined world of universal peace and mutually reconciled indifference in all respects—the fusion, so speak, of the two visions Immanuel Kant tentatively offered in his two late works *The End of All Things* (1794) and *Toward Perpetual Peace: A Philosophical Sketch* (1795).[105] Some might possibly want to find faint echoes of such an outlook in the more unguardedly optimistic sections of *Gaudium et Spes*.[106] However this may be according to the wishful thinking that informs much of the pre-

105. Precisely because these texts and their programmatic vision have sunk into the collective subconscious of the secularized West, it is still worth returning to them for a careful study, a study that will make patent Kant's own profound and commendable uncertainty and ambiguity about the realizability of this programmatic vision. The more this vision has become the utopian horizon that drives the present techno-industrial progress, the less nuanced and more certain it has become. Kant's *The End of All Things* may best be found in Immanuel Kant, *Religion within the Boundaries of Mere Reason. And Other Writings*, ed. Allan Wood and George di Giovanni (Cambridge: Cambridge University Press, 2004), 193–205. His *Toward Perpetual Peace: A Philosophical Sketch* may best be found in Immanuel Kant, *Toward Perpetual Peace and Other Writings on Politics, Peace, and History*, ed. with intro. by Pauline Kleingeld, trans. David L. Colclasure (New Haven, Conn.: Yale University Press, 2006), 67–109.

106. It would be quite salutary to submit to a careful *re-lecture* of Karl Rahner's "Animadversiones," his stridently critical analysis of Schema 13 (the draft document that eventually became *Gaudium et Spes*), which he presented to the German bishops gathered at Fulda on August 31, 1965, criticisms renewed in a lecture six months before his death in 1984, "Christian Pessimism" (Karl Rahner, *Theological Investigations*, vol. 22 [New York: Crossroad, 1991], 155–62). For a helpful narration and analysis of

sentist hermeneutics of Vatican II, it is quite clear that Kant's vision—embraced by all the great lights of German liberal Protestantism before World War I—of an immanent, and for some even imminent, *eschaton* of global republican peace and enlightened perfection of culture, is nothing but a theologically and philosophically unsupportable and historically unrealistic messianic secular humanism with its characteristic millennialist outlook on the future.[107] "For," as Newman reminds us with proper eschatological sobriety, "Christ will never reign visibly upon earth."[108]

Ecclesial presentism and its ecumenical specification, "early victory enthusiasm," are nothing but instantiations of millennialist hopes and pretensions. Proper Christian hope in genuine ecumenical progress must not be confused or conflated with, or co-opted by, the complacently self-congratulatory somnambulant belief in an irresistible cultural and techno-industrial progress, a belief as unreflective as it is deep-seated in the world of late modern global capitalism, mesmerized as it is by the false promises of subjective sovereignty and haunted by the "*luctus et angor*," the "griefs and anxieties" (*Gaudium et Spes* §1), that our state of advanced ecological, cultural, and social self-destructiveness unavoidably elicits.[109]

The two most urgent and difficult challenges—one world-wide for ecumenism and the other for the proclamation of the gospel in North America and Europe—seem to me not to be a divided Christianity (the late modern world is increasingly indifferent about that, indeed, welcomes it as a contribution to an ever-increasing plurality of options) but rather two very different forms of presentism. The first is a rapidly growing worldwide form of Christian charismatic presentism, that is, neo-Pentecostalism, a third wave of Pentecostalism that emerged in the 1980s. Neo-Pentecostalism is intensely syncretistic, preaches a gospel of material success and prosperity and a complete emancipation from the traditional norms related to holiness—the moral rigorism and the ascetic way of life characteristic of classical Pentecostalism. In many parts of the world that tend to be hostile to traditional

---

Rahner's critique of *Gaudium et Spes*, see Brandon Peterson, "Critical Voices: The Reactions of Rahner and Ratzinger to 'Schema XIII' (*Gaudium et Spes*)," *Modern Theology* 31, no. 1 (2015): 1–26.

107. For a still-pertinent theological critique of such a secularized millennialism, one could do worse than read again the recently re-issued late *opus magnum* of Henri de Lubac, SJ, *La postérité spirituelle de Joachim de Flore: De Joachim à nos jours* (Paris: Cerf, 2014) and to reconsider two small but pertinent philosophical works by Josef Pieper, his 1950 work, *The End of Time: A Meditation on the Philosophy of History*, trans. Michael Bullock (San Francisco: Ignatius Press, 1999) and his 1967 work, *Hope and History: Five Salzburger Lectures*, trans. David Kipp (San Francisco: Ignatius Press, 1994).

108. John Henry Newman, *Fifteen Sermons*, Sermon V, nr. 36, p. 97.

109. See Pope Francis's 2015 encyclical letter *Laudato Si'*, §§20–52.

Catholicism and Protestantism and that are at best indifferent and at worst inimical to the ecumenical movement, neo-Pentecostal communities are often organized similarly to large enterprises and international corporations. Their overall success and their ongoing growth leads to what one might call the pentecostalization of Christianity, including the Catholic Church, in many parts of the world, a pentecostalization that is synonymous with an increase in syncretism across the board.[110]

While this first form of presentism is found increasingly among the poorer *strata* of the so-called developing world, the second form of presentism reigns in the wealthy segments of North America, Europe, and their elite satellites in other parts of the world. This ever-intensifying collective state of presentism is driven by the omnipresence of social media and preoccupied with the instant satisfaction of the ever-new desires which the relentless dynamic of consumer capitalism fuels. Aided by the dominant self-image of subjective sovereignty—that is, consumer sovereignty—this presentism absorbs history, future, and transcendence into the ever-changing immanent "now," a vortex of free-playing wills, desires, and instant gratifications resulting in an existential state of constant distraction and dissipation. In such a setting, genuine intentional unbelief—as profoundly problematic as it is—would actually be a kind of achievement compared to the seemingly impenetrable indifference this presentism breeds. This is an exceedingly hard ground for the seeds of the gospel to take root and the saplings of the faith to grow.

Both forms of presentism display strong millennialist pretensions. But only to their own detriment may Christians forget that, since the Ascension of the Incarnate Lord, this world—while being sustained by the loving patience of divine mercy—is moving ever closer to nothing but God's judgment, which will coincide with the *terminus* of history and the world as we know it. Given this eschatological horizon, the irrevocable ecumenical commitment of the *ecclesia militans*—funded by a faith ever-watchful and free from the presently pervasive forms of presentist sleepwalking—is an act of

110. On this important topic, see Jacob E. Thorsen, *Charismatic Practice and Catholic Parish Life: The Incipient Pentecostalization of the Church in Guatemala and Latin America* (Leiden: Brill Academic Publisher, 2015); Alan H. Anderson, *To the Ends of the Earth: Pentecostalism and the Transformation of World Christianity* (Oxford: Oxford University Press, 2013); *Pentekostalismus: Die Pfingstbewegung als Anfrage an Kirche und Theologie*, ed. Peter Rethmann and Tobias Keßler (Salzburg: Pustet, 2012); Philip Jenkins, *The Next Christendom: The Coming of Global Christianity* (New York: Oxford University Press, 2011); Roberto J. Schuler, *Pfingstbewegungen in Brasilien: Sozio-politische Implikationen der neuen Pluralität* (São Leopoldo: EST, 2004); and with reference to North America in particular, Kate Bowler, *Blessed: A History of the American Prosperity Gospel* (New York: Oxford University Press, 2013).

Catholic eschatological faithfulness with all those who are ordained, called, and ordered to the one, holy, catholic and apostolic Church. Any visible fruit that this irrevocable ecumenical commitment of the Catholic Church—in a truly catholic scope—yields is nothing but an anticipatory sign of the eschatological gathering of the nations, a gathering that will be increasingly challenged by the ever more destructive work of the Antichrist and will be accomplished finally only by God's own direct intervention. "And yet, when the Son of Man comes, will he find faith on earth?" (Lk 18:8). For the Catholic Church in her hierarchy of theological and ecclesial priorities, what stands at the very top is the living divine and Catholic faith, *the very object of which is God as the First Truth Speaking* (prima veritas loquens) *through his revelation definitively communicated in the holy scriptures and in holy tradition and authoritatively communicated by way of the Church's living apostolic preaching and teaching*. Any genuine and lasting ecumenical progress can occur only in faithfulness to this first theological and ecclesial priority. Although he would have disagreed about the nature and scope of it, Karl Barth would have strongly agreed to put faith at the top of the hierarchy of theological and ecclesial priorities, an agreement Newman most certainly would have shared. In *Ut Unum Sint*, Pope John Paul II articulates and affirms in all desirable clarity this first theological and ecclesial priority that directs the Catholic ecumenical commitment:

> Full communion of course will have to come about through the acceptance of the whole truth into which the Holy Spirit guides Christ's disciples. Hence all forms of reductionism or facile "agreement" must be absolutely avoided. Serious questions must be resolved, for if not, they will reappear at another time, either in the same terms or in a different guise. (*UUS* §36)

False ecumenism under the dominant condition of this pervasive sociopolitical and cultural presentism takes the all too familiar form—encouraged and applauded by the secular media—of walking down the broad and easy path of a comprehensive "reconciled diversity." The reigning normative sociopolitical and cultural pluralism, the other side of presentism, welcomes, indeed mandates, the universal acknowledgment of "reconciled diversity" and thereby turns religious or confessional differences into options of individual preference expressive of subjective sovereignty. The iron logic of the market of unlimited consumer possibilities will unavoidably transform what might have been a well-intended, nuanced, and clearly circumscribed "unity in reconciled difference" into an undifferentiated state of reconciled diversity, that will ineluctably glide into a state of lukewarm indifference about the truth of revelation and the intimately connected truth about the Church. False ecumenism is simply the submission of ecumenism to this dominant market dynamic. Declaring reconciled diversity as the telos and terminus of ecumenism does nothing but extend the range of private judgment, individual preference, and sovereign consumer choice to virtually all aspects of the Christian faith and its ecclesial constitution.

True ecumenism resists the temptation to succumb to the spirit of the age, the dominant condition of presentism, and will climb patiently and irrevocably the narrow and steep path of the unshakable commitment to the truth, the unity it yields, and to the dialogue, encounter, and common inquiry to which the truth beckons and commits. True ecumenism cannot be nudged along by diplomatic manipulations or other contraptions but requires common prayer, mutual charity, indeed, brotherhood, and long-suffering patience under the guidance of the Holy Spirit in a shared eschatological horizon. True ecumenism is exceedingly unpopular because it defies the logic of presentism, by being deep in history, hopeful toward a future prepared by God, and in the presence of a transcendent reality that is already on the other side of all ecumenical efforts, the Church in heaven. True ecumenism defies the normative pluralism and the self-image that funds it, subjective sovereignty. True ecumenism defies the dominant utilitarianism, because it cannot be submitted as one more welcome means that serves the overarching end, the greatest possible flourishing—here and now—of the greatest number of sovereign subjects. In light of the ruling utilitarian scale of values, true ecumenism is utterly useless and will therefore be met with growing impatience, ridicule, and even hostility, not only in the wider secular society but also in the so-called mainline denominations that find themselves already in a state of reconciled diversity and, hence, indifference with each other. True ecumenism will be judged as intolerant, judgmental, fundamentalist, sectarian, and ultimately as anti-ecumenical. In season and out of season, true ecumenism will be committed to one principle and one principle only, a principle in which genuine unity is already inchoately present:

> The unity willed by God can be attained only by the adherence of all to the content of revealed faith in its entirety. In matters of faith, compromise is in contradiction with God who is Truth. In the Body of Christ, "the way, and the truth, and the life" (*Jn* 14:6), who could consider legitimate a reconciliation brought about at the expense of the truth? (*UUS* §18)

This principle is increasingly a sign of contradiction, a stumbling block to ecclesial, and foolishness to secular, presentists; but to those for whom the ecumenical commitment is a consequence, indeed, an irrevocable consequence, of the commitment to the One who says of Himself, "I am the way, and the truth, and the life," the very root of this ecumenical principle, its warrant, and the hope, patience, and joy to which it gives rise, is nothing but the power of God and the wisdom of God.

Chapter 12

True and False Ecumenism at an Apostolic Threshold of the Church

Richard Schenk, OP

Polemic, however, if it is accurate, loyal, and irenic, can be a form of dialogue.

—Yves Congar

Ecumenical Discourse and the Uses of History

In his second set of *Untimely Reflections*, from 1874, "On the Use and Abuse of History,"[1] Friedrich Nietzsche distinguished three forms of history, the utility of which for our own present and future lives is said to depend in part on how certain limited forms of remembering the past are matched to certain limited forms of forgetting it.[2] Nietzsche identified the three forms of history as its monumental, antiquarian, and critical senses. Karl Barth's visit to Rome fifty years ago and his questions for a Roman Catholicism that in the Second Vatican Council had just sought to reorient itself call for our reflection on all three forms of history, since each of them enters into ecumenical discourse both in useful and in detrimental ways.

Epigraph is from Yves Congar, *True and False Reform in the Church*, trans. Paul Philibert (Collegeville, Minn.: Liturgical Press, 2011), 7.

1. Friedrich Nietzsche, *Die Geburt der Tragödie. Unzeitgemäße Betrachtungen I-IV. Nachgelassene Schriften 1870–1873* (Kritische Studienausgabe, vol. 1, ed. Giorgio Colli and Mazzino Montinari (Munich/Berlin/New York: DTV/De Gruyter, 1988), 243–334.

2. Nietzsche, *Die Geburt der Tragödie*, 258–70.

Monumental History

What Nietzsche calls "monumental" or exemplary history, perhaps something like what is known today as Whig history, demands a double forgetting: a forgetting of some of the weaknesses that conditioned the great figures and discourses of the past and a forgetting of some of our worries that, because of our own weaknesses, we could never measure up to those whose greatness we commemorate and claim as our antecedents. We need to set aside here the worry that we could increase at least in our own eyes only if our predecessors could be diminished by comparison.[3] This failure to set aside some of our self-doubts shows itself in the dynamics of ecumenical dialogue in the familiar tactic which suggests that we can reach an amicable understanding with one another today only by claiming that earlier opponents, for all their own pioneering work, had to a large degree simply misunderstood one another. Unlike ourselves, they did not speak to one another's real concerns.

To give an example: Some of the most prominent studies that prepared the "Joint Declaration of the Doctrine of Justification" (hereafter, JDDJ) at the end of the last century made programmatic the recurrent claim of misunderstanding as the first step toward a rapprochement that identified the positions once criticized as "nicht getroffen," not "hit" or understood, so that the criticisms were "not applicable." The conflictual partner was not touched, much less engaged, by the critique of the opponents.[4] Against the trend of other historical disciplines, which had tended to suspect division beneath apparent harmony, and despite occasional, explicit *dementis*, harmony was asserted here beneath apparent conflict with such programmatic consistency, that the more historically oriented critics of the new harmony were obliged to retrace how the positions of the sixteenth century were in fact in serious conflict.[5] The 1992 anonymous, unpublished, and semi-secret consultation or expertise commissioned by the Pontifical Council for Promoting Christian Unity, which was listed in the "Common Official Statement" of 1999 in first place among contemporary writings as a "source"

3. Nietzsche, *Die Geburt der Tragödie*, 258–65.

4. Cf. the 1986 study, *The Condemnations of the Reformation Era: Do They Still Divide?* ed. Karl Lehmann and Wolfhart Pannenberg (Minneapolis, Minn.: Fortress Press, 1989).

5. The study elicited responses aimed at documenting that the conflictual partners were in fact more than just "touched" by critique of their opponents, e.g., the much-debated response of the Protestant faculty in Göttingen: *Überholte Lehrverurteilungen? Die Gegensätze in der Lehre von Rechtfertigung, Abendmahl und Amt zwischen dem Konzil von Trient und der Reformation—damals und heute*, ed. Dietz Lange (Göttingen: Vanderhoeck & Ruprecht, 1991).

for the JDDJ,[6] began with a reference to the first article of Thomas Aquinas's treatise on faith (*ST* II-II, q. 1, a. 1): that faith regards chiefly the first truth and not historical enunciations or statements. But it is silent about the next article, which adds that, as linguistic animals, we are closer to the first truth with, rather than without, enunciations, however finite they might be. This "beginner's mistake" in drawing on Thomas's writings may have been one reason why the pontifical council chose to keep the authors, the basis for their selection, and the text itself hidden from public scrutiny and allow merely the publication of press comments about the expertise that supported the trend toward the JDDJ by quite nearly denying not just the fact, but even the possibility of abiding disagreement among believers. Through the suggestion that our understanding today would demand the widespread mutual misunderstanding of earlier disputants, the path toward reconciliation had become longer and more arduous.

Admittedly, not every self-doubt *vis-à-vis* our history is destructive. There can be something salutary, for example, in the trepidation about contributing to a volume that seeks to form a synthetic theological judgment about the remarkable if imperfect event that was the Second Vatican Council; and about the remarkable if imperfect theologian who was Karl Barth; and, above all about what the remarkable if imperfect, "critical-irenic"[7] conversation between the two might tell us about the dynamics of an ecumenism that might improve upon much of what has become common practice today, hopeful that we can learn from the strengths and even from the weaknesses of Barth's Roman conversations in the 1960s without diminishing the strengths or hiding from the weaknesses of official and less official efforts at ecumenical conversation since then. We need enough monumental history to acknowledge the abiding significance for all of Christianity of the conflicts of the sixteenth century. To belittle them as misunderstandings would be to impoverish Christianity, and not just in the West.

Antiquarian History

Marking his own departure from the conventional scope of classical philology, Nietzsche showed the least sympathy for what he calls "antiquarian"

6. Cf. "Lehrverurteilungen: Positives Votum aus dem Einheitsrat," *Herder-Korrespondenz* (April 1993): 175–77.

7. Cf. Karl Barth, *Ad Limina Apostolorum* (Zurich: Evangelischen Verlags Zollikon, 1967), trans. Keith R. Crim as *Ad Limina Apostolorum: An Appraisal of Vatican II* (Eugene, Ore.: Wipf and Stock, 2016). (Hereafter, *ALA*, citing the English-language page numbers.)

history. It appeared to him to be the least useful of the historical methods, for it forgets the forest for the trees; misses the significance of historical contexts by excessive devotion to their concrete details; gives its "conserving and venerating soul" over to often well researched but minor features of the past that it portrays as a prescriptive template for our present and future existence. Antiquarian history in this sense is less interested in advancing the spirit of the past than in recording its letter and trying to feel at home within it.[8]

One might assume in an ecumenical conversation sponsored by the Thomistic Institute and the Center for Barth Studies that antiquarian history in this sense describes a theological vice familiar only to Roman Catholic scholars. Admittedly, it is a vice from which Barth, John Calvin, and Reformed theology generally, given their greater ease with a hermeneutic of suspicion about their own traditions, are in comparison to the most prominent Catholic schools of theology relatively free.[9] The late work by Paul Ricoeur on *Memory, History, and Forgetting*,[10] one of the best philosophical accounts of the need to move beyond antiquarian history and even *Wirkungsgeschichte* for a more self-critical blend of both memory and forgetting, reflects the legacy of Calvin's abiding dialectic of justification and sanctification.

And yet, for all that, the temptation to antiquarianism is also no stranger to theologians of the various Reformational traditions. The antiquarian spirit that Nietzsche describes breathes again for example in recent appeals for a programmatically noncritical use of history and narrative, including "identity-establishing myths," a term borrowed from texts for the Calvin jubilee of 2009 by the recent, ecumenically abstinent basic text (*Grundlagentext*) of the Evangelical Church in Germany for the Luther celebrations around the 500th anniversary of the Reformation in 2017: *Justification and Freedom*.[11] Despite the passing acknowledgment of the need for an "appro-

8. Nietzsche, *Die Geburt der Tragödie*, 265–69.

9. For an example cf. Karl Barth, "Zum 400. Todestag Calvins," *Evangelische Theologie* 24, no. 5 (Munich 1964): 225–29.

10. Kathleen Blamey and David Pellauer translated the work as Paul Ricoeur, *Memory, History, Forgetting* (Chicago: University of Chicago Press, 2004). For Ricoeur's comments on Nietzsche's three senses of history with the uses and abuses of each cf. especially pp. 141–43, 287–92.

11. Evangelical Church in Germany, ed., *Rechtfertigung und Freiheit. 500 Jahre Reformation 2017* (Gütersloh: Gütersloher Verlagshaus, 2014, fourth edition 2015). The vaguely formulated exception on page 99 confirms the rule of ecumenical abstinence, in that confessional plurality is presented exclusively as a consequence of the Reformation's new appreciation of freedom. For the fourth edition, a reference to recent ecumenical discussions along established paths was added in response to public criticism (1f.): *Vom Konflikt zur Gemeinschaft. Gemeinsames lutherisch-katholisches Reformationsgedenken im Jahr 2017*, ed. Karlheinz Diez and Eero Huovinen (Leipzig/Paderborn: Evangelische Verlagsanstalt/Bonifatius, 2014).

priate balance between tradition and innovation," the programmatic focus of this organizational plan is the reaffirmation of familiar if admittedly fictional narratives of the early years of the Reformation.

The spirit of excessive antiquarian history is perceptible as well in a second example, the single-minded goal of Donald Norwood's conversational study of the topic of this book in his *Reforming Rome: Karl Barth and Vatican II*,[12] in which the benchmark of theological progress, including Barth's own, is the growing conformity to the more familiar features of Reformational theology and practice. Admonitions of the Roman Catholic ecumenical partners and the call for their transformation to an established alternative are isolated here from other key ecumenical tasks, such as the affirmative discovery of "the other" or sustained attempts at self-reform. The embrace of the project of self-reform as a task for each partner in ecumenical dialogue distinguishes Barth's approach to the Vatican Council from Norwood's study. In his essay from 1963, "Thoughts on the Second Vatican Council," which the English translation has added to *Ad Limina Apostolorum*,[13] Barth reflects on the tumultuous events of the first session of the Council and notes: "The way to unity of the Church can only be the way of her renewal. But renewal means repentance. And repentance means turning about: not the turning of those others, but one's own turning."[14] Barth presents here a notion of ecumenism "quite freed from the thought that the brethren separated from us might become 'evangelical' in our sense and style."[15] Directly in the context of Barth's visit *ad limina apostolorum*, Eberhard Busch's reflections on the course of Barth's life in light of his correspondence would cite Barth at some length on the shallowness of seeking the conversion of the partner rather than first of all self-reform by growing "conversion ... to Jesus Christ, the Lord of the one, holy, catholic and apostolic Church. It is a matter of principle that on each side it has to be a matter of how each and every Christian in his or her place in his or her Church allows his or her self to be called to faith in the one Lord and to his service."[16] We all "need to do

12. Donald Norwood, *Reforming Rome: Karl Barth and Vatican II* (Grand Rapids, Mich.: Eerdmans 2015).

13. Karl Barth, "Überlegungen zum Zweiten Vatikanischen Konzil," in *Ende der Gegenreformation? Das Konzil—Dokumente und Deutung, ed.* Johann Christoph Hampe (Stuttgart/Mainz: Kaiser/Grünewald, 1964), 406–15, included by Keith R. Crim as "Thoughts on the Second Vatican Council," in *ALA*, 63–79, following the publication in *The Ecumenical Review* 16, no. 4 (July 1963): 357–67.

14. *ALA*, 78ff..

15. *ALA*, 77, translating "den von uns getrennten Brüdern."

16. Eberhard Busch, *Karl Barths Lebenslauf. Nach seinen Briefen und autobiographischen Texten* (Munich: Kaiser, 1986), 497–503, here 498ff.

some thorough sweeping on our own front steps (*peccatur intra muros et extra*)."[17] Barth's worry that the Reformational side might neglect this aspect of ecumenically motivated self-reform could hardly have been dispelled by Norwood's more antiquarian study.

Contrary to standard expectations, Roman Catholic perspectives on ecumenism do often incorporate, but need not be restricted to, something like the antiquarian use of history.[18] At times ecumenism is endangered not by an excess, but by a deficiency of antiquarian history. Close attention to the Roman Catholic past can discover important instances of greater affinity to the initial Reformational stress on grace, faith, revelation, and Christ than what is to be found in some of the more recent trends in Roman Catholic teaching and practice. It is here that Conciliar "ressourcement" had and has its particular place. A second questionable tactic not unknown in common ecumenical efforts since the Council has been to follow the claim of earlier misunderstandings with the complementary assertion that, even where the confessions might have genuinely disagreed in the sixteenth century, these differences no longer exist today, at least not in matters or degrees that could continue to divide the Church (leading to the debate on what would constitute fundamental disagreement, or *Grunddissens*).[19] One of the many problems with this tactic is that it passes too quickly over too many of the counterexamples of divisions that arguably have become greater with time. These examples are not limited to Vatican Council I and the Marian dogmas. The response prepared in 1992 by the Protestant faculty in Göttingen for the emerging Catholic-Lutheran agreement on justification identified several issues of growing diversity, such as the dominant priesthood of the local bishop, which in the wake of Vatican II had become more rather than less defining for the Roman Catholic community.[20]

Barth experienced firsthand during his trip to Rome how Roman Catholicism can suffer from an unexpected lack of exemplary or antiquarian his-

17. Busch, *Karl Barths Lebenslauf,* 498ff.

18. For the unity of these three senses of history cf. Martin Heidegger, *Sein und Zeit*, 19th ed. (Tübingen: Niemeyer, 2006), 396 (II 5, §76).

19. *Grundkonsens—Grunddissens. Studie des Straßburger Instituts für Ökumenische Forschung. Ergebnisse und Dokumente*, ed. André Birmelé and Harding Meyer (Frankfurt/Paderborn: Lembeck/ Bonifatius, 1992); and *"Kein Anlaß zur Verwerfung!" Studien zur Hermeneutik des ökumenischen Gesprächs. Festschrift für Otto Hermann Pesch*, ed. Johannes Brosseder and Markus Wriedt (Frankfurt: Lembech, 2007).

20. *Überholte Lehrverurteilungen? Die Gegensätze in der Lehre von Rechtfertigung, Abendmahl und Amt zwischen dem Konzil von Trient und der Reformation—damals und heute*, ed. Dietz Lange (Göttingen: Vanderhoeck & Ruprecht, 1991), 132ff.

tory. At least as related by Eberhard Busch in his journal of these years,[21] Barth met in Rome with a group of Dominican friars, apparently in good part from the *curia* at Santa Sabina,[22] but in the absence of their official representative to the Council, Master Aniceto Fernandez. Busch states that the meeting was "with one of the highest ranking general vicars," which still leaves the friar at the head of the Dominican delegation difficult to identify.[23]

A brief aside might help to situate Barth's Roman discussions with the Dominicans. Barth and Busch mention no friars by name in attendance at this meeting, but one might have expected the participation of Jerome Hamer, OP (†1996). From the remarks by Barth and Busch, it is unclear whether Hamer in fact attended the meeting at all, much less what he might have contributed to it. A relator for the Secretariat for Christian Unity and a consultor on ecumenical and interreligious matters during the Council, the Belgian friar became adjunct secretary to the Secretariat for Christian Unity in 1966 and full secretary in 1969, before serving in the Congregations for Faith (from 1973) and Consecrated Life (from 1984). Well into 1966, Hamer was still part of the Dominican *curia* at Santa Sabina, serving as the *socius generalis* for studies in the Order and as the general assistant for Francophone territories: one of the highest ranking general *socii*. Busch will note in his journal for the following year (June 10, 1967) Barth's disappointment in Hamer, beginning apparently soon after the 1949 publication of Hamer's dissertation in Fribourg on the "occasionalism" of Barth's theology of revelation. Barth interprets "occasionalism" in the sense of Malebranche, which he dismisses as "abstruse." Indeed, Hamer fails to explain what he means by "theological occasionalism," but he is employing and transforming a category drawn, as he tells us, from medieval disputes on sacramental causality.[24] Hamer

21. Eberhard Busch, *Meine Zeit mit Karl Barth. Tagebuch 1965–1968* (Göttingen: Vandenhoeck & Ruprecht, 2011), 88 (October 5, 1966). The author wishes to thank Professor Bruce L. McCormack for his reference to this work, which provides important context for Barth's Roman visit and for the preparatory questions he dictated to Busch and discussed with him.

22. Congar learns shortly beforehand that such a meeting on the constitution *LG* will take place without him at Santa Sabina on Monday afternoon, September 26, 1966; cf. Yves Congar, *My Journal of the Council* (Collegeville, Minn.: Liturgical Press, 2012), 888ff. (September 24, 1966).

23. Fr. Gomez of the province of Greece seems to have been the *vicarius magistri generalis* at the time. The author wishes to thank the Angelicum Professors Bernhard Blankenhorn, OP, and Francesco Campagnoni, OP, for the references to the curial work of Fathers Gomez and Hamer.

24. This lack of a closer description of occasionalism holds true even for the nearly half page dedicated to "b) L'occasionalisme théologique" in chapter 11 of the first edition, 170: Jerome Hamer, *L'Occasionalisme théologique de Karl Barth* (Paris: Desclée de Brouwer, 1949), translated by and cited in the following according to Dominic M. Maruca, SJ, under the simplified title *Karl Barth* (Westminster, Md.: Newman Press, 1962). The closest Hamer comes in this work to a definition of "theological occasionalism" is on p. vi of the 1949 introduction: "If someone were to request a brief definition of Barth's

seemed to have in mind the disputes over the gracious consequences of the sacramental rites. These could be attributed in covenantal theories to the quasi contractual self-binding of God to provide grace to those celebrating the prescribed rites; or graciousness on the basis of a divine ordination but brought about by the intrinsic mediation by an instrumentally efficient causality of the rite itself; in another interpretation, the rites are seen as nothing other than the more or less frequent occasion for God's free gifts (grace given *occasionaliter*, or *ex beneplacito*, at will). Of these three interpretative alternatives, this third form of graciousness comes arguably the closest to Barth's later sense of the sacraments, which Hamer already in the early 1960s was interpreting as thoroughly consistent with Barth's unfolding but never self-contradictory theology of revelation and the Word of God: Scripture viewed as the occasion for the revelation of the "Word of God." Barth's disappointment with Hamer's claim of "occasionalism" would not have been assuaged by Hamer's thirty-eight page introduction to the American edition in 1962, in which the author expanded upon and provided the "indispensable" key to his reading of Barth in relation to other Catholic studies on Barth that had appeared since his own, notably by H. U. v. Balthasar, H. Küng, and—nearer to Hamer's own interpretation—H. Bouillard.[25] Hamer offered a more unified picture of Barth's development than had Balthasar. The link between *Church Dogmatics* and the second edition of Barth's commentary on Romans, the abiding presence of Kierkegaard, as well as the continuity between Barth's views on Church and sacraments and his theology of revelation are all stressed by Hamer, whose sense of Barth's distance from genuinely Roman Catholic views has more in common with Bouillard than with Balthasar or Küng. Despite his affinities with Bouillard, Hamer does not address in either edition of his Barth study that polar extreme to charitological occasionalism, Teilhard de Chardin, or similar views found in Karl Rahner and elsewhere of the immanent supernatural dynamic of *de*

method, we would characterize it as a *theological occasionalism*. Perhaps some will be astonished to see us summarize his basic orientation by this formula. Does not this term pertain more to sacramentality than to supernatural knowledge? Since revelation, according to Barth, is rather a force than an enrichment of the intelligence, it seems to us that *theological occasionalism* expresses adequately a theory which reduces Scripture, limited in its claim to contain divine truth, to a simple appeal to that mysterious energy which Barth designates by the expression 'Word of God.'" For the threefold distinction in medieval theology of the gracious fruitfulness of the sacraments as the consequence of intrinsic instrumental causality, of extrinsic covenantal causality, or of mere occasionalism, cf. Robert Kilwardby, *Quaestiones in librum quartum Sententiarum*, ed. R. Schenk, Veröffentlichungen der Kommission für die Herausgabe ungedruckter Texte aus der mittelalterlichen Geisteswelt 17 (Munich: Bavarian Academy of Sciences, 1993), e.g. Quaestiones 32 et 39 (pp. 134–42, 191–213); and William J. Courtenay, *Covenant and Causality in Medieval Thought* (London: Variorum Reprints, 1984).

25. Hamer, *Karl Barth*, xi–xxvii.

facto nature, human or cosmic. Barth worries during his Roman sojourn that the stress on an immanent, historical dynamism to the absolute in Conciliar and post-Conciliar Roman Catholicism has done little to improve upon the immanent, naturalistic temptation of post-Vatican I scholasticism.[26]

At least some of the friars in attendance at the meeting with Barth on the Aventine hill, including the unnamed highest ranking member of the Dominican *curia* present, allegedly tried to impress Barth by identifying themselves emphatically with positions of a then still fashionable Jesuit theology that the Jesuits (notably, Juan Alfaro) told Barth during his visit they themselves were beginning to question. As Barth related it to Busch, the friars who were present boasted that they were now all followers of Teilhard and therefore rejected any "apocalyptic" view of the *eschaton* that saw salvation coming from above rather than in Rahnerian terms as evolving from below as the fruition and harvest of free human deeds.[27] Somehow Hamer's more nuanced *votum* seemed to go unheard. The curial embrace of more contemporary Roman Catholic majority trends in theology predictably failed to impress Barth, though he found the discussions with the Jesuits there to be a high point of his Roman visit. The accommodating and well-meaning friars might have done better to recall their Thomistic tradition, which toward the end of the sixteenth century was denounced as crypto-Calvinist, but which, if freed from antiquarianism in a manner suggested in the first edition of Hamer's study of Barth, might have better addressed Barth's concerns in that lecture, "Inhaerens vestigiis," to which Congar would invite him and which is now also included in *Ad Limina Apostolorum*.[28] They would then have been better able to follow the traces of both the Concilium Tridentinum *and* the Second Council of Orange, with their pronouncements on grace and election, to the point where their paths join and head in a direction less counter to Barth's own than could any form of Teilhardian-Rahnerianism with its far greater distance from charitological or epistemological "occasionalism." The friars' fear of antiquarianism had led them in this instance in a direction that was less ecumenical and, as the discussions on justification twenty years later would show, less "up to date." By assimilating what it could not integrate, their position not only exerted less conservative

26. Cf. the entry in Busch's journal for August 26, 1966; *Tagebuch*, 73ff.

27. Barth would come to see Rahner's nonapocalyptic (Barth says noneschatological) optimism and his all-too-close identification of the singular Christ with the evolving Christic Church and world as a manifestation of just how shaky (*wackelig*) progressive Catholicism had become. He predicts that Catholics will turn increasingly to the same remedy invoked in their need by no less shaky Protestants: the Holy Spirit; cf. E. Busch's journal for November 11, 1967; *Tagebuch*, 504).

28. *ALA*, 41–55.

influence on the past, but failed to be antecedent of genuine future development. For reasons of his own, Barth was not amused, and the conversation must be counted, along with the visit to Cardinal Bea, as one of the mishaps or breakdowns ("eine *wirkliche Panne*") of an otherwise successful visit.[29]

And yet, even where it has occurred among the various Christian communities, a growing convergence of theology or pastoral practice increasing after the sixteenth century is not of itself a guarantee of the deeper commitment to grace, faith, revelation, or Christ. The "chronic vigor" and steady transformation of the *ecclesia semper reformanda* (*semper purificanda, semper augenda, LG* §§8, 18) is a necessary, but not a sufficient, condition of genuine development. Indeed, one of the many reasons for Roman Catholic theologians to study Reformed theology is better to locate the genuinely Roman Catholic possibilities of discerning developments from corruptions even in more recent and dominant trends of Roman Catholic theology and practice, including the varied aspects of its recent ecumenical dynamics, the methods and goals of which to date need not be viewed as the new prize of antiquarian rigor. *Methodus oecumenica est semper reformanda.*

Critical History

The Roman Catholic proponents of the need to transcend the limitations of antiquarian history without simply forgetting the past have not always found theirs an easy task. John Henry Newman had anticipated Nietzsche's critique of antiquarian history by insisting that the necessary continuity in the principles of faith requires at some point a kind of limited forgetting or discontinuity regarding some of the earlier concrete doctrinal formulations of those principles. The preservation of a type of Christian existence—say, of the existential importance of intercessory prayer—demands at times novelty in its outward practice. *Genesis* always implies a certain *steresis;* or, as Matthew 16:25 reminds us, the very attempt to save a form of life can lose it. Newman illustrates how precisely the failure to develop by this mix of memory and forgetting had, to use Nietzsche's terms, amounted to the kind of antiquarian abuse of history that can in the end destroy both all that had so admirably grown up in the past and the common if hidden roots that could foster further growth into the future.

Even prior to the Council, Yves Congar had ordered his vast and detailed reading of patristic and medieval sources around a sense of development

29. Cf. Busch's journal for October 5, 1966; *Tagebuch*, 87.

constructed, as he tells us in his pre-conciliar study *True and False Reform in the Church*, with insights drawn from Newman, Johann Adam Möhler, and Thomas Aquinas.[30] In this work, Congar identifies two forms of false reform in unambiguous antiquarianism or unambiguous revolution. Like the later "hermeneutic of reform" for reading the texts of Second Vatican Council, true reform in Congar's sense here must both live with the ambiguity and take up the synthetic task of holding and thinking continuity and discontinuity together. Both would find their place in the agreed, compromise texts of the Council, or in terms that Newman takes from Möhler, *Gegensätze* without *Widersprüche*, i.e., noncontradictory opposites that have developed over time. Recalling a brief but "precious" exchange on Mariology between Rahner and Ratzinger during his Roman visit, to which Barth also refers in his final question on *LG*, Barth related to Eberhard Busch his impression that "one noticed in this exchange how thoroughly trained the Catholics are in dialectical-differentiating thought, so that opposites are not really opposites but differences, complementing rather than excluding one another. Here and elsewhere the same line is repeated, time and again: 'We need to distinguish here!'"[31] Despite his greater ease with clear-cut contradiction, Barth, too, arguably has his own way of practicing this art, e.g., with praise and criticism of such important sources as Calvin or Kierkegaard, and, of course, the emerging thought of Karl Barth. A studiously ambivalent stance toward the past, perhaps more congenial to Roman Catholic thought, comes closer to the best possibilities suggested by Nietzsche's brief description of the third or "critical" use of history.

Admittedly, the destructive element in Nietzsche's passionate desire to overcome the legacy of the post-heroic past for the sake of a bold new future goes beyond what all but the most aggressive of ecumenists would intend for established Christian traditions. From his amicable and largely harmonious conversations with Hans Küng immediately before and after the trip to Rome, Barth gladly made his own a number of questions and viewpoints suggested by Küng, notably in Küng's soon to be published book on the Church.[32] These included the inversion of the hierarchical pyramid (during the mishap of the conversation with Bea, recounted in the journal *Tagebuch*, 79ff., 89); the apology to Muslims (80, 87); the prefigurement of the Roman Catholic Church in the limited faction around Cephas (79, 88ff.);

30. Congar, *True and False Reform*, 10.

31. Cf. Busch's journal for October 5, 1966; *Tagebuch*, 91.

32. Cf. Busch, *Tagebuch*, 79–89; and Hans Küng, *The Church* (New York: Sheed and Ward 1968), cf. idem, *Die Kirche*, Sämtliche Werke 3 (Freiburg:, Herder, 2015), 103–5.

the description of the different factions at and after Vatican II;[33] and the primacy among papal titles of "Servus servorum," which Barth included in the dedication for each of the four *opuscula* that he presented to Paul VI during the Roman visit (80, 82). At the same time, Barth expressed criticism of Küng's "liberal" adoption of the divorce of the Christ of faith from the Jesus of history. Barth worried about Küng's lack of distance from troubling developments within recent Protestant theology (80). Following a visit by Jan Willebrands and Johannes Feiner in Basel to prepare Barth's trip to Rome, during which the two visitors spoke *inter alia* for an elimination of the custom of the rosary and the doctrine of transubstantiation (75), Barth expresses more concern than his compatriot Küng that, "for the Reform wing of Catholicism, everything is in motion" and that the Roman Catholic community might be collapsing like an animal without bones or a ship without nails (71, 75, 79). Even after the critical remarks by Willebrands, Barth is skeptical that Küng's proclamation that Marian and Mariological discourse is now just a *mausoleum* ("Totenhaus") had met with widespread acceptance in the Roman Catholic community (89). Despite their many points of agreement, Barth "worries about a modernist, liberal trend in the reforming wing of Catholicism."[34] Barth's choice of beginning in Rome with questions rather than with countertheses came about in part due to his conviction, that "in Protestantism things are no better at the moment than in all the commotion of contemporary Catholicism" (76). Barth's sense of critical history is perceptibly less destructive in its aims than Nietzsche's or Küng's.

Although Benjamin Dahlke's recent study *Karl Barth, Catholic Renewal and Vatican II* barely mentions Yves Congar's interest in Barth, the case of Congar would have only confirmed what is arguably one of the strengths of Dahlke's study: its insight into just how much of the dynamic in ecumenical discourse is a result of intramural controversies among theologians on each side about what to retain and what to dismiss within their own traditions.[35] The critique in 1993 by Protestant theologians in Göttingen of the Roman Catholic sense of the *magisterium* (and the sense of justification it expressed)[36] reflected current Protestant worries about that novel claim to a teaching au-

33. *Tagebuch*, 85ff. Küng was surely right to assure Barth that Paul VI's complaints about the burdens of the papal office during his conversation with Barth had little or nothing to do with the latter's own questions in Rome but was meant as a reference to the inner-Catholic disputes around some of the same issues.

34. Busch, *Tagebuch*, 79, 85ff., and *ALA*, 20.

35. Benjamin Dahlke, *Karl Barth, Catholic Renewal and Vatican II*. T&T Clark Studies in Systematic Theology, ed. John Webster et al., vol. 16 (London, Bloomsbury 2012).

36. Cf. D. Lange, *Überholte Lehrverurteilungen?* 115–33.

thority by the World Lutheran Federation which would in fact come to be expressed by the "Common Official Statement"[37] and by its critique in the open letter of more than two hundred fifty Lutheran university-level instructors in October of 1999.[38] How internal critiques have transformed the understanding of Barth and his legacy within Reformational theology today is a question especially for our Protestant partners.

Mutatis mutandis, internal Roman Catholic readings of the Council, following the historical research at its fortieth anniversary, have established a clear sense of the compromise character of the sixteen documents themselves, something that Barth had referenced already at several points of his questions.[39] What is a matter of renewed controversy today among Roman Catholic theologians and within the Catholic episcopacy is whether the task at hand is a synthesis of these opposed Conciliar positions (in accord with one of the first principles of practical reason, "pacta sunt servanda") or alternatively whether the assignment of a privileged status for positions of discontinuity is called for (this latter option entailing a hermeneutic of rupture, a "forgetting" or dismissing of the agreed moments of continuity and perhaps even demanding in the near future a "purer" Vatican Council III and so a rejection of the Council as it was with all its compromises and its complex reception). Rejection in Catholic circles of the historically accessible Council is not limited to those nearest to Levebvre. Addressing theological developments within the communities of the Reformation in recent years, Dahlke's treatment of how we can view Barth and the Council suggests how a fuller statement of ecumenical methodology would demand the identification and serious—not necessarily the neutral—transparency and engagement of the spectrum of discussion partners on both sides of the dialogue.

The work by Congar just cited, written in the first five years after the Second World War, was published in late 1950 after the promulgation of *Humani Generis*. In light of the encyclical, it was banned by the Roman authorities in 1954, in part at the urging of more antiquarian Dominican theologians.[40] Following his intimate involvement at the Council, made possible by papal

37. Cf. Nr. 4 of the "Annex" to the Common Official Statement.

38. Cf. Votum der Hochschullehrer zur "Gemeinsamen Erklärung zur Rechtfertigungslehre," in *epd-Dokumentation* 1998/7; und: Professoren sagen "Nein" zur Rechtfertigungserkläung, in *epd-Doku mentation* 1999/45, 23ff.

39. Cf. especially Nr. 7: "Durch eine Unterzeichnung der GOF würden die für Lehrfragen verantwortlichen Mitgliedskirchen des LWB übergangen: Keine ihrer Synoden hat je zur GOF Stellung genommen, geschweige denn, sie bejaht. Weder die in ihr enthaltene Interpretation der GER und der lutherischen Lehre noch die Absicht, die GER 'in ihrer Gesamtheit' zu bestätigen, kann sich auf die offiziellen Voten zur GER aus den Mitgliedskirchen stützen."

40. Cf. Aidan Nichols, "Thomism and the *nouvelle théologie*," *The Thomist* 64, no. 1 (2000): 1–19.

influence, Congar was able to publish a second version of *True and False Reform* in 1967. In his preface to the post-Conciliar edition, Congar regretted that he was now compelled by time restrictions to reprint the third section of this study, "The Reformation and Protestantism," with merely minor revisions. The English translation of the second edition saw itself forced to omit without compensation Congar's account of the Reformation as unnecessary for understanding his discussion of true reform. While regretting the "hints of polemic" in his own presentation of Protestantism, Congar makes clear that he is not in principle against every use of critical confrontation or even polemic, but he reverses precisely the very three attributes that Nietzsche associated with and celebrated in his own more destructive brand of critical history: a history that for Nietzsche must be willfully unjust, impious, and without mercy or grace.[41] As Congar articulates his alternative, "Polemic, however, if it is accurate, loyal, and irenic, can be a form of dialogue."[42] Congar mentions here only one theologian by name whose work he would especially have needed to reconsider in a more adequate study of Protestantism. If Congar were to rework this third part of his study toward a more adequate application of critical history, so he tells us in the 1967 preface to the second edition of *True and False Reform*, he would have "nuanced here several stereotypical expressions" and would have spoken "more positively about the meaning of the church, about the role of the ecclesial community in the reading of the Bible, about Karl Barth's current views, etc." He would have presented "somewhat differently certain Catholic views opposed to those of Protestantism, not so as to reject those which I had held before, but in order to expand upon them and nuance certain points. The ecclesiology that is implicit in this third part is not sufficiently expressive of *Lumen Gentium's* teaching on the People of God, a people gifted in its entirety with spiritual charisms."[43]

It belongs to the central goals of the essays collected here, as I understand them, to take up the conversation where Congar indicated it should go, asking, with reference to Roman Catholic and Reformational thought, how Barth's questions for the Council and for its reception might help us to better discern true and false reform in the Church, and as part and parcel of that, true and false forms of ecumenical dialogue. We can ask what the content, character, and spiritual charism of Barth's questions at the thresh-

41. Nietzsche, *Die Geburt der Tragödie*, 269ff.
42. Congar, *True and False Reform*, 7.
43. *Congar, True and False Reform*, 7.

old moment of the Second Vatican Council can tell us about an ecumenical conversation that is capable today of progress, precisely in as far as it is accurate, loyal and irenic. The first two of these attributes (i.e., accuracy and loyalty) involve resisting the temptation to portray the discussion partner as being too distant from or too proximate to one's own position to offer a distinctly viable form of the living faith. The third attribute (i.e., irenicism) seeks to relate the other two accounts of distance and proximity. Taken together, the three qualities characterize what might be called "relational ecumenism" as an alternative to prominent forms of conversion or reductive convergence.

Ecumenism and Critical History

Barth's Questions and the Quality of Ecumenical Justice

Critical history can fail by our applying an unbridled "exclusivist" hermeneutic of suspicion, exaggerating the distance between the positions of the other and what we hold to be a more genuine understanding of the faith. Admittedly, any portrayal of what characterizes the other's grasp of the faith will draw on its sense of what distinguishes the other from itself. In our text, for example, it is impossible to draw too sharp a distinction between Barth's questions of understanding the Council and his critical questions about its intentions. The former questions reflect the latter ones and prepare their better articulation. Without prejudice to the other studies in this volume, my impression is that Barth's description of the Council and the Roman-Catholic self-understanding that it expressed never transgressed the demands of justice and accuracy, with the possible and not particularly polemical misunderstanding of *Dignitatis Humanae*.

The now accessible knowledge of the Conciliar debates confirms that the declaration was a programmatic rejection of the kind of opportunistic and selective admission of religious liberty which Barth suspects is the intended aim of *DH*.[44] Barth's suspicion is nevertheless understandable, given that it does reflect the policy that had dominated Roman Catholic practice during the century prior to the Council, particularly following the introduction by

44. Cf. Martin Rhonheimer, *Christentum und säkularer Staat. Geschichte—Gegenwart—Zukunft* (Freiburg im Breisgau: Herder, 2012), 142–91; Roman A. Siebenrock, *Theologischer Kommentar zur Erklärung über die religiöse Freiheit* Dignitatis humanae, in Peter Hünermann and Bernd Jochen Hilberath, ed., *Herders Theologischer Kommentar zum Zweiten Vatikanischen Konzil*, vol. 4 (Freiburg im Breisgau: Herder, 2005), 125–218.

Carlo Maria Curzi and the other contributors to the semi-official periodical *La Civiltà Cattolica* of the distinction between the substantial "thesis" of an ideal rejection in principle of religious freedom, to be applied in lands with Catholic majorities, and the very contingent "hypothesis" of a merely pragmatic demand for religious toleration in other territories.[45] In his questions on *DH*, Barth is more accurate with his description of the type and provenance of arguments offered by the Declaration: the accommodation of Enlightenment insights into human rights was an expression of the power of assimilation that the Council affirms and Barth denies for the Church. But as regards not the argument from human rights and natural law but the intended conclusion in declaring universal religious freedom, Barth failed to recognize the novel proximity between his own position and the Declaration's chief point. In an exception that confirms the rule, the proximity between Barth and the Council's desire for universal religious freedom could be identified and enhanced by the exposure of a simple misunderstanding.

More characteristic and less obvious, however, are the ecumenical opportunities that are first made possible by Barth's usually more accurate comments about the intentions of the Council. They point to the difficulty of locating among all the many accidents and properties of alternate traditions something like the "differentia specifica" that truly separates one tradition from the others. When and only when accurately described, can the differences that are so identified be used to address two distinct *genera* of features proper to the other community: features that the partners *can* and other features that the partners *cannot* easily reform without forfeiting what has been characteristic of their manner of embracing the Gospel. Each genus is of ecumenical importance, but even here the twin thesis seems evident and not especially hazardous. Corresponding to the two *genera* are two essential constituents of genuine ecumenical encounter: the desire for self-reform and the *Vorgriff* or "anticipation" of its likely parameters.

We can explicate this ecumenical dynamic by listening to Barth's general questions. Barth had prefaced his sets of dual questions of understanding and critique about nine of the sixteen documents of the Council with seven general questions, not yet divided into the discrete categories of understanding and critique.[46] In all but possibly the first two of these seven

45. Cf. Giovanni Miccoli, "II. Zwei Schwierige Problemfelder: Die Religionsfreiheit und das Verhältnis zu den Juden," in *Geschichte des Zweiten Vatikanischen Konzils (1959–1965)*, vol. IV, ed. Giuseppe Alberigo and Günther Wassilowsky (Mainz/Leuven: Grünewald/Peeters, 2006), 110–229, esp. 115.

46. *ALA*, 20.

general questions, Barth seeks to explore thematically the accommodation or updating (*aggiornamento*) intended by the Council and its unfolding reception. He shows that he is well aware of two lines of thought present in the Conciliar texts: one with a greater attention and attraction *ad extra* to non-Catholic and non-Christian movements, the other, with greater attention to the Church *ad intra*. Barth points out the often overlooked parallels to disagreements within the communities of the Reformation and their own struggle for clarity, self-critique, and self-reform. Along the lines suggested by Dahlke and Congar, Barth confirms that ecumenical dialogue demands an awareness of intra-confessional differences on both sides of the table.[47] There is one theme connecting the final five general questions:

3. What does *aggiornamento* mean? "Accommodation" to what?
4. Was the main concern
   a) a renewal of the Church's theoretical and practical understanding of itself in the light of the revelation on which it is founded, or
   b) a renewal of her thinking, speaking, and acting today in the light of the modern world?
5. If both, in the interests of the pastoral task, which was it primarily?
6. On which of these two types of renewal will the stress be placed in the period after the Council?
7. Are the adherents of the "progressive" majority of the Council, who opt for the latter (for b.), aware of the danger that this might result in an undesired repetition of the errors committed in modern Protestantism?[48]

The issue of accommodation that dominates Barth's general questions accurately names an overarching issue at and soon after the Council. It was a question about which the Catholic awareness of contemporary Protestant, and in particular Reformed, responses influenced the Conciliar texts and can still be of use in understanding them today.

Barth's questions here echo the admonitions of the Reformed theologian Lukas Vischer (†2008), on the problematic surrounding an initially naive restriction of the phrase "signa temporum" to the more welcome historical developments in the cultural and political communities of that modernity in which many of the faithful of "the First World" were living in 1965. Representing the World Council of Churches as an official observer at the Council since 1963, Vischer had been involved especially in the discussions

47. *ALA*, 20.
48. *ALA*, 20.

around what would become *GS*, discussed initially as Schema 17 and from mid-1964 on as Schema 13. Vischer had articulated verbally and in writing his criticisms of the way in which the phrase "signs of the times" was being proposed in the drafts of the pastoral constitution.[49] Vischer argued that the lack of recognition of the biblical ambivalence about such signs in the early drafts reflected a systematic lack of ambivalence about evaluating the signs of our own times. Because the draft "gives too innocent a picture of the world, it cannot mediate any real hope."[50] In good part on the basis of these and similar objections raised notably by Vischer in 1964, a compromise was sought. When no consensus could be reached on expanding and deepening the notion of the *signa temporum*, "the term was largely eliminated from the draft, surfacing in the final text (of *GS*) just this one time, in the first paragraph of article 4, where it is further qualified by the remark that these signs need to be read in the light of the Gospel."[51] The verb *perscrutandi* was restored to the draft, emphasizing just this need for examination.

The critique by the Catholic German theologians in the final months of the Council was formulated most effectively and most surprisingly by Karl Rahner. His "Animadversiones" from May of 1965, presented to, and discussed with initial general approval by, the German bishops gathered in Fulda on August 31 of that year, argued with uncharacteristic emphasis that the draft of *GS* was indeed too optimistic about the possibilities and *élan* of human achievement to be promulgated.[52] Recommended alternatives in-

49. Cf. Lukas Vischer's undated Memorandum, "Signa temporum," seemingly from October 1964, in Archives du Conseil Oecuménique des Églises, Genf, 5.17; it is also to be found among the papers of Bishop Marcos McGrath, now in the University of Notre Dame Archives: Marcos McGrath Papers, Box 1, Folder 3, University of Notre Dame Archives (CMCG 1/03, UNDA). Charles Moeller refers in his commentary (cf. below, 260A) as well to similar arguments in a letter by Vischer from May 29, 1964. Cf. in addition Lukas Vischer, *Überlegungen nach dem Konzil*, Polis 26 (Zürich: Evangelischen Verlags Zollikon, 1966), 12.

50. Cf. the penultimate sentences of Vischer's Memorandum: "Das Schema ... ist in seiner jetztigen Gestalt zu flach und bringt die Bedeutung des Kommens Christi für den Gang der Geschichte zu wenig zum Ausdruck. Es unterschätzt den 'dramatischen' Charakter der Geschichte und gibt ein zu harmloses Bild von der Welt. Gerade darum vermag es aber auch keine wirkliche Hoffnung zu vermitteln."

51. Charles Moeller's commentary on *Gaudium et Spes* in Volume III of the supplement to the second edition of *Lexikon für Theologie und Kirche*, vol. XIV (Freiburg im. Breigau: Herder, 1968), 260; cf. the translation by Lalit Adolphus et al., in *Commentary on the Documents of Vatican II*, ed. Herbert Vorgrimler (London/New York: Burns and Oates/Herder and Herder, 1967–1969).

52. Cf. Giovanni Turbanti, *Un concilio per il mondo moderno. La redazione della constituzione pastorale "Gaudium et spes" del Vaticano II* (Bologna: Società editrice il Mulino 2000), 617–26: "1. L'episcopato tedesco contro lo schema." The Karl-Rahner-Archiv in Munich (Nr. 476) has preserved the 13-page typograph circulated during the interim in May of 1965 and presented in Fulda in August, as well as Rahner's handwritten text (Nr. 453). Finally, this important intervention has now been published thanks to Albert Raffelt in Karl Rahner, Sämtliche Werke: Ergänzungen 32/1 (Freiburg: Herder, 2016), XVIII–XIX and 289–323; see also 334–35. For a summary of Rahner's arguments cf. Hans-Joachim Sander, "Theologischer Kommentar zur Pastoralkonstitution über die Kirche in der Welt von heute

cluded the suggestion of reducing the status of *GS* from a constitution to an open letter on unfinished work or assigning the entire task to a post-Conciliar *coetus*. This self-critique owed much not only to the memory of misguided consciences during the Second World War, but in significant degree to the voices of Protestant theology at the Council. It is anticipated and echoed in Barth's initial reflections and his general questions on the Council, but most particularly in his questions on *GS*. While, in the end, at the urging of the French episcopate and it theological advisors, the text of *GS* was accepted with less significant revision than the German Catholic theologians had urged, a basis had been established by this critique for a more nuanced and fruitful reception of the Pastoral Constitution, making it more plausible both for the post-1960s culture of the West and for emerging social and economic readings in the Third World. The admonition for Catholic self-reform in this regard from voices of the Reformed tradition, as it was articulated between Barmen and the Council, continues to offer a needed counterpoint to recurring Catholic impulses in segments of theology and the episcopate to perceive the signs of the times as the "voice of God" or to see in societal facticity a source (another *fons*!) of normative doctrine.[53] It can remind us of the admonition implied in the second part of Barth's final question on *Gaudium et Spes*: "Where is the prophetic function of the Council to be found in the real problems that surfaced in the middle of the 20th century?"[54] It is also a question that today's post-Barthian Protestant theology will need to answer for itself.

Lukas Vischer later suggested that the Declaration of Barmen remained for Barth the model of ecumenical collaboration for the churches in the world of our times.[55] The measured but cautionary word on the sources,

---

Gaudium et spes," in *Herders Theologischer Kommentar zum Zweiten Vatikanischen Konzil*, vol. 4, ed. Peter Hünermann and Bernd Jochen Hilberath (Freiburg: Herder, 2005), 581–886, esp. 650–63: "7. Die Opposition der deutschen Bischöfe und Theologen—der Streit um die soteriologische Qualität der pastoralen Ortsbestimmung."

53. For the Catholic segments in theology, cf. Hans-Joachim Sander, "Die Kirchenkonstitution Gaudium et spes. Die pastorale Ortsbestimmung kirchlicher Identität," in *Kontroversen. Worum es sich in der Seelsorge zu streiten lohnt*, ed. Bernhard Spielberg und Astrid Schilling (Würzburg: Echter, 2001), 13–18; and idem, "Theologischer Kommentar zur Pastoralkonstitution über die Kirche in der Welt von heute Gaudium et spes," in *Herders Theologischer Kommentar zum Zweiten Vatikanischen Konzil*, vol. 4. For those in the episcopate, see Radio Vatican http://www.archivioradiovaticana.va/storico/2015/04/10/d_theologische_debatte_zu_lebenswirklichkeit,_glaubenssinn/de-1135806.

54. In Barth's distinction of questions of understanding from questions of critical evaluation, "A" refers to Barth's questions of understanding, "B" to his questions of critique. On *GS*/B §3: "Where is the prophetic function of the Council in the face of the real problems in the middle of our century?" *ALA*, 28.

55. Lukas Vischer, "Raum für Gottes Plan" (2006), cited here from http://karlbarth.unibas.ch/fileadmin/downloads/letter8.pdf.

standards, and limits of accommodation is communicated here as an admonition based on an accurate assessment of "the other," neither glossing over nor magnifying the distance separating it from needed self-reform. The Reformed admonition names here an area for Roman self-critique and self-reform that was well within reach and was in fact embraced by the Catholic partners, at least here and there, off and on—which makes this kind of critical question of lasting use. Barth's questions, however, also touch on questions for the remaining two features of ecumenical collaboration: first, questions characterized by the quality of ecumenical loyalty, when the possibilities of growing conformity seem to have reached their limit, and then by questions exemplifying the quality of ecumenical relationality and its implications for the self-understanding of a Roman Catholic Church that seems to be in continual need of external admonition to reach her ideal center. Let us turn to these other two features of critical exchange.

Barth's Questions and the Quality of Ecumenical Loyalty

Critical history can also fail by our applying an unbridled "inclusivist" hermeneutic of retrieving the insights of "the other" as mere approximations to our own, exaggerating the proximity between the positions of "the other" and our own sense of the genuine faith. While Nietzsche had called for critical history "to march right over all pieties" by cutting off the past at its very root as no longer an option for the future,[56] that is not the only form of impiety toward "the other." "The other" can be eradicated by an excessive proximity not prepared or mediated by a prior awareness of distance, by a theoretical and/or practical denial of the alterity of "the other," which can lead in the end to the atrophy of a now nonrelational self.[57] It is the danger latent in the method suggested by the semi-secret expertise of 1992 cited above.[58]

Barth's *Ad Limina Apostolorum* does not include explanatory background to his questions. Out of consideration for a more Roman than Reformational perception of "discretion," Barth decided in advance of his trip not to report on the content of his Roman discussions. As Eberhard Busch

56. "reitet man grausam über alle Pietäten hinweg . . ." Vischer, "Raum für Gottes Plan."

57. Cf. Richard Schenk, "The Place of Mimesis and the Apocalyptic: Toward a Typology of the 'Far and Near,'" *Contagion* (Spring 2013), 1–24; now also in *Transcending Boundaries. Practical Philosophy from Intercultural Perspectives*, ed. Walter Schweidler, West-östliche Denkwege, 26. (Sankt Augustin: Academia, 2015), 219–36.

58. Cf. n. 7 above.

tells us, Barth also—alas!—soon set aside the passing thought of composing outlines or theses for counter-schemata or counter-decrees.[59] But especially in the repetition of certain issues in his questions on the nine documents, Barth indicates where he sees a need for admonition even on issues where consensus might well prove to be elusive. Barth's willingness to pose unglossed questions in Rome, unsure of their chances to move the partner to self-critique and self-reform or alternatively to elicit in that partner greater clarity of self-understanding, did not seem to diminish the overall cordiality with which Barth was welcomed at this threshold moment in Roman Catholic history. Such unharmonized topics included:

1. The place and significance of the Eucharist and baptism for Christian existence.[60] (Barth's final volume of *Church Dogmatics* on baptism would appear the same year as *Ad Limina Apostolorum*, suggesting that the rite should be viewed as human response and human witness to an invisible baptism in the Spirit, not far from what J. Hamer had described in 1949 and 1962.)

2. Questions on the primacy of Scripture in relation to tradition, *magisterium* or such "loci alieni" as reason and history.[61]

59. Busch, *Tagebuch*, 74, 76.

60. On the place and sense of Eucharist and baptism cf. *SC*/B §§1, 2, 4 (*ALA*, 21ff.), *LG*/B §§2, 3 (*ALA*, 23ff.), *DV*/B §2 (*ALA*, 26), *AG*/A §4 (*ALA*, 33). The notion that the ecclesial rite of water baptism, even for adults, is a human response to a prior divine activity (baptism in the Spirit) is famously the central topic of the final volume of *Church Dogmatics* IV/4, published in the same year as *Ad Limina Apostolorum*. The extension of this view of the ecclesial rite of baptism to the rite of the Lord's Supper as a human response to the Living Bread given in faith would mean that the "efficacy" of the outward "sacraments" has a different sense for Barth than in the Roman Catholic or Eastern Church traditions, but perhaps also otherwise than in other, less "Zwinglian" traditions of Reformed theology. The question of intra-confessional differences is once again of importance. The trajectory of Barth's account of the sacraments could see "ecumenical" changes in the ritual practice more "manageable," but only if the alternative understanding is ignored or denied, perhaps by members of those other communities themselves. Cf. the alternative argumentation by Eberhard Jüngel, whose proposals in 1988 come closer to a "conversion" model, in that the common celebration of the Lord's Supper implies the denial of the difference between the common and the ordained priesthood (presupposing the affirmation of an exclusively passive—"indicative, not imperative"—sense both of justification and of the Lord's Supper: Jüngel, "Church Unity Is Already Happening: The Path towards Eucharistic Community," *Dialog: A Journal of Theology* 44, no. 1 (2005): 30–37. There is arguably room here for partial convergence and for the self-reform of post-conciliar Catholicism. Jüngel and Barth recognize something that has not always been at the forefront of post-conciliar Catholic thought: that what is most decisive about genuine sacramentality is that the ecclesial community is the subject of the liturgical celebration only in a secondary sense. Jüngel notes in his talk in *Dialog* a point where the two sides seem to have been closer in the sixteenth century: "On the basis of these statements (at the Tridentinum) about the character of the sacramental action as uniquely representing Jesus Christ, it must be possible to reach basic agreement between the Lutheran churches and the Roman Catholic Church that Jesus Christ makes himself present in the Lord's Supper and that he is the one who really acts in the sacramental action, making us to be recipients."

61. On *fides et ratio/historia* cf. *DV*/A §§2, 3, 4, 5, (*ALA*, 25ff.); *GS*/A §§ 2, 3, 4, and *GS*/B §§1, 2, 3

3. Questions around ministry, especially the difference between the common priesthood of the people and something like a hierarchy.[62]

4. Questions with and beyond those concerning the place and understanding of the Church as sacrament and/or as an effect of grace.[63]

5. Questions about the proper understanding of Mary and what she has to say or not to say about ecclesiality as a whole.[64]

6. Questions about the relation of the parts of the Church to the whole.[65]

In addition to those listed above, the longest questions involve the relationship of Christianity to non-Christian religions or to the general idea of religiosity.[66] They surface particularly in Barth's questions on *NA* and *DH*, but also in the questions he had prepared on what seems to be the document that arguably most intrigued him, *AG*, unfortunately the only document that in the end was not discussed during the Roman visit. Barth notes that he did not raise the vexed questions of papal primacy during the Roman visit.[67] The "critical-irenic" questions that Barth did raise are dealt with in greater detail by the other essays in this volume. Here it suffices to see how Barth's unglossed questions, polemical or not, aim at a critical use of history without succumbing to the temptation "to march right over all pieties" by strategies of exaggerated alienation or harmonization.

Without diminishing the importance to ecumenism of Edinburgh in 1910 or the attempts at self-reform in the Vatican Council, the history of ecumenism and self-reform has a longer history. To take one example, in his study of the ultimately unsuccessful ecumenical movement toward ecclesial reunion in the seventeenth century, notably that series of negotiations organized by Gerhard Wolter Molanus and Christoph de Rojas y Spinola, to which Leibniz came at an advanced stage of the conversations,[68] Paul Eisenkopf distinguished the discrete ecumenical strategies articulated by

(*ALA*, 27ff.); on tradition and magisterium cf. *DV*/A§§1, 6, *DV*/B §1 (*ALA*, 25ff.); for further questions on accommodation to secularity: *SC*/A §1e (*ALA*, 21), *GS*/A §1 (*ALA*, 27), *AG*/A §4 (*ALA*, 33), *DH*/A §1, *DH*/B §§ 1, 2, 3, 4, 5, 6, 7 (*ALA*, 35ff.).

62. For questions on ministry, laity, and hierarchy cf. *SC*/A §1f., *SC*/B §§1–2 (*ALA*, 21ff.), *LG*/A §§1, 2, 3, 4, 5, *LG*/B §§1, 3 (*ALA*, 23ff.), *AA*/A §§1, 2, 3, *AA*/B 1, 2, 3 (*ALA*, 31ff.).

63. On the Church as source and sacrament of grace and/or its fruit cf. *SC*/A §2 (*ALA*, 21), *LG*/B §§1, 2, 3, 4 (*ALA*, 21ff.), *AG*/A, §§1–3, *AG*/B §§1, 2, 3 (*ALA*, 33ff.).

64. On Mary cf. *LG*/A 5, *LG*/B §5 (*ALA*, 23ff.), *AA*/B §2 (*ALA*, 32), *AG*/A §4 (*ALA*, 33).

65. On parts/whole respecting the *fratres seiuncti*: *SC*/A §2 (*ALA*, 21), *LG*/A §§1–4 (*ALA*, 23), *UR*/A §§1a–c, 2, 3, 4, 5, *UR*/B §§1, 2, 3, 4, 5, 6 (*ALA*, 29ff.).

66. Religion: *NA*/A §1, *NA*/B §§1, 2, 3, 4, 5, 6, 7, 8 (*ALA*, 35ff.).

67. Busch, *Tagebuch*, 85f.

68. Cf. *Die Reunionsgespräche im Niedersachsen des 17. Jahrhunderts. Rojas y Spinola—Molan—Leibniz*, ed. Hans Otte and Richard Schenk (Göttingen: Vandenhoeck & Ruprecht 1999).

Leibniz which were in good part responsible both for the initial success and for the ultimate failure of the negotiations. To these belonged, alongside self-reform and preliminary union, *synkatabasis* or *condescendence* and its chief tool, interpretation.[69] In what was intended as a benevolent (if not condescending) reading of the oppositions, each position was to be interpreted to appear as close as possible to its apparent counterposition. The grasp of the problem, however, was regularly lost without gaining much of use to either side. One hundred fifty years after the beginning of the Reformation, neither Leibniz nor Molanus appeared still to be aware of the *proprium* of a Reformational theology of justification,[70] and critics on each side set about reiterating positions that they recognized had been forgotten. With that, if unintentionally, interpretations based on excessive *synkatabasis* had made the path to unity much longer and more arduous.

This parabolic dynamic is not unknown in our own times. Many of the more vigorous reactions to discussions on justification preparing the JDDJ in 1999 had expressed frustration with the rigor with which the tripartite template of (1) initial misunderstandings, (2) growing convergence, and (3) present consensus on each major question was applied to interpret all potentially divisive issues; so much so, that where the template appeared all too artificial, notably in the issues of sacraments and ministry, the topics were withdrawn from the discussion of their implications for the doctrine of justification.[71] Older and more recent experience with the counterproductive effects of quasi-Leibnizian interpretative strategies of harmonization make it unlikely that a path to the common table of the Lord will be found by "interpreting" the opposing positions on Eucharistic sacrifice merely as a consequence of a misunderstanding of *memoria* prevalent in the sixteenth century but overcome in our own. Establishing as a preliminary goal that

69. Paul Eisenkopf, *Leibniz und die Einigung der Christenheit. Überlegungen zur Reunion der evangelischen und katholischen Kirche,* Beiträge zur ökumenischen Theologie 11 (Munich: Schöningh, 1975), 111–71.

70. Cf. H.W. Krumwiede, "Molans Wirken für die Wiedervereinigung der Kirche," *Jahrbuch für niedersächische Kirchengeschichte* 61 (1963), 72–114.

71. The method of interpretative *synkatabasis* reached its zenith to date on Roman Catholic side with the semi-secret expertise commissioned in 1992 by the Papal Council on Unity that was mentioned above. For the reaction to this strategy well into October 1999 cf. the "Stellungnahme theologischer Hochschullehrer zur geplanten Unterzeichnung der Gemeinsamen Offiziellen Feststellung zur Rechtfertigungslehre"; and the literature cited by Ulrich Winkler, "Ökumenisch leben. Neuerscheinungen für die Praxis," *SaThZ* 7 (2003): 72–99, where chapter four of "Dominus Jesus" and the Protestant faculty responses to "Communio sanctorum" are included in the list of such reactions. Cf. also Richard Schenk, "The Unsettled German Discussions of Justification: Abiding Differences and Ecumenical Blessings," *Dialog. A Journal of Theology* 44, no. 2 (2005): 153–64, which relies in part on debated accounts now found in Dorothea Wendebourg, "Zur Entstehungsgeschichte der Gemeinsamen Erklärung zur Rechtfertigungslehre," in *Die eine Christenheit auf Erden* (Tübingen: Mohr Siebeck, 2000), 225–60.

theological dialogue should be loyal enough to other Christian communities to acknowledge in them remaining moments of alterity—without resorting to something like conversion (as Jüngel's proposals in 1998 for intercommunion on the basis of a joint acceptance of the purely passive sense of justification, ministry, and the Lord's Supper);[72] or to merely pragmatic sanction or official and unofficial forms of Church-order activism; or to misguided *synkatabasis*—seems the more likely approximation to that unity of the body of Christ which Augustine identified as the intended grace of the Lord's Supper. Both sides are in principle agreement with the axiom: *Deus non alligavit potentiam suam sacramentis*.[73] That common conviction makes all the more obvious the crassly political character of demanding of dialogue partners a specified *Gastgeschenk* or "gift of hospitality" as the price for their ecumenical welcome, as was perceived in 2011 in Nikolaus Schneider's highly publicized (later qualified) expectation of an ecumenical gift (*Gastgeschenk*) that required the visitor to present immediate and universal recognition of a particular understanding of sacrament and ministry.[74]

Barth's Questions and the Quality of Ecumenical Peace

The most sharply dialectical qualification of Congar's vision of an ecumenically fruitful form of critical history comes with the coincidence of irenic and polemic. Irenic might seem from a distance as the less likely description of Barth's mindset in accepting the invitation *ad limina apostolorum*. He is skeptical of that familiar kind of ecumenism which sees itself along the lines of negotiated peace or trade agreements between two sovereign parties. Despite the skepticism that Barth expresses in the essay of 1963 and elsewhere, it speaks for the culture of debate within the World Council of Churches that, despite this critique, Willem Adolf Visser't Hooft and Lukas Vischer continued to seek Barth's involvement in Roman-Reformed dialogue. It is

72. Cf. the address of Eberhard Jüngel noted in n. 73 above, read together with Jüngel, *Justification: The Heart of the Christian Faith. A Theological Study with an Ecumenical Purpose* (Edinburgh: T&T Clark, 2001).

73. For the scholastic use and qualification of the axiom prior to the Reformation cf. Peter Lombard, *IV Sent.* dist. 1, cap. 5 (II 235); *Summ. sent.*, cap. 7, tract. V (PL 176, 133 D); Hugo de St, Victor, *De sacram.*, lib. I, p. 9, cap. 5 (PL 176, 323 C–324 A); William of Auvergne, tract. 1, quaest. 2, ad 5 (ed. Col. 26, 4, lin. 44–47); Bonaventura, *Breviloquium*, p. 6, cap. 1 (ed. Quaracchi, V 265); Robert Kilwardby, *Quaestiones in lib. IV Sententiarum*, Q 39 (ed. Schenk, 195, l. 80); Thomas Aquinas, *In lib. I Sententiarum* d. 42 q. 42 q. 2 a. 2 ad 1; *In lib. III Sententiarum* d. 3 q. 1 a. 1 qc 3 ad 1; *In lib. IV Sententiarum* d. 1 q 1 a 2 qc 1 co., d. 2 q. 2 a. 4 ad 3; d. 3 q. 1 a. 2 qc. 2 co.; d. 5 q. 2 a. 3 qc. 2 co.; d. 6 q. 1 a. 1 qc. 2 co.; *ST* I-II q. 113, a. 3 obj. 1.

74. http://m.thueringer-allgemeine.de/web/mobil/blaulicht/detail/-/specific/Papstbesuch-Kein-oekumenisches-Gastgeschenk-im-Augustinerkloster-1311942597

hard to think of the Roman dicasteries issuing their invitations to Barth in 1964 and 1966 without his known rapport with these two figures in Geneva. The questions that Barth carried to Rome in his storied satchel were not all of a kind, by which a peaceful refiguration—or "reformation"—of the partner could be effected or even expected. The invitations presented him a chance to bear theological witness to the Gospel that both partners confessed and so to see first of all how evangelical believers could better answer their own calling, spurred onwards by Roman Catholic attempts at self-reform and by those Roman Catholic developments that would best serve as a contrast -program and so an aid to the Christian identity set in relief by a new parsing of ancient grammars. Precisely because of this, Barth's interest in the Council was also well suited to serve secondary purposes such as providing a sounding board to chart just how far the Conciliar examination of Reformational convictions might lead the Roman Catholic community or learning to what degree it was a "reform council."[75] And yet the chief purpose of Barth's questions was to sharpen, by comparison and contrast, the Reformational search for where the Spirit was leading it. We would therefore miss the irenic motive of Barth's initiative if we reduced ecumenism to the *concordiae* negotiated by more institutionalized ecumenical bodies with the magisterial authority that has often been a point of internal contention among the partners on each side of the table.[76] Already Thomas Aquinas knew that we need to distinguish between genuine peace and mere concord (or concords). *Concordiae* are agreements between two parties, urged at times by very external factors (even violence), whereas peace demands that hearts on each side attain what they long for.[77] For Thomas as for Barth, this εἰρήνη is possible only by the gift of each partner's growing conversion to God.

Barth's rejection of the model of ecumenism chiefly as a conversion from one confession to another implies also the rejection of a merely external convergence of institutions that would leave their members more indifferent to the source of their unity and so further behind on the path toward that peace which the world cannot give. In the negotations referred to above

75. Cf. Barth's second general question (*ALA*, 20).

76. Cf. nn. 48ff. above.

77. Cf. Thomas Aquinas, *ST* II-II q. 29, a. 1, c.: "Peace includes concord and adds something to it. Hence wherever peace is, there is concord, but there is not peace, wherever there is concord, if we give peace its proper meaning. . . . The human heart is not at peace, so long as it has not what it wants, or, if having what it wants, there still remains something for it to want, which it cannot have at the same time. On the other hand, this union is not essential to concord: wherefore concord denotes union of appetites among various persons, while peace denotes, in addition to this union, the union of the appetites even in each one."

for reunification of the churches in the seventeenth century, the initiators of largely political plans "knew" that they were the irenicists in this business (*negotium*), and they named themselves as such without hesitation or qualification, although their failure to acknowledge differences within and between the confessions was a significant cause of the continued divisions.

As Augustine tells us, peace is the *tranquillitas ordinis*, and a legitimate if elusive goal of the remarkable ecumenical movement of the last hundred years has been to identify what kind of ordering should be sought, from organic unity to unity in a—now more, now less—reconciled form of diversity. Among Barth's contributions to the future of ecumenism should be counted his example of how, even prior to settling collectively on a definitive statement of ecumenical goals, and without any overt or latent decision that all open questions are to be declared incidental in the end, a profoundly amicable encounter is possible that can avoid the excesses of estrangement and harmonization. That gave Barth's ecumenical method something of an exploratory character, well expressed in the initial form of questions, none of which is entirely "innocent."

Despite his own initial willingness in 1963 to employ the term, "seiuncti fratres,"[78] Barth's many irritated references to the questionable implications of the term, including his own ironic use of the term in one of the book-dedications for Paul VI,[79] point to his deeper questions about the Council's notion of "Church." These questions address the central topic of *LG*, but here let us note: although the Council's use of the term "subsistit" is not discussed in Barth's questions, his issue with the *seiuncti fratres* revolves around the degree to which the Roman Catholic community should be viewed as the part of a greater whole which is the Church. Parallel to Congar's remark on "spiritual charisms,"[80] Barth asks about the ecclesiological implications of the fact that Catholicism has learned of the essential importance of ecumenism from the Protestant churches. As suggested above, the list of benefactions to the Roman Catholic community could be lengthened to include the need to scrutinize the signs of the times, inside and outside the Church; the need to acknowledge an extrinsic source of grace, the non-identity of self-salvation and salvation through another, and Christ as the first subject of genuine sacramentality, as well as the necessity of historical critical methods.

78. Cf. n. 17 above.
79. Cf. Busch, *Tagebuch*, 86.
80. Cf. n. 54 above.

Ad Limina Apostolorum does not attempt to provide direct answers to the questions raised here, and perhaps the "perfect peace" of a final answer is not yet today even within our reach. Despite Barth's criticism of the Conciliar call to devote extensive attention to Thomas Aquinas in its plans for the theological formation of priests,[81] one further remark by Thomas on peace might be allowed here. Thomas wrote that it is important to distinguish between perfect and imperfect peace and to pursue both.[82] The eschatological reserve which nevertheless encourages the pursuit of different levels of attainable—but admittedly imperfect—peace, implies that the idea of the preliminary goals in the seventeenth century, if at the time arguably not "preliminary" enough (the Gallican model was all too final), is not altogether implausible. Do not these genuine correctives and enrichments of major trends in Roman Catholic thought and practice by the affirmation and admonition of Reformatonal theologians suggest as a fitting, if provisional, ecclesial model the *totum potestativum*, the "potential whole" made up not of homogeneous but of heterogenous parts, not all of which express the whole to equal degrees and about which we might continue to debate, but all or at least several of which in their heterogeneity are needed for the whole to thrive? To be a *locus* of subsistence and to be a part in need of other parts are not mutually exclusive attributes. Until the perfect order of the different confessions to one another becomes clear, we will be *ad limina* in Victor Turner's sense of the betwixt and between, in a state of liminality.[83] During that time we will need (!) to rely on friends who share and model for us the *fides quaerens intellectum* of the gospel, friends who are different enough to be for and with us in justice, loyalty, and with a view toward an "eirene" not just of our own fabrication.

81. Cf. Busch, *Tagebuch*, 74.

82. *ST* II-II, q. 29, a. 3 ad 4. See also *ST* II-II, q. 29, a. 2 ad 4: "Since true peace is only about good things, as the true good is possessed in two ways, perfectly and imperfectly, so there is a twofold true peace. One is perfect peace. It consists in the perfect enjoyment of the sovereign good, and unites all one's desires by giving them rest in one object. This is the last end of the rational creature, according to *Psalm 147*:3 'Who hath placed peace on thy borders.' The other is imperfect peace, which may be had in this world, for though the chief movement of the soul finds rest in God, yet there are certain things within and without which disturb the peace."

83. Victor W. Turner, "Betwixt and Between. The Liminal Period in *Rites de Passage*," in *Symposium on New Approaches to the Study of Religion*, ed. June Helm (Seattle: University of Washington Press, 1964), 4–20.

Bibliography

Alberigo, Giuseppe, and Joseph A. Komonchak, eds. *History of Vatican II*. 5 vols. Maryknoll/Leuven: Orbis/Peeters, 1995–2006.

Allison, Gregg R. *Roman Catholic Theology and Practice: An Evangelical Assessment*. Wheaton, Ill.: Crossway, 2014.

Anderson, Alan H. *To the Ends of the Earth: Pentecostalism and the Transformation of World Christianity*. Oxford: Oxford University Press, 2013.

Ashworth, E. Jennifer. "Aquinas, Scotus and Others on Naming, Knowing, and the Origin of Language." In *Logic and Language in the Middle Ages: A Volume in Honor of Sten Ebbesen*, edited by Jakob Leth Fink, Heine Hansen, and Ana María Mora-Márquez, 257–72. Leiden: Brill, 2013.

Aslan, Reza. *Zealot: The Life and Times of Jesus of Nazareth*. New York: Random House, 2013.

Ayres, Lewis. *Nicaea and Its Legacy: An Approach to Fourth-Century Theology*. Oxford: Oxford University Press, 2004.

———. "The Memory of Tradition: Post-Conciliar Renewal and One Recent Thomism." *The Thomist* 79, no. 4 (2015): 511–50.

———. "The Word Answering the Word: Opening the Space of Catholic Biblical Interpretation." In *Theological Theology: Essays in Honor of John B. Webster*, edited by R. David Nelson, Darren Sarisky, and Justin Stratis, 37–53. London: Bloomsbury, 2015.

Balthasar, Hans Urs von. *Karl Barth. Darstellung und Deutung seiner Theologie*. Cologne: Verlag Jakob Hegner, 1951.

———. *Theo-Drama: Theological Dramatic Theory*. Vol. 3, *The* Dramatis Personae*: The Person in Christ*. Translated by Graham Harrison. San Francisco, Calif.: Ignatius Press, 1992.

———. *Theo-Logic: Theological Logical Theory*. Vol. 2, *Truth of God*. Translated by Adrian Walker. San Francisco, Calif.: Ignatius, 2004.

———. *The Theology of Karl Barth: Exposition and Interpretation*. Translated by Edward T. Oakes, SJ. San Francisco, Calif.: Ignatius, 1992.

Baptism, Eucharist, and Ministry. Faith and Order Paper 111. Geneva: World Council of Churches, 1983.

Barnes, Elizabeth. *The Minority Body: A Theory of Disability*. Oxford: Oxford University Press, 2016.

Barth, Karl. *Ad Limina Apostolorum*. Berlin: Evangelische Verlagsanstalt, 1967.

———. *Ad Limina Apostolorum*. Zurich: EVZ-Verlag, 1967.

———. *Ad Limina Apostolorum. An Appraisal of Vatican II*. Translated by Keith R. Crim. Louisville, Ky.: John Knox Press, 1968.

———. *Ad Limina Apostolorum: An Appraisal of Vatican II*. Translated by Keith R. Crim. Edinburgh: St. Andrews Press, 1969.

———. *Ad Limina Apostolorum: An Appraisal of Vatican II*. Translated by Keith R. Crim. Eugene, Ore.: Wipf and Stock, 2016.

———. *Church Dogmatics*. 4 vols. Edited by G. W. Bromiley and T. F. Torrance. London: T&T Clark, 1936–75.

———. *Church Dogmatics*. 4 vols. Edited by G. W. Bromiley and T. F. Torrance. London: T&T Clark, 2004.

———. *The Göttingen Dogmatics: Instruction in the Christian Religion*. Vol. 1. Grand Rapids, Mich.: Eerdmans, 1991.

———. "Die Kirche und die Offenbarung (1923)." In Karl Barth, *Gesamtausgabe*. Vol. III.1, *Vorträge und kleinere Arbeiten 1922–1925*, edited by Holger Finze, 307–48. Zurich: Theologischer Verlag Zürich, 1990.

———. *Letters 1961–1968*. Edited by Jurgen Fangmeier and Hinrich Stoevesandt. Translated by G. W. Bromiley. Grand Rapids, Mich.: Eerdmans, 1981.

———. "Roman Catholicism: A Question for the Protestant Church." In *Theology and Church*. Translated by Louise Pettitbone Smith, 297–333. London: SCM, 1962.

———. *Der Römerbrief*. 2nd edition 1922. Zurich: Theologischer Verlag Zürich, 1976 (11th reprint).

———. "Der römische Katholizismus als Frage an die protestantische Kirche." In Karl Barth, *Die Theologie und die Kirche*, 329–63. Munich: Kaiser, 1928.

———. *Überlegungen zum Zweiten Vatikanischen Konzil*. In *Ende der Gegenreformation? Das Konzil—Dokumente und Deutung*, edited by Johann Christoph Hampe, 406–15. Stuttgart/Mainz: Kaiser/Grünewald, 1964.

———. "*Unterricht in der christlichen Religion*." In Karl Barth, *Gesamtausgabe*. Vol. II, *Die Lehre von der Versöhnung/Die Lehre von der Erlösung 1925/1926*. Edited by Hinrich Stoevesandt, 349–50. Zurich: Theologischer Verlag Zürich, 2003.

———. *Witness to the Word: A Commentary on John 1*. Translated by Geoffrey W. Bromiley. Grand Rapids, Mich.: Eerdmans, 1986.

———. "Zum 400. Todestag Calvins." *Evangelische Theologie* 24, no. 5 (1964): 225–29.

Bathrellos, Demetrios. *The Byzantine Christ: Person, Nature, and Will in the Christology of Saint Maximus the Confessor*. Oxford: Oxford University Press, 2004.

Bauckham, Richard J. "The Worship of Jesus in Philippians 2:9–11." *Where Christology Began: Essays on Philippians 2*, edited by Ralph P. Martin and Brian J. Dodds, 128–39. Louisville, Ky.: Westminster John Knox, 1998.

Baur, Jörg. *Einig in Sachen Rechtfertigung? Zur Prüfung des Rechtfertigungskapitels der*

Studie des Ökumenischen Arbeitskreises Evangelischer und Katholischer Theologen, Lehrverurteilungen, kirchentrennend? Tübingen: Mohr Siebeck, 1989.

———. *Frei durch Rechtfertigung: Vorträge anläßlich der römisch-katholisch lutherischen "Gemeinsamen Erklärung."* Tübingen: Mohr Siebeck, 1999.

Bea, Augustin. *The Church and the Jewish People: A Commentary on the Second Vatican Council's Declaration on the Relation of the Church to Non-Christian Religions.* Translated by Philip Loretz, SJ. New York: Harper and Row, 1966.

———. *The Word of God and Mankind.* London: Geoffrey Chapman, 1967.

Becker, Werner. "History of the Decree." In Vorgrimler, *Commentary on the Documents of Vatican II*, vol. 2, 1–62.

Bellarmine, Robert. *Disputationes de Controversiis Christianae Fidei adversus hujus temporis Haereticos.* Naples: Giuliano, 1857.

Bender, Kimlyn J. *Karl Barth's Christological Ecclesiology.* Aldershot: Ashgate, 2005.

Benedict XVI, Pope. "Address of His Holiness Benedict XVI to the Roman Curia, December 22nd 2005 Offering Them His Christmas Greetings." http://w2.vatican.va/content/benedict-xvi/en/speeches/2005/december/documents/hf_ben_xvi_spe_20051222_roman-curia.html.

———. *General Audience from March 5, 2008.* http://w2.vatican.va/content/benedict-xvi/en/audiences/2008/documents/hf_ben-xvi_aud_20080305.html.

Berkouwer, G. C. *Nabetrachting op het Concilie.* Kampen: Kok, 1968.

Birmelé, André, and Harding Meyer, eds. *Grundkonsens—Grunddissens. Studie des Straßburger Instituts für Ökumenische Forschung. Ergebnisse und Dokumente.* Frankfurt/Paderborn: Lembeck/Bonifatius, 1992.

Bockmuehl, Markus, and Alan J. Torrance, eds. *Scripture's Doctrine and Theology's Bible: How the New Testament Shapes Christian Dogmatics.* Grand Rapids, Mich.: Eerdmans, 2008.

Boersma, Hans. *Nouvelle Théologie and Sacramental Ontology: A Return to Mystery.* Oxford: Oxford University Press, 2009.

———. *Violence, Hospitality, and the Cross: Reappropriating the Atonement Tradition.* Grand Rapids, Mich.: Baker Academic, 2004.

Bouillard, Henri. *Conversion et grâce chez S. Thomas d'Aquin: Étude historique.* Théologie 1. Paris: Aubier, 1944.

Bowler, Kate. *Blessed: A History of the American Prosperity Gospel.* New York: Oxford University Press, 2013.

Bowlin, John. "Elevating and Healing: Reflections on Summa Theologiae I-II q. 109, a. 2." *Journal of Moral Theology* 3, no. 1 (2014): 39–53.

Brague, Rémi. *On the God of the Christians (and on one or two others).* Translated by Paul Seaton. South Bend, Ind.: St Augustine's Press, 2013.

Brosseder, Johannes, and Markus Wriedt, eds. *"Kein Anlaß zur Verwerfung!" Studien zur Hermeneutik des ökumenischen Gesprächs. Festschrift für Otto Hermann Pesch.* Frankfurt: Lembech, 2007.

Brunner, Emil, and Karl Barth. *Natural Theology.* Eugene, Ore.: Wipf and Stock, 2002.

Bruston, Henry. "L'Église et la Vocation Humaine." In *Points de Vue de Théologiens Protestants: Études sur les décrets du Concile Vatican II*, edited by J. Bosc et al., 173–203. Paris: Cerf, 1967.

Bullivant, Stephen. *Mass Exodus: Catholic Disaffiliation in Britain and America since Vatican II.* Oxford: Oxford University Press, 2019.

Bullivant, Stephen, Hannah Vaughan-Spruce, and Catherine Knowles, *Why Catholics Leave, What They Miss, and How They Might Return.* New York: Paulist Press, 2019.

Busch, Eberhard. *Karl Barths Lebenslauf. Nach seinen Briefen und autobiographischen Texten.* Munich: Chr. Kaiser, 1975.

———. *Meine Zeit mit Karl Barth: Tagebuch 1965–68.* Göttingen: Vandenhoeck & Ruprecht, 2011.

Cagin, Michel, OSB. "La théologie des religions chez Charles Journet." *Revue thomiste* 106, no. 1–2 (2006): 173–203.

Cahill, Thomas. *Pope John XXIII: A Life.* London: Penguin, 2002.

Capéran, Louis. *Le problème du salut des infidèles.* 2 vols. 3rd ed. Toulouse: Grand Séminare, 1934.

Casel, Odo. *The Mystery of Christian Worship and Other Writings.* Edited by Burkhardt Neunheuser. London: DLT, 1962.

Cassidy, Edward Idris. *Ecumenism and Interreligious Dialogue:* Unitatis Redintegratio, Nostra Aetate. New York: Paulist Press, 2005.

Catechism of the Catholic Church. 2nd ed. Vatican City: Libreria Editrice Vaticana, 1997.

Congar, Yves, OP. *Chrétiens Désunis; Principes d'Un "Oecuménisme" Catholique.* Paris: Cerf, 1937.

———. "The Church, Universal Sacrament of Salvation." In Yves Congar, *This Church That I Love*, translated by Lucien Delafuente, 39–61. Denville, N.J.: Dimension Books, 1969.

———. *Diversity and Communion.* Translated by J. Bowden. London: SCM Press, 1984.

———. "Dogme christologique et Ecclésiologie. Vérité et limites d'un parallèle." In Yves Congar, *Sainte Église; Études et approaches ecclésiologique*, 84–101. Paris: Cerf, 1963.

———. *The Meaning of Tradition.* Translated by A. N. Woodrow. San Francisco, Calif.: Ignatius Press, 2004.

———. *My Journal of the Council.* Collegeville, Minn.: Liturgical Press, 2012.

———. *Tradition and Traditions: An Historical and a Theological essay.* Translated by M. Naseby and T. Rainborough. London: Burns and Oates, 1966.

———. *True and False Reform in the Church.* Translated by Paul Philibert. Collegeville, Minn.: Liturgical Press, 2011.

———. *Vraie et fausse réforme dans l'église.* Paris: Cerf, 1950.

———. *Vraie et fausse réforme dans l'Église.* Paris: Cerf, 1968.

Congregation for the Doctrine of the Faith. *Dominus Jesus: On the Unicity and Salvific Universality of Jesus Christ and the Church*. August 6, 2000. www.vatican.va.

———. *Letter on Certain Questions Concerning Eschatology*. May 17, 1979. www.vatican.va.

———. "Responses to Some Questions regarding Certain Aspects of the Doctrine on the Church." *Acta Apostolicae Sedis* 99 (2007): 604–8.

Courtenay, William J. *Covenant and Causality in Medieval Thought*. London: Variorum Reprints, 1984.

Cuchet, Guillaume. *Comment notre monde a cessé d'être chrétien. Anatomie d'un effondrement*. Paris: Seuil, 2018.

Dahlke, Benjamin. *Karl Barth, Catholic Renewal and Vatican II*. London: Bloomsbury, 2012.

Damascene, John. *On the Orthodox Faith*. Translated by S. D. F. Salmond. Nicene and Post-Nicene Fathers, vol. 9. Oxford: James Parker, 1899.

De Lubac, Henri, SJ. *Catholicism: Christ and the Common Destiny of Man*. Translated by L. Sheppard and E. Englund. San Francisco, Calif.: Ignatius, 1988.

———. *Catholicisme: Les aspects sociaux du dogme*. 4th ed. Paris: Cerf, 1947.

———. *The Church: Paradox and Mystery*. Translated by James R. Dunne. Staten Island, N.Y.: Ecclesia Press, 1969.

———. *La postérité spirituelle de Joachim de Flore: De Joachim à nos jours*. Paris: Cerf, 2014.

———. "The Problem of the Development of Dogma." In *Theology in History*. Translated by Anne Englund Nash, 248–80. San Francisco, Calif.: Ignatius Press, 1996.

———. *Splendor of the Church*. Translated by Michael Mason. New York: Sheed and Ward, 1956.

———. *Splendor of the Church*. Translated by Michael Mason. San Francisco, Calif.: Ignatius Press, 1999.

———. "The Total Meaning of Man and the World." *Communio* 35 (Winter 2008): 613–41.

Denzinger, Henry. *The Sources of Catholic Dogma*. Translated by Roy J. Deferrari. Saint Louis, Mo.: Herder, 1955.

Diez, Karlheinz, and Eero Huovinen, eds. *Vom Konflikt zur Gemeinschaft. Gemeinsames lutherisch-katholisches Reformationsgedenken im Jahr 2017*. Leipzig/Paderborn: Evangelische Verlagsanstalt/Bonifatius, 2014.

DiNoia, J. A., OP. *The Diversity of Religions: A Christian Perspective*. Washington, D.C.: The Catholic University of America Press, 1992.

Duby, Steven J. *Divine Simplicity: A Dogmatic Account*. London: Bloomsbury, 2018).

Dulles, Avery Cardinal, SJ. *John Henry Newman*. London: Continuum, 2002.

———. "Nature, Mission, and Structure of the Church." In Lamb and Levering, eds., *Vatican II: Renewal within Tradition*, 25–36.

Eastern Orthodox/Roman Catholic Consultation in the United States. "An Agreed

Statement on the Lima Document: Baptism, Eucharist, Ministry." http://www.usccb.org/beliefs-and-teachings/ecumenical-and-interreligious/ecumenical/orthodox/statement-lima-baptism-eucharist-and-ministry.cfm.

Echeverria, Eduardo. *Berkouwer and Catholicism: Disputed Questions*. Studies in Reformed Theology 24. Leiden: Brill, 2013.

———. *Dialogue of Love: Confessions of an Evangelical Catholic Ecumenist*. Eugene, Ore.: Wipf and Stock, 2010.

Ehrman, Bart D. *How Jesus Became God: The Exaltation of a Jewish Preacher from Galilee*. New York: HarperCollins, 2014.

Eisenkopf, Paul. *Leibniz und die Einigung der Christenheit. Überlegungen zur Reunion der evangelischen und katholischen Kirche*. BöT 11. Munich/Paderborn: Schöningh, 1975.

Ernesti, Jörg, and Wolfgang Thönissen, eds. *Die Entdeckung der Ökumene: Zur Beteiligung der katholischen Kirche an der ökumenischen Bewegung*. Paderborn/Frankfurt: Bonifatius/Lembeck, 2008.

Ernst, Harold E. "The Theological Notes and the Interpretation of Doctrine." *Theological Studies* 63, no. 4 (2002): 813–25.

Evangelical Church in Germany, ed. *Rechtfertigung und Freiheit. 500 Jahre Reformation 2017*. 4th ed. Gütersloh: Gütersloher Verlagshaus, 2015.

Feldmeier, Reinhard, and Hermann Spieckermann. *The God of the Living: A Biblical Theology*. Waco: Baylor University Press, 2011.

Ferracci, Luca, ed. *Toward a History of the Desire for Christian Unity: Preliminary Research Papers*. Proceedings of the International Conference at the Monastery of Bose (November 2014). Vienna: LIT, 2015.

Flannery, Austin, OP, ed. *The Basic Documents, Vatican Council II: Constitutions, Decrees and Declarations*. Northport, N.Y./Dublin: Costello Publishing Company/Dominican Publications, 1996.

———, ed. *Vatican Council II*. Vol. 1: *The Conciliar and Post Conciliar Documents*. Rev. ed. Northport, N.Y.: Costello Publishing Company, 1996.

Garrigou-Lagrange, Réginald, OP. "La Nouvelle théologie, où va-t-elle?" *Angelicum* 23 (1946): 126–45.

———. *Reality: A Synthesis of Thomistic Thought*. Translated by Patrick Cummins, OSB. Lexington, Ky: Ex Fontibus, 2009.

Garrigues, Jean-Miguel. *L'Epouse du Dieu Vivant; Marie plenitude trinitaire de l'Église*. Paris: Parole et Silence, 2000.

George, Timothy. "*Unitatis Redintegratio* after Fifty Years: A Protestant Reading." *Pro Ecclesia* 25, no. 1 (2016): 53–70.

———, and Thomas G. Guarino, eds. *Evangelicals and Catholics Together at Twenty: Vital Statements on Contested Topics*. Grand Rapids, Mich: Brazos, 2015.

Goutagny, Frère Étienne. "Histoire du Groupe des Dombes." http://www.arccis.org/downloads/groupedesdombesi.pdf.

Gregory, Brad S. *The Unintended Reformation: How a Religious Revolution Secularized Society*. Cambridge, Mass: Harvard University Press, 2012.
Gregory, Eric. *Politics and the Order of Love: An Augustinian Ethic of Democratic Citizenship*. Chicago: University of Chicago Press, 2008.
Guarino, Thomas G. *Foundations of Systematic Theology*. New York: T&T Clark, 2005.
———. "Henri Bouillard and the Truth-Status of Dogmatic Statements." *Science et Esprit* 39 (1987): 331–43.
———. *Revelation and Truth: Unity and Plurality in Contemporary Theology*. Scranton, Ohio: University of Scranton Press, 1993.
Gushee, David. "A Christian Theological Account of Human Worth." In *Understanding Human Dignity*, Proceedings of the British Academy, edited by Christopher McCrudden, 275–88. Oxford: Oxford University Press, 2013.
Hamer, Jerome. *L'Occasionalisme théologique de Karl Barth*. Paris: Desclée de Brouwer, 1949.
Hare, John E. *God's Command*. Oxford: Oxford University Press, 2015.
Harnack, Adolf von. *Marcion: The Gospel of the Alien God*. Translated by John E. Steely and Lyle D. Bierma. Durham, NC: Labyrinth Press, 1990.
Hauerwas, Stanley. "The Politics of Justice: Why Justice Is a Bad Idea for Christians." In *After Christendom? How the Church Is to Behave If Freedom, Justice, and a Christian Nation Are Bad Ideas*, 45–68. Nashville, Tenn.: Abingdon Press, 1991.
Heidegger, Martin. *Sein und Zeit*. 19th ed. Tübingen: Niemeyer, 2006.
Hellin, Francisco Gil. *Concilii Vaticani II Synopsis. Constitutio Dogmatica De Divina Revelatione Dei Verbum*. Città del Vaticano: Libreria Editrice Vaticana, 1993.
Herms, Eilert, and Lubomir Žak, ed. *Grund und Gegenstand des Glaubens nach römisch-katholischer und evangelisch-lutherischer Lehre*. Tübingen/Rome: Mohr Siebeck/Lateran University Press, 2008.
———, and Lubomir Žak, ed. *Taufe und Abendmahl im Grund und Gegenstand des Glaubens*. Tübingen/Rome: Mohr Siebeck/Lateran University Press, 2017.
———, and Lubomir Žak, ed. *Wort und Sakrament im Grund und Gegenstand des Glaubens*. Tübingen/Rome: Mohr Siebeck/Lateran University Press, 2012.
Heyking, John von. *Augustine and Politics as Longing in the World*. Columbia, Mo: University of Maryland Press, 2001.
Hick, John. *An Interpretation of Religion: Human Responses to the Transcendent*, 2nd ed. New Haven: Yale University Press, 2004.
Hipp, Stephen A. *The One Church of Christ: Understanding Vatican II*. Steubenville, Ohio: Emmaus Academic, 2018.
Hittinger, Russell. "Natural Law and Public Discourse: The Legacies of Joseph Ratzinger." *Loyola Law Review* 60, no. 4 (2014): 241–271.
Hünermann, Peter, ed. *Heinrich Denzinger: Enchiridion Symbolorum: A Compendium of Creeds, Definitions, and Declarations of the Catholic Church* [Latin-English]. 43rd ed. San Francisco, Calif: Ignatius Press, 2012.
———. *Das Zweite Vatikanische Konzil. Konstitutionen, Dekrete und Erklärungen*. New

Edition. Edited by Peter Hünermann. Darmstadt: Wissenschaftliche Buchgesellschaft, 2014.

Hütter, Reinhard. "Barth between McCormack and von Balthasar: A Dialectic." *Pro Ecclesia* 8, no. 1 (1999): 105–9.

———. *Bound for Beatitude: A Thomistic Study in Eschatology and Ethics*. Washington, D.C.: The Catholic University of America Press, 2019.

———. *Bound to Be Free: Evangelical Catholic Engagements in Ecclesiology, Ethics, and Ecumenism*. Grand Rapids, Mich: Eerdmans, 2004.

———. "Karl Barth's 'Dialectical Catholicity': Sic et Non." *Modern Theology* 16, no. 2 (2000): 137–57.

———. *Suffering Divine Things: Theology as Church Practice*. Grand Rapids, Mich: Eerdmans, 2000.

Imbelli, Robert P. *Rekindling the Christic Imagination: Theological Meditations for the New Evangelization*. Collegeville, Minn: Liturgical Press, 2014.

International Theological Commission. *Memory and Reconciliation: The Church and the Faults of the Past*. http://www.vatican.va/roman_curia/congregations/cfaith/cti_documents/rc_con_cfaith_doc_20000307_memory-reconc-itc_en.html.

Jackson, Timothy P. *The Priority of Love: Christian Charity and Social Justice*. Princeton: Princeton University Press, 2003.

Jaeger, Lorenz. *A Stand on Ecumenism: The Council's Decree*. Translated by Hilda Graef. New York, N.Y.: Kenedy, 1965.

Jenkins, Philip. *The Next Christendom: The Coming of Global Christianity*. New York: Oxford University Press, 2011.

Jenson, Robert. *A Theology in Outline: Can These Bones Live?* New York: Oxford University Press, 2016.

John Paul II, Pope. "Ecclesia de Eucharistia." *Acta Apostolicae Sedis* 95 (2003): 433–75.

———. *Spiritual Pilgrimage: Texts on Jews and Judaism 1979–1995*. Edited by Eugene J. Fisher and Leon Klenicki. New York: Crossroad, 1995.

John XXIII, Pope. "Gaudet Mater Ecclesia." *Acta Apostolicae Sedis* 54 (1962): 786–95.

Joint Statement of the Evangelische Kirche in Deutschland and the Deutsche Katholische Bischofskonferenz. *Erinnering heilen—Jesus Christus bezeugen: Ein gemeinsames Wort zum Jahr 2017*. http://www.dbkshop.de/media/files_public/hpldvggu/DBK_624.pdf.

Joint Working Group of the Roman Catholic Church and the World Council of Churches. "The Notion of 'Hierarchy of Truths': An Ecumenical Interpretation." Faith and Order Paper n. 150. Geneva: WCC Publications, 1990.

Journet, Charles. *Destinées d'Israël: A propos du salut par les Juifs*. In *Œuvres completes de Charles Journet*, vol. 11, 17–431. Paris: Desclée de Brouwer, 2015.

———. *L'Église du Verbe Incarné*. Vol. 1, *La hiérarchie apostolique*. Paris: Saint Augustin, 1998.

———. *L'Église du Verbe Incarné*. Vol. III, *La structure interne de l'Eglise et son unite catholique*. Paris: Saint-Augustin, 2000.

———. *Théologie de l'Église*. In *Œuvres complètes de Charles Journet*, vol. 15. Paris: Éditions Lethielleux, 2017.

———. *Theology of the Church*. Translated by Victor Szczurek, O.Praem. San Francisco, Calif: Ignatius Press, 2004.

Jüngel, Eberhard. "Church Unity Is Already Happening: The Path towards Eucharistic Community." *Dialog: A Journal of Theology* 44, no. 1 (2005): 30–37.

———. *Justification: The Heart of the Christian Faith*. Translated by Jeffrey F. Cayzer. Introduction by John Webster. London/New York: Bloomsbury T&T Clark, 2006.

Kant, Immanuel. *The End of All Things*. In Immanuel Kant, *Religion within the Boundaries of Mere Reason. And Other Writings*, edited by Allan Wood and George di Giovanni, 193–205. Cambridge: Cambridge University Press, 2004.

———. *Toward Perpetual Peace: A Philosophical Sketch*. In Immanuel Kant, *Toward Perpetual Peace and Other Writings on Politics, Peace, and History*, translated by David L. Colclasure, edited with introduction by Pauline Kleingeld, 67–109. New Haven, Conn.: Yale University Press, 2006.

Kasper, Walter. *Pope Francis' Revolution of Tenderness and Love: Theological and Pastoral Perspectives*. Translated by William Madges. New York: Paulist Press, 2015.

Ker, Ian. *Newman on Vatican II*. Oxford: Oxford University Press, 2014.

Kilwardby, Robert. *Quaestiones in librum quartum Sententiarum*. Edited by Richard Schenk. Veröffentlichungen der Kommission für die Herausgabe ungedruckter Texte aus der mittelalterlichen Geisteswelt 17. Munich: Bavarian Academy of Sciences, 1993.

King, Martin Luther, Jr. "Letter From a Birmingham Jail." *I Have a Dream: Writings and Speeches that Changed the World*, edited by James Melvin Washington, 83–100. San Francisco, Calif: HarperCollins, 1986.

Kirwan, Jon. *An Avant-garde Theological Generation: The* Nouvelle Théologie *and the French Crisis of Modernity*. Oxford: Oxford University Press, 2018.

Knobel, Angela McKay. "Can Aquinas's Infused and Acquired Virtues Coexist in the Christian Life?" *Studies in Christian Ethics* 23, no. 4 (2010): 381–96.

Krumwiede, H. W. "Molans Wirken für die Wiedervereinigung der Kirche." *Jahrbuch für niedersächische Kirchengeschichte* 61 (1963): 72–114.

Kühn, Ulrich, and Otto H. Pesch. *Rechtfertigung im Disput: Eine freundliche Antwort an Jörg Baur auf seine Prüfung des Rechtfertigungskapitels in der Studie des Ökumenischen Arbeitskreises evangelischer und katholischer Theologen: "Lehrverurteilungen - kirchentrennend?"* Tübingen: Mohr Siebeck, 1991.

Küng, Hans. *The Church*. New York: Sheed and Ward, 1968.

———. *Die Kirche*. Sämtliche Werke, vol. 3. Freiburg im Breisgau: Herder, 2015.

Lamb, Matthew L., and Matthew Levering, eds. *Vatican II: Renewal within Tradition*. New York: Oxford University Press, 2008.

Lamb, Michael. "Augustine and Republican Liberty: Recontextualizing Coercion." *Augustinian Studies* 48 (2017): 119–59.

Lange, Dietz, ed. *Überholte Lehrverurteilungen? Die Gegensätze in der Lehre von*

Rechtfertigung, Abendmahl und Amt zwischen dem Konzil von Trient und der Reformation—damals und heute. Göttingen: Vanderhoeck & Ruprecht, 1991.

Lash, Nicholas. *Change in Focus: A Study of Doctrinal Change and Continuity*. London: Sheed and Ward, 1973.

———. *Newman on Development. The Search for an Explanation in History*. London: Sheed and Ward, 1975.

La Soujeole, Benoît-Dominique de, OP. "The Economy of Salvation: Entitative Sacramentality and Operative Sacramentality." *The Thomist* 75, no. 4 (2011): 537–53.

———. *Introduction to the Mystery of the Church*. Translated by Michael J. Miller. Washington, D.C.: The Catholic University of America Press, 2014.

———. *Le sacrament de la communion: Essai d'ecclesiologie fondamentale*. Paris and Fribourg: Cerf and Éditions Universitaires Fribourg Suisse, 1998.

Lehmann, Karl, and Wolfhart Pannenberg, eds. *The Condemnations of the Reformation Era: Do They Still Divide?* Minneapolis, Minn.: Fortress Press, 1989.

Leppin, Volker, and Dorothea Sattler, eds. *Reformation 1517–2017: Ökumenische Perspektiven*. Freiburg im Breisgau: Herder, 2015.

Levenson, Jon D. *The Hebrew Bible, the Old Testament, and Historical Criticism: Jews and Christians in Biblical Studies*. Louisville, Ky.: Westminster John Knox Press, 1993.

———. *Inheriting Abraham: The Legacy of the Patriarch in Judaism, Christianity, and Islam*. Princeton: Princeton University Press, 2012.

Levering, Matthew. *Engaging the Doctrine of Revelation: The Mediation of the Gospel through Church and Scripture*. Grand Rapids, Mich.: Baker Academic, 2014.

———. *The Indissolubility of Marriage:* Amoris Laetitia *in Context*. San Francisco, Calif.: Ignatius Press, 2019.

———. *An Introduction to Vatican II as an Ongoing Theological Event*. Washington, D.C.: The Catholic University of America Press, 2017.

———. *Proofs of God: Classical Arguments from Tertullian to Karl Barth*. Grand Rapids, Mich.: Baker Academic, 2016.

Lindbeck, George. "Le Cadre du Désaccord Catholique-Protestant." In *Théologie d'aujourd'hui et de demain*, edited by P. Burke, H. de Lubac et al., 191–206. Paris: Cerf, 1967.

———. *Dialogue on the Way: Protestant Report from Rome on the Vatican Council*. Minneapolis, Minn: Augsburg, 1965.

———. *The Future of Roman Catholic Theology: Vatican II—Catalytst for Change*. Philadelphia: Fortress Press, 1970.

———. *The Nature of Doctrine: Religion and Theology in a Postliberal Age*. 2nd ed. Louisville, Ky.: Westminster John Knox, 2009.

———. "The University and Ecumenism." In *Justification and the Future of the Ecumenical Movement: The Joint Declaration on the Doctrine of Justification*, edited by William G. Rusch, 1–13. Collegeville, Minn.: Liturgical Press, 2003.

Lombardi, Riccardo, SJ. *The Salvation of the Unbeliever*. Translated by Dorothy M. White. Westminster, Md.: Newman Press, 1956.

Lutheran World Federation and the Roman Catholic Church. *Joint Declaration on the Doctrine of Justification*. Grand Rapids, Mich.: Eerdmans, 2000.

Lynch, Reginald. *The Cleansing of the Heart: Sacraments as Instrumental Causes in the Thomistic Tradition*. Washington, D.C.: The Catholic University of America Press, 2017.

Malloy, Christopher J. *Engrafted into Christ: A Critique of the Joint Declaration*. New York: Peter Lang, 2005.

———. "*Subsistit In*: Nonexclusive Identity or Full Identity?" *The Thomist* 72, no. 1 (2008): 1–44.

Mansini, Guy, OSB. *Fundamental Theology*. Washington, D.C.: The Catholic University of America Press, 2018.

Maritain, Jacques. *On the Church of Christ: The Person of the Church and Her Personnel*. Translated by Joseph W. Evans. Notre Dame, Ind.: University of Notre Dame Press, 1973.

Markus, Robert. *Saeculum: History and Society in the Theology of St. Augustine*. Cambridge: Cambridge University Press, 1970.

Marshall, Bruce D. "Aquinas, Postliberal Theology, and the Universal Offer of Salvation in Christ." *The Thomist* (forthcoming).

———. "Christ and Israel: An Unsolved Problem in Catholic Theology." In *The Call of Abraham: Essays on the Election of Israel in Honor of Jon D. Levenson*, edited by Gary A. Anderson and Joel S. Kaminsky, 330–50. Notre Dame, Ind.: University of Notre Dame Press, 2013.

———. "Do Christians Worship the God of Israel?" *Knowing the Triune God*, edited by James J. Buckley and David S. Yeago, 231–64. Grand Rapids, Mich.: Eerdmans, 2001.

———. "Elder Brothers: John Paul II's Teaching on the Jewish People as a Question to the Church." In *John Paul II and the Jewish People: A Christian-Jewish Dialogue*, edited by David Dahlin and Matthew Levering, 113–29. Lanham, Md.: Rowman and Littlefield, 2008.

———. "Religion and Election: Aquinas on Natural Law, Judaism, and Salvation in Christ." *Nova et Vetera* (English edition) 14, no. 1 (2016): 61–125.

———. *Trinity and Truth*. Cambridge: Cambridge University Press, 2000.

Maruca, Dominic M., SJ. *Karl Barth*. Westminster, Md.: Newman Press, 1962.

Mathewes, Charles. *The Republic of Grace: Augustinian Thoughts for Dark Times*. Grand Rapids, Mich.: Eerdmans, 2010.

Mattes, Mark C. *The Role of Justification in Contemporary Theology*. Foreword by Klaus Schwarzwäller. Grand Rapids, Mich.: Eerdmans, 2004.

Mattison, William. "Can Christians Possess the Acquired Cardinal Virtues?" *Theological Studies* 72, no. 3 (2011): 558–85.

McCormack, Bruce L. "The Identity of the Son: Karl Barth's Exegesis of Hebrews 1:1–4 (and Similar Passages).” In *Christology, Hermeneutics and Hebrews: Profiles from the History of Interpretation*, edited by Jon C. Laansma and Daniel J. Treier, 155–72. London: T&T Clark, 2012.

———. *Karl Barth’s Critically Realistic Dialogical Theology: Its Genesis and Development 1909–1936*. Oxford: Clarendon, 1995.

———. “Karl Barth’s Version of an ‘Analogy of Being’: A Dialectical No and Yes to Roman Catholicism.” In *The Analogy of Being: The Invention of the Antichrist or the Wisdom of God?* edited by Thomas Joseph White, OP, 88–144. Grand Rapids, Mich.: Eerdmans, 2010.

———. *Orthodox and Modern: Studies in the Theology of Karl Barth*. Grand Rapids, Mich.: Baker, 2008.

McCrudden, Christopher. “In Pursuit of Human Dignity: An Introduction to Current Debates.” In *Understanding Human Dignity*, Proceedings of the British Academy, edited by Christopher McCrudden, 1–58. Oxford: Oxford University Press, 2013.

McDowell, John. “Avoiding the Myth of the Given.” In John McDowell, *Having the World in View: Essays on Kant, Hegel and Sellars*, 256–72. Cambridge, Mass.: Harvard University Press, 2009.

Meszaros, Andrew. *The Prophetic Church: History and Doctrinal Development in John Henry Newman and Yves Congar*. Oxford: Oxford University Press, 2016.

Miccoli, Giovanni. “Zwei Schwierige Problemfelder: Die Religionsfreiheit und das Verhältnis zu den Juden.” In *Geschichte des Zweiten Vatikanischen Konzils (1959–1965)*, vol. 4, edited by Giuseppe Alberigo and Günther Wassilowsky, 110–229. Mainz/Leuven: Grünewald/Peeters, 2006.

Moorhead, James H. “Beyond the Battle for the Bible: What Evangelicals Missed in Van Til’s Critique of Barth.” In *Karl Barth and American Evangelicalism*, edited by Bruce L. McCormack and Clifford B. Anderson, 42–72. Grand Rapids, Mich.: Eerdmans, 2011.

———. “Redefining Confessionalism: American Presbyterians in the Twentieth Century.” In *The Confessional Mosaic: Presbyterians and Twentieth-Century Theology*, edited by Milton J. Coalter, John M. Mulder, and Louis B. Meeks, 59–83. Louisville, Ky.: Westminster/John Knox, 1990.

Morali, Ilaria. “Salvation, Religions, and Dialogue in the Roman Magisterium: From Pius IX to Vatican II and Postconciliar Popes.” In *Catholic Engagement with World Religions*, edited by Karl J. Becker and Ilaria Morali, 122–42. Maryknoll, N.Y.: Orbis, 2010.

Morerod, Charles, OP. “The Decree on Ecumenism, *Unitatis Redintegratio*.” In Lamb and Levering, eds., *Vatican II: Renewal within Tradition*, 311–41.

———. *Tradition et Unité des Chrétiens. Le dogme comme condition de possibilité de l’oecumenisme*. Paris: Parole et Silence, 2005.

Morrisey, Francis G. *The Canonical Significance of Papal and Curial Pronouncements*. Hartford, Conn.: CLSA, 1974.

———. “Papal and Curial Pronouncements: Their Canonical Significance in the Light of the 1983 Code of Canon Law.” *The Jurist* 50, no. 1 (1990): 102–25.

Newman, John Henry. *Apologia Pro Vita Sua*. New York: Penguin, 2004.

———. *Briefe und Tagebücher bis zum Übertritt zur Kirche 1801–1845*. Introduction by Francis Bacchus and Henry Tristram. Translated by Edith Stein. Edited by Erich Przywara, SJ. Munich: Theatiner, 1928.

———. *Discourses Addressed to Mixed Congregations*. London: Longmans, Green and Co., 1906.

———. *An Essay on the Development of Doctrine*. Foreword by Ian Ker. Notre Dame, Ind.: University of Notre Dame Press, 1989.

———. *Fifteen Sermons Preached Before the University of Oxford*. Edited by J. D. Earnest and G. Tracey. Oxford: Oxford University Press, 2006.

———. *Fifteen Sermons Preached before the University of Oxford between A.D. 1826 and 1843*. Introduction by Mary Katherine Tillman. Notre Dame, Ind.: University of Notre Dame Press, 1997.

———. *Rise and Progress of Universities and Benedictine Essays*. Introduction and Notes by Mary Katherine Tillman. Notre Dame, Ind.: University of Notre Dame Press, 2001.

Nichols, Aidan, OP. *From Newman to Congar: The Idea of Doctrinal Development from the Victorians to the Second Vatican Council*. Edinburgh: T&T Clark: 1990.

———. “Thomism and the *nouvelle théologie*.” *The Thomist* 64, no. 1 (2000): 1–19.

Nietzsche, Friedrich. *Die Geburt der Tragödie. Unzeitgemäße Betrachtungen I-IV. Nachgelassene Schriften 1870–1873*. Kritische Studienausgabe, vol. 1, edited by Giorgio Colli and Mazzino Montinari, 243–334. Munich/Berlin/New York: DTV/De Gruyter, 1988.

Noll, Mark, and Carolyn Nystrom. *Is the Reformation Over? An Evangelical Assessment of Roman Catholicism*. Grand Rapids, Mich.: Baker, 2005.

Norwood, Donald W. *Reforming Rome: Karl Barth and Vatican II*. Grand Rapids, Mich.: Eerdmans, 2015.

Nygren, Anders. *Agape and Eros: The Christian Idea of Love*. Translated by Philip S. Watson. London: SCM Press, 1956.

O’Donovan, Oliver. *The Desire of the Nations: Rediscovering the Roots of Political Theology*. Cambridge: Cambridge University Press, 1996.

Otte, Hans, and Richard Schenk, eds. *Die Reunionsgespräche im Niedersachsen des 17. Jahrhunderts. Rojas y Spinola—Molan—Leibniz*. Göttingen: Vandenhoeck & Ruprecht 1999.

Panaccio, Claude. *Le discours intérieur: De Platon à Guillaume d’Ockham*. Paris: Seuil, 1999.

Pannenberg, Wolfhart. *Jesus—God and Man*. 2nd ed. Translated by L. L. Wilkins and D. A. Priebe. Philadelphia: Westminster, 1968.

Pasquier, Jean-Marie. *L’Eglise comme Sacrement. Le development de l’idée sacramentelle de l’Eglise de Moehler à Vatican II*. Fribourg: Academic Press Fribourg, 2008.

Pelikan, Jaroslav. *Christianity and Classical Culture: The Metamorphosis of Natural Theology in the Christian Encounter with Hellenism*. New Haven, Conn.: Yale University Press, 1993.

Peterson, Brandon. "Critical Voices: The Reactions of Rahner and Ratzinger to 'Schema XIII' (*Gaudium et Spes*)." *Modern Theology* 31, no. 1 (2015): 1–26.

Pettit, Philip. *Republicanism: A Theory of Freedom and Government*. Oxford: Oxford University Press, 1997.

Pieper, Josef. *The End of Time: A Meditation on the Philosophy of History*. Translated by Michael Bullock. San Francisco, Calif.: Ignatius Press, 1999.

———. *Hope and History: Five Salzburger Lectures*. Translated by David Kipp. San Francisco, Calif.: Ignatius Press, 1994.

———. *Tradition: Concept and Claim*. Translated by E. Christian Kopff. South Bend, Ind.: St. Augustine's Press, 2010.

Pius XI, Pope. *Mortalium Animos*. *Acta Apostolicae Sedis* (1928): 5–16.

Pius XII, Pope. *Humani Generis*. *Acta Apostolicae Sedis* (1950): 561–78.

Przywara, Erich, SJ. *Analogia Entis: Metaphysics—Original Structure and Universal Rhythm*. Translated by John Betz and David Bentley Hart. Grand Rapids, Mich.: Eerdmans, 2014.

Rahner, Karl, SJ. "Anonymous Christians." In Karl Rahner, *Theological Investigations*, vol. 6, 390–98. New York: Crossroad, 1982.

———. "Atheism and Implicit Christianity." *Theological Investigations*, vol. 9, 145–64. London: Darton, Longman and Todd, n.d.

———. "Christianity and the Non-Christian Religions." *Theological Investigations*, vol. 5, 115–34. Baltimore: Helicon Press, 1966.

———. "Christian Pessimism." *Theological Investigations*, vol. 22, 155–62. New York: Crossroad, 1991.

———. "The Development of Dogma." *Theological Investigations*, vol. 1, 39–77. London: Darton, Longman and Todd, 1961.

———. "Dogmatic Notes on 'Ecclesiological Piety.'" *Theological Investigations*, vol. 5, 336–65. Baltimore: Helicon Press, 1966.

———. "Zur Frage der Dogmenentwicklung." *Schriften zur Theologie*, vol. 1. Einsiedeln: Benziger Verlag, 1954–84.

———. *The Trinity*. Translated by J. Donceel. London: Burns and Oates, 1967.

———. *Das Zweite Vatikanum. Beiträge zum Konzil und seiner Interpretation*. Edited by Günther Wassilowsky. Sämtliche Werke 21/1 und 22/2. Freiburg: Herder, 2012.

———, Josef Ratzinger et al., eds. *Das Zweite Vatikanische Konzil: Dokumente und Kommentare*. 3 vols. Ergänzungsbände zu *Lexikon für Theologie und Kirche*. Freiburg: Herder, 1967.

Ratzinger, Joseph. *Eschatology: Death and Eternal Life*. 2nd ed. Translated by Michael Waldstein. Washington, D.C.: The Catholic University of America Press, 1988.

———. *Jesus of Nazareth: From the Baptism in the Jordan to the Transfiguration*. Translated by Adrian J. Walker. New York: Doubleday, 2007.

———. *Jesus of Nazareth*, Part Two: *Holy Week: From the Entrance into Jerusalem to the Resurrection*. Translated by Vatican Secretariat of State. San Francisco, Calif.: Ignatius Press, 2011.

———. *Jesus of Nazareth: The Infancy Narratives*. Translated by Philip J. Whitmore. New York: Random House, 2012.

———. *Theological Highlights of Vatican II*. Translated by Henry Traub, SJ. New York: Paulist Press, 2009.

Rawls, John. *A Theory of Justice*. Cambridge: Harvard University Press, 1971.

Rethmann, Peter, and Tobias Keßler, eds. *Pentekostalismus: Die Pfingstbewegung als Anfrage an Kirche und Theologie*. Salzburg: Pustet, 2012.

Revel, Jean-Philippe. *Traité des sacraments I. Baptême et sacramentalité 1. Origine et signification du baptême*. Paris: Cerf, 2004.

Rhonheimer, Martin. *Christentum und säkularer Statt. Geshichte—Gegenwart—Zukunft*. Freiburg im Breisgau: Herder, 2012.

Riccardi, Andrea. *Il secolo del martirio. I cristiani nel Novecento*. Milan: Mondolibri, 2000.

———. *Ils sont morts pour leur foi. La persécution des chrétiens au XXe siècle*. Paris: Omnibus, 2002.

———. *Salz der Erde, Licht der Welt: Glaubenszeugnis und Christenverfolgung im 20. Jahrhundert*. Freiburg: Herder, 2002.

Ricoeur, Paul. *Memory, History, Forgetting*. Chicago: University of Chicago Press, 2004.

Root, Michael. "Aquinas, Merit, and Reformation Theology after the Joint Declaration on the Doctrine of Justification." *Modern Theology* 20, no. 1 (2004): 5–22.

———. "Remembering the Reformation—with the Pope." *The Christian Century*. www.christiancentury.org/article/2016-08/catholics-gathering.

Rosen, Michael. "Dignity: The Case Against." In *Understanding Human Dignity*, Proceedings of the British Academy, edited by Christopher McCrudden, 143–54. Oxford: Oxford University Press, 2013.

Sander, Hans-Joachim. "Die Kirchenkonstitution Gaudium et spes. Die pastorale Ortsbestimmung kirchlicher Identität." In *Kontroversen. Worum es sich in der Seelsorge zu streiten lohnt*, edited by Bernhard Spielberg and Astrid Schilling, 13–18. Würzburg: Echter, 2001.

———. "Theologischer Kommentar zur Pastoralkonstitution über die Kirche in der Welt von heute Gaudium et spes." In *Herders Theologischer Kommentar zum Zweiten Vatikanischen Konzil*, vol. 4, edited by Peter Hünermann and Bernd Jochen, 581–886. Freiburg im Breisgau: Herder, 2005.

Scheeben, Matthias. *The Mysteries of Christianity*. Translated by Cyril Vollert, SJ. London and St. Louis: Herder, 1947.

Schenk, Richard. "The Place of Mimesis and the Apocalyptic: Toward a Typology of the 'Far and Near.'" *Contagion* (Spring 2013): 1–24.

———. “The Unsettled German Discussions of Justification: Abiding Differences and Ecumenical Blessings.” *Dialog. A Journal of Theology* 44, no. 2 (2005): 153–64.
Schillebeeckx, Edward. *Christ the Sacrament of the Encounter with God*. Translated by Paul Barrett, OP. London: Sheed and Ward, 1963.
Schleiermacher, Friedrich. *The Christian Faith*. 2 vols. Edited by H. R. Mackintosh and J. S. Stewart. Edinburgh: T&T Clark, 1968.
Schuler, Roberto J. *Pfingstbewegungen in Brasilien: Sozio-politische Implikationen der neuen Pluralität*. São Leopoldo: EST, 2004.
Schwahn, Barbara. *Der Ökumenische Arbeitskreis evangelischer und katholischer Theologen von 1946 bis 1975*. Göttingen: Vandenhoeck & Ruprecht, 1996.
Schwöbel, Christoph. *Christlicher Glaube im Pluralismus, Studien zu einer Theologie der Kultur*. Tübingen: Mohr Siebeck, 2003.
———. “Gottes Ökumene. Über das Verhältnis von Kirchengemeinschaft und Gottesverständnis.” In *Befreiende Wahrheit. Festschrift Eilert Herms*, edited by W. Härle, M. Heesch, and R. Preul, 449–66. Marburg: N. G. Elwert, 2000.
———. “The Same God? The Perspective of Faith, the Identity of God, Tolerance and Dialogue.” In *Do We Worship the Same God? Jews, Christians, and Muslims in Dialogue*, edited by Miroslav Volf, 1–17. Grand Rapids, Mich.: Eerdmans, 2012.
Second Vatican Council. Decree on Ecumenism, *Unitatis Redintegratio*. www.vatican.va.
———. Dogmatic Constitution on the Church, *Lumen Gentium*. www.vatican.va.
Sellars, Wilfrid. “Empiricism and the Philosophy of Mind.” In Wilfrid Sellars, *Science, Perception, and Reality: Variations on Kantian Themes*, 127–96. London: Routledge and Kegan Paul, 1963.
Sesboüe, Bernard. *Hors de l’Église pas de salut: Histoire d’une formule et problèmes d’interprétation*. Paris: Desclée de Brouwer, 2004.
Sherwin, Michael. *By Knowledge and by Love: Charity and Knowledge in the Moral Theology of Thomas Aquinas*. Washington, D.C.: The Catholic University of America Press, 2011.
Siebenrock, Roman A. *Theologischer Kommentar zur Erklärung über die religiöse Freiheit Dignitatis humanae*. In *Herders Theologischer Kommentar zum Zweiten Vatikanischen Konzil*, vol. 4, edited by Peter Hünermann and Bernd Jochen Hilberath, 125–218. Freiburg im Breisgau: Herder, 2005.
Singer, Peter. *Animal Liberation*. New York: HarperCollins, 1990.
Slenczka, Notger. “Die Kirche und das Alte Testament.” In *Das Alte Testament in der Theologie* (Marburger Jahrbuch Theologie XXV), edited by Elisabeth Gräb-Schmidt and Reiner Preul, 83–119. Leipzig: Evangelische Verlagsanstalt, 2013.
Slenczka, Reinhard. “Dogma und Kircheneinheit.” In *Handbuch der Dogmen- und Theologiegeschichte*, vol. 3, edited by Carl Andresen, Adolf M. Ritter, and Gustav A. Benrath, 426–603. Göttingen: Vandenhoeck & Ruprecht, 1984.
———. “Das evangelisch-katholische Gespräch in Deutschland.” *Zeitwende* 33 (1962): 815–25.
Smith, Richard F. “Inspiration and Inerrancy.” In *Jerome Biblical Commentary*,

vol. 2, edited by Raymond S. Brown, Joseph A. Fitzmyer, and Ronald E. Murphy, 499–514. Englewood Cliffs, N.J.: Prentice-Hall, 1968.

Smulders, Peter, SJ. "L'Eglise Sacrement du Salut." In *L'Église de Vatican II. Études autour de la Constitution conciliaire sur l'Église*, vol. II, edited by G. Baraúna and Y. Congar, 313–38. Paris: Cerf, 1966.

Söhngen, Gottlieb. "The Analogy of Faith: Likeness to God from Faith Alone?" Translated by Kenneth Oakes. *Pro Ecclesia* 21, no. 1 (2012): 56–76.

———. "The Analogy of Faith: Unity in the Science of Faith." Translated by Kenneth Oakes. *Pro Ecclesia* 21, no. 2 (2012): 169–94.

Stout, Jeffrey. *Democracy and Tradition*. Princeton, N.J.: Princeton University Press, 2004.

Stransky, Thomas. "The Observers at Vatican II: A Unique Experience of Dialogue." *Centro pro Unione Bulletin*, no. 63 (Spring 2003): 8–14.

Sullivan, Francis A. *Creative Fidelity: Weighing and Interpreting Documents of the Magisterium*. New York: Paulist Press, 1996.

Tanner, Norman, SJ, ed. *Decrees of the Ecumenical Councils: Volume II (Trent–Vatican II)*. Washington, D.C.: Georgetown University Press, 1990.

Teuffenbach, Alexandra von. *Die Bedeutung des subsistit in (LG 8): Zum Selbstverständnis der katholischen Kirche*. Munich: Herbert Utz Verlag, 2002.

Thomas Aquinas. *S. Thomae Aquinatis Super Evangelium S. Ioannis Lectura*. 5th ed. Edited by Raphael Cai, OP. Turin: Marietti, 1952.

Thorsen, Jacob E. *Charismatic Practice and Catholic Parish Life: The Incipient Pentecostalization of the Church in Guatemala and Latin America*. Leiden: Brill Academic Publisher, 2015.

Tilley, Terrence W. *The Disciples' Jesus: Christology as Reconciling Practice*. Maryknoll, N.Y.: Orbis Books, 2008.

———. *Inventing Catholic Tradition*. Maryknoll, N.Y.: Orbis Books, 2000.

Tolkien, J. R. R. "On Fairy-Stories." In J. R. R. Tolkien, *Tree and Leaf*, 11–70. London: George Allen and Unwin, 1964.

Torrell, Jean-Pierre, OP. *Saint Thomas Aquinas*. Vol. 2, *Spiritual Master*. Translated by Robert Royal. Washington, D.C.: The Catholic University of America Press, 2003.

Tracy, David. *The Analogical Imagination: Christian Theology and the Culture of Pluralism*. New York: Crossroad, 1981.

Tschipke, Theophil. *L'humanité du Christ comme instrument de salut de la divinité*. Translated by P. Secrétan. Fribourg: Academic Press Fribourg, 2003.

Turbanti, Giovanni. *Un concilio per il mondo moderno. La redazione della constituzione pastorale "Gaudium et spes" del Vaticano II*. Bologna: Società editrice il Mulino, 2000.

Turner, Victor W. "Betwixt and Between. The Liminal Period in *Rites de Passage*." In *Symposium on New Approaches to the Study of Religion*, edited by June Helm, 4–20. Seattle: University of Washington Press, 1964.

Urban, Hans Jörg, and Harald Wagner, eds. *Handbuch der Ökumenik*. 3 Parts in 4 Vols. Paderborn: Bonifatius, 1985–1987.

Van Buren, Paul M. *A Theology of the Jewish-Christian Reality. Part 1: Discerning the Way*. San Francisco, Calif.: Harper and Row, 1980.

———. *A Theology of the Jewish-Christian Reality. Part 2: A Christian Theology of the People of Israel*. San Francisco, Calif.: Harper and Row, 1984.

———. *A Theology of the Jewish-Christian Reality. Part 3: Christ in Context*. San Francisco, Calif.: Harper and Row, 1988.

Vatican II. *Unitatis Redintegratio. Acta Apostolicae Sedis* 57 (1965): 90–112.

———. *Die Menschheit Christi als Heilsorgan der Gottheit*. Freiburg im Breisgau: Herder, 1940.

Volf, Miroslav. *Allah: A Christian Response*. New York: Harper One, 2011.

———. "Wheaton Professor's Suspension Is about Anti-Muslim Bigotry, not Theology." *The Washington Post*, December 17, 2015.

Vischer, Lukas. *Überlegungen nach dem Konzil,* Polis 26. Zurich: Evangelischen Verlags Zollikon, 1966.

———. "Raum für Gottes Plan" (2006). http://karlbarth.unibas.ch/fileadmin/downloads/letter8.pdf.

Vorgrimler, Herbert, ed. *Commentary on the Documents of Vatican II*. Vol. I. Translated by L. Adolphus et al. New York: Herder and Herder, 1967.

———, ed. *Commentary on the Documents of Vatican II*. Vol. II. Translated by R. A. Wilson. New York: Herder and Herder, 1968.

———, ed. *Commentary on the Documents of Vatican II*. Vol. III. Translated by William Glen-Doepel et al. London: Burns and Oates, 1969.

———, ed. *Commentary on the Documents of Vatican II*. Vol. V, *Pastoral Constitution on the Church in the Modern World*. Translated by W. J. O'Hara. London: Burns and Oates, 1969.

Wainwright, Geoffrey. "*Unitatis Redintegratio* in a Protestant Perspective." *Pro Ecclesia* 15, no. 2 (2006): 172–85.

Waldron, Jeremy. "Citizenship and Dignity." In *Understanding Human Dignity*, Proceedings of the British Academy, edited by Christopher McCrudden, 327–43. Oxford: Oxford University Press, 2013.

———, with Wai Chee Dimock, Don Herzog, and Michael Rosen. *Dignity, Rank, and Rights*. Edited by Meir Dan-Cohen. Oxford: Oxford University Press, 2012.

Ward, Wilfrid. *The Life of John Henry Cardinal Newman*. Vol. II. London: Longmans, Green and Co., 1912.

Washburn, Christian D. "The Theological Priority of 'Lumen Gentium' and 'Dei Verbum' for the Interpretation of the Second Vatican Council." *The Thomist* 78, no. 1 (2014): 107–34.

Wawrykow, Joseph. *God's Grace and Human Action: "Merit" in the Theology of Thomas*. Notre Dame, Ind.: University of Notre Dame Press, 1996.

Weigel, George. *Evangelical Catholicism: Deep Reform in the 21st-century Church.* New York: Basic, 2014.

———. "Re-Viewing Vatican II: An Interview with George A. Lindbeck." *First Things* 48 (December 1994): 44–50.

Welch, Lawrence J. "*Quaestio Disputata* Reply to Richard Gaillardetz on the Ordinary Universal Magisterium and to Francis Sullivan." *Theological Studies* 64, no. 3 (2003): 598–609.

Wendebourg, Dorothea. "Zur Entstehungsgeschichte der Gemeinsamen Erklärung zur Rechtfertigungslehre." In *Die eine Christenheit auf Erden*, 225–60. Tübingen: Mohr Siebeck, 2000.

Wendebourg, Ernst-Wilhelm. *Die Christusgemeinde und ihre Herr: Eine kritische Studie zur Ekklesiologie Karl Barths*. Berlin/Hamburg: Luthersches Verlagshaus, 1967.

White, Thomas Joseph, OP. *The Incarnate Lord: A Thomistic Study in Christology.* Washington, D.C.: The Catholic University of America Press, 2015.

———. "The Precarity of Wisdom: Modern Dominican Theology, Perspectivalism, and the Tasks of Reconstruction." In *Ressourcement Thomism: Sacred Doctrine, the Sacraments, and the Moral Life*, edited by Reinhard Hütter and Matthew Levering, 92–123. Washington, D.C.: The Catholic University of America Press, 2010.

———. "The Virgin Mary and the Church: The Marian Exemplarity of Ecclesial Faith." *Nova et Vetera* (English Edition) 11, no. 2 (2013): 375–405.

Winkler, Ulrich. "Ökumenisch leben. Neuerscheinungen für die Praxis." *Salzburger Theologische Studien* 7 (2003): 72–99.

Witte, Pieter de. *Doctrine, Dynamic, and Difference: To the Heart of the Lutheran–Roman Catholic Differentiated Consensus on Justification*. London: T&T Clark International, 2012.

Wittman, Tyler R. *God and Creation in the Theology of Thomas Aquinas and Karl Barth*. Oxford: Oxford University Press, 2018.

Wolterstorff, Nicholas. *Justice: Rights and Wrongs*. Princeton, N.J.: Princeton University Press, 2008.

Contributors

Lewis Ayres is professor of Catholic and historical theology at Durham University.

Hans Boersma is St. Benedict Servants of Christ Professor in Ascetical Theology at Nashotah House Theological Seminary.

John R. Bowlin is Robert L. Stuart Associate Professor of Philosophy and Christian Ethics at Princeton Theological Seminary.

Reinhard Hütter is ordinary professor of fundamental and dogmatic theology at the Catholic University of America.

Matthew Levering is James N. and Mary D. Perry Jr. Chair of Theology at Mundelein Seminary.

Bruce D. Marshall is Lehman Professor of Christian Doctrine at Perkins School of Theology, Southern Methodist University.

Bruce L. McCormack is Charles Hodge Professor of Systematic Theology at Princeton Theological Seminary.

Francesca Aran Murphy is professor of theology at the University of Notre Dame.

Richard Schenk, OP, is honorary professor at Albert-Ludwigs-Universität, Freiburg im Breisgau.

Christoph Schwöbel is chair of divinity at the University of St. Andrews.

Katherine Sonderegger is William Meade Chair in Systematic Theology at Virginia Theological Seminary.

Thomas Joseph White, OP, is professor of theology and director of the Thomistic Institute at the Pontifical University of St. Thomas Aquinas (Angelicum).

Index

Dogma and Ecumenism: Vatican II and Karl Barth's *Ad Limina Apostolorum*
was designed in Meta Serif Pro with Meta Pro display type and composed by
Kachergis Book Design of Pittsboro, North Carolina. It was printed on
60-pound House Natural Smooth Web and bound by
Sheridan Books of Chelsea, Michigan.